Rivalries that Destroyed the Roman Republic

For Olivia

Rivalries that Destroyed the Roman Republic

Jeremiah McCall

PEN & SWORD
HISTORY

First published in Great Britain in 2022 by
Pen & Sword History
An imprint of
Pen & Sword Books Ltd
Yorkshire – Philadelphia

ISBN 978 1 52673 317 7

A CIP catalogue record for this book is
available from the British Library.

Typeset by Mac Style
Printed and bound in the UK by CPI Group (UK) Ltd,
Croydon, CR0 4YY.

MIX
Paper from
responsible sources
FSC
www.fsc.org
FSC® C013604

Pen & Sword Books Limited incorporates the imprints of Atlas,
Archaeology, Aviation, Discovery, Family History, Fiction, History,
Maritime, Military, Military Classics, Politics, Select, Transport,
True Crime, Air World, Frontline Publishing, Leo Cooper, Remember
When, Seaforth Publishing, The Praetorian Press, Wharncliffe
Local History, Wharncliffe Transport, Wharncliffe True Crime
and White Owl.

For a complete list of Pen & Sword titles please contact

PEN & SWORD BOOKS LIMITED
47 Church Street, Barnsley, South Yorkshire, S70 2AS, England
E-mail: enquiries@pen-and-sword.co.uk
Website: www.pen-and-sword.co.uk

Or

PEN AND SWORD BOOKS
1950 Lawrence Rd, Havertown, PA 19083, USA
E-mail: Uspen-and-sword@casematepublishers.com
Website: www.penandswordbooks.com

Contents

Acknowledgments

In addition to my deepest gratitude to Olivia, who makes this all possible and worthwhile, I would like to take a moment to thank Junietta McCall and John Pearson. They have faithfully and lovingly been my early draft proof-readers for several books now, and I am so grateful for their support.

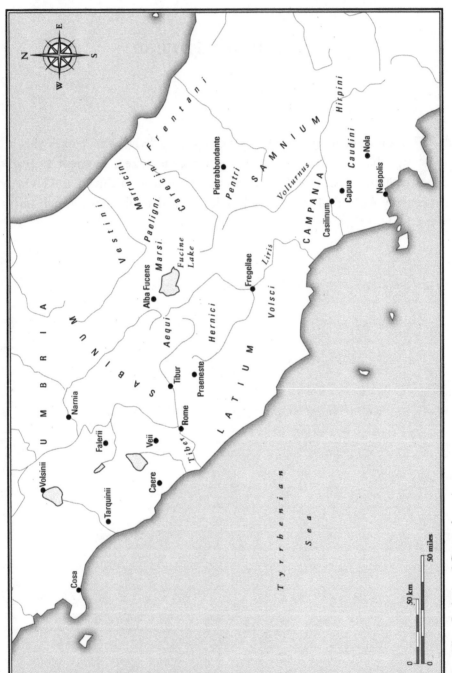

Republican Latium and Campania.

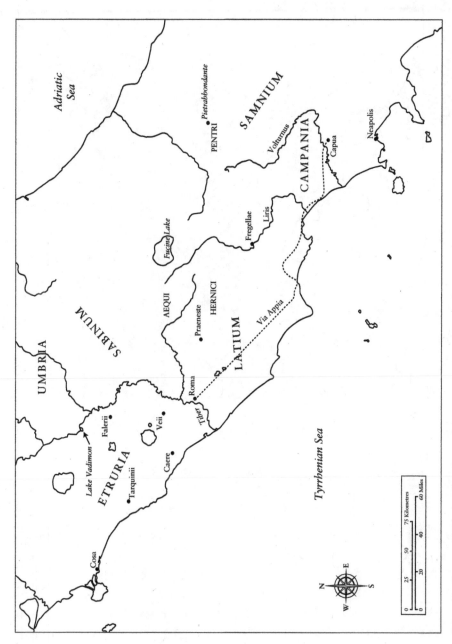

Rome, Latium, and Surrounding Regions.

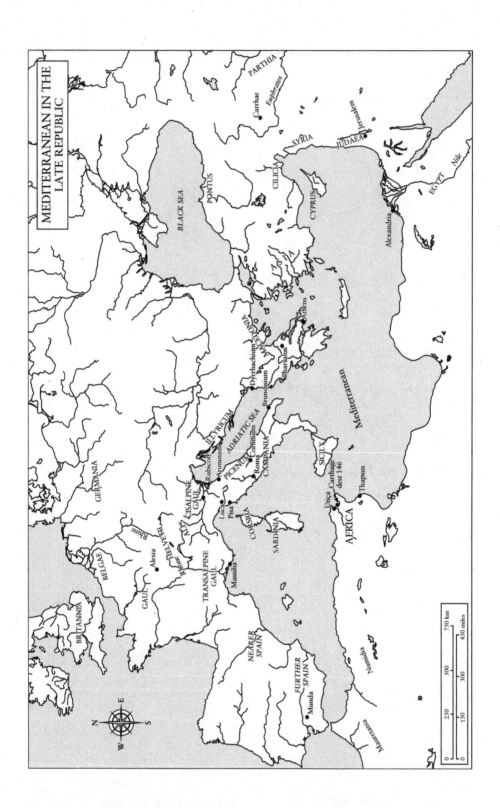

MEDITERRANEAN IN THE LATE REPUBLIC

PARTHIA
Euphrates
Carrhae
SYRIA
CILICIA
JUDAEA Jerusalem
CYPRUS
EGYPT Nile
Alexandria
BLACK SEA
PONTUS
Mediterranean
ILLYRICUM
Dyrrhachium
Brundisium
Pharsalus
Athens
ADRIATIC SEA
Rubicon
Ariminum
PICENUM
Rome Corfinium
CAMPANIA
SICILY
Utica Carthage
dest 146
Thapsus
AFRICA
GERMANIA
ALPS
CISALPINE GAUL
Luca
Pisa
CORSICA
SARDINIA
Rhine
BELGAE
HELVETII
Alesia
Rhône
TRANSALPINE GAUL
Massilia
GAUL
BRITANNIA
NEARER SPAIN
FURTHER SPAIN
Munda
Numidia
Mauretania

N
E
S
W

0   250   500   750 km
0   150   300   450 miles

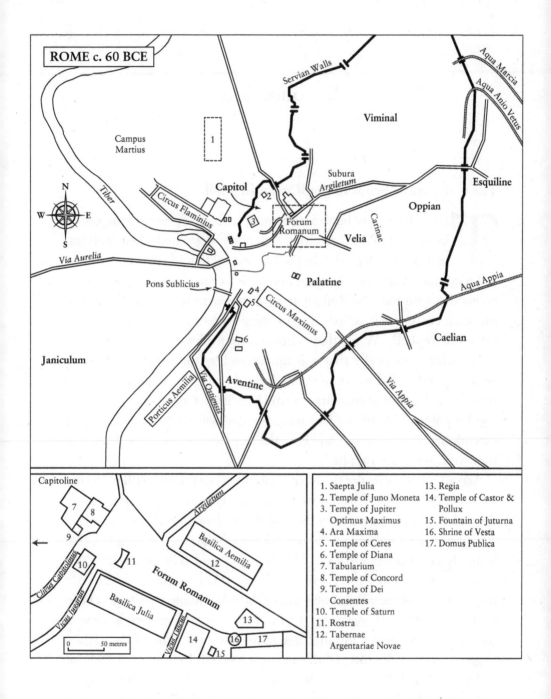

ROME c. 60 BCE

Servian Walls

Aqua Marcia

Aqua Anio Vetus

Viminal

Campus
Martius

1

Capitol

Subura

Argiletum

Esquiline

Circus Flaminius

2

Oppian

Tiber

3

Forum
Romanum

Carinae

Velia

Via Aurelia

Palatine

Pons Sublicius

4

5

Circus Maximus

Aqua Appia

6

Caelian

Janiculum

Aventine

Via Appia

Porticus Aemilia

Via Ostiensis

Capitoline

Argiletum

7

8

9

Basilica Aemilia

11

Forum Romanum

12

Clivus Capitolinus

10

Vicus Iugarius

Basilica Julia

Vicus Tuscus

13

14

16

17

0   50 metres

15

1. Saepta Julia
2. Temple of Juno Moneta
3. Temple of Jupiter
   Optimus Maximus
4. Ara Maxima
5. Temple of Ceres
6. Temple of Diana
7. Tabularium
8. Temple of Concord
9. Temple of Dei
   Consentes
10. Temple of Saturn
11. Rostra
12. Tabernae
    Argentariae Novae

13. Regia
14. Temple of Castor &
    Pollux
15. Fountain of Juturna
16. Shrine of Vesta
17. Domus Publica

Introduction

The Origins and Scope of the Roman Republic

This is the story of how some Roman aristocrats grew so competitive in their political rivalries that they destroyed their political system, the Republic, in the late second to mid first century BCE. That it was only some Romans, not all, is a critical point.[1] The Roman political system that the Roman aristocracy began to craft at the end of the sixth century was called the *res publica* – literally 'public affairs'. We call it the Republic. While that political system allowed a range of people to participate politically that was unmatched by the monarchies of the ancient world, it did not even remotely allow everyone to participate. So first, it is important to consider who did and did not get to take part in the regular political life of the Republic, the decisions about laws and their execution, wars and peace, and how the resources of the state, limited as they were, were to be applied.

According to the stories the Romans told, at least the ones still preserved in the scraps of their histories we have, the city of Rome was founded in the eighth century BCE. 753 is the traditional date, though since the very dating system of BCE and CE did not exist when the city was founded, that is simply a convenient estimate. The city was founded by groups of ethnic Latins – people who spoke Latin and practised Latin customs – who built small settlements of villages on some of the hills around a particular bend in the Tiber River. Over time, the hill settlements developed a sense of community and began to build shared architecture. One of the earliest projects was the draining of the swampy lowland between the Palatine and Capitoline hills to create the space that became the centre of public and political life in the Republic: the Forum. Here the Romans built many important shared religious, political, economic, and social structures.

Traditional stories tell us the government of the early city of Rome was a monarchy. Kings ruled with more or less participation (depending on the king) from the aristocracy, those descended from the great families whose origins were lost to time. There was some idea of a formal voting assembly of male citizens, not aristocrats, but those wealthy enough to supply their own infantry, weapons and armour and thus serve in the Republic's armies. Much of the formal political power, however, seems to have been in the hands of the king. And so, under the control of their kings, the Roman city developed many of its political and economic institutions. It also formed relations with nearby peoples, first in the surrounding region of Latium, where Latins lived, and then in central Italy.

Human societies are complex and diverse interlocking systems, and all members have roles; this is certainly true of the Romans. And it is absolutely the case that all of Roman society had roles, critical roles, in the broad political, military, familial, economic, and cultural systems and processes of Roman society. Yet when it came to formal political and military institutions under the kings or later, only some Romans could participate directly. Even though the sources, focused as they are most often on aristocratic males, provide scant information, it would be wholly misleading here at the start to pass over in silence the excluded Romans, the majority of society.

Consider, then, even if only for a moment, those important peoples the Roman state excluded from formal roles in its political systems. Women were not, so far as we know, consulted formally in political or military decisions. They were not required to serve in the military, nor were they eligible to vote in the early assemblies that granted formal approval for royal acts and served as the juries for public crimes. The Roman Republic, like so many ancient political systems, was firmly patriarchal and excluded women from these formal political roles. Nor were the many enslaved peoples of Rome allowed to participate formally in political and military processes. Those peoples – first Italians, then over time people throughout the Mediterranean – by incurring insurmountable debts or losing battles, had their freedom taken from them by Romans. The poorest among free Romans had little formal political role and for centuries very little formal military role either. And it is a matter of considerable debate, even now, how much political power and participation Roman male citizens of modest means had, those who could vote in the citizen assemblies. Taken together, this majority of Roman society was fundamental to the broader political, economic, military, familial, and cultural systems (and many more), but they were mostly excluded from formal political and military roles. We will try to note the rare occasions when their informal political and military roles appear in the sources. It is important to recognize, in any case, that even when our limited sources – most often focused on war, formal politics, and aristocrats – pass over these politically excluded Romans, they existed and mattered.

Formal political power is also an important caveat here. A reasonably comprehensive understanding of politics includes most, if not all, activities involved in the access, distribution, and use of power, or more simply: Who can (has the right to) do stuff, how much can (should) they do, And what do they (should they) do when they can? These questions involved all in any society, whether at Rome or elsewhere. Accordingly, we will see instances in the sources where people outside the enfranchised minority played critical roles in political decisions and actions. But when it came to the formal political powers of kings, of legislation, of war making, of how the resources of the early state were to be allocated, only freeborn males with sufficient property were invited to formally participate. And, ultimately, the end of the Republic was mostly a shift in the formal political powers of a small group of people, who, nevertheless have left us with most of our documentary evidence.

Of these, Roman aristocrats, those from the highest ranked, most prestigious families, had the greatest amount of formal political power. But, as best we can determine from the legends and myths that surround the earliest period of Rome, at least some became dissatisfied with the limits a king imposed on their opportunities to exercise power and earn distinction. And so, the ancient stories say, at the end of the sixth century, 509 BCE, to use another conventional, but imprecise, date, at least some aristocrats rebelled against the final king of Rome, Tarquinius Superbus, 'Tarquin the Proud'. According to several stories, his son, also named Tarquinius Superbus, was a morally bankrupt royal youth. Most horrifically, he raped the noble and virtuous Lucretia, the wife of the aristocrat Lucius Tarquinius Collatinus. She, Roman tale-tellers said, killed herself to atone for the dishonour, though her husband insisted she had done nothing wrong. The shock of Tarquinius' assault and Lucretia's decision drove Collatinus, his close friend Marcus Junius Brutus, and other aristocrats to band together and drive out the last king of Rome.

In place of a monarchy, the Roman aristocrats crafted the beginnings of a new political system, the Republic. Ancient writers often spoke as if the Republic's institutions were fully formed in 509 BCE, but the reality is that the Republic developed over centuries and really never stopped developing until it was destroyed. At first only the noblest aristocrats were allowed to hold offices and, in their role as senators, advise the magistrates. Their families were called patricians. One tradition developed later that the patricians were descendants of those first 100 prestigious Romans the first king, Romulus, selected to be his advisors in the senate. However it may have been perceived in the sixth and fifth century, the patricians were the social and political elite.

A larger group of free Roman peoples were also a critical part of the city's daily rhythms: the plebeians. Neither ancient sources nor modern historians have been able to decisively define plebeian status, but it seems to be safe to say that plebeians were not descended from patrician families and, initially, they did not have access to the political offices of the Republic. This caused a considerable amount of friction for the wealthiest plebeians, those who came from the same social and economic circles as the patricians but lacked the distinction of high birth. There also was a considerable amount of friction between the wealthy, whether patrician or plebeian, and the poor plebeians who made up the majority of Roman society. Poorer plebeians it seems – though again our evidence is fragmentary and often legendary – struggled with crushing debt and debt enslavement and wanted political and legal protections from wealthy creditors. These frictions sparked a lengthy period of social and political disorder and disruption that later authors called the Struggle of the Orders – the patrician and plebian orders. By the early third century BCE, these struggles had transformed the Republic so that both patricians and plebeians could participate politically. The aristocracy, the political and social elite, now became a blend of patrician and plebeian families.

The Origins of the 'Classical' Republic, c. 300 BCE

By the start of the third century, let's say 300 BCE, the political system that we call the Republic seems to have had the following features. First, a set of yearly magistrates, elected by assemblies of male citizens. The most powerful of these yearly magistrates were the two consuls. Consuls served as chief executives, carrying out the policies of the senate and leading senatorial debates. They also had the power to summon the voting and electoral assemblies of citizens. But they also wielded the critical *imperium*, 'power', which could mean many things to Romans but, most importantly, the right to have one's commands obeyed and the right to levy and command armies (*imperium* is a critical term throughout this history; it and other critical terms are defined in the glossary in the appendices).

So, for much of the Republic, the consuls spent most of their time as military commanders engaging in the essentially endless string of wars that the Romans prosecuted, the processes that gained them a Mediterranean empire. Beneath them in rank were the praetors. Like the consuls they had the power to summon assemblies, and they had *imperium*, though typically it seems they commanded smaller armies than consuls. Their primary functions were judging legal cases and, as the Roman empire expanded, governing territories the Romans dominated.

The various assemblies were made up of free male citizens. They elected consuls, praetors, and all the other yearly magistrates. They also voted on bills, and by the early third century, the principle was fixed that laws were only laws if they had been approved by the necessary assembly. Two forms of citizen assembly were most important for this history. The centuriate assembly and the tribal assembly. The centuriate assembly, *comitia centuriata*, organized male citizens according to wealth so that the wealthiest voters had considerably greater voting power than the poorer, and the poorest were almost completely excluded. The centuriate assembly elected consuls and praetors yearly, and declared war and peace. Occasionally they would vote laws into being. The tribal assembly, *comitia tributa*, on the other hand, allowed all male citizens to vote and was organized so that all voters, regardless of wealth, had a roughly equal vote. The tribal assembly mostly passed laws and elected other important magistrates like the tribunes of the plebs.

The tribunes of the plebs, by c. 300 BCE, were the ten yearly elected officials whose job was, conventionally, to protect the rights of the plebeians, especially the commoners that were most of the plebeians. The wealthy plebeians, who had access to resources and political offices, could pretty much take care of themselves. Several powers were critical for the tribunes to carry out their responsibilities. First they had the right of intercession. Quite simply, they could prevent anyone, a creditor for example, from laying hands on a plebeian simply by physically interceding. This is because the tribunes of the plebs enjoyed sacrosanctity: their bodies were inviolable. In practice this meant that anyone who assaulted a tribune, which seems not to have happened for a sizeable chunk of the Republic's history, faced the collective wrath of the plebeians. Tribunes' second power was their ability to veto. A single tribune could veto – the word means 'I forbid' in Latin – any law in the process of being proposed or voted upon, or even a senatorial deliberation, as well as other political processes. Finally, tribunes had the right to propose bills directly to the tribal assembly. In other words, strictly speaking, tribunes could draft proposals and make legislation directly through the tribal assembly. Conventionally, tribunes were charged with using these powers to defend the rights of plebeians, most often common plebeians. Wealthy plebeians already had access to wealth and influence to protect themselves.

In addition to annually elected officials and assemblies, the Republic was directed by the senate. Unlike modern representative governments, senators in the Republic were not elected officials. Rather, senators were simply those most prestigious citizens who had acquired the status of senator. In other words, when the censors, the pair of officials elected every five years to conduct the formal Roman census, wrote down the senators names, they had some form of mark indicating that they had the status of senator. This status brought with it two critical privileges not enjoyed by the vast majority of Roman society: the right to attend meetings of the senate (the collective of people with senatorial status) and the right to give one's opinion in the senate. By about 300 BCE, we think, censors regularly chose Romans who had held elected office to have senatorial status, and that status lasted a lifetime, so long as no subsequent censors demoted the individual out of the senate.

So, the senate was an informal government body. The Roman constitution – not written but a collection of laws, precedents, and, equally important, conventions – gave them no formal power. Informal power, for the Romans, could be quite formidable power. But ever since their creation in the monarchy, the senate had served as the *de facto* guiding body of government. That certainly continued after 300 BCE. Senators tended to be older – the word comes from the word for 'elder' – and, almost always, former office holders. They had experience with political processes and, by 300 BCE, essentially lifetime positions. This meant, in practice, the senators provided continuity of decision-making and guidance that the yearly elected magistrates simply could not provide. And so the senate served to guide the magistrates. More specifically, the senate tended to exercise power in two areas: foreign policy and diplomacy, including determining the military provinces consuls and praetors would govern and how treasury funds could be allocated to Republic officials and projects.

The Political Aristocracy

So the group that led the way to create the Republic, the successful military expansion of that Republic's empire, and, through excessive competition, the political disintegration conventionally called 'The Fall of the Republic' were the aristocratic citizens. These people came from aristocratic families that produced sons who held one or more elected offices and, accordingly, had senatorial status. These aristocrats are the focus of this book.

But why study this group, a tiny proportion of Roman society? There are many reasons, but two seem most relevant for this book. First, quite simply, is the limitations of our sources. As we will see, Roman writers tended to be male and tended to write about formal politics, war, and religion – particularly as that religion linked to politics and war. It is, therefore, exceedingly difficult to find sufficient evidence for the Classical Republic (let's say 300–49 BCE) about anyone who was not an aristocrat engaged in political, military, and religious affairs. Thus, the most detailed histories of the Republic pretty much by necessity focus a great deal on these aristocrats.

But there is another answer that I hope to make clear here at the start. Individuals in the Roman political aristocracy competed intensely, and quite often aggressively, for political offices and honours. And there is good reason to suppose that the seeds of aristocratic competition that were sown in the classical Republic led to the ultimate demise of the Republic. And while objective history – to the extent anyone can achieve that – is not really supposed to be a morality tale or offer predictive power over our present and future, it does give us context, perspective, and insight into the variety of human experience and behaviour. Many readers in the present, I hope, will find interesting the story of intensely competitive politicians craving offices and honours and in the process destroying their political system and ushering in the imposition of a dictatorship. So, with that hope in mind, let us examine aristocratic competition in the Republic and get to the start of this book proper.

(Political) Aristocratic Competition in the Roman Republic

Roman aristocrats competed about all sorts of things: ancestry, progeny, resources, luxuries, education, connections, and so on. Many members of the socio-economic elite of Rome lacked the name or funds to hold the highest political offices. Many must not even have wanted to hold those offices (just as today we do not all desire political office). But we are primarily focused on the small group that did want high office and had the ability to win election through persuading the voting assemblies. For these aristocrats, it can be useful to consider political competition as a form of game – a competition governed by rules with winners and losers – so long as we understand that it was in no way trivial for the players.

One of their animating concepts was *dignitas*, the dignity that came with family, heritage, wealth, and achieving political and military honours, and having ancestors who had these marks of distinction. Aristocrats kept careful track of their own achievements and those of their ancestors. Lineage and achievement, and the resulting honours accrued in the service of the Republic, were the foundation of *dignitas*. This is found across the sources for ancient Rome but is perhaps best embodied in the custom of the aristocratic funeral, described for us by Polybius, a Greek observer of the Republic from the second century BCE. He begins his description noting,

> One example will be sufficient of the pains taken by the Roman state to turn out men ready to endure anything to win a reputation in their country for valour. Whenever one of their illustrious men dies, in the course of his funeral, the body with all its paraphernalia is carried into the Forum to the Rostra, as a raised platform there is called, and sometimes is propped upright upon it so as to be conspicuous, or, more rarely, is laid upon it.[2]

Then a close relative of the deceased, usually a son, sometimes a daughter or some other relation, mounted the speaker stand in the Forum called the Rostra and gave a speech about the deceased's virtues and deeds – two critical components of *dignitas*. But this was only the beginning. Aristocrats made wax death masks, called *imagines*, of their family members when they passed away. These were housed in a special cabinet in each aristocratic household most of the time but were brought out at funerals. Says Polybius,

> When any illustrious member of the family dies, they carry these masks to the funeral, putting them on men whom they thought look as much like the originals as possible in height and other personal features. And these substitutes assume clothes according to the rank of the person represented ... These representatives also ride themselves in chariots, while the fasces and axes, and all the other customary insignia of the particular offices, lead the way, according to the dignity of the rank in the state enjoyed by the deceased in his lifetime.[3]

The actors representing the deceased's ancestors and achievements were supplemented by speeches retelling those achievements. After the achievements of the deceased were recounted, the speaker

> starts upon the [other ancestors] whose representatives are present, beginning with the most ancient, and recounts the successes and achievements of each. By this means the glorious memory of brave men is continually renewed; the fame of those who have performed any noble deed is never allowed to die; and the renown of those who have done good service to their country becomes a matter of common knowledge to the multitude, and part of the heritage of posterity.[4]

Polybius' description illustrates very well what we will see time and time again. Roman aristocrats competed for marks of distinction and status that would add to their and their families' *dignitas*. They cared **deeply** about their status, how their peers and subordinates viewed it, and whether they sufficiently honoured them for it.

The most important marks of distinction for the political aristocracy were marks of *virtus* – the origin of our term virtue – though for Romans of the Republic it meant something more like 'manliness in war'. And the sure way to exhibit *virtus*, as Roman aristocrats saw it, was to behave courageously in battle and earn distinction, first as a soldier, then, if the individual were successful, as an officer, and finally as a commander of armies, a praetor or consul. Military distinction, *gloria* as the Romans termed it, was the single best way to earn a reputation to increase one's *dignitas*. But it was not just any form of military distinction; it was distinction earned, so aristocrats claimed, in the service of the Republic.

So, to follow the game analogy, Roman aristocrats competed for distinctions and honours by stressing their distinguished ancestry and stressing the service those ancestors and they themselves did for the Republic. The prizes were elected offices; they were awarded by the voters. These prizes brought great distinction and honour, not least an important role in guiding the state and a position among the senatorial elite. But the highest offices, like the consulship, also brought with them opportunities for aristocrats to earn even more fame and distinction, through successful military achievements, victories, and conquests in the name of the Republic. In such a competitive system, rivalries were commonplace. They were understood and encouraged as an important part of political life. After all, in this competition, there were a limited number of offices and honours.

This, then is the story of how this competitive political system functioned, failed to function, and ultimately collapsed under the weight of rivalries in the final century of the Republic. It focuses on individual aristocrats who struggled with each other in the political arena for prestige, for status, for *dignitas*. Through these stories of these rivals, we will trace the Republic from what are normally understood as its solid functioning foundations – as an intensely competitive political system – in the third century BCE to a series of bitter rivalries that seem increasingly to have led to the failure of the system in a series of politically motivated murders, proscriptions, police actions, and civil wars. These were most often sparked by aristocrats who wanted to increase their power, status, and influence.

This Book is an Investigation

I have found myself over the years as a historian and teacher largely incapable of writing books on the Roman Republic as anything other than investigations. For those not familiar with the body of evidence we have available for the Republic, it can be shocking, or perhaps dismaying, how few of our ancient sources have survived, how fragmentary they often are, and how much we simply do not know about the past. In a nutshell, our situation as regards the evidence is like this. For the direct workings of the Republic itself and the aristocrats in it, most of our evidence comes from Livy, Polybius, Plutarch, Valerius Maximus, Appian, Dio Cassius, and others whose names will become familiar throughout this book. For the most part, with the occasional exception of Polybius, none of them witnessed any of the events they describe, events from the years c. 205 to 49 BCE.[5] Many of them wrote decades and even centuries after the events they reported. It is often not clear what sources they had access to. It is almost always the case that those earlier sources do not survive, certainly not the primary sources. Frankly, most of the secondary accounts we do have are in fragments and the fragments we have are not the originals. Rather they are the bits copied by hand by mostly monastic scribes in medieval and Renaissance Europe over more than a millennium – but let's not dwell on that unsettling point and forge ahead to investigate.

In all honesty, that is part of the fun of delving into this history, the lure of mystery. We use what we have. We use it because we want to know about the Roman Republic and because there is almost nothing else: archaeological and inscriptional evidence is so valuable in learning about the ancient world, but can tell us very little about the functioning Republic in Rome. And so we use what we have: Roman writings. And we can reasonably discuss many events in the past referred to by these writings. But it is critical to remember from the outset: our sources are opinionated individuals with varying motivations, using sources no longer extant to talk about the topics we are studying.

And so this history, like all histories – certainly histories of the Republic – is an investigation of mostly later sources to construct an interpretation of an earlier past. Accordingly it is critical to know where our information comes from as much as what it says. At the same time, this investigation is meant to be inviting and enjoyable for anyone who wants to think about the Republic. And so the balance for the author must be somewhere between hedging every statement with endless uncertainties, stylistically unsatisfying, and narrating without comment as if the evidence were easy to gather and interpret. I hope it is a balance I have struck.

Our story begins at the very end of the second century BCE, the conclusion of the Second Punic War against Hannibal and the Carthaginians. It ends with the civil war between Caesar, Pompey, and their adherents. It is an exploration into the political lives of aristocrats and, most of all, their competitions for offices and honours and their rivalries with their fellow aristocrats. The end of our story is more or less at 49 BCE. It is a plausible end for the Republic – many end dates could be nominated – the years just before Julius Caesar made himself dictator for life. It was a short life after Caesar seized that power, for he was murdered soon after the announcement, ushering in even more civil wars that swept away the Republic and brought Caesar's adopted son, Augustus, to power as the first *princeps*, the first Roman Emperor.

But at the start of our investigation, about 205 BCE, the Roman Republic, by most understandings, functioned effectively as a political system. Effectively for what it was intended to do. It was intended to preserve and defend the state, handle the very basic functions of ancient governments, and allow aristocrats to compete for offices and honours while leading it. It was designed to allow aristocrats to compete but to prevent anyone from being powerful enough to return Rome to a monarchy. A monarchy meant the end of the free competition for offices and honours that the aristocrats cherished. At this time, 205 BCE, the Romans of the Republic were still locked in a life-or-death struggle with the powerful empire of Carthage in North Africa and the skilled Carthaginian general Hannibal Barca. Our story begins with a rivalry between an aging aristocrat of unparalleled fame and dignity, Quintus Fabius Maximus, and a very young, up-and-coming aristocrat, Cornelius Scipio, who desired a prestigious consulship even though he had not achieved the traditional prerequisites for such an office.

Chapter 1

The Warhorse and the Prodigy: Fabius Maximus and Cornelius Scipio

Publius Cornelius Scipio's bid for the Consulship

In 205 BCE, Publius Cornelius Scipio aimed to invade Africa, an ambitious step that could end the long war against Hannibal and Carthage one way or another. Did he need the approval of the senate, that august group of elders who guided the Roman state? Certainly there was little Scipio had needed from the senate in his short, but spectacularly successful, rise to glory. No, assembly voters were the source of his glory. They had elected him *aedile* in 213, the first rung of an aristocratic career. So far he had a normal enough career, if anything could be considered normal in the more-than-decade during which the Carthaginian Hannibal marched hostile armies of Spanish, Gallic, and African soldiers through Italy.[1]

Then in 211 BCE, a new catastrophe struck for Scipio and the Republic. His father and uncle, Publius and Gnaeus Cornelius Scipio, had successfully battled the Carthaginian empire in Spain, but in 211 the tide turned. The Carthaginian and Spanish forces crushed both Roman armies in the region, slaying their commanders in the process. That catastrophe spurred the second time the assembly had supported Scipio. This time they catapulted him ahead of many senior aristocrats. They had granted him, son and nephew of the slain commanders, the *imperium* of a consul and command of Roman forces in Spain. He had never held any of the prerequisite offices for accepting such a command; he was not even old enough, at 25 to be a praetor, let alone a consul. He was not even a magistrate at the time of the appointment. He may not even have yet been granted senatorial status.[2] Yet he had dared to go, when so many far more experienced – and eligible – senators feared to. The centuriate assembly was inspired by his courage and voted him the command.[3]

And Scipio's successes in Spain were stunning. He took command
of a Spanish army in fragments and imposed rigorous training to hone
the soldiers – many of whom were older than him. He reorganized the
workings of cohorts and maniples to make the army more tactically
effective. Then with his reinvigorated fighting force, Scipio captured
the strategically important New Carthage in 209. More victories against
the Carthaginians followed, including a smashing victory at Ilipa – all
testimony to his successful efforts to reform the army. By the end of the
year 206, Scipio had shattered, it seemed, Carthaginian forces in Spain
and laid the foundations for lasting Roman influence in the peninsula.
Triumphant, the young man, now a bit over 30, returned to Rome, his
ambitions set on holding one of the two consulships for 205.[4]

The *populus*, the Roman voters, had propelled Scipio's successful
career. Now, fresh from victory in Spain, Scipio sought an even greater
honour: to be elected consul, one of the chief magistrates of the Republic.
If he won, he would leap over any number of older senators who had
held the praetorship, the conventional prerequisite office to a consulship.
In a meeting of the senate, the young proconsul-who-had-never-been-
consul recounted his achievements and asked the senate for permission
to celebrate a triumph, that spectacular military parade awarded to senior
commanders who had won important victories. The senate denied the
request. Scipio acquiesced: he knew no one had ever celebrated a triumph
who had not held a regular magistracy. Undaunted however, Scipio
entered the city on foot in a style that could only be called triumphal,
wagons of spoils and silver preceding him. Spectators flocked around
him on election day, following him to his house, and joining him on
the Capitoline when he sacrificed 100 oxen to Jupiter. Once again, the
voters favoured him with an unusual honour: they elected him consul
years ahead of his time and without having held the office of praetor.[5]

If anything, this honour stoked Scipio's ambition further. The senate,
exercising its customary power, established Bruttium in Southern Italy
and Sicily as the two provinces for the consuls of 205. Ordinarily Fate
– in the form of casting lots – determined which consul would go to
each province. But the consul Crassus was pontifex Maximus and
could not leave Italy; therefore he was assigned to Bruttium. That left
Sicily for Scipio. But Scipio had no intention of spending the war in a
largely pacified province. His sights were higher: invade Africa; put the

Carthaginians on the defensive; force Hannibal to abandon Italy to save his precious homeland. Who better to do it than the precocious Scipio? And so he planned to persuade the senate that the Republic was best served if he invaded Africa rather than cooling his heels in Sicily. Not that he would wholly depend on that guiding body. Scipio had investigated a backup plan and either the news slipped out or, perhaps, he had spread it: if the senate denied him the African command, he would simply go back to the centuriate assembly, the voters who had always supported him, and be voted that command against the senate's wishes.[6]

And so the seeds of conflict were planted when consul Scipio convened the senate to discuss the matter. First though, as the president of the senate, he determined the order of other business. This business included receiving ambassadors from the Spanish city of Saguntum who had come to declare thanks to Rome, and to Scipio, for ending the Carthaginian threat. In addition to the polished diplomatic flattery of the ambassadors, the Saguntines also wished to dedicate a golden wreath to Jupiter on the Romans' behalf. After these opening items of business, the time came to discuss the issue most important to Scipio. He wished the senate to shift his province from Sicily to Africa. In other words, he intended to invade Africa, and in doing so win the decisive victory over the Carthaginians.[7]

Quintus Fabius Maximus' Counter

Scipio made his case; now it was time for the senate to respond. Following the hierarchy of speaking in the senate, the first opinion was delivered by the *princeps senatus*, 'the leader of the senate', an honorary position granted to a venerable senator. But the princeps happened to be Scipio's *de facto* rival, the venerable aristocrat and general Quintus Fabius Maximus Verrucosus. Fabius had particular ideas about this young Roman and his audacity; misplaced audacity, he and a number of senior senators thought.

Scipio and Fabius Maximus' personalities, if we can glean anything about them, seem to offer a study in political opposites. Where Scipio had never been praetor or consul, Fabius had held five consulships, the first over 25 years ago when Scipio was just a toddler. In some of the darkest days of the war, after the disastrous Roman defeat to Hannibal at Lake Trasimene (217 BCE), Fabius had been named dictator by the Roman assembly, an established political and military office for state emergencies.

Famously in that year, he adopted a strategy of *cunctatio*, 'delaying.' He shadowed Hannibal through central Italy, biding time while his soldiers regained their nerve and the Republic rallied from two disastrous losses. When his dictatorship ended and the Romans opted again to head into a decisive battle, the disaster at Cannae was the result. Tens of thousands of Roman soldiers were trapped and butchered on an August day in 216 BCE. Fabius again proved instrumental in the recovery, helping the city regain its balance and slowly tilt power away from Hannibal and back to the Republic. In short, Fabius was as decorated a noble as one could be in the middle Republic and had largely succeeded politically and militarily by practising cautious restraint and prudently avoiding great risks.[8] Some regarded him as the saviour of the Republic.

Now Fabius, as *princeps*, had the right to speak first. What would he say? How would he persuade the senate to curb the rash Scipio and follow a more measured strategy to conclude the war? The late first century BCE historian, Livy, reports a blistering harangue. Perhaps the original speech survived the pair of centuries between Fabius and Livy, but the speech we have has all the hallmarks of a dramatic work Livy or one of his sources constructed for the story. Still, it is difficult to deny that the points of Fabius' speech as Livy presents them seem to well represent the core of Fabius' opposition.

So, as Livy relates it, Fabius launched a tirade. Many senators, he opined, believed Sicily was nothing more than a staging ground, and that it was a settled matter that Scipio would readily move from it to invade Africa. Fabius, however, did not take it as a given and declared that Africa should in no way be Scipio's province explicitly or implicitly. Some might say Fabius was simply acting as the *cunctator*, the delayer. One who did not know his reputation might dismiss him as timid. He cared not: the Romans had regained control of Italy and Sicily through careful planning and deliberate action, a strategy that Fabius was instrumental in forming. Others might suspect that Fabius was simply old and jealous, begrudging the young Scipio whose star was on the rise. He cared not. Five consulships – a record practically unmatched in the Republic we should note – spoke to his own *dignitas* and rank. There was no need for Fabius to covet the younger man's glories. Scipio was no rival; he was little more than a boy, younger than Fabius' own son. And Fabius himself was far too old and tired to claim the African command for himself.[9]

Rhetorical embellishments notwithstanding, Livy's version of Fabius' speech plausibly gets to the heart of the historical Fabius' objection. Hannibal seemed to be on the defensive, waiting with his army in Bruttium, but as long as he commanded an army in Italy, the Republic was in danger. The soundest course was for the consuls to meet the great foe in Bruttium. If they focused their attention elsewhere, then Hannibal might threaten the very city itself. For good measure, in Livy's version, Fabius pivoted to the historical example of Marcus Atilius Regulus' failed invasion of Africa in the first war against Carthage, a failure that saw the army defeated and Regulus captured. Then Fabius contrasted Scipio's Spanish theatre, where Rome had some allies and local support, with Africa, where there would be neither. Essentially for Fabius, Scipio was an impetuous youth who underestimated the threat of Hannibal and the enormity of invading Africa. Scipio was no king. He was an elected consul of the Republic; he served that Republic. Let him best serve, then, keep the province of Sicily, and stay out of Africa.[10]

A number of senators regarded Fabius' speech favourably, and it is not difficult to see why.[11] The calm measured advice of the old aristocrat must have reassured many. Then there was the matter of age and custom. The Romans tended to idolize – unlike modern societies oft focused on perpetual youth – the seniors in age, the tried and tested leaders. Indeed the word 'senate,' *senatus*, comes from the word for elder and refers to that august body as a group of elders. Scipio was young, very young. But the other former aediles – the only magistracy Scipio had earned through election – were junior in prestige in the senate.[12] The majority who had been elected praetor or consul in the traditional fashion had, presumably, climbed the ranks in the time-honoured way, by growing older, listening to their elders, and earning the support of voters over time. Scipio was a bypass: he held the honours and ranks without the necessary commitment of time, energy, and homage to his elders.

Livy, of course, provided a rebuttal speech for Scipio, and, again, there is good reason to suppose it is not the original words Scipio uttered that day. But it seems a good synopsis of what Scipio's arguments must have been. Well, perhaps not Scipio's first point. Livy has him begin by respectfully, yet firmly, accusing Fabius of jealousy and asserting that he, Scipio, saw Fabius as a rival, for Fabius was at the pinnacle of a successful aristocratic career and the pinnacle was where Scipio planned to be. This sounds more like Livian character-building than a sound rhetorical tactic. At any rate, the rest seems to follow better what must have been the arguments at the time. Scipio had achieved great things out of the disaster in Spain; he was more than capable of handling the present dangers. It was time for Africa to be ravaged, not Italy, which had suffered the depredations of Hannibal for well over a decade. Hannibal would surely leave Italy and follow Scipio to Africa; he could do nothing else as a defender of his country.[13]

Scipio, the Tribunes of the Plebs, and the Authority of the Senate

Apparently, however, Scipio's intentions to undermine the senate and go directly to the assembly had circulated by now among the senators. The 'junior' Scipio (the term for men under the age of 45) had essentially said he would not respect the decision of his elders. Quintus Fulvius Flaccus, a most distinguished aristocrat with four consulships and a censorship to his name, pressed Scipio. Would he respect the Senate's decision in assigning provinces or would he put the question to the people? Scipio, no fool, begged the question: he would pursue the interests of the Republic. Fulvius was no fool either and pressed the point home. Clearly Scipio, he asserted, was not asking the senate for guidance – as Fulvius surely was implying would have been the appropriate, respectful, conventional path. No, he simply wished to take their temperature. If they denied him the province of Africa, he was ready to go immediately to the assembly and override the senate's decision.[14]

It is important to note that the fundamental accusation Fulvius threw at Scipio, the core issue, would be a point of disagreement, contention, and even violence in the late Republic. Unlike modern countries with written constitutions, the Roman Republic's laws and rules of operation were mostly unwritten, preserved in the memories of the political class. Of course, those memories could be faulty. There was a very strong sense among Romans, however, that they followed binding conventions set by the *mos maiorum*, the 'customs of the ancestors'. One of those customs, rather firmly entrenched, was that the senate, not the people, had the power and authority to determine the consular provinces of the year. And while it is true that there were at least two laws in the time before Scipio, explicitly stating that any motion passed by an assembly was binding on all Romans, this did not change the fact that convention – powerful, weighty convention – dictated that the people did not interfere with the senate's right to assign provinces.

So Fulvius was pressing Scipio on an important point, not just of constitutional law, but of the senate's collective dignity and authority. If Scipio would not answer the question, then Fulvius would not offer his opinion. That needs a bit of unpacking. The senate functioned as a deliberative body where everyone present of senatorial rank had the right to speak their opinion. Indeed, it may be helpful to think of senators not as officials at all, but as Romans who had been granted, by the censors acting on behalf of the Roman people, the right of attending the senate meetings and offering an opinion there. Fulvius, a senior senator, had been called to give his opinion presumably either because Scipio, probably the presiding consul, had just asked him to give his opinion, or because his rank gave him the right to opine at that point. However it may have been, Fulvius refused to offer his opinion, something like refusing to vote. If Livy's account is accurate on this point, Fulvius seems to have thought that refusing to offer his opinion when asked was unorthodox if not illegal. For he called upon the tribunes of the plebs to support his right not to speak: what was the point anyway if the consul would not accept the guidance of the senate?

Scipio insisted the tribunes had no right to intervene on this matter: it was Fulvius' turn to offer his opinion, and so offer his opinion he must at the time warranted by his status. The tribunes, presumably, must have taken at least a moment to confer, then made a ruling. They wished the consul to follow the decision of the senate about provinces and would not allow Scipio to propose the province of Africa before the assembly. Scipio must not have been prepared for that because he called a day-long recess so that he might confer with his colleague Crassus. They conferred and Scipio subsequently yielded to the senate's decision about consular provinces.[15]

We are assuredly missing something in Livy's account, for the next thing he says is that one province was Bruttium and the war against Hannibal. The other province, Livy asserts, was Sicily, along with permission to invade Africa if the consul deemed that to be best for the Republic. In other words, Scipio got what he wanted. Presumably there must have been more political negotiations in the day of recess that are lost to us.[16]

Still, though Fabius did not get his way in this instance, his opinion must have had some traction because the senate did not authorize Scipio to levy any new troops. With military authorisation but insufficient troops beyond the garrisons in Sicily, Fabius and like-minded senators could still check Scipio's invasion. Undaunted, Scipio asked and received permission to recruit volunteers. When he did, 7,000 soldiers flocked to him. He also received permission to seek donations from Rome's allies to build a larger fleet than the thirty quinqueremes he had been allocated. The donations proved plentiful, allowing him to build and fully equip an additional thirty ships.[17] Actors outside the senatorial elite enabled Scipio.

But it was not Fabius' last chance to stop Scipio. Not yet. He was still convinced the young consul should be curbed. Carthaginian operations in 205 in Italy could only have underlined this reality as Fabius saw it. While Scipio prepared his forces in Sicily for an invasion, Hannibal's brother Mago sailed with thirty warships and captured Genoa, some 250 miles up the coast, with a modest army. From there he worked to spark yet another rebellion in Gaul, the north Italian region inhabited largely by Celtic peoples. News of Scipio's preparations hardly diverted him. He dispatched twenty warships to guard the Carthaginian coast and continued with his plans. Not only did the Carthaginians appear unimpressed by Scipio, they continued active operations in Italy. Meanwhile, Scipio spent the whole of his consulship preparing to invade. He forged a new army between his volunteers and the veterans of the Sicilian garrison. His new warships were dry-docked to season the newly-chopped timbers. Gaius Laelius, Scipio's trusted lieutenant, raided the African coast with a fleet to sow fear and gain intelligence. And so the invasion might soon have been launched without a hitch.[18]

The Pleminius Affair

Except for Gaius Pleminius. At some point in 205, Scipio had spied the opportunity to recover the south Italian city of Locri. He did so and put his legate, Pleminius, in charge of the city. He proved a terrible governor, at least to the Locrians. Livy notes that Pleminius inflicted 'unspeakable abuse' on the Locrians, and while one might reasonably suspect that unspeakable meant, unprovable, with what else is known about Pleminius the indictment seems to stick.[19] Through his deficiencies as a governor, Pleminius stirred up a hornet's nest of trouble.[20]

It began with a puzzling Roman situation in Locri, presumably set up by Scipio after recovering the city. Livy insists that there were two independent commands at Locri, one under Pleminius, the other under a pair of Scipio's military tribunes. It seems like a shockingly bad idea to govern a city in wartime with a confused command hierarchy, so perhaps the tribunes were just ill-informed or recalcitrant about Pleminius' command. In any event, one of Pleminius' soldiers pilfered a silver cup from a Locrian. The tribunes Sergius and Matienus stopped him in the act and ordered him to return the cup. The pilferer refused. Friction heated to altercation as nearby soldiers, according to their loyalties, joined the tribunes or the pilferer. A streetfight broke out, and the tribunes and their troops won. Pummelled and looking for payback, the pilferer and his comrades found Pleminius to complain about their mistreatment.[21]

Pleminius ... overreacted. On his orders, the tribunes were arrested and he ordered his lictors to strip them in preparation for a flogging, a staple of Roman military discipline. The tribunes resisted arrest and called on those nearby for aid. Soldiers loyal to the tribunes joined the fracas, subdued the lictors, and gathered round Pleminius to cut and beat him, mutilating his ears and nose and leaving him for dead. Word reached Scipio, who could not have been pleased. He took a ship to Locri to settle the mess. The tribunes he clapped in irons to be judged by the Roman senate. Pleminius he judged free of wrongdoing and confirmed at his post. The necessary orders given, Scipio returned to Locri.

Scipio had not reckoned with Pleminius' pain, humiliation, and rage. He assumed Pleminius would follow his orders; he had not personally seen the tribunes off to Rome. Pleminius did not follow orders, and the tribunes never made it. He had the tribunes seized, brutally tortured, and killed when he was satisfied they had suffered enough; their corpses he ordered cast in the street to lie unburied. That was just the start. Pleminius had a world of grievance stored up and he unleashed it on the Locrians. The soldiers in his command were let loose to rape and pillage the defenceless inhabitants of the city, brutally assaulting Locrians, stealing and destroying. Pleminius even affronted the gods and looted the sacred treasury of Proserpina, testified the Locrian embassy that escaped to Rome to report the misdeeds of the governor.[22]

Fabius, rightfully as the *princeps senatus*, began to interrogate the delegation. Had they informed Scipio of his heavy-handed governor? In the process Fabius uncovered the whole nasty business of mutilated Pleminius and the murdered tribunes. Indeed, the Locrians were confident that the whole military debacle was proof of divine Proserpina's wrath. After the ambassadors left the senate, Fabius and those who supported him launched what would be a final push to discredit Scipio. He was an unfit commander, and his corruption produced unfit soldiers. He had no business even being in Locri since it was outside his province. They even claimed that Scipio had a love for Greek clothing and culture, essentially a jab at Scipio for being too soft, too unRoman. Fierce debate roiled the senate with many supporting Scipio and many thinking he was a corrupt upstart. So many opinions were offered that the senators present could not all speak that day.[23]

Fabius' push to recall Scipio ultimately failed. A compromise solution, suggested by Quintus Metellus, prevailed. A commission would investigate the matter on scene. If it became clear that Scipio ordered and condoned Pleminius' rampage against the Locrians, he would be relieved of command. If not, he should be left to prepare for the African invasion. The results of the investigation were predictable. When interviewed by the commissioners, the Locrians suggested Scipio should have supervised Pleminius more closely. Fearing potential reprisals, they were not willing to suggest Scipio himself was the problem. With nothing to build a case upon, the commission exonerated Scipio. And Pleminius? He died in a Roman prison before his trial concluded.

Ultimately, the distinguished Quintus Fabius Maximus Cunctator, the elder statesman who demonstrably led the Roman recovery against Hannibal, the one 'who by delaying saved our cause', as the poet Ennius once eulogized, failed to check the precocious commander Publius Cornelius Scipio.[24]

Scipio's invasion army landed in Africa in spring 204 at Utica, a city to the north of Carthage. For reasons that are unclear, the Carthaginians did not challenge the fleet from Sicily or the army's landing. Carthage dispatched a couple of cavalry forces to harry the Romans, and though they were driven off, the Romans made little progress during the campaign season. Scipio raided the lands near Utica and ultimately began a siege of the city itself. When a Carthaginian-Numidian army arrived, Scipio broke his siege. The armies did not engage however, and late in 204 all three forces established winter camps. There were some talks, but not serious ones, at least not to Scipio who began 203 with a surprise attack on the enemy camps. The Romans torched the camps and the flames caught thousands in their sleep. The Carthaginian and Numidian armies were destroyed. Scipio then returned to his siege of Utica and Hasdrubal and Syphax were free to recruit another Carthaginian army. They journeyed to the Great Plains and Scipio eventually followed and won a victory. Then Scipio raided some more and offered peace terms to the Carthaginian government. Carthage accepted and a treaty was struck, but, for reasons that are not entirely clear, the treaty did not last. Meanwhile Hannibal finally departed Italy and arrived in Africa with a small army late in 203.[25]

In the midst of Scipio's campaign in Africa, in 203 BCE, Fabius died. He never saw Scipio's ultimate victory and we cannot say what he would have felt – though even had he lived through it all those feelings would almost certainly be lost to us. Envy; relief; admiration? Whatever it might have been, Fabius died a highly distinguished aristocrat. His inability to check Scipio using the constitutional machinery available did not tarnish his reputation, likely not with contemporaries, certainly not with posterity. When Livy pauses to note the great Cunctator's death, he offers a far more substantial eulogy than he gave to many an aristocrat:

This year also saw the death of Quintus Fabius Maximus. He had reached a very great age, if it is true, as some writers have stated, that he held the office of augur for sixty-two years. What is indisputable is that he was worthy of the name Maximus, and would have deserved to be the first of his line to bear it. He held more magistracies than his father, and the same number as his grandfather. His grandfather Rullus enjoyed the fame of more victories and greater battles, but to have had Hannibal as one's enemy is enough to equal or outweigh them all. Fabius has been stigmatized as a cautious soldier, never quick to act; but though one may question whether he was a 'delayer' by nature or because delaying tactics happened to suit the campaigns he was engaged in, this, at least, is certain, that, as the poet Ennius wrote, 'One man by his delaying saved the State.' His son Quintus Fabius Maximus succeeded him as augur, and as pontifex (for he had held two priesthoods) he was succeeded by Servius Sulpicius Galba.[26]

After Fabius died, late in 202, Scipio and Hannibal's forces clashed at Zama in North Africa. The Romans won decisively.[27] When the senate heard the news of Scipio's smashing victory at Zama, they declared three days of thanksgiving and notified the public through an assembly. The rivalries of Roman aristocrats, and inspired manoeuvrings, continued nevertheless. After the centuriate assembly elected the consuls for 201, Gnaeus Cornelius Lentulus and Publius Aelius Paetus, there was some jockeying to undermine Scipio's glory. Consul Lentulus essentially refused to allow public business to be conducted until the matter of the consular provinces was settled by the senate. He insisted that he should be assigned to Africa, currently proconsul Scipio's province. His hope was to steal Scipio's glory by mopping up the enemy and the war, either by conducting operations that would be made quite easy thanks to Scipio's great victory, or simply by being the one who formally got to impose a victorious peace on Carthage. His colleague Paetus offered Lentulus no resistance, not out of any loyalty but simply because he was convinced Lentulus' plan to steal credit would fail. Two tribunes of the plebs, however, Quintus Minucius Thermus and Manius Acilius Glabrio countered that the assembly had already granted Scipio proconsular *imperium* the year before to conduct the war, so Lentulus' demand was improper. Debates continued on the matter of the African command, and ultimately the matter was left to the senate. They assigned a peculiarly precise province to the consul who left Italy. He would command the fleet of fifty warships based in Sicily. If there was any fighting left to do in Africa, Scipio would command the land forces, and the consul would command the fleet. If peace terms were to be forged, the tribunes would ask the assembly whether the consul or Scipio should be authorized to craft the treaty and have the honour of leading the Roman army in Africa home.[28]

Then the senate arranged the rest of the provinces for 201 and met with envoys from Macedonia, for King Philip of Macedon had allied with the Carthaginians against Rome. Then the time came to receive the embassy from Carthage. The Carthaginians gave their speeches, hoping Rome would be merciful in victory. The senate was resolved to grant peace, but Lentulus vetoed the resolution, still hoping to keep the war against Carthage in play for his own personal glory. Consuls vetoing senatorial resolutions does not occur often in our sources, but that veto gained him nothing. The tribunes Acilius and Minucius simply summoned the tribal assembly and asked them if they favoured peace and which commander should conclude the treaty and bring the army home. The tribes voted for Scipio to end the war and bring the soldiers home. The senate accordingly dispatched a ten-person commission to advise Scipio on the terms he would set for Carthage. The *fetiales*, those Roman priests whose job was to take care of the sacred aspects of declaring war and peace, were also sent with their customary flint knives and special sacred herb-bunches to sanctify the treaty.[29]

And so Scipio concluded the treaty and the fetials did their holy work. The Carthaginians surrendered their ships and war elephants, along with Roman deserters they had sheltered and prisoners of war. Scipio gave the orders: the Latin deserters were beheaded and the Romans crucified. The fleet – some 500 oared craft of all kinds – Scipio ordered burnt at sea. Later Scipio would relate that had not Lentulus set out to undermine his victory and usurp his command, he would have destroyed Carthage outright.[30] As it was, the humbled city persisted until the Romans finally destroyed it in 146 BCE.

The peace concluded, Scipio led the troops home. Most of them he sent the quick way by sea. He, on the other hand, took a leisurely land route home, savouring and celebrating his victory to the fullest. He travelled through Italy. His route was mobbed by well-wishers from the cities and the farms. Livy says his triumph was the most grand ever, but offers no details.[31] Fortunately for us, second century CE Appian of Alexandria describes the procession. First trumpeters and wagons filled with the spoils of war led the procession. Models of towers symbolized the cities Scipio had captured, and painted scenes illustrated his battles next; then the masses of coins and precious metals and the various victory crowns grateful allies and Scipio's own soldiers had awarded him. Then a series of white oxen for the sacrifice followed by captured war elephants. The captive leaders of Carthage and Numidia trudged along, followed by lictors wearing purple. Next a series of musicians adorned with gold, pacing the march with rhythmic music. Then bearers of incense perfuming the area. Only after all these spectacles had passed came the great spectacle of Scipio, imperator, the general himself

> on a chariot embellished with various designs, wearing a crown of gold and precious stones, and dressed, according to the fashion of the country, in a purple toga embroidered with golden stars. He bore a sceptre of ivory and a laurel branch, which is always the Roman symbol of victory. Riding in the same chariot with him were boys and girls, and on horses on either side of him young men, his own relatives. Then followed those who had served him in the war as secretaries, aids, and armour-bearers.[32]

Following all of this, at last, marched Scipio's victorious army unit-by-unit, all crowned, all carrying branches of laurel, with those who had won spoils in battle carrying them along for good measure. According to the rules of the triumph, the soldiers could speak freely and so they praised some officers and mocked others. The lengthy parade travelled through Rome until Scipio arrived at the Capitoline Hill. There he held a victory banquet attended by his friends. Perhaps most striking of all in the history of a highly competitive Roman aristocracy, Scipio was the first Roman commander to be nicknamed after the land he had conquered. Africanus. Who coined it and made it stick was never quite clear, but the glory it conferred was clear to all.[33]

The rivalries and conflicts around the details of Scipio's bid for an African command helpfully illuminate several features of the aristocratic political arena in the Middle Republic. They involved the efforts of one aristocrat, young Scipio in this case, striving for *gloria*, and rivals, not least Fabius, gathering to curb him. The arguments were not just about rivalry – there were disagreements about strategy and competency in this stage of the war. But it is hard to escape the impression that senior consulars like Fabius and Fulvius did not think such important commands and potential honours should go to an aristocratic upstart. A more self-interested effort at stealing honours came when Scipio had defeated Hannibal and Carthage, and consul Lentulus attempted to swipe Scipio's command and secure credit for officially ending the war himself.

In these and many other disagreements, the senate fulfilled its traditional role as the body moderating conflict between individuals and curbing the excessive claims to power and prestige that any of its members might make. And so it mediated the rivalries between Scipio and these aristocrats. Ultimately, though, Scipio achieved a level of *gloria* largely unmatched by any so young in the Republic. He had rather nimbly sidestepped the traditions that governed and slowed any individual's rise among the ranks of the aristocrats. Commanding armies with the *imperium* of a consul at 25 – unheard of – he had pacified, at least for a little while, Spain and Carthaginian forces there. But when he sought a triumph, the senate checked him: he had not held the prerequisite offices they decreed. Scipio of course, concerned with his rising star, his rising *dignitas*, and his claims to *gloria* walked into the city on foot in what may have been the most triumphal non-triumph to date.

And then the wranglings in the senate. Senators like Fabius and Fulvius, highly distinguished consulars, did their best to limit Scipio, to restrain him from receiving full permission for an African command in 205. And the senate moderated a compromise, perhaps not a compromise fully to Fabius' liking, but still a compromise. Yes, assign Scipio to Sicily but allow him to invade Africa if he thought it best. Limit his forces and resources however, acts fully within the traditional authority of the senate. And Scipio, as most exceptional aristocrats did, pushed against those limits; ultimately successfully, he gained the forces he needed through donations and volunteers.

But none of this amounted to a substantive challenge to the power structures in the Republic. Scipio was no renegade general determined to get his way, damn the costs. At least two important decisions kept the systems working, kept the aristocracy cohesive and the senate in its authoritative role. First, the tribunes agreed to veto any effort Scipio might make to circumvent the senate. And second, Scipio, when he saw the constitution arrayed to reinforce senatorial prerogatives, agreed to follow the dictates of the senate. Not that Scipio probably had any serious choice in the matter. There were few, if any, precedents of individual aristocrats seizing commands that the senate had not authorized. Scipio had magnificent prestige, but not a power base of the sort that would allow him to ignore the senate and seize a command through the support of the assemblies. A century and more later, it would come to that, as some aristocrats indeed used such power for rebellion. For now, however, the system had allowed Scipio to be magnificent, but not monarchic. Indeed, even the great Scipio could find himself slighted in the competitive world of senatorial politics, as we shall see in the next chapter.

Chapter 2

The Censor and the Corrupt Nobles:
Cato, the Scipios, and Flamininus

Cato never grew clumsy in his political prosecutions, and his rivals never stopped trying to silence him. Even at the venerable age of 86, sometime in the 150s BCE, Cato's rivals charged him with a capital offence. The fire of his oratory had not cooled, however, and Cato's foes could not make the charges stick. A few years later in 149, his final year as it happened, Cato prosecuted Servius Sulpicius Galba, who, as governor of Spain, lured 8,000 Lusitanians to be slaughtered after inviting them to parley.[1] Over the decades, Cato had carefully crafted a reputation for traditional Roman virtues like honesty, simplicity, and selfless service to the Republic. The high standards he set for himself left his rivals little margin for error in their own conduct and Cato clashed frequently with those he disdained for misconduct. Among these rivals was reportedly Publius Cornelius Scipio Africanus, conqueror of Hannibal and arguably the most distinguished Roman of the day.[2] Nor did Cato seem to have much use for Scipio's brother Lucius Cornelius Scipio Asiaticus, conqueror of the Syrian Seleucid King Antiochus IV. At least no use for him after that war concluded and Asiaticus was accused of taking bribes from the king. So, when a series of tribunes in the 180s charged these two noble magnates with corruption, word naturally spread that Cato had instigated the indictments.[3]

These efforts to disgrace Lucius Asiaticus and his brother Africanus were spectacles that captured Roman attention. It started with Lucius. In 187 two tribunes of the plebs both named Quintus Petilius – presumably cousins – charged Lucius in the senate with misappropriating funds seized in the recent war against Antiochus, king of the Seleucid Empire (192–188 BCE). This charge also tarnished the great Africanus by association since he had served as his brother's legate and bookkeeper on that campaign. The accusations against Lucius Scipio were dropped in the senate but swiftly picked up by the tribune Gaius Minucius Augurinus, who indicted Asiaticus in front of an assembly; quite a scene. Convicted and unable to pay the stiff fine, Lucius would have been publicly hauled off to prison if not for the timely protection of another tribune, Tiberius Sempronius Gracchus.[4] Several years later, in 184, the political attack shifted directly to Africanus, also accused of embezzlement during that Syrian campaign. Africanus ultimately did not dignify the charges with a response. At least, not a direct one; but, as we will see, he created a spectacle of his own to counter the charges, a swansong as it happened. Then he left Rome, with less-than-sterling dignity, to his estate in Liternum, where he soon died.

Whether Cato in fact lay behind these prosecutions of the Scipio brothers, these incidents still serve as an excellent instance of the senate regulating its members and attempting to check those who had grown mighty.[5] More than that, Cato's career and rivalries, like those of Scipio and Fabius before him, illustrate effectively the intense political struggles between Roman aristocrats that took place in the century before the troubles of the late Republic. Aristocrats wrangled, but the political systems of the Republic withstood the strain. At least at this point.

The Rise of a New Man

Our most detailed source for Cato's life is the Greek priest and biographer Plutarch's *Life of Cato the Elder* from the early second century CE. As often is the case, it is difficult to establish a clear chronology from Plutarch's general statements, but this seems reasonably solid. Cato came originally from Tusculum, a Latin city south of Rome. He grew to adulthood on an estate in Sabinum. As a youth he developed two notable talents. He was a skilled advocate who took the cases of those in need without a fee, and thus built a reputation for honour and talent in the villages around Rome where he plied his craft. He was apparently no less talented as a soldier, making his mark as a cavalry trooper, military tribune, and quaestor in the years when Hannibal stalked the hills and plains of Italy. His chest, Plutarch tells us, was marked by honourable wounds. The politics of the Republic often revolved around aristocrats claiming to have greater *virtus* than their rivals, and thus being of greater service to the Republic. It was not unheard of – and may have been very common for all our paltry evidence suggests – for aristocrats to show their battle scars as proof of their *virtus*. So, Cato had the goods, the scars to prove he could stand his ground and take a hit in the service of the Republic.[6] Roman culture, not by any means uniquely, emphasized the importance of moral role models, suggesting that youth should learn both whom to mimic and whom to not in order to instil the proper virtues. Reports suggested that Cato found inspiration early on, from the life and reputation of Manius Curius Dentatus. His modest house and small farm abutted Cato's land, bringing him to the young man's mind, and his legend – a modest frugal Roman even though he had celebrated three triumphs – served as inspiration. If not Dentatus then there were many other lionized Romans who reportedly – and almost certainly exaggeratedly – cared nothing for softness and luxury and were simple strong hard folk who served the Republic well.

These mannerisms aided Cato well, for he was a *novus homo*, as the Romans termed it, a 'new man'. A new man lacked the consular ancestors that defined the nobles, and without that pedigree faced serious obstacles to climbing the political ladder. He had to build a reputation and political relationships, with little to start from. His skill as an orator and steadfastness as a soldier served him well in this. These qualities Rome valued highly during the war against Hannibal that defined Cato's youth. He first entered the military and political world at Rome where larger-than-life figures like Fabius Maximus and Scipio Africanus led the efforts to defeat the invader. The sources do not fully agree on his military posts during the war, but they do not conflict either. Cato's first military campaign, it would seem, was in the year when Fabius Maximus and Claudius Marcellus were consul, 214 BCE.[7] Subsequently, Cato served as a military tribune in Sicily, probably under the command of Marcellus, who campaigned against the Greeks and Carthaginians there from 214 to 210.[8] He served under Fabius as the latter retook the Greek city of Tarentum (209). Cato rose from trooper to military tribune to staff officer of Claudius Nero in a short time. Nero, in 207 BCE, joined forces with co-consul Marcus Livius Salinator to inflict a devastating defeat on the Carthaginian army at the Metaurus River, the last major battle of the war in Italy.[9]

Young, politically hopeful Romans not uncommonly attached themselves to elder aristocrats for guidance, and Plutarch explicitly attaches Cato to Quintus Fabius Maximus. They may have met during the siege of Tarentum. Plutarch asserts that, in the later years of the war, Cato adopted Fabius as a role model. Adopting Fabius' rivals followed, so Cato opposed Publius Cornelius Scipio, who was no more than a handful of years older than Cato himself. Where Cato worked steadily up the political ladder, Scipio had catapulted to distinction commanding his slaughtered father's army in Spain and defeating Carthaginian forces there (as we saw in the last chapter). Regardless of any inherited rivalry, the initial break between the two young aristocrats, Plutarch relates, came in 205 when Cato reportedly was Scipio's quaestor – essentially a treasurer – in Sicily.[10] Thrifty and austere Cato was offended not only by Africanus' attraction to theatres and all manner of luxuries he secured for himself, but by the money he lavished on his troops. The two quarrelled, and Cato returned to Rome, dismissed. There he joined Fabius' cause to check Scipio and secure his recall.[11]

The decades-long bitter rivalry between Cato and Scipio seems destined from their first meeting in Plutarch's biography of Cato. The eternally frugal Cato had, as a new man, to earn his traditional path to office through exceptional service. Meanwhile Scipio had hurtled past the normal requirements of office holding, jumping from aedile to proconsul in Spain, to consul (205 BCE) without any of the intervening requisite offices and under the minimum age. Surely the two must have been bitter rivals? A good story, to be sure, and one that sets the seeds of the conflicts between the two in the 180s that are otherwise more difficult to explain. An archetypically austere Cato could not help but clash with archetypically profligate Scipio upon their first encounters late in the war. Still, this episode, this initial clash of wills, is unlikely to have been serious, if it occurred at all. As it happens, a series of other sources suggest Cato served with distinction in Scipio's African campaign. Livy asserts that Cato was Scipio's quaestor in 204, not 205, and commanded part of the fleet of Roman ships Scipio used that year to invade Africa.[12] First century CE stratagem collector Frontinus offers an additional nugget: Cato and his soldiers seized control of some Carthaginian ships and used them to deceive and sink other ships.[13] Frontinus' rough contemporary, the great encyclopedist Pliny the Elder, suggests Cato learned the military arts from Scipio and Hannibal in Africa, as well a quaestor might, suggesting that Cato served in the campaign even after the naval crossing.[14] There is little reason to doubt these sources, while the same cannot be said for Plutarch and Nepos. Even beyond the weight of opposing evidence, their version is problematic. The idea that Scipio, who had successfully turned his African campaign into something of a private venture, would have been forced to accept a bad quaestor strains credibility, just as it strains credibility to suppose that Cato would risk his precarious political career – he was, after all, a new man – by turning on his commander, to whom he was duty-bound, in his very first elected office.[15] While seeds of conflict may have been sown here, accounts of a fundamental breach should probably be ignored.

Certainly Cato's successful tenure as soldier, officer, and quaestor built the foundation for him, a new man, to win a praetorship in 198. In that office he continued to pursue his personal policy of austere moderation – whether affected or innate. He was assigned to the province of Sardinia by the lot and was dispatched with a supplementary force of infantry and cavalry to govern the island. Livy and Plutarch agree that Cato, exceptionally among his governor peers, opted to have no large retinue or lavish transportation and accommodation while praetor, thus saving the Sardinians a fair amount of expense. Plutarch waxes more on Cato's temperance and frugality in ways that are hard to pin to specific acts, but Livy notes that Cato expelled those money-lenders engaged in extortion from the island, presumably also to the advantage of the Sardinians.[16]

Roman Women Protest the Oppian Law

Steadily climbing the cursus, the new man Cato won election to the consulship swiftly, in 195, alongside his fast-friend Valerius Flaccus. Just two years had passed since his praetorship ended, the customary minimum gap between these offices. That year, Roman resistance in Spain had reached such a pitch that the senate designated Further Spain as a consular province and Cato drew lots to receive it as his command.[17] Before he left for Spain, however, consul Cato was involved with a fascinating, though brief, political episode at Rome. And though it does not fall neatly under our investigation of Cato's career and rivalries, it does corroborate Cato's consistent emphasis on reactionary Roman virtues in his politics and serve as another glimpse into the legislative process and the role of tribunes, systems that are crucial for understanding the later rivalries of the Republic. It also happens to provide one of those exceedingly rare glimpses at Roman women that goes beyond the stock stereotypes of our ancient sources – that is when they comment on women at all.

This was the situation: following the Roman massacre at Cannae in 216 BCE, when Hannibal encircled and slaughtered as many as 50,000 soldiers, the Republic was short not only on soldiers but on funds to continue the fight. In addition to various other responses, tribune Gaius Oppius passed a law through the assembly. There are two different versions of this Oppian law preserved in the sources. Livy and Valerius Maximus suggest these terms: Roman women could not possess more than half an ounce of gold, wear clothing that was multicoloured – and thus expensive – or ride in a horse-drawn carriage in cities or towns unless they were engaged in a public sacrifice or other public religious act.[18] Zonaras, our sometimes helpful thirteenth century CE chronicler, suggests that the restriction was on wearing, not owning the gold, but he seems to miss the essential point: the law was designed not only to check women's luxury, but also to generate revenues for the war effort.[19] The war stretched on for more than a decade, until the final Roman victory at Zama. The law lasted longer, still in effect when Cato took office. Granted that this sumptuary law applied mostly to the wealthiest Roman women, there still seems to have been broad support for repealing the law. Otherwise it is difficult to explain what happened next. Two of the tribunes of 195, the Brutus brothers, made it known that they would veto any attempt to repeal the Oppian Law, suggesting they believed there was enough support in the assembly to repeal the law.

One or more debates were held publicly in the Forum, likely in a *contio*, an assembly where not voting occurred and magistrates informed those who came about some political issue. Since these were public, women nearby could readily hear. Cato, true to his stance as a traditionalist, spoke against the law. Cato did publish speeches that survived to Livy's day, the stance fits, so perhaps Livy preserved something close to Cato's actual words. Repealing the law, he grumbled, would not only encourage frivolous luxury, it would set the bad precedent of empowering women to question the laws the men made when they should be legally and practically subservient. Not all shared Cato's overwhelming preoccupation with patriarchy. The tribune Lucius Valerius, says Livy, advocated repealing the law, arguing that the need for the law had vanished and that it was unjust to put Roman women under stricter economic limits than men. The day after these politicians spoke to the assembly, a large crowd of women appeared in the city and a number specifically targeted the houses of the Brutus brothers, besieging them, says Livy, until the tribunes gave up their veto. They did so swiftly, and the assembly promptly repealed the Oppian Law. It may not have been a transcendent moment of gender equity, but it did illustrate the significant, if informal, political influence Roman women could muster.[20]

Cato's Consulship in Spain

Following this, Cato went to his province of Nearer Spain (*Hispania Citerior*) with an army and engaged in the grim business of crushing the Spanish tribes and towns that had rebelled against Roman rule. The description of Cato's highly competent year in command that Livy passes on may be from Cato's very own writings. Still, his success was corroborated, by the senate, which declared that three days of thanksgiving sacrifices be devoted to the gods for Cato's victories. Cato also celebrated a splendid triumph with spoils of war and the loot of newly acquired silver mines.[21]

It was reportedly at the close of Cato's consulship and the start of Africanus' in 194 that the two had another quarrel. Africanus was elected consul for 194 alongside Tiberius Sempronius Longus. Though both tried to persuade the senate to declare Macedonia a province to counter the Seleucid king Antiochus IV, the senate persisted in declaring Italy as the province for both consuls. Longus was active against the north Italian Gauls, says Livy, but his sources were split on whether Scipio joined him or did nothing at all worthy of record during his consulship.[22] Plutarch, however, weaves a whole conflict between Scipio and Cato that likely never happened. At the end of Cato's consulship in Spain, says Plutarch, this happened. Scipio was assigned the province of Spain by the lot. Hoping to stop Cato's successes and take control of his new province, Scipio sped to Spain and relieved Cato of his command. Cato left the army and returned to Rome escorted by several thousand infantry and a few hundred cavalry. Along the way, however, he defeated the fractious Lacetani and recaptured and executed 600 Roman deserters for good measure. Scipio was angered by

Cato's actions and complained, but to no avail: the senate accepted all of Cato's arrangements in Spain.[23]

Plutarch or his source almost certainly fabricated this anecdote. It conflicts directly with Livy's more detailed account and chronology, in which Scipio was assigned to Italy as a province along with his consular colleague. Equally important, the anecdote suffers from inconsistencies within it.

First, Cato had finished his campaigns, dispatched a letter to the senate, and earned days of thanksgiving, all before Scipio was elected. It strains credibility to think Scipio had any hope of going to Spain as a province and stealing Cato's glory. Second, Cato's defeat of a minor tribe on the way home from his province would have no bearing at all on Cato receiving the glory for his prior campaign in Spain. Third, wars with Spain continued for decades and Scipio could surely have found some tribes or towns to bully in order to claim military honours, regardless of Cato's success in the province. Indeed Sextus Digitius, praetor of Further Spain in 193, found that many tribes and towns had revolted once Cato had left the province.[24] So this anecdote seems to have no historical grounding and simply illustrates that Plutarch or his sources could embellish or even construct details to enliven a story of lifelong political rivalry between Africanus and Cato.[25]

The next major episode in Cato's career was the war against Antiochus. A bit of background: as soon as the peace treaty was forged that decisively subordinated Carthage to Rome in 201 BCE, the Roman senate looked east to Macedonia. There King Philip V – descendant of Alexander the Great's general Antigonus – reigned unchallenged, despite having joined Hannibal's war against the Romans and sparking the ultimately inconclusive First Macedonian War (215–205 BCE). Now with Hannibal's threat ended, the senate dispatched the consul Publius Sulpicius to the centuriate assembly to secure a declaration of war against Philip. Strikingly enough, the seemingly perpetually bellicose Romans rejected the declaration when first petitioned, nearly unanimously. This is worth a pause. Roman assemblies almost never voted against any measure approved by the senate.[26] Indeed this episode is often referred to because of its exceptional nature. Livy notes, no doubt rightly, that war exhaustion was a real factor after almost two decades fighting Hannibal in Italy, Sicily, Spain, and Africa. He also identified the tribune Quintus Baebius as an instigator. Baebius chastised the senate for refusing even a moment's peace to the people: here on the tail end of one brutal war, they eagerly committed Rome's citizen-soldiers to another. The senate, however, was determined and so collectively castigated Baebius until the tribune yielded, another instance of the senate resolving conflict within the aristocracy. Baebius cowed, the consul addressed a second assembly and warned that Philip would launch his own war against Rome soon enough, if left alone, and be all the more powerful for the respite. The centuriate assembly listened and dutifully voted to invade Philip's kingdom; the Second Macedonian War had begun in 200.[27] The conflict lasted several years until the forces commanded by the proconsul Titus Quinctius Flamininus defeated the Macedonian army decisively at Cynoscephalae (198). Philip was forced to make peace, and the Romans, perhaps somewhat unwittingly, became the new arbiters of Greek international politics. This new status for Rome, in turn, increasingly irritated the Seleucid king Antiochus IV, another grandson of an Alexandrian general. Antiochus contested Roman influence in Greece with an army, and the Romans retaliated eagerly with a war against him. The random lot gave consul Manius Acilius Glabrio (191 BCE) the command against Antiochus in Greece. Glabrio, aided by no less a distinguished staff officer than the former consul Cato, drove Antiochus out of Greece.[28] Even for Cato, who had cultivated a reputation for steadfast service to the Republic and traditional virtue, it was striking to see a former consul serve as a tribune, but his service appears to have been distinguished enough. Ultimately it was another way the new man could trumpet his *virtus*, and in doing so set himself against any political rivals among the nobles.

Cato Runs for Censor

At this point, Cato's career had been quite spectacular. He had climbed the *cursus honorum* and even earned a triumph while consul in Spain. But Cato was not finished: he set his eyes on the censorship. Perhaps his service in Glabrio's legions was designed to keep him fresh with the voters. Regardless, at the end of 190 he ran for the censorship, the highest elected office. It was the last political office open to an aristocrat, held customarily by former consuls and only two of them every five years at that, a grand feather in a very successful political career. Livy notes that year stood out for the number of candidates to the censorship and for their distinction. For patricians there were Titus Quinctius Flamininus, who had defeated Philip of Macedon at Cynoscephalae, Scipio Africanus, and Lucius Valerius Flaccus, Cato's stalwart ally. For plebeians, the distinguished plebeian Marcus Claudius Marcellus, whose father was the near-legendary commander from the war against Hannibal, and Manius Acilius Glabrio, a new man like Cato, who as consul in 191 had recently driven Antiochus out of Greece.[29]

Glabrio seemed to be the people's choice, Livy notes, because he had freely spread gifts and money to those around him. This offended the nobles, a new man taking the lead in the election to the censorship. Accordingly, the tribunes Publius Sempronius Gracchus and Caius Sempronius Rutilus indicted Glabrio for misappropriation of funds, failing to deposit in the Republic's treasury a substantial amount of booty seized from Antiochus. Cato served as witness, declaring that treasure he had seen in Antiochus' camp did not materialize in the public display that was Glabrio's triumph. Glabrio may have hoped for some sense of solidarity with Cato since the latter had served under his command and also faced the prejudices the nobles held against political new men. He received no such courtesy. Only when Glabrio abandoned his candidacy for the censorship did the tribunes drop their suit. But Cato was not the only new man to run for censor. The voters passed him over; perhaps as Livy suggested, they saw his testimony against Glabrio as petty political rivalry against another new man in a contested election. The assembly passed over his comrade Flaccus for good measure, electing instead Flamininus and Marcellus to be censors.[30]

The Trials of Scipio Asiaticus and Africanus

We return at last to the trials of Scipio Asiaticus around 187 and Africanus in 184. Did Cato engineer these attacks, and, if so, why? Four sources suggest that Cato was the architect of these political indictments.[31] He certainly seems to have been in Rome at the time and could easily have motivated the necessary tribunes to attack the Scipios. Lacking the particular office to make the largest impact, he worked with what he had, finding some agreeable tribunes.[32] What about the motive? It's reasonably clear that the account offered by Plutarch, pursued throughout his biography, in which Cato and Scipio were antagonists from the start, a continuation of the rivalry between Fabius and Scipio simply does not withstand scrutiny. Contradictory evidence from Livy and others, and the implausibility of the scenarios Plutarch offers, suggests that these two Romans, whatever their feelings about each other, were not destined to be enemies.

By the same token, deflating the narrative in which Cato and Scipio were sworn rivals does not mean the two were amicable. Cato had a reputation for traditional Roman virtue that he fostered all his life. Surely connected to this reputation was Cato's distinction for lifetime involvement in over forty lawsuits – both as prosecutor and indicted – the last in his 80s. He was known for seeking vengeance for misconduct and corruption. He testified against Glabrio for misappropriating booty and indicted Galba for embezzlement in his Spanish province. It requires little imagination to suppose that Cato instigated the indictment of Scipio Asiaticus so soon after a similar charge against Glabrio. After all, the evidence does not suggest that Asiaticus' and Africanus' accounting was particularly scrupulous, and, indeed, neither seems to have supplied evidence supporting their innocence. If Cato had suspicions, he seems exactly the sort of person who would pursue them.

The details of the accusations against these two prominent political brothers, Africanus and his younger brother Lucius Scipio, are a thicket for historians. Certainty eludes us. Livy provides the fullest account of the trials, but offers a confusing conflation of events; he complains that the sources were at odds. Indeed, after laying out one chronology of events, he offers an entirely alternative version.[33] Other sources provide some checks to Livy but have their own problems. Some refer only to Africanus' indictment; others only mention his brother, Lucius. Too much is hidden, and the available sources conflict too much to establish a certain chronology. What follows then is a version reconstructed by historians that has some consensus and seems to make the best sense of the existing evidence.[34]

The affair began in 190. Lucius Scipio, consul, succeeded Glabrio and campaigned against Antiochus in Asia Minor. Lucius' brother, the famous Africanus, accompanied him as a legate. The Romans decisively defeated Antiochus' army at the battle of Magnesia in 189, forcing the king to come to terms.[35] Part of the ultimate treaty stipulated that

Antiochus immediately surrender to Lucius the quite large sum of 500 talents of silver – literally tons. Further payments as war reparations were set for the coming years.[36] Lucius Scipio had made good political use of his victory at Magnesia, adopting the agnomen 'Asiaticus' to commemorate his victory in Asia, just as his brother Africanus had done a decade before to commemorate his victory against Carthage. But rumours persisted that he and his brother had defrauded the Republic out of its just profits from the war. Those 500 talents became the subject of an intense debate and senatorial inquiry. Was that money essentially war booty, loot seized by the victorious army and not subject to government oversight, or was it the first official payment of Antiochus' reparations and thus meant to be deposited in the public treasury? In 187 it seems the Petilius cousins – several sources say at Cato's urging – raised the question in the senate whether Lucius Scipio had misappropriated funds by treating the reparations as if they were personal booty.[37] Africanus, however, leapt to his defence, possibly cutting short an embassy mission he had been sent on in Etruria and hurrying home to defend his brother.[38] He promptly waded into the senatorial interrogation. Beyond his concern for his younger brother, Africanus probably felt the sting of the charge himself since he had apparently kept the accounts while legate on his brother's campaign. Africanus now made a show in the face of the inquiry, requesting that Lucius bring him his account books for the Magnesia campaign. When Lucius handed him the ledger, Africanus dramatically tore it apart in the senate, outraged that their dignity was slighted in this way when they had brought so much wealth to the Republic's treasuries and renown to its people.[39]

A good show for those watching in the senate certainly, but Africanus' theatrics hardly settled the issue. Though the matter was dropped in the senate, a tribune, perhaps Gaius Minucius Augurinus, soon called an assembly and summoned Lucius before it: the Roman people would have an account of these funds one way or another.[40] Lucius was in a bind. The ledger was destroyed, along with any potentially exonerating proof, and Scipio's brother, Africanus, had imperiously set the tone that they were beyond reproach. Lucius refused to account for the funds. And now Augurinus convinced the assembly to fine Lucius a sum he could not afford. Accordingly, he refused to pay the fine, and the tribune ordered him hauled off to prison. It was a bitter ignominy for him and no cause for

celebration among the nobles: one of their own, Lucius Scipio, victor at
Magnesia, imprisoned like a common debtor. Only a sympathetic tribune
could keep Lucius out of prison. The eight other tribunes, however, were
content to let Scipio be jailed. Only the tribune Tiberius Sempronius
Gracchus objected. On the record as Scipio's enemy – Aulus Gellius
indeed says he swore an oath to it – still Gracchus interposed his veto. In
Livy's assessment, Gracchus refused to see the ruling class so humiliated,
to see Asiaticus imprisoned in the same cells that held defeated enemies.
Far better to end this fiasco now.[41]

Rumours persisted and the challenge did not drop; not completely. In
184 Africanus himself became the target of a formal indictment for the
misappropriated funds. This time the tribune Marcus Naevius – if one
accepts this version of events; Livy mentions an alternative – brought
the charges against Africanus, again instigated, some said, by Cato.[42]
Accusations of misconduct had dogged Africanus at least since his
brother's trial in 187. Seeing few viable options and inspired with the
boldness that had spurred him to defeat Hannibal, Africanus doubled
down on his dramatic ledger destruction in the senate a few years before.
He appeared in the Forum on the day scheduled for his trial. Not alone:
an entourage of clients and well-wishers outstripping any in memory
accompanied Africanus.[43] The famous general, it seems, spoke first.
He opted, however, not to address the specific charge of embezzlement
levied by Naevius. Instead he recounted his career, eloquently according
to the tradition Livy preserves. Unsurprisingly: when indicted in public
trials, distinguished aristocrats quite commonly tended to wax on their
achievements as a defence. What could be more fitting, from a Roman
perspective, than a speech about one's service to the Republic to counter
what in essence was a charge of impropriety, a charge of harming the
Republic? So Africanus' supporters might say. His detractors, of course,
probably judged the whole nostalgia trip an effort to dodge the serious
issue of maladministration by an agent of the Republic.

The tribune presented his suit. Unwilling to waste material, opponents
dusted off the old standards: Africanus' troublingly opulent quarters in
Syracuse before the final campaign against Carthage and the Pleminius
fiasco. To these they added new allegations. Africanus' son was captured
in the Syrian campaign and released without ransom, suggesting the
father had influence with Antiochus. While in the east, Africanus had

behaved more like a dictator than a legate as he sought to persuade the Greeks that the Republic followed his bidding closely; he would decide whether there would be war or peace.[44] The speeches took the whole of the day, and, when the day waned, the assembly adjourned to meet again in the morning.

That next morning, Scipio was summoned again to defend himself at the Rostra. He approached, again with a sizeable entourage. Then he spoke. Today happened to be the 15th anniversary of his victory at Zama. On such a day of celebration, Scipio judged it would be inappropriate to spend the time in legal wrangles, so he announced he would ascend the Capitol and sacrifice there in thanksgiving to Jupiter, Juno, and Minerva. The final touch, Livy says, was this invitation:

> I also invite you, citizens of Rome, all of you for whom it is convenient, to come with me and to pray the gods that you may have leaders like me; but I invite you on this assumption, that if from my seventeenth year up to my old age you have always been in advance of my years in promoting me to posts of honour, I on my part have anticipated those honours of yours by my achievements.[45]

Then Scipio ascended the Capitoline Hill. The crowd followed, says Livy, leaving all but the probably-apoplectic tribune and his enslaved servants behind at the Rostra.[46]

This was Scipio's swansong. He travelled to his villa at Liternum in Campania, an estate so grand that two-and-a-half centuries later a philosopher on vacation raved about it in a letter.[47] He did not return to defend himself against the charges of Naevius. His brother, Lucius, reported that Africanus was ill and, because of this, could not return to Rome to face the charges. Naevius would have none of it and summoned an assembly to condemn him, but Lucius appealed to the other tribunes. They decreed that Africanus' illness was legitimate, and the trial would be postponed until he was able to return.[48] The assembly adjourned, and the matter dropped. Scipio Africanus never returned. He spent the short remainder of his life enjoying the pleasures of Liternum.

Reports about where Africanus was buried varied, Livy notes. According to some sources, he had his tomb at his villa in Liternum. His funeral was conducted there away from the city, a fitting spite, perhaps, for one indicted by a Republic he had done much to save. So Livy reports, and adds a brief eulogy for that larger-than-life Roman.[49] No more than two chapters below in his history, however, Livy allows that some sources claim Scipio's funeral in fact was in Rome, and some even claimed he had been buried in Rome.[50] Confusing the matter more, Livy asserts that cenotaphs and statues of Africanus could be found both in Rome and Liternum. So much for certainty when it came to the tomb of the great Africanus.

Did Cato orchestrate these publicly embarrassing investigations of the Scipios and, if so, for what reason? Four sources say Cato purposefully instigated the inquiries: Livy, Plutarch, Aulus Gellius, and Cassius Dio.[51] Cornelius Nepos goes further, asserting that Cato and Scipio Africanus were at odds their entire careers. Plutarch concurs and, as we have seen, his biography of Cato is punctuated by places where Cato and Scipio allegedly clashed. Once the fabricated story is dropped that Scipio and Cato were antagonists from the moment they first worked together, the question of motive remains. Why encourage an attack on Africanus so long – six or seven years – after the Syrian campaign? Perhaps it was to gain some traction for Cato's second attempt to win the censorship with his friend and ally Valerius Flaccus. Asiaticus was involved in a campaign against Antiochus that Cato was personally involved in, and perhaps Cato got a bit obsessed with the idea that Antiochus had fantastic wealth, far more than Glabrio and Asiaticus had fairly accounted for. For a Roman so engaged in the competitive ethos of the aristocracy and one who had built so much on a reputation for righteousness, it requires little explanation. So it seems reasonable to suppose Cato did instigate the prosecution of Asiaticus, as the sources suggest.[52]

Cato the Censor

The trial of 187 was a spectacle, and so would the trial of 184 be, but perhaps not much more than when Cato announced his candidacy for the censorship of 184. The news sparked a fair amount of apprehension. Nobles and new men alike wondered who might face the wrath of Cato's stylus as they drafted the list of citizens and senators. The year was marked, like the last censor elections, for the number of distinguished aristocrats who ran for the office. With the exception of Flaccus, Cato's staunch ally, the candidates strove against Cato in particular. Some because Cato was a new man; others because they feared that the censor would call them to account for their immoralities. Small wonder the prospect of Cato as the censor incited concern; Cato had regularly challenged his peers and rivals of wrongdoing without the power of office; what would he do when invested with the official authority to supervise Roman morality? All told, those who preferred Cato not to become censor found no fewer than seven rival candidates. Each made an appeal to the voters. Cato made his own brand of pledge. He would punish the corrupt and excise the immoral from the body politic. If the voters wanted to see the corrupt squirm, he promised, they should elect him – of course with Valerius Flaccus as his partner. The voters obliged.[53]

As censors, Cato and Flaccus struck seven senators from the census-lists, demoting them out of the senate.[54] Livy noted that, since the practice of noting the transgression next to the name of the person who had been demoted this way had not yet been established, Cato had left a number of speeches indicating the sources of dishonour.[55] Lucius Quinctius Flamininus was by far the most famous of the demoted senators. Consul in 192 BCE, he was the brother of famed Titus who had defeated Philip V and his army at the battle of Cynoscephalae in 198, wrapping up the second war against Macedonia. Lucius' activities while consul drew the censors' censure. Cato and Valerius levied more than one accusation that day, but the most damning was this. Flamininus was enamoured with a prostitute named Philip, apparently well known and prosperous. He persuaded Philip to accompany him on campaign in Gaul even though that meant missing the entertainments of the City, a gladiatorial contest in this case. One evening the wine had flowed and inhibitions evaporated when word came to Flamininus that a noble from the Gallic Boii tribe had just defected to the Roman cause. He sought assurances directly from Flamininus that he would be protected. And so, accompanied by an interpreter, the Boian entered and appealed. Flamininus allegedly interrupted the Gaul and asked Philip: since he had missed seeing the gladiators, would he like to see this Gallic noble die, right there, right then? Philip nodded; seriously or in jest did not matter, for he was not the one on trial. Flamininus drew his sword and struck the Gaul's head as he spoke. The blow was not fatal, and the Gaul fled the tent, begging for protection in a camp full of Roman soldiers. Flamininus followed and finished the murder swiftly. Livy claimed to have pulled the details of this accusation straight from Cato's preserved speech on the topic. The first century BCE historian Valerius Antias, however, offered a slightly different version. In this variant, Flamininus was enamoured of a prostitute whose name was not reported, but who indeed joined him at dinner, still in Gaul. Flamininus recounted his successes as a prosecutor and bragged that he would condemn a number of Romans to be beheaded when he returned to the city. His guest noted that she had never seen a beheading and would very much like to. Obligingly, Flamininus ordered a condemned prisoner brought before him and removed his head personally with an axe – or ordered a subordinate to do it. Either way, even for the Romans – who forced the enslaved to fight to the death for their amusement and had enshrined in their earliest law code that an insolvent debtor could be physically cut up and distributed to their creditors – killing a person at a dinner party for the amusement of a prostitute seemed particularly morally lax.[56]

Loyal brother Titus, says Plutarch, would not let the matter drop. After all, his brother had been stripped of his rank, publicly humiliated. It was hardly good for the family's honour. He pressed Cato to justify in a public assembly his choice of Lucius Flaminius for demotion. Cato was willing enough, and the speech he delivered seems to have survived to Livy's day. When Cato recounted the sordid details of that murderous night, however, Lucius denied it and called him a liar. Cato did not flinch. He challenged Lucius to a judicial wager, a *sponsio*, at the end of his speech. Romans did this from time to time. Essentially two parties wagered money that they were in the legal right on some contested issue. After the bet had been made, both spoke to an arbiter who decided whose case was the stronger, who won the bet.[57] But Lucius had no stomach for the risk and relented. The case closed, Lucius Flamininus was a senator no more. Though apparently some felt he had got a bad deal. Plutarch recounts that Lucius once entered the theatre and walked past the senatorial seating only to have the crowd pity him and demand he sit among the senators as he once did.[58] As for the rest of the disgraced senators, we know almost nothing, though tradition preserved that one promising senator, Manilius, lost his rank for daring to kiss his wife in the daytime with their daughter looking on. This sounds suspiciously like the setup for a joke. Plutarch continues by offering some wit: 'Cato claimed that for his part he never embraced his wife except after a loud clap of thunder, and he said as a joke that Jupiter's thunder made him a happy man.'[59]

The censors only started with expelling senators. Then they directed their fierce gaze to the next rank of privilege, the most distinguished *equites* who maintained a publicly subsidized warhorse. This was Cato's chance to further humble Lucius Scipio Asiaticus, either wreaking double vengeance or harping on the Roman not long after his brother's death. Declaring him unfit to hold the privilege, he struck him off the list of the *equites equo publico*. Unlike Flamininus, however, Asiaticus seems to have kept his senatorial rank. However, he was effectively declared unfit for honourable service as a cavalry trooper, a humiliation.[60] The Scipios had fallen far in a short time, though their star would soon rise with a new generation.

Revising citizen lists and, in the process, handing out marks of ignominy to the ostensibly corrupt were perhaps the flashiest of the censors' duties, but hardly the only matters under their purview. The censors were also responsible for auctioning contracts for tax collection. Private companies of agents called *publicani* would bid and pay a certain sum in return for the right to collect taxes on behalf of the Roman state. Two aspects of this process merited mention by Livy and Plutarch. First Cato and Flaccus set very high prices for tax collection, resulting in extra revenue for the Republic and less profit for the *publicani*, the tax collectors. But the censors stipulated an array of sumptuary taxes for luxury items ranging from expensive decorative furnishings and women's dresses to overly expensive carriages and enslaved adolescents whose owners had paid over a certain amount to acquire them. The censors also targeted those property owners who took advantage of public lands. They ordered pipes destroyed that siphoned the public water supply to private dwellings. They ordered demolished any buildings that overreached their owners' property boundaries and made inroads onto public land. They also supervised the construction of public works ranging from temples to cisterns to sewers. Most famously, Cato supervised the construction of the Porcia Basilica.[61] This famous structure served to house the tribunes of the plebs, giving them an important place next to the senate's meeting place and the *Comitia* where assemblies voted.[62]

People, Plutarch suggests, approved heartily of Cato and Flaccus' measures in the censorship, going so far as to dedicate a statue to Cato with the inscription 'When the Roman constitution was in a state of collapse and decline, he became censor and set it straight again by effective guidance, sound training, and sensible instruction.'[63] Hyperbolic, certainly, but an indication that his lifelong political tack, embodying and enforcing traditional Roman virtue – at least as he saw it – earned him a great deal of political support. Indeed, Cato seems to have become a household synonym for virtue, and his descendants would struggle to live up to the standards he set. He held no more political offices, but there was no need. He had ascended the *cursus honorum*, a spectacular political success for a new man from Tusculum. He continued, however, to play an active role in the senate, opining on matters of foreign and domestic policy in the eventful years that led up to the final war against Carthage (149–146).

Cato represents a textbook competitor from the middle Republic. He took on rivals real and potential without hesitation. He affected – or embraced – a life of Roman virtue and gloried in his own achievements in that sphere. Successful orator and soldier, successful commander, and scrappy political fighter, yet for all of those scraps with rivals, his behaviour seems to have remained within the accepted conventions of political competition. Though he was spectacularly successful for a new man, he held his offices at the conventional age in the conventional order, and in the conventional amounts. He competed with his rival of the moment in the assemblies and courts. At the risk of being reductionist, none of his Roman rivals died in their fierce struggles with Cato. That infamy of killing a rival would belong to Cato's contemporary Scipio Nasica, who, more than a decade after Cato had passed, would beat a tribune to death in an assault on an assembly, and usher in the political violence of the late Republic.

Chapter 3

The People's Tribune and the Reactionary: Tiberius Gracchus and Scipio Nasica

It would end in a bloodbath. Tiberius Sempronius Gracchus, tribune of the plebs, pushed too far. Rousing the rabble with a law designed to rob land from the wealthy and squander it among the poor, he had successfully thwarted all the aristocracy's attempts to rein him in. He illegally deposed his colleague, tribune Marcus Octavius, when the latter sought to veto his law. Vetoes were commonplace enough, but never had a tribune been stripped of his power by another tribune. Dancing nimbly around the senate's legitimate efforts to restrain him, Tiberius seemed to recognize no authority but the Roman people, the very Roman people that did his bidding. Now he had thrown his name into the ring to run for a second consecutive tribunate, a violation of law and convention that would enable him to effectively subjugate the senate like a conquering general. No, worse, like a KING, that most horrid of words in the Roman political lexicon. Kill Gracchus, save the Republic. It was the only way.

Certainly Publius Cornelius Scipio Nasica saw it in those terms. And when the consul, Lucius Calpurnius Piso, proved reluctant to put Gracchus down, Nasica took matters into his own hands. Calling on like-minded senators to join him, he led his gang into the assembly convened to elect the new tribunes. Bludgeoning their way to Tiberius and his supporters, they proceeded to beat them to death. It was the first time for the Romans that political difference had ended in the murder of a Roman official, a tribune for that matter whose person was supposed to be sacrosanct. A grim precedent, but the murder was the end of a tribunate grown increasingly radical for Gracchus.

To understand Gracchus and Nasica's positions on that fateful day, consider the whole of the tribune's brief life. Any investigation of the revolutionary tribunes, Tiberius and his younger brother Gaius Gracchus – who would meet his own brutal end a decade later – has to begin with their exceptional mother, Cornelia.[1] Just the fact that Plutarch not only mentions her, but devotes most of the first chapter of his biography of the Gracchi to her, marks her as exceptional, especially since our sources are almost exclusively elite male writers who tended not to discuss the women of the Republic.

Cornelia, an Epic Roman Mother

She was clearly a powerful figure in elite Roman circles in the late second century BCE. She was the daughter of that most famous of early second century aristocrats Publius Cornelius Scipio Africanus, the commander who had ended Hannibal's threat on the North-African plans of Zama (see chapter 1). That alone made her a powerful partner in any marriage alliance, for the Romans, as many aristocrats then and since, used marriage ties to bind together powerful families for political, social, and sometimes economic purposes. Tiberius Sempronius Gracchus, twice consul, twice triumphed, even a censor, succeeded in his hope to marry Cornelia, much to the distinction of his family. Cornelia was so much more, however, than a prestigious spouse. Gracchus was significantly older than Cornelia and died long before her. A story circulated at Rome that Gracchus had received an omen, a male and female snake slithering on his furniture. The priests interpreted: either he or his young wife must die: kill the male snake, kill himself; kill the female, and kill Cornelia. Tiberius loved his wife, killed the male snake, and departed the realm of the living.[2]

Cornelia was left behind with considerable responsibilities. Her twelve children were still alive – very unusual for a Roman household where 40 to 50 per cent of children died before the age of 10 – and she was in charge of the house and property she had shared with Gracchus. Yet she managed those formidable management tasks expertly. To the outside world she showed nothing but propriety as a Roman matron. Her reputation for excellence flew beyond the confines of Italy. Indeed Plutarch tells us that Ptolemy, king of Egypt, proposed marriage to her, but she declined and remained a widow for the rest of her life, so far as we know.[3] Plutarch may be mistaken about the royal marriage proposal, but Cornelia merited what was, in Roman terms, such a flattering story. As Plutarch describes,

She had a wide circle of friends and her hospitality meant that she was never short of dinner guests. She surrounded herself with Greeks and scholars, and used to exchange gifts with kings from all over the world. Her guests and visitors used particularly to enjoy the stories she told of the life and habits of her father, Africanus.[4]

She was educated, charismatic, capable, and a Roman who seems to have fully valued her station and connections. So, when Plutarch suggested that she urged her boys Tiberius and Gaius Gracchus to win her the fame of being mother of the Gracchi rather than simply the daughter of Africanus, he probably did not miss the mark.

So Tiberius was raised a *nobilis* – a descendant of consular ancestors on both parents' sides. His name and pedigree alone suggested he could anticipate a splendid journey up the *cursus honorum*, buoyed by his family's dignity. Instead he would hold the dubious honour of a radical tribune, the first to be murdered. The start of what would end as a tragedy was, perhaps, a war gone wrong. The Romans had fought a series of long, bitter wars in Spain, slowly asserting their control over the peninsula, as tens of thousands of Roman soldiers faced extraordinarily long and harsh terms of service, or lost their lives far from their Italian homes. Tiberius, as many young aristocrats did, engaged in a stint of military service, probably required to do so by a law that stipulated any office holder must first complete ten campaigns of military service.[5] He served with distinction under Publius Cornelius Scipio Africanus, his brother-in-law through his sister Sempronia. This Scipio was the biological son of the great Aemilius Paullus, and had been adopted into the Scipio Africanus clan, whose progenitor had defeated Hannibal at Zama two generations before. Tiberius had the honour of sharing Scipio's tent, a prestigious honour for a young staff officer. When the Roman forces at Carthage made the final push (146 BCE), scaling the walls and storming the city that had excited their fears for a century, Tiberius was the first to top the battlements, a sign of his courage and his willingness to share the hardships of the average soldier. Unsurprisingly, he was reported to have a strong connection with the soldiers he commanded.[6]

Debacle in Spain: The Mancinus Treaty

But then came Spain, and a hitch under Gaius Hostilius Mancinus at the Spanish stronghold of Numantia (137 BCE). Mancinus managed to get the soldiers under his command trapped. Desperate to prevent their slaughter, Mancinus sought to parley with the Numantines. Plutarch reports that they would only negotiate with Tiberius, Mancinus' quaestor, for they remembered that his father had honorably struck a treaty with them years before. Tiberius, in this version, was thus personally responsible for an agreement that saved some 20,000 Roman soldiers from slaughter far from home. The Roman senate, however, found nothing to celebrate in the treaty; it spoke of Roman weakness. A movement pushed to return Mancinus and his officers, including Tiberius, back to the Numantines. The logic behind this: when a Roman commander made a treaty, he did so on his own authority with no guarantee that senate and assembly would accept his terms. If it turned out that senate and assembly did not accept those terms, the commander could be sent back to the enemy, life forfeit, and the Romans considered themselves free of any obligation.[7] Tiberius narrowly escaped this fate, plucked from the fires of disaster by his former commander, the influential Scipio, now destroyer of Carthage. Mancinus was not so fortunate. Shackled and weaponless, the former consul was delivered to the Numantines to do with as they wished. The Numantines simply cast Mancinus out, refusing to take the deal, and considered the Romans oath breakers.[8]

The significance of this political storm over Mancinus depends on the source. Velleius Paterculus, a Roman officer and aristocrat of the early Empire writing a *Roman History* some century and a half later, asserts that this episode, and his close shave with death, drove Tiberius to become a tribune so that he could avoid any further fallout from the episode or any similar punishment.[9] The far later and probably confused third century CE aristocrat and writer Dio Cassius similarly suggests the Mancinus treaty moved him to become a demagogue.[10] He suggests, however, that Tiberius had hoped to win a triumph for his treaty, and since there is no evidence to suggest any Republican quaestor, a minor subordinate officer, was ever eligible for a triumph, nor any reason to suppose that a forced surrender and treaty would qualify for that most prestigious military celebration, we need not pause on Dio. There may well be a kernel of truth in his account, however, that Tiberius gained some enemies in this affair, senators who would have gladly surrendered him to the enemy.

The Problem of Available Farmland and Military Readiness

Tiberius might have had a normal career from this point, full of rivalries and competition, capitalizing on his noble status. Larger forces, however, were at work. Rome seemed in the second half of the second century BCE to observers of the time to be caught in a demographic crisis. There was not enough land available for the small farmer citizens in the peninsula to work. The ancient sources suggested this was the result of rapacious wealthy plantation farmers. They seized the Italian lands of peasant soldiers when they unwillingly neglected them owing to lengthy stints in the army overseas and incorporated the fields into large *latifundia*, plantations usually worked by the enslaved.[11] More recently it has been well argued that what really happened, unbeknownst to the ancients, was a demographic swell in the Italian small-farmer class with insufficient Italian land to provide farms. The political result was the same: tens of thousands of Roman citizens had too little farmland to subsist and demanded more.[12] Yet for reasons that are not clear, the Romans had not settled colonies, the traditional way they mitigated land pressures, since 177.[13]

Though modern historians have debated the exact nature and causes of this agrarian problem for over a century, Tiberius' sincere belief that there was a problem with insufficient land for small farmers is reasonably well attested by the evidence.[14] Plutarch draws from a pamphlet Tiberius' younger brother Gaius drafted, presumably after Tiberius had been bludgeoned to death in an electoral brawl. According to this, Tiberius waxed eloquently how, when he first travelled to Numantia by way of Etruria, he saw the land depopulated of free farmers, and now only worked by the enslaved.[15] And he continued to champion, it appears, the cause of the soldiers who lacked the land to properly support themselves when their service to the Republic was over. Plutarch attributes these words to a speech of Tiberius:

> The wild animals of our Italian countryside have their dens ... Each
> of them has a place of rest and refuge, but those who fight and die for

Italy have nothing – nothing except the air and the light. Houseless and homeless they roam the land with their children and wives. And they make liars of our military commanders: 'The enemy must not be allowed near our tombs and temples,' our leaders say, to inspire their troops in battle, but none of all these Romans has an ancestral altar or a family tomb. No, they fight and die to protect the rich and luxurious lifestyle enjoyed by others. These so-called masters of the world have not one clod of earth that they can call their own.'[16]

While other sources add this and that element, the core message seems to be consistent. Men eligible for military service appeared harder to find, the free farmers who provided military service seemed on the wane, and there were a troubling number of enslaved farmhands about.[17] We live in an age when the dangers of assuming that what a politician claims truly reflects reality are clear, and it is risky to assert that Tiberius' claim truly reflected a large-scale problem. But it seems to have rung true for many, for the call for land for veterans and small-famers would not end while the Republic lasted.[18]

Writers like Velleius Paterculus add that Tiberius proposed a law to give citizenship to all Italians, and Dio persists in making wilder assertions: Tiberius ended jury membership for the law courts on provincial mismanagement and other aristocratic crimes for senators and awarded it to *equites*, the wealthy class of Romans who served in the cavalry. Neither, however, pursues these assertions in their sparse narratives.[19] It's reasonable to suppose they are confused, since a decade later younger brother Gaius seems to have made such proposals. Tiberius, however, if we follow the evidence for how his brief career played out, seems to have focused wholly on his agrarian law, which he drafted and moved to pass in 133 BCE.

Tiberius' Agrarian Law

He did not simply rush out a draft bill and throw it into the mix. His choice of co-drafters indicates he was no hotheaded rebel but a careful reformer. Plutarch identifies a no-less distinguished list of allies than the soon-to-be pontifex maximus Marcus Licinius Crassus (who would hold the consulship in 131), the distinguished legal expert Publius Mucius

Scaevola, praetor in 136 and now consul for 133, and Appius Claudius, his father-in-law, fellow augur, and consul of 143.[20] These were high ranking senators, to be sure, all *nobiles*. The initial terms of the agrarian law as Plutarch presents them seem to warrant his hyperbole that 'no law was ever more moderately or mildly worded'.[21] In his version, Romans holding more than the maximum 500 *iugera* of public land (around 300 acres) permitted by law according to the over two-centuries-old Sexto-Licinian law would be compensated for giving up the excess land – excess that was held illegally it should be noted. That excess would then be divided and provided to poor small-farmers so that they would have sufficient land for they and their families to subsist.[22] Second century CE Appian of Alexandria gets into greater detail on specific acreages and notes that landowners with sons might have higher maximums. He makes no mention of compensation to the landowners for their excess land.[23] How we understand the impact of Tiberius' agrarian law, however, clearly hinges on this point: would the wealthy squatters receive compensation for their illegal holdings, the gentlest possible way this law could have played out, or would they simply be required to surrender those extra *iugera*, regardless of how many generations had occupied and improved that excess land?

Surely it would have been a far more cautious calculated risk for the drafters, themselves wealthy senators, to go with the compensation method. Even with the compensation clause, they were making a proposition that could gain them considerable political clout with the landless poor who benefitted from the measure. Even with compensation their measure would meet stiff resistance in the senate. None of this amounts to proof, but if we must take a stand on the poor evidence, this seems the firmer ground.[24]

When the law was introduced, the problems started. The political details, specifically how exactly tribune Tiberius went about passing this law, are hidden by Plutarch and Appian's vague accounts. The evidence does not suggest, however, that Tiberius proposed the bill to the senate for discussion and amendment – or outright rejection – before it was submitted to the tribal assembly for a vote into law. Tactically this was both a reasonable and an incendiary move at the same time. Reasonable because the senate, consisting of wealthy landowners, would almost certainly smother the proposal. Incendiary because the senate, though not constitutionally guaranteed the right to debate potential legislation before it was passed to the appropriate legislative assembly, was regularly accorded that privilege.

Instead, it appears Tiberius spent the time between the announcement of the bill and the vote – a required interval of three market days or around twenty days – working the crowds with persuasive speeches.[25] He spent time at the Rostra, the speaker's platform in the Forum adorned centuries earlier with the bronze rams of defeated warships – a perfectly Roman construction.[26] Here he gave speeches, perhaps to the crowds passing by, perhaps to formally summoned audiences, *contiones*, who would listen to Roman officials' arguments. Here he put his oratory to use, decrying the plight of soldiers and farmers, warning of the dangers a growing enslaved population posed to Roman security. Meanwhile, opponents of the law reared their heads and made their own claims: this was nothing less than revolution, the redistribution of land from the propertied to the indigent. Plutarch would have it that they could not compete with Tiberius' honest zeal, and, truly, it is difficult to imagine the common Romans in the Forum feeling more sympathetic to the claims of the wealthy that they deserved their land.[27]

Octavius Vetoes the Agrarian Law

The sources, whether late and confused or more consistent in their narrative, all agree what happened next. Obstructionist senators found an agreeable tribune to check Tiberius: Marcus Octavius. Octavius' connection to Tiberius is not clear. Plutarch calls him a close friend, Dio a family enemy. The others are silent beyond the point that Octavius was a tribune – he had to be for what came next – and he was coopted by opponents of Gracchus' land law. This was a standard political action: senators opposed to some legislation would find a tribune to veto the law so it could not be passed in the assembly.[28]

So when Tiberius came to the official day when he would put the law to an assembly vote, Octavius vetoed the proceedings, as his tribunician power entitled him to do. There was little Tiberius could do. Appian has it that Tiberius simply adjourned the assembly until the following day. But Octavius vetoed again and the two began to quarrel along with their followers and were begged to appear in the senate like petulant schoolchildren to sort out their differences. This was a time-honoured role of the senate, smoothing out disagreements between members of the ruling aristocracy. Appian's altercation in Dio's account amounts to civil violence in the streets, Rome becoming practically an armed camp.[29] He probably exaggerated, but maybe not completely. Plutarch offers a critical detail of strife the oppositional tribunes sparked: because Octavius would not yield on his veto, Tiberius declared that no magistrates could conduct city business until the assembly was allowed to vote on the agrarian law. Further, Tiberius personally sealed the Republic's treasury kept in the Temple of Saturn and forbade magistrates to withdraw or deposit funds in the course of their duties. These were serious measures: a single tribune effectively proposed that his official powers enabled him to bring the government to a halt if he chose. And though the other sources do not mention these political mechanisms – enforced public holidays and a locked up treasury – their reference to fierce wrangling suggests these details may be authentic. A fair amount of political theatre spiced up Tiberius' already unorthodox actions. Wealthy landowners wore mourning-clothes in the Forum to advertise their plight. Less publicly, it was rumoured, they hired thugs to murder Gracchus, requiring him to wear a dagger under his toga for safety.[30]

It is important to remember that there must have been a great deal of support for Tiberius' agrarian law, support from Roman citizens who had insufficient land to subsist alone or with their families. It is also illuminating to remember that the senators must have included a fair number of wealthy landowners who were opposed to the law for personal financial reasons. The agrarian law revealed a Republic riven by class conflict on this issue. Small wonder that Rome was up in arms about the duelling tribunes, for they fought over a matter of great import to many: those with more than enough resources jealously kept those resources from those in need. Yet it is equally important to remember that Gracchus and his aristocratic backers were all senators and all, no doubt, wealthy, so an individual Roman's sympathies for the agrarian bill and the inequity it was designed to redress could not be predicted simply by considering their socio-economic status.

At a certain point – perhaps a few days into the conflict, perhaps a few weeks, we do not know – Gracchus agreed – perhaps due to the pleas of some former consuls – to seek some resolution from his fellow senators.

Appian suggests Tiberius thought it a great idea. Not likely, for Tiberius had not bothered to put the agrarian bill before the senate in the first place. Sure enough, as it turned out, the senate, itself divided on the issue, offered no solution to the deadlock.[31]

Tribune Octavius Deposed

Tiberius had exhausted the options available to him by conventional practices. The legislative machinery was paralyzed by Octavius' veto and Tiberius' willingness to use his tribunician powers creatively to force the issue. But there was no way to counter a tribune's veto for it was their nigh-sacred power to defend the plebeians against harmful interests. Nor was there sufficient momentum in the senate to direct the tribunes either way, though the senatorial elders must have been irked by the fiasco the young tribunes had created. Deadlocked, and with no senatorial resolution, Tiberius ventured beyond the political pale. He summoned another assembly with Octavius present, importuned Octavius to yield, and when Octavius refused, proposed that the assembly vote to strip Octavius of his powers as tribune. Whether the assembly responded with a roar, a gasp, or the indecipherable murmurings of crowds, the proposal was disruptive, perhaps even revolutionary. So far as we know, no tribune had ever been stripped of his power in office, certainly not to eliminate his veto.[32]

Was this even legal? Rome had no written constitution, and, as we have seen, senators and magistrates debated and reinterpreted political convention time and time again in the Republic. The gold standard was the *mos maiorum*, the customs of the elders, the idealized rules established by idealized ancestors that Roman politicians argued must be followed – at least when they felt the ancestors approved of their actions and not those of their rivals. Again, though, the Romans had no written constitution, and their Republic, including the powers of the governing bodies and the magistrates, evolved over centuries. It was often very much an open matter what convention dictated, if it dictated anything at all.

Even so, Tiberius' action was, so far as we know, unheard of and the ancient sources punctuated the novelty and illegality of his act. Certainly the Roman crowds knew he was in uncharted territory. The majority of the assembly, however, was game enough. Officials called out the majority vote of each tribe in order; the very first tribe voted to strip Octavius of his office. A shot across the bow. Now Tiberius begged Octavius to desist in his veto. Octavius refused to budge, though he must have been on the verge of panic. Sixteen more tribes registered their vote; sixteen more tribes agreed that Octavius had to go. In the assembly, once a majority vote from the 35 tribes was reached the citizens were dismissed. One more yes vote would abrogate Octavius' command. Tiberius paused the voting again and begged Octavian not to go down this way. Arguably quite sincerely. If he could just get Octavius to yield in what he saw as stubborn folly, the law could pass, and no disturbing precedents would be set, insofar as Octavius would not actually lose his position. Plutarch adds a detail that captures the drama of the moment. Octavius was in a state, trapped and wanting nothing more than to yield to Tiberius, but he looked over to the clique of wealthy landowners he took orders from and steeled his resolve. The eighteenth tribe voted to depose Octavius, and so he became the first tribune ever to be stripped of his office. Perhaps Octavius simply slunk away unnoticed, as Appian had it, but the air was so charged it is more likely that Plutarch captures the authentic details: Tiberius ordered one of the freedmen in his entourage to pull Octavius from the Rostra. The gravity of his act deserves a moment's pause. Octavius as tribune was sacrosanct, yet here he was being forced from the Forum. Whether that could legitimately be done depended entirely on whether one thought Octavius had been legitimately deposed.[33] Clearly a number did, and angry crowds sought to harm the obstinate former tribune, but Tiberius and a number of senators intervened to give the broken tribune safe passage out of the assembly. Then it was over. Tiberius had found a novel and, ultimately, explosive means to counter a tribune's veto.[34]

He followed up by passing the agrarian law, a move well supported by the voters. According to the provisions of the law, a committee of three men, *triumviri* as the Romans called them, was set up to manage surveying and redistributing of land to small holders. Tiberius himself, his father-in-law Appius Claudius, and his younger brother Gaius were the initial commissioners. Appius Claudius' appointment is important for it suggests that still, even with Tiberius' wrangles with Octavius and his arguably revolutionary act to depose him, the former consul still politically supported his son-in-law. This suggests that Tiberius was not conclusively seen as a political pariah at this point by senators, but a young fractious tribune out to make his name with the people. Fair enough: the senate and Gracchus' opponents who led it still had manoeuvres open to them. They were the ones who traditionally controlled and distributed the finances needed for the works of the state.[35] And so they granted a pittance – less than the price of a modest dinner – to Tiberius' committee to carry out its work, effectively strangling the commission created by the law.[36]

The Roman Inheritance of Asia and The Agrarian Law

And there the impact of Tiberius' agrarian law might have ended, blocked by the senate's traditional control of the treasury. The Roman Republic, with its systems designed to check excessive action, appeared to have blocked the tribune who had thwarted his fellow tribune's power of veto, and deposed him in the process. Chance intervened in the tense standoff. As it happened, Attalus III, king of the Roman ally in Asia Minor, Pergamum, died in 133, during Tiberius' tenure as tribune. So did countless others, but Attalus also formally willed his kingdom to the Roman people. What exactly this meant was a matter of interpretation. Tiberius, a clever-enough strategist, would propose a law to the assembly dividing up the wealth of Pergamum to fund the distribution of land according to his agrarian law.[37] A bold move: he would sidestep the senate's lock on finances and fund the law through this bequest, presumably with the almost-assured permission of Roman voters.

And now his senatorial opponents pulled out the stops. In the senate, the accusations grew and flew, and Plutarch offers some of the juicier ones. Quintus Pompeius claimed that Eudemus of Pergamum, Attalus III's son presumably, sent Tiberius a purple robe and royal diadem, knowing he would soon be king of Rome. This was no idle talk to Tiberius' enemies in the senate. To them he must at the very least have seemed a demagogue bent on disrupting and ignoring the traditional authority of the senate and carrying out a dangerous populist agenda through the assembly. That some would accuse him of royal aspirations is not much of a stretch. Moral slander, as usual, accompanied the accusations. Quintus Metellus noted that when Tiberius' father was censor Romans walked home from parties in the dark lest they reveal themselves too drunk to navigate the road home, but his son, tribune Tiberius, walked home with common people holding torches all the way.

The Debate with Titus Annius

The challenges to Tiberius' methods grew more serious. Titus Annius moved beyond the riled aspersions of the senators. He began his verbal assault in the senate, demanding Tiberius prove that he had not violated Octavius' sanctity and inviolability as tribune. Whether Tiberius answered the charges then and there is not clear, but he stormed from the senate and arraigned Annius in front of the assembly. Or perhaps Annius challenged him. It has the appearance of a *sponsio*, a judicial wager, like the one Cato proposed to Lucius Flamininus fifty years before.[38] Plutarch's account of the exchange surely captures the substance of Annius' argument:

> Since he was no match at all for Tiberius either in eloquence or in popularity, Annius took refuge in his strong point and invited Tiberius to answer a few questions before the speeches began. Tiberius gave him permission to put his questions, and silence fell. Then Annius said, 'Let's imagine that you want to expel me from my office and insult me. Now, suppose I call on one of your fellow tribunes, and suppose he mounts the rostra to defend me, which makes you angry: would this make you remove him from office?'[39]

Annius' question cut to the heart of Tiberius' deeds. If Tiberius answered 'yes' he essentially would admit there was no check on his power as tribune so long as the voters supported him. It is difficult to see how answering 'no' would save him from further scrutiny: for it still suggested his deposition of Octavius was a serious breach of the Republican constitution.

Annius' verbal thrust, Plutarch suggests, so disturbed Tiberius that he was speechless. It's not a stretch to suspect this was the case. Tiberius' agrarian law originated as a bold proposal authored by respectable Roman aristocrats designed to redress a serious imbalance for the soldiers and small farmers that were the backbone of the Republic. Now Tiberius found himself in a most extreme, and probably untenable, political position, accused of aims at monarchy, slandered as a demagogue. Yet if he submitted to the senate, the good that he felt his law could do for

Rome and its farmers would be lost. Did he despair at this point and wonder how things had gone so wrong?

Even if he flirted with despair as he reflected on his situation, his actions were those of one determined to keep moving, to recover his political footing, to justify his revolutionary action. It has not gone unnoticed that unlike the many past tribunes who yielded to the oligarchy's wishes, Tiberius was unusually attached to his land law.[40] Plutarch reports he addressed a citizen assembly and made the case that Octavius was in fact no longer a tribune when he acted to block a proposal so clearly desired by the Roman people.[41] No other source mentions this, but they are all highly condensed versions of Tiberius' tribunate, and it is reasonable to suppose that with the senate up-in-arms about Tiberius' deposition of Octavius, he sought to recover his strength with the assembly voters by justifying his acts.

A Second Tribunate?

The year had sped by, and the time approached for the election of tribunes for 132. Tiberius made a fateful decision: to run for a second consecutive tribunate. The annuality of offices was a critical limit on individual power in the Republic and had seldom been overridden, and not ever, so far as we know, by a fractious tribune seeking a second year of personal sacrosanctity and legislative power. Tiberius' choice was unconventional at best; it would take no effort at all for his enemies to argue it was illegal. Why poke the bear of senatorial wrath? Appian and Plutarch agree Tiberius feared he would be vulnerable to his enemies if he did not have the shield of tribunician power to block them, an indication of his steadily deteriorating political situation.[42] Plutarch suggests that Tiberius tried to court the assembly by passing laws appealing to the common citizens, but there is no evidence that any of these laws succeeded, if they were even proposed.[43]

The day for elections approached. It was harvest time however, and Tiberius could not rally his supporters, labouring in the fields at the most critical time, to come to the city and support his second tribuneship. No doubt dismayed, Tiberius canvassed among the urban plebs, promising them that he fought for them too, not just the landless farmers.[44] It is not clear whether he had any success. Certainly it did not keep him alive.

The electoral assembly for the tribunes of 132 was a contentious arena. Plutarch and Appian differ on significant details. For Plutarch, voting began and the lack of Tiberius' supporters quickly grew clear as the voters supported his opponents for tribune. So Tiberius' supporters blocked the voting by castigating his enemies and dissolving the assembly for the day. Presumably this means Mummius dismissed it, the tribune ally of Tiberius who had replaced Octavius and had the power to do so. Appian claims the opposite: The voting initially swayed Tiberius' way, as the first two tribes out of thirty-five chose him. Then some opponents who Appian vaguely labels 'the Rich' objected, declaring Tiberius' bid for a second tribunate unlawful. Rubrius, the tribune chosen by lot to preside over the electoral assembly, waffled. Mummius pushed to take over the assembly himself. Other tribunes objected, and an argument broke out. Then Tiberius dissolved the assembly until the next day. The two accounts suggest different levels of support for Tiberius' second tribunate among the voters. Both, however, suggest Tiberius or his supporters dissolved the assembly until the following day, and so they probably did.[45]

The morrow loomed with the promise of a new assembly, and Tiberius went to the Forum and begged for support. He sought protection too, claiming his enemies might kill him in the night. He may well have added the touch of walking round with his son and begging bystanders to watch over him when he was dead.[46] Was this political theatre or a serious fear of assassination? It is difficult to know, and the hindsight that Tiberius would fall murdered the next day, rather than illuminating, obscures any clearer picture. If Tiberius indeed believed he was safe from his enemies only if he continued to wield the power of a tribune, this dissolved fractious assembly was a bad sign for him.

Omens before the Assembly

Plutarch and his sources are probably reasoning from hindsight, for he reports a series of threatening omens Tiberius witnessed the next day. Or maybe episodes that seemed harmless enough on the morning of the fateful assembly later appeared ominous as Romans sought to make sense of the bloody political violence that was about to erupt in their city. As he walked, the omens flocked:

- The keeper of the sacred chickens used to divine the gods' will before the assembly found that the birds would not leave the safety of their cage to eat – a bad sign.
- Tiberius reportedly stubbed his toe violently on the threshold of his door, splitting the nail and causing blood to flow out from his sandal.
- Crows to his left, squabbling, struck a roof tile loose that fell next to Tiberius, barely missing him.

Only the reproval of his friend the philosopher Blossius from the Campanian town of Cumae, Plutarch says, steeled Tiberius to ignore the omens and trek to the Capitoline Hill where the assembly gathered.

It would likely have taken less to persuade Tiberius that day would be fateful, so even if these omens were not noticed until later, the tribune may well have been uneasy. After a first round of electoral squabbling, Tiberius had clearly signalled his intent the day before to friend and foe alike to run for a second, essentially illegal, tribunate. So far his political enemies had been unable to check his manoeuvres. What might they do to prevent him extending his reign – for that seems to be how they saw it – with a second tribunate?

Did he feel trapped? Did he even consider it an option to give up his plan for re-election and make amends with his foes in the senate? Could he beg his father-in-law, the respectable Appius Claudius, to restore him to the senatorial fold? Would his other allies help him if he sought peace? The allies that Plutarch and his sources took pains to note helped Tiberius craft his law – all respectable senators – do not appear in the sources after drafting the law, except for Appius Claudius, who was appointed to the three-person commission called for by the agrarian law. If they had not abandoned Tiberius by now, they had at least found it untenable to openly support him. When had he lost their support? During the initial wrangling with Octavius when Tiberius sealed the treasury and forbade public business? Unlikely; though exaggerated, these early manoeuvres fell within the realm of tense political competition and Tiberius' three distinguished allies certainly must have known what opposition they would stir up with the proposed law. After the deposition of Octavius? Perhaps not at first, but as this dubiously constitutional deed drew the ire of more senators, it may have become impossible for senior senators like these three to save face and still support Tiberius. Now, whenever their open support waned, or dissolved altogether, Tiberius did not have the protection of any powerful senators. Might he throw himself on his friends' mercy and seek a less revolutionary course?

Maybe, but that would likely mean abandoning his agrarian law, and that appears to have been inconceivable. The law, after all, seemed to be decent and just, an attempt to remedy the plight of some poor Roman farmers at the expense of those who illegally held more than enough land. It is the difficult charge of historians to suspend moral verdicts, to seek to understand the cultures and people of the past on their own terms, and, as much as possible, not apply our own standards. That begins with avoiding, as much as possible, imposing our values on the Romans simply because that judgment clouds our ability to understand how and why Romans acted as they did in their world. The story of Tiberius Gracchus strains that attempted objectivity. It is exceedingly difficult not to see him as a tragic figure, a moral reformer who was driven to extreme measures in his desire to do right.

And there is some truth to that image, even for contemporary Romans. Certainly Plutarch's biography is custom-made to present Tiberius' life as a tragedy. And that's the problem. Our sources are laden with a bias that is not always easy to detect. And, as students hoping to understand Roman politics and their rivals, we need to seek the other side, the other point of view. In this space, however, it is not hard to find. Tiberius' senatorial opponents, many of them at least, had been senators longer, held higher offices, and came from families as distinguished or more distinguished than his own. They belonged to the governing body of the Republic, the senate, the authority figures who were to morally guide the citizens of the Republic to stability and prosperity, or so they would have it. Tiberius was an upstart, but tribunes had been proposing radical legislation and challenging the established senatorial hierarchy for centuries. Indeed it could almost be expected that a tribune would challenge the status quo. To a point. Tribunes hoping to join the august body of the senate – a decision that hinged on the censors – and seeking further magistracies, could not provoke the senate as a whole too far, and seriously challenge the power of the institution itself. Nor could they step on the toes of the senior magistrates too much. Such actions would effectively be political suicide for an upwardly-inclined tribune. These, however, were exactly the actions Tiberius took. Using his tribunician powers at every turn to make sure his law, his agenda, succeeded, he had essentially ignored altogether the long-lasting traditional checks on any individual official's power in the Republic:

- The common role of the senate as a sounding board for any legislation before it went to the assembly and as a force of moderation and consensus between fractious aristocrats.
- The convention-honoured collegial veto that allowed any magistrate to oppose an equal-ranked magistrate.
- The tribunician veto, an extra source of conservatism stopping proceedings deemed pernicious.
- The senate's power over finances.

Now the last check on excessive power, the annual term limits on magistrates, was about to be overcome. In what way, his opponents might well have reasoned, would Tiberius *not* be a king, if he had overcome the last limitation? Why *couldn't* he simply rule through the assembly, unstoppable and inviolable?

The Day of the Final Assembly: Plutarch's Version

These thoughts must have been among the many that occurred in the city that morning, the morning of the second assembly. What happened next though, is difficult to reconstruct exactly. Plutarch and Appian have very different accounts of the election assembly. Nor are their differences superficial. And they paint very different portraits of Tiberius' final hours.

First, Plutarch's account. When Tiberius reached the foot of the Capitoline Hill, he heard the cheers of his supporters, and it must have galvanized him, at least a bit. They flocked round him, forming a barrier to ward off any wishing him harm. When they reached the assembly place, the consul Mucius Scaevola was already calling on the tribes to make their votes. The consul presided today surely because yesterday's assembly had ended in disorder. Tiberius and his supporters tried to work their way into the assembly, but there was pushback, shoving and jostling. Then Marcus Fulvius Flaccus, certainly an ally of Tiberius' younger brother Gaius and likely a friend to Tiberius at this point, gestured to him, hoping to catch his attention across the assembly and speak with him. Flaccus told him that the wealthy senators, unable to persuade the consul to kill Tiberius, determined to do the deed themselves and had armed a mob of their enslaved servants and followers to do the job. Tiberius passed the news to his associates, and they prepared for a battle in the assembly. The voluminous folds of togas were cinched up to allow freedom of movement. The staves Tiberius' deputies had carried they broke into small clubs and distributed.[47]

But Plutarch either got confused at this point, intentionally stepped back in time to narrate earlier events at the meeting of the senate, or both. Flaccus had already told Tiberius that the consul – presumably Lucius Calpurnius Piso since Scaevola was in charge of the assembly – refused the senate's demands that he (the consul) kill Tiberius, and the senate had responded by gathering an armed mob and marching up the Capitoline to the assembly. But then Plutarch's account gets problematic. In response to Flaccus' news that the senatorial mob was approaching, out for blood, Tiberius attempted to gesture to the farther reaches of the crowd – out of earshot in the commotion the assembly was in – to indicate his life was in danger. He touched his head. His enemies, however, *ran to the meeting of the senate and reported Tiberius asked for a royal diadem, that he sought now to be king.* This news outraged the senate and **now** senator and *pontifex maximus* (chief priest) Publius Cornelius Scipio Nasica demanded that the consul 'put down the tyrant', but the consul calmly replied that he would not kill a citizen without trial, but he would not recognize any election results Tiberius persuaded the Roman people to take. Nasica – 'pointy nose' – appears in Plutarch's sources a bit earlier as a holder of excess land who, consequently, took the lead in closing the Republic's purse.[48]

Little evidence survives to attest to Nasica's career. He must have had considerable weight in the senate however. He became *pontifex maximus*, chief of the priestly college of *pontifices*, in 141, and consul in 138.[49] He was grandson of the Gnaeus Cornelius Scipio who had fought in Spain alongside the father of Africanus in the war against Hannibal, and son of the censor who had adorned the Capitol with porticoes.[50] Velleius Paterculus, writing in the early first century CE, depicted him as a noble Roman putting the welfare of the Republic before his own familial loyalties. Plutarch identified him as an opponent of the agrarian law because he stood to lose land. So ran some of the many opinions.

Interestingly, he was cousin not only to the great Scipio Aemilianus who had destroyed Carthage but to Tiberius himself.[51]

Scipio and Gracchus' family links had just snapped under political pressure. Enraged, Nasica called for supporters, urging those senators who wanted to protect the Republic to follow him. A band of senators and their supporters accompanied him in a murderous mood and strode purposefully up the Capitoline Hill to stop Tiberius.[52]

Which is the order of events? One possibility is:

1. Some senators prepared to kill Tiberius themselves after the consul refused to do so
2. Flaccus went to the Capitoline ahead of the senators and warned Tiberius
3. Tiberius and his followers prepared to fight

If so, Plutarch is confused: in reality the senators chose to murder Tiberius before he and his followers armed themselves. They instructed the consul to act. When the consul refused, Nasica goaded the senators into a murderous rage. Flaccus warned Tiberius, and the addition that Tiberius had made a monarchical sign that initially provoked the senators to act is altogether false, or out of place in the narrative.

The other possibility is that Tiberius warned Gracchus of looming trouble, but Plutarch is mistaken that the senators had already formed their mob and were approaching. In this case, Tiberius responded to Flaccus' warning, his followers prepared for a brawl, and this news reached a reactionary senate, which then unsuccessfully called upon the consul to act and finally formed a mob of armed henchfolk, both enslaved and free.

Appian's Version

The thicket of evidence entangles even more, for Appian has a different start to the second assembly than Plutarch. Far from being afraid and seeing omens everywhere, Tiberius awoke in good spirits. Still, he was ready for trouble. Gathering his followers, he showed them the signal he would give if violence were called for. In other words he was ready for a fight. Leading his band up the Capitoline, he claimed the centre ground of the assembly. When he found that his opponents would not allow the assembly to vote, he signalled his mob. Some banded around as a personal bodyguard while others, tying up their togas, seized the fasces and staffs from lictors present – an assault on their office. Tiberius' personal army of thugs drove off 'the rich', the general term Appian uses to label his opponents, and the other tribunes. Rumours raced through the city that Gracchus had deposed his fellow tribunes, or perhaps he had claimed a second tribunate without an election. Appian's version paints Tiberius more as a ready brawler determined to get his second tribunate, even by illegitimate violence. Now the Senate convened at the temple of Fides, also on the Capitoline, probably very close to where the assembly currently met. Appian simply notes his amazement that they did not appoint a dictator, but says nothing about Nasica's attempt to have the consul stop Gracchus. He vaguely notes the senate reached a decision and Nasica led the senators to the nearby assembly urging those who wanted to save the Republic to follow him.[53]

What Did Happen?

Picking one version over the other depends to a large extent on how one views the mindset, not only of Tiberius and his followers, but also of Nasica and his senatorial mob. It is also important to visualize how the narrative sources attempt to impose a causal order that may not fully reflect the chaos of the assembly and simultaneous meetings of senate and electoral assemblies. So what can be said about the events leading to Nasica's march? First, Tiberius probably did not occupy the assembly and chase away the other tribunes and the rich. Why not? He would make the assembly illegitimate in the eyes of enemies and bystanders alike, and thus his second tribunate would appear illegitimate. More reasonably, he came to the assembly with his supporters, perhaps prepared for violence, in order to run for a second tribunate. Who first escalated to physical violence? Events were happening simultaneously in the nearby temple of Fides – no more than 100 yards away – where the senate met and at the assembly gathering. No doubt different witnesses saw different things, and, in the aftermath of the chaos, partisans on both sides chose the details they preferred, one blaming Tiberius for violence, the other faulting the reactionary Nasica and his senatorial colleagues.

Plutarch and Appian agree, in any event, that Nasica led senators to form a mob and enter the Capitoline assembly space, and other sources agree.[54] For Nasica, his cousin was no longer a Roman politician governed and protected by the rules of politics at Rome. No! He was a tyrant, and tyrants must die to keep the Republic safe.

Nasica, once he had gained a following of senators and armed supporters, prepared for urban battle. Velleius Paterculus notes he wrapped his toga around his left arm – both to keep the folds from tripping him and to provide a makeshift shield. Plutarch and Appian agree he pulled the hem of his toga over his head like a hood – Appian speculates he wanted to stand out for followers to see or to protect his head or to shield his identity from the gods because of guilt. The last seems the least likely. Nasica seems to have been unwavering in his purpose from the moment he demanded the consul put down Gracchus.[55]

What began as a political competition between Tiberius, his allies, and his opponents over an agrarian law, ended in a brutal street fight. The senators armed themselves with the legs of smashed seats in the assembly as supporters gathered sticks and clubs. They arrived at the assembly and forced themselves into the crowd, clubbing their way towards Tiberius and his followers. Tiberius' group could not withstand the assault and fled the assembly grounds. A number were killed.

And Tiberius? Senatorial mobs beat him to death, reportedly finding him huddled against the nearby temple to Jupiter Capitolinus, surely terrified, likely broken in spirit.[56] He died next to the temple door located by the statues of the kings, Appian reports, but that may have come from a hostile source eager to paint Tiberius as a royal revolutionary to the end. Plutarch's sources did not even give Tiberius that long to live. He tried to escape the assembly area, shedding his toga when a foe seized the garment. He fell over a body and stumbled to his feet, but the tribune Publius Satyreius first struck his head with a club, and Lucius Rufus bragged about landing the second blow. Along with Tiberius, 300 others were beaten to death by stones or improvised clubs. Velleius has him die in flight almost randomly, suggesting he was fleeing down the steps of the Capitoline when he was struck dead by a bench fragment. The horrors of the deaths he and his supporters on the Capitoline faced were compounded by the dishonour heaped upon his corpse. Though his brother Gaius asked for permission to recover Tiberius' body and bury it properly, the senate refused and all the Gracchan corpses were dumped into the Tiber like so much garbage.[57] Tiberius' senatorial foes had just begun their quest for blood however. In the following months, they exiled some of Tiberius' comrades without trial, violating their rights as Roman citizens. They were, perhaps, the more fortunate ones. Others, the senators summarily executed.[58]

But some Romans stood against Tiberius' enemies and protested their heavy-handedness. Their pressure was sufficient to force compliance with Tiberius' agrarian law. A new appointee, Publius Licinius Crassus, already father-in-law of younger brother Gaius Gracchus, replaced Tiberius on the three-person committee to redistribute land. The committee was allowed to begin its work of redistributing public land properly. Nasica, an easy target because of his leadership of the brutal mob, risked prosecution for his deeds, if not worse: he became a pariah as passers-by on the streets insulted him. Soon, Nasica, who was legally not allowed to leave Italy because of his sacred duties as *pontifex maximus*, fled the city and sailed east, dying in Pergamum within a year.[59]

And so Tiberius Gracchus' brief political career ended. He was and is an ambiguous figure. Fully a Roman aristocrat, a person of his place and time and circumstances, he was proud of his family name, sought a reputation for military virtue, built connections with important elder senators, and clearly sought to be a distinguished part of the ruling class. His agrarian law, though highly controversial, was not the work of a revolutionary. He had drafted it with support from highly respectable senators. He was not the first to draft such a law. Though he initially skirted senatorial opposition by going straight to the assembly with his proposal, this too had probably been done before. If anything he was playing the established role of tribune of the plebs, an office for the relatively young, new to their aristocratic political career. Shaking things up, proving a bit obstinate, taking on big fish, these were all well within the realm of a tribune. When these issues are considered, Tiberius appears as an earnest social reformer, or at most a cynical aristocrat who, like many before, had used reform to further his own climb up the ladder of the senatorial elite.

But then we are faced at the same time with Tiberius Gracchus the revolutionary. Shutting down public business and sealing the treasury to force a vote on his agrarian law saw him pushing the limits. Deposing Octavius was the step beyond the pale. And once this had happened, the political situation at Rome degraded rapidly for Tiberius. Appropriating the wealth of Pergamum for the agrarian law was perhaps not as radical as deposing a fellow tribune, but it built on the revolutionary nature of Tiberius' political position. He was not subject to fellow tribunes; he could not be contained by the senate. Petitioning the assembly to be tribune for a second consecutive year was a final straw for Nasica and his whipped-up crowd. And so Tiberius, and many of his supporters, died.

But Roman small farmers' demands for land to farm and a way to subsist, did not disappear. Nor were these the only complaints the citizens and allies of the Republic had against the system as it was, run by the senatorial elite. Less than a decade later, Gaius Gracchus, younger brother of Tiberius, would mount the Rostra as a tribune, and initiate a larger, more comprehensive effort to address the grievances of those the senate governed, beyond the modest-in-comparison efforts of the slain Tiberius. And to that younger brother's clash with the powerful we now turn.

Chapter 4

The Reformer and the Reactionary: Gaius Gracchus and Lucius Opimius

The final decree of the senate: the consul should take any actions necessary to save the Republic. This dire edict gave the consul for 121 BCE, Lucius Opimius, exactly what he wanted: leave to exterminate Gaius Gracchus, Fulvius Flaccus and their rabble, who even now fortified the Aventine Hill in rebellion. They rejected the label of rebels, to be sure, but Opimius controlled the spin on events, at least from the senatorial perspective. He wasted no time. When the rebels' leaders sent Flaccus' son as a herald seeking terms not once but twice, Opimius arrested the youth and put him under a guard. There would be no peace. They could surrender or die. And the time had passed for surrender. Opimius mustered legionaries and a detachment of Cretan archers. He declared that he would pay anyone who brought him Flaccus and Gracchus' heads their weight in gold. The soldiers approached the Aventine civilians. Meanwhile, Gaius was at his wits' end. Younger brother of Tiberius Gracchus and twice tribune of the people, Gaius now found himself in a deadly spiral not wholly unlike the one that claimed the life of his elder brother just a decade ago. And all for championing a more equitable distribution of the spoils of empire to the many outside the senatorial class.

The archers started the grim business, showering the Aventine civilians with arrows that pierced their bodies and drove them to flight. The soldiers pursued, and, for the second time in a decade, a bloodbath ended the life of a Sempronius Gracchus. But not without a lethal chase. Flaccus died caught in the vacant bathhouse in which he hid. But Gaius still lived. He had remained apart from the hillside combat and stayed at the Temple of Diana on the Aventine. Opimius' forces were carving into the Gracchan supporters. Defeat certain and perhaps even death as far as Gaius was concerned, he opted to end his life then and there on the

Aventine. Two of his comrades, Pomponius and Licinius persuaded him to flee instead.

And he ran. Gaius hurtled down the Aventine into the Forum Boarium (Cattle Market) and reached the ancient, wooden Sublician bridge across the Tiber. Those comrades pushed him onward and stopped at the bridge to slow his pursuers. They were cut down. And Gaius ran.

Outside the walls to the grove of trees sacred to the ancient Roman goddess Furrina, Gaius stopped, out of breath or simply out of hope. There he instructed the enslaved Philocrates (though his name might have been Euporous) to kill him. And either he managed the grim final task, or they were caught and murdered. Either way, Gracchus could no longer run.

Gaius Gracchus' Early Career

A more fatalistic Roman might pronounce the death of Gaius as ordained. But it was by no means certain that Gaius would even enter the political realm, certainly not to take up the mantle of his elder brother, certainly not to expose himself to the rivalries and enmity of those who hated the Gracchan programme of addressing the needs of the citizens and subjects outside the senatorial elite. Or at least Plutarch makes it seem uncertain. He asserts that Gaius initially wanted no part of politics and kept to his private affairs. This is understandable: his brother had been murdered by politics. Despite Plutarch's comment, however, Gaius clearly had some political duties. After all, he was one of the three commissioners of the agrarian law his brother had passed at such great personal cost. There is reason to suppose that law still had strong supporters.[1] To that extent, at least, Gaius must have involved himself in public business. So Plutarch may just have meant that Gaius, not yet 20, lay low in the aftermath of Tiberius' sacrifice, for he soon discusses the young man's entry into public life.[2] On the other hand, there is no reason to accept at face value Dio's hatchet job. In his account, unlike his once-upstanding brother, Gaius 'was naturally turbulent and played the rogue voluntarily... his designs were more mischievous, his daring more spontaneous, and his arrogance greater'.[3]

Indeed, Gaius seems to have been politically active enough to argue publicly with the great Scipio Aemilianus. Sometime in the years following Tiberius' murder, the tribune Gaius Papirius Carbo proposed a law allowing an individual to be elected to the tribunate multiple times. Unsurprisingly, Gaius backed the law since to do otherwise would be to accuse his murdered brother of illegally seeking a second tribunate. The distinguished Scipio Aemilianus challenged the law and asserted that Tiberius seemed to have been justly slain for his deed.[4]

The reality, however, is that Gaius spent a considerable amount of his early adulthood away from Rome in military and political service.[5] So he was certainly engaged in the Republic, but still too young and usually too far away to get embroiled in city politics. Unfortunately Plutarch is our only detailed source for the start of Gaius' career, but his account is plausible enough. Gaius began, as so many young aristocratic senate-hopefuls did, by working the law courts as an advocate and appears to have distinguished himself as a gifted orator. Indeed decades later, Cicero, no slouch of an orator himself, asserted that, with time, Gracchus would have become the greatest Roman orator.[6] Gaius won election to the quaestorship and accompanied the consul Lucius Aurelius Orestes to the island of Sardinia in 126 BCE, where apparently the island-dwellers were in revolt.[7] Gaius proved that, just like his older brother, he had the skills and temperament for military life and distinguished himself for bravery. But he also, Plutarch asserts, became known for his fair dealings with Roman subjects in Sardinia, and this seems likely since Gaius' political career was marked by an intense concern for the wellbeing of those governed by the Roman aristocracy.[8]

Demands for Italian Citizenship

As he left the city for his quaestorship in 126, the sparks of a different political conflagration were struck. A tribune of 126, Marcus Junius Pennius, passed a law ejecting all without Roman citizenship from the city.[9] We do not know exactly why. Some have suggested it was connected to the proposal the consul of 125, Fulvius Flaccus, would make to grant citizenship to the Italian allies – that same Fulvius Flaccus who eventually died in a bathhouse when Opimius crushed the Gracchans. The logic in this case: Pennius ejected non-citizens in 126, before Flaccus was consul, to anticipate Flaccus' proposal and prevent Italians from pressuring citizens to vote in their favour. But the chronology is far from certain.[10]

It is important to unpack Flaccus' citizenship proposal because it illustrates some of the social and political pressures the Republic faced at this point. He proposed granting citizenship to the Italian allies and providing those who did not wish citizenship with the right to appeal sentences to the Roman people.[11] The Romans, for centuries, had developed relationships with the peoples of Italy as their power spread throughout the peninsula and then the Mediterranean. Early on, Rome, one Latin city-state in Latium, was part of an alliance with the other Latin states. Eventually relations soured and war broke out between the Romans and their fellow Latins. With difficulty the Romans subjugated their former friends and in 338 BCE transformed the old Latin League into a new settlement that would shape Roman influence in Italy for centuries. Rome simply absorbed the smaller Latin states and made their citizens Roman citizens. The two largest Latin foes, Tibur and Praeneste, however, were assigned the status of Latin allies. As states with 'Latin Rights' they could manage their own internal affairs, trade and intermarry legally with Roman citizens, and even move to Rome and receive full Roman citizenship. In return they had to follow Roman foreign policy and supply troops to Roman armies. In time this package of Latin Rights became a legal status rather than an ethnic one. When Rome founded new colonies, with the exception of a small handful of citizen colonies, colonists had Latin Rights.[12]

Latin Rights were three:

- The right to have one's contracts enforced in Roman courts (*ius commercii*) – this was essential to trade and other business partnerships.
- The right to have legal marriages and heirs recognized (*ius connubii*).
- And finally, the right of a Latin to move to the city of Rome and gain full Roman citizenship with voting rights (*ius migrationes*).

The Latin states whose citizens enjoyed these rights ceded their control over any independent foreign policy: they were at peace and war with anyone Rome said they must be. The Latin states also had to supply troops for the Roman armies, an important source of personpower as Roman influence expanded in Italy. [13]

As the Romans continued to extend their authority along the peninsula, they categorized the peoples of Italy who were not full Roman citizens into three basic groups:

- the Latins who held the legal package of Latin Rights,
- citizens without the right to vote (*civitas sine suffragio*),
- and allied Italians.

The status of citizenship without the vote was granted to various peoples. Fundamentally it was similar to Latin status in that these non-voting citizens had the same rights and could relocate to Rome and become full citizens. They also shared the obligation of Latins and full citizens to provide soldiers at the annual levies when summoned. This status was imposed forcefully on some peoples for disloyalty to Rome, as in the case of Capua in the late third century war against Hannibal. The Capuans were more clearly considered subjects and yearly they were under the governance of a Roman praefect elected for the task.[14]

Finally, the allies (*socii*) were those states and peoples who did not have the full package of rights that the Latins and non-voting citizens did. These Italian states provided troops as needed to Roman armies. Traditionally historians have accepted that Rome extracted troops from these allies through a series of bilateral treaties the city state signed with each ally. More recently that view has been challenged, and it has been suggested the relationship between Romans and allies was strong but informal and not treaty-based. However it may have been, the contributions of Latins and allies to the ceaseless Roman war efforts was substantial. At the time the Greek historian Polybius wrote in the second century BCE, allied states supplied half the soldiers in any Roman army, with citizens supplying the other half. By the end of the second century that ratio went up to two thirds.[15]

Over time the burden increased of not being a Roman citizen in Italy. As noted, the Latins and allies provided ever growing proportions of soldiers to Roman citizens, and allied troops seem to have been more likely to serve for longer stretches than citizens. In a very real sense the Latins and allies were the conquerors of an empire just as much as the Romans, if not more. With greater military burdens, however, the cities and towns of Italy did not receive a greater benefit from the spending of conquered loot; that seems to have been lavished upon Rome itself.[16]

Increasing Desires for Citizenship

The lack of Roman citizenship was an issue of equity for Italians as much as anything. It may well not be the case that most Italians wanted Roman citizenship, but it is reasonable to suppose that they did not want to be treated as Roman subjects, inferior to citizens. By the late second century a growing number of incidents punctuated the reality that even distinguished Italians, aristocrats and gentlefolk in their local municipalities, were insignificant compared to the Roman senatorial elite. The stinging support for such claims came from the whip. A Roman magistrate could not beat a private citizen without due process. But they could flog a Latin or another form of Italian ally. Gaius detailed a few examples in one of his speeches, which we have in fragments thanks to Cicero's quotations decades later. Gaius paints a troubling picture. The leading magistrate of the Latin colony of Teanum Sidicinum? Publicly flogged. The charge? The local public bath had not been fully vacated and cleaned when the wife of a consul in town wanted to bathe. Reportedly, the nearby colony of Cales took no chances and passed a law forbidding its citizens to use their public baths if a Roman magistrate were visiting. In another poignant episode, a Roman officer travelled by closed litter, prompting a Venusian farmer to joke that the litter bearers looked like they were heading to a funeral. An over-eager young Roman officer took the comment as a mortal insult to his commander and had the poor farmer publicly whipped to death. True, these are highly provocative examples that Gaius used for rhetorical effect, but they are not the only egregious examples of the whip being used to reinforce the lower social status of non-citizens.[17]

Why were many Romans opposed to granting citizenship to Latins and Italians? It is difficult to say, but several factors were likely in play. First Roman aristocrats, whose status depended on their ability to benefit from the electoral system, probably did not welcome the inclusion of thousands of new citizens and the reconfiguration of the voters that would entail. Then too, some aristocrats must have been wary of the assumed political boost a Flaccus or a Gaius would gain at the polls once all these newly-enfranchised – thanks to them – citizens voted. As for the average Roman citizen, it is far less clear what the concern would be. Perhaps they were persuaded that their interests would no longer be represented when all these new voters registered? Whatever the reasons, granting full citizenship to Latins, the allies, or all Italians, was political dynamite.[18]

So Flaccus sought to remedy the resentment of Italians by extending citizenship to them. The senate refused.[19] Frustrated to breaking-point, the Latin colony of Fregellae revolted against Roman rule in 125 BCE. There is a hint in the sources that some of the elite of the colony stayed loyal to Rome throughout the short-lived rebellion. We do not know. Either way, the revolt was little short of suicide. A praetor of 125, Lucius Opimius, destroyed the city.[20] Several years later, as consul, he would destroy Gaius. Reportedly Opimius claimed, but did not receive, a triumph for his efforts. It is striking that he would have claimed a triumph over Latins, peoples so closely connected to Rome, and it may be a hint of his later stance against Gracchus, who championed the non-citizens of Italy.[21] Regardless, some Romans, Plutarch opines, pinned Gracchus to the revolt of Fregellae. These accusations amounted to nothing, but they illustrate the heat of the political climate.[22]

Gaius' Run for Tribune

By the end of 124, Gaius was ready to seek the tribunate. It is hard to view that choice without some foreboding, even not knowing the outcome of Gaius' brief career. His older brother had been murdered in a political brawl stemming from his tribunate; surely it would be wiser to avoid taking the same office a decade later? But Gaius clearly had talent, clearly had an aristocratic pedigree that could only be maintained if he and future generations held public office, and clearly had concerns about the peoples of Rome and Roman Italy outside the senatorial clique. The burden of Tiberius' moral example may have been too weighty to ignore. Romans were fond of pointing out moral exemplars and failures to their children to inculcate desired virtues. Cornelia had reportedly told her children that she wanted to be known as the mother of the Gracchi. So perhaps it was more than empty rhetoric when Gaius reportedly was pulled from his preferred quiet life by a dream: phantasmal Tiberius proclaimed that fate had marked Gaius to be a champion of the people, just as he had been.[23] But it will not do to just give the sympathetic sources voice. Dio – even though he seems to have little appreciation of political nuance more than three centuries before his time – derides Gaius as the better orator than his brother but also the greater scoundrel and so more arrogant and disruptive to Roman politics.[24] It is difficult to see this accusation, however, as more than the slander of Roman sources who thought the subordinated classes of Italy – common Romans, Italian allies, landless peasants, urban poor – deserved no more than what the senate generously deemed fit to give them, and thus Gracchus' attempts to champion these groups amounted to little more than insurrection.

The opposition was fierce: Romans lumped together by sources as the 'people of note' sought to nip Gracchus' political rise in the bud; Plutarch suggests that Gracchus had the support of many Italians – presumably non-Roman citizens in the peninsula – and that crowds of them flocked to Rome to support Gaius' bid for tribune.[25] They could not vote in elections, however, so their support must have been limited to campaigning and increasing the size of Gaius' entourage, a mark of an influential Roman. He also may well have had the support of Fulvius Flaccus, consul the year before. They shared an interest in granting citizenship, with all its legal rights and protections, to all of Italy, and clearly worked together subsequently. Flaccus seemed to have been a divisive character, but tribunes were known for stirring the pot politically, and even a divisive supporter of consular rank was far better than no support at all. Gaius won the election. Whether he came in a resounding first or a more modest fourth – the sources disagree – Gaius would be a tribune in 123.[26]

The timeline of Gaius' career as tribune is a bit unclear. He held the tribunate in 123 BCE, then, as we will see, he was re-elected without seeking office to the tribunate of 122 – and without being clubbed to death. He passed legislation in both terms, but Plutarch and Appian disagree not only on the laws but their order. The following chronology of his two tribunates essentially follows Plutarch's version of Gracchus' legislative programme because it is more detailed and coherent than Appian's. Still, it is only a likely version, not a certainty.

The First Tribunate

Gracchus hit the ground running as tribune, addressing crowds and condemning the unlawful execution of his brother to gain sympathy with the voters for his legislative agenda. He had an axe to grind and needed to set the stage. The first bills Gracchus attempted seem to have been purely political, or, to put it in Roman terms, purely personal, crafted for no other purpose than to exact vengeance against his brother's foes. The first bill would prohibit any magistrate stripped of an office by the people from holding a future office. So far as we know, only one person fitted that bill: Marcus Octavius, the former tribune whom Tiberius had ejected from office. But why? Was this purely for revenge or was Octavius still a potentially important player in the political melees at Rome? Or perhaps Gaius sought to strike at an enemy and intimidate future opponents all at once, paving the way for a radical legislative package? Or was it just for show, a flex of political muscle? Plutarch asserts that Gaius not only withdrew this bill from consideration after proposing it but announced that he spared Octavius only at the request of his mother, Cornelia.[27] A shot across the bow then, of any would-be enemies? Probably; certainly any enemies would see it that way. The second bill targeted 'any magistrate who had banished a Roman citizen without trial,' and the target, though apparently not named in the bill, was clear enough: Publius Popillius Laenas, consul in 132 who led the senatorial investigation of Tiberius' network of supporters and inflicted punishments summarily. Popillius read the voters, and voluntarily exiled himself to avoid a worse fate.[28]

Gaius was a powerful orator, which helps explain the effect he had on friends and rivals. The sources essentially claim he pioneered a new style of dramatic oratory: ranging back and forth on the Rostra, striding up and down the assemblies he addressed, pulling back his formal toga and baring his arms and shoulders – which we must infer was an indecent practice – employing vigorous language and an equally vigorous delivery.[29] He bared his emotions and appealed to the emotions of his listeners, especially their sense of outrage. He either initiated or continued the recent precedent of turning as speaker to the Forum instead of the senate, to indicate the power and importance of the people, not the elite.[30] Indeed the sources felt clearly that Gaius was the supreme orator of the two Gracchi, the one far more aptly branded as a demagogue.[31] Whether or not Gaius' dramatic style was truly new in Rome, it was clearly rather effective.

A legislative agenda the likes of which the Romans had not seen followed these initial jabs at his rivals. First, Gracchus worked on a law requiring the state to provide subsidized grain to the urban plebs, a constituency his elder brother Tiberius had never really appealed to. Fulvius Flaccus, the consul of 125 who sought to expand Roman citizenship, also supported Gaius' grain law. Flaccus is a fascinating character about whom we know so very little. He was older than Gracchus by a fair margin, and the scion of a distinguished family. He must have been a junior senator at the time Tiberius was elected tribune. It is likely that he was the same Fulvius Plutarch mentioned warning Tiberius of the senate's intentions on that fateful day when that elder brother was beaten to death. Clearly he was close enough to the Gracchi that he received a seat on Tiberius' land commission when that one's father-in-law, Appius Claudius, died in 130.[32] In 129 Flaccus had harangued Scipio Aemilianus publicly to the point that some even suspected he had a hand in that great man's mysterious death, though their suspicions amounted to nothing in the way of prosecution or penalty.[33] He had held the praetorship by 128 and successfully won the consulship in 125. At this point, Flaccus proposed citizenship for the Italians in some form but failed to get the measure passed. He then went on to battle the Gauls of modern day Provence and returned to Rome to triumph in 123, where he ran into the newly minted tribune, Gracchus, with sympathetic political interests. Their friendship ended with their deaths.[34]

Gracchus also passed an agrarian law of his own.[35] Since Tiberius' law and land commission were still in effect, it seems reasonable to suppose that this law expanded on his elder brother's work for poor farmers. The terms are not clear. It may simply have empowered the three land commissioners in the original law to found colonies in order to distribute public land rather than simply grant plots to individuals. At long last, after a decades-long hiatus that surely had contributed significantly to the unrest the Gracchi were responding to, the Republic would plant colonies again.[36]

These laws suggest that Gaius did more than simply follow his brother's agrarian agenda. Indeed, a historian of Rome once deemed Gracchus' legislation practically 'an entirely new constitution'.[37] He launched a legislative programme that systematically addressed the concerns and interests of less economically fortunate Romans. Land for poor farmers was the extent of Tiberius' programme, and Gaius expanded on addressing that with the founding of new colonies, where Romans could gain land in return for pioneering. But Gaius reached out to new classes of Roman citizens. He proposed food for the poorest citizens, which amounted to a substantial number of Rome's urban inhabitants.[38] He also targeted the economic burden of military service. At an earlier point in the Republic, Roman citizen soldiers were expected to provide their own equipment and clothing but were paid and provided with food while on campaign.[39] Arguably, in the course of the second century, that state had come to supply soldiers with basic weapons and some form of protection. Otherwise one would expect Gaius to have legislated that the state would supply the more expensive weapons and armour rather than the much smaller cost of clothes. So, it may well be that Gaius' proposal removed the final economic burdens of providing military service. He went further in this area and prevented juveniles from being drafted into the army, though we cannot know the extent to which this was an issue at the time. He also may have passed a law restricting the severity of military punishments.[40] Road construction would prove of benefit to those engaged in travel and trade within and outside Roman dominions, a boon to the wealthier classes of citizens. Gaius, in short, proposed a series of state-sponsored benefactions a step closer to modern welfare states than the ancient Republic had been.

His more controversial proposals confirmed that Gaius planned to reach a far greater circle of constituents than Tiberius had dreamed of. There is some uncertainty here. Though the sources vary significantly and some suggest Gracchus proposed giving full citizenship to all Italians, a safer reading suggests Gracchus proposed full citizenship for the Latins and Latin rights for allied Italians, essentially an upgrade in each groups' current status.[41] The measure had merit in offering some equity for the non-citizens who had carried so much of the burden of expanding Roman power throughout the Mediterranean. This proposal, however, would shake up the voting assemblies at least a bit with the influx of new citizens and would likely make a number of new voters great supporters of Gracchus. Of course, it is not at all clear whether this influx of voters simply raised fears or actually would have produced practical effects.

The Judicial Law

These laws may have disgruntled some among the elite senators at Rome who did not particularly want to care for the needs of the common Roman, but Gracchus' move to undercut the judicial privileges of the senators must have earned him more permanent enemies. How exactly he did this is unclear; the evidence is problematic and highly confused.[42] Here is what we know. In 149 BCE the tribune Lucius Calpurnius Piso legislated the creation of a permanent court to try Roman governors who had defrauded their provinces. The court consisted of a jury composed of senators. A criticism of the day was that senatorial jurors would be quite unlikely to convict one of their own. Whether that was the case, a number of senators clearly felt that a governor should only be tried by those of his own class: senators. But at least some among the *equites*, the wealthy cavalry class whose members not uncommonly had considerable interest in effective management of the empire, wished to check extortionate governors by placing some of their number on the extortion juries. Gracchus' law brought this about. Instead of the list, the *album* as it was called in Latin, of 300 senators as potential jurors, Gaius proposed to double the number of jurors by choosing 300 equestrians to add to the album.[43]

Or did he? Appian suggests Gaius went further, removed senators from the juries altogether, and replaced them with *equites*.[44] Livy's summarizer offers a mutually exclusive third option: Gaius proposed enrolling 600 equites as senators, increasing the membership of the senate to 900 and doubling the influence of new equestrian interests over established senatorial interests – not that their interests always diverged.[45] Deciding which of these variants for the law courts Gaius proposed becomes tricky because the composition of the law court juries – either all *equites*, all senators, or a mix – was the subject of a variety of laws and political wranglings after Gracchus. Though certainty is impossible, our best guess is that Appian's claim was the authentic one: 300 *equites* would now form the album of jurors, no longer senators. Two important additions put some teeth into the extortion court, clearly showing that Gracchus intended the *equites* to check fraudulent senators. First his law established that convicted governors would now pay back double to provincials what they had extorted. But the greater blow was this. As long as the court had been a matter of senators trying their own, the penalty for conviction had been less substantial. With equestrians on the jury, however, the *repetundae* court became a public court and thus a conviction brought with it *infamia*, and thus effectively barred the convicted from ever holding office or ever sitting in the senate again.[46]

Additionally, Gaius passed laws planting colonies outside Italy, a means to distribute the benefits of Roman conquests to poorer farmers; laws to construct new high-quality roads; and laws establishing granaries, presumably to help regulate the price of grain subsidies and help during shortages. He even showed an interest in the provincials beyond his revision of the extortion court. When Fabius Maximus acquired a great deal of grain from Spain to supply Rome, word on the street said Fabius had coerced the Spanish in his province to supply the grain. Gaius accordingly proposed to sell the grain, give the profits to the involuntary Spanish suppliers, and censure Fabius.[47]

Gaius certainly kept himself busy implementing his laws in 123. Taken together, Gaius' measures suggest that he sought to redistribute some of the benefits and just a bit of the power in the Republic. He may not have been revolutionary, but he was definitely radical. The senatorial aristocracy of noble Roman families feared losing their lock on voters through the expansion of citizenship and their lock on policing their own through the loss of the juries to the *equites*. The wealthy would be checked in their ability to hold public land and the poor granted redistributions of land. Even the poorest Romans, the urban poor, would receive grain for free or at a reduced rate. The Republic would, in short, be forced to operate at least a little bit for the welfare of those outside the dominant political class.

Clearly, Gaius' legislative programme, and second consecutive tribunate, would have inspired opposition. But the descent into martial law and Lucius Opimius' barely legalized murder of Gracchus and his supporters, was still some time in coming. Indeed, there was no reason to suspect after the year of his first tribunate, in 123, that Gaius would meet his brother's fate.

By the close of 123 BCE, Gaius had earned the support of many outside the senate and arguably had alienated a number of senators in the process. There was speculation that Gaius might overstep himself. Gaius, Plutarch suggests, declared in a speech that he had a favour to ask that he dearly hoped the people would grant. Rumours abounded that Gaius would seek the consulship for 122, a move that would be illegal by pretty much any standard – not only as a jump between offices without any time in between but also because he would have skipped the mandatory aedileship and praetorship. On the day that candidates for the consulship declared themselves, however, Gaius accompanied and campaigned for Gaius Fannius. Fannius won election, assuredly buoyed by Gaius' support.

As for Gaius, he seems to have planned to step down from the tribunate when his term expired, perhaps unsurprising given the brutal end Tiberius met when running for a second consecutive tribunate. The plebeian assembly would have none of it, however, and named him tribune for 122, even though he was not a candidate. Gaius Gracchus became tribune a second consecutive time in 122. Tiberius had been bludgeoned to death when he ran for that office twice. The closest to such a law: Papirius Carbo, as tribune in 131 or 130, tried to legalize second tribunates, and Gaius Gracchus supported him. The measure failed however, not least because the distinguished Scipio Aemilianus proclaimed during the debates that Tiberius Gracchus had been lawfully killed.[48] How is it that Gaius could be elected tribune a second time and yet escape senatorial lynch mobs claiming to defend the constitution? Appian suggests a law had been passed where the Roman people were empowered to select anyone as tribune if insufficient candidates ran for the office. There are at least two barriers to supposing Appian got this right. First, none of the other sources even comment on such a law, unlikely in itself. But second, if indeed a law existed saying that voters could choose their own tribunes if insufficient candidates – ten, that is – ran for office, it would have been absurdly easy for Gracchus' opponents to find enough straw people to fill the gap. Casting further doubt on Appian is the fracas of 110 BCE, centring on two tribunes who aimed for a second term and second year of office.[49] The political squabbles over the legality of this closed public business for a time at Rome. How could this have happened if a law less than two decades old had been passed allowing tribunes to hold a second term of office? Appian's assertion does not float, though that leaves us in the dark.

There were good reasons, beyond the outrage it might provoke, for Gaius to pass on a tribunate for 122. That year would see a difficult set of legislative struggles that Gaius could probably predict, most notably over the extension of citizenship. He may have hoped to hand his programme over to Fulvius Flaccus, who did win election to the tribunate for 122 – an irregularity to be sure, for Flaccus had already been a consul. Fannius the consul-elect also appeared to owe Gaius a favour or two. And Gaius seems to have planned to travel to Carthage and supervise the foundation of the

Junonia colony. Perhaps Gaius felt his interests supported enough that he could go abroad without a second tribunate.[50] Perhaps he felt it would be too provocative to seek the second term that had killed his brother.

So, Gaius got away with being elected tribune for a second consecutive term, perhaps because he had made no claim to it and perhaps because of the voters' regard for endorsing Fannius.[51]

Gaius' Second Tribunate

However it may have happened, Gracchus and Flaccus were tribunes for 122, and Gracchus took this opportunity to introduce legislation granting citizenship to those Italians of Latin status. If he had calculated an easy victory because of his allies, he soon learned better. Fighting fire with fire, Gaius' political opponents in 122 found an agreeable tribune to aid them in Marcus Livius Drusus. Drusus had the pedigree: son of an aristocratic family line with a sterling reputation. He also must have possessed at least solid oratory skills.

The strategy: detach Gaius' support and neutralize his political power by proposing popular counter-measures to the assemblies. When Gaius' proposed two colonies for citizens with modest resources, Drusus countered by proposing twelve colonies for the destitute. And when Gaius proposed citizenship for the Italians, Drusus countered with a lesser, but still important, sign of respect: a ban on flogging Latins even in military service. Drusus also proposed the poor farmers who received public land would not pay any rent for it.[52] Throughout his speeches, Drusus assured the voters that the senate fully approved of his measures. But he made clear that he would not be personally involved in the planting of the new colonies or indeed in administering any of his legislative projects. It was a clever move: Gaius personally involved himself in his various legislative projects – from planting colonies to distributing land and building roads – probably because he was a concerned micromanager who wanted to make sure things were done correctly. By standing apart from his proposed colonial projects, however, Drusus could imply that Gaius sought to gain personally from his popular legislation, whereas he, Drusus, simply did what was best for the people. And here it is worth considering Plutarch's analysis fully: 'In this way the senate made it perfectly clear that it did not disapprove of Gaius' measures per se, but wanted to destroy him or, failing that, to humiliate him utterly.'[53] It is reasonable to suppose those outside the senatorial class saw it this way: purely personal politics.

Whether Drusus actively vetoed Gaius' measures or simply forestalled their proposal with the threat of veto, Gaius seemed to have accomplished little legislation at the start of his second tribunate in 122. Soon he was needed to supervise the foundation of the new colony at Carthage – whether because he was on the land commission or had been formally selected to supervise the founding is not clear.[54] Either way, off Gaius went. His absence proved a liability for legislative efforts at home. Drusus continued to cultivate votes. He also went out of his way to attack tribune Flaccus in the assemblies. Even on his best days, Flaccus does not seem to have had Gaius' talent as a speaker, which must have made him an easier target for Drusus.[55]

It's worth pausing again to consider Flaccus and his role in the civil conflagration that would claim his life and that of Gaius. As noted above, he was a land commissioner and a Gracchan ally, and he had proposed citizenship for the Italian allies in 125 BCE when consul. These items in his pedigree would suffice to earn the disapproval of many senators.

What else do we know? Plutarch is scathing in his assessment:

[Flaccus] was a disruptive influence ... and as well as being openly hated by the senate he was also widely suspected of fuelling allied discontent and of secretly fomenting revolt among the Italians. Although there was no evidence or proof to support these claims, Fulvius [Flaccus] himself gave them plausibility by his insane and revolutionary policies.[56]

Clearly Plutarch and his sources did not think much of Flaccus. The charge of 'insane and revolutionary policies', howerver, ignores the simple fact that in 125 Flaccus won election to the consulship through the favour of the centuriate assembly that was arranged so that Romans of some property strongly influenced the outcomes. Yet his shift from holding the consulship to running for the lower office of tribune was a pretty radical move, suggesting he was concerned more with his legislative goals than his traditional dignity. Flaccus remains something of an enigma.

Drusus had help in his pressure play against Gaius and Flaccus. Lucius Opimius, the praetor who had destroyed the Latin colony of Fregellae three years ago, had sought the consulship for 122 but lost the election to Fannius. In no small part, word on the street said, this was because Gaius had campaigned so effectively for him. Opimius was determined to win the office at his next opportunity, the summer elections for the consulship of 121. He also made no secret that he would dismantle Gaius' legislative programme and cancel his colonies.[57] Why? Opimius' treatment of Fregellae and especially his claim for a triumph against former allies may point to a more general conviction against policies elevating the Latins. More generally, a number of senators opposed Gaius' policies, and Opimius may just have been a part of that cohort that happened to win election to consul at a decisive moment in time.

Meanwhile, all sorts of problems and inauspicious omens had plagued the African colony of Junonia. Plutarch passes on the murmurings:

> The work was often disrupted, and they say that this was the gods' doing. For instance, the standard that was leading the procession was caught in a gust of wind, and when the bearer held onto it with all his strength, it broke into pieces; the entrails lying on the altars were scattered by a wind-storm and carried here and there beyond the stakes marking the new city's boundaries, which had already been traced; and the markers themselves were attacked, uprooted, and carried a long way off by wolves.

Whether these ill omens occurred or were embellished by his adversaries, Gaius persisted in sorting out the settlement procedures after several months at it. Then he returned to Rome, likely in no small part to defend his political position and dignity against the likes of Drusus and Opimius.[58]

The End of the Second Tribunate

The final months of Gaius' tribunate in 122 BCE pose a tangled knot to historians. Appian has Gaius essentially step off the boat and head directly to an assembly convened by Opimius, an assembly that could only have taken place after January 1st of 121 when Opimius became consul.[59] That chronology does not work for there were assuredly some months left in Gaius' tribunate of 122 after he returned from Africa. Appian, it seems, ignores some important final details of Gaius political efforts in 122. Plutarch may supply the missing details for those final months. Gaius returned to find Flaccus politically overwhelmed and indeed his own influence waning. It's not difficult to understand why. Gaius had been gone over two months and Drusus had been hard at work undermining him with the help of consul-elect Opimius. It is reasonable to suppose the voters lost some of their fire for Gracchus when Drusus offered such similar legislative benefits. In an effort to shore up his base, Gaius moved from his domus on the ritzy Palatine to a spot near the Forum, making no secret that he did so to be closer to his constituents, average Romans. Then he circulated details of his forthcoming legislation.[60]

The air was charged as 122 passed. Gaius had returned to Rome and announced a new legislative programme while Drusus challenged his position as the people's orator and Opimius made known he would repeal Gaius' acts. It appears part of Gaius' final legislative push was the move to grant citizenship to the Latins, a proposal near and dear to Flaccus. For Plutarch reports that Italian friends and supporters of Gaius flooded into the city after he announced his future legislation, and surely only the franchise would move such interest. These allies could not vote, of course, but they could canvas voters, and they could use whatever influence they might have with their Roman patrons to help Gaius pass the measure.[61]

The senate grew reactionary, however, and persuaded the consul Fannius – supposedly beholden to Gaius – to expel all non-citizens from Rome. Perhaps the crowds were too daunting. Perhaps there had been disorder. Perhaps there was fear that some Italians would pass themselves off as legal voters. Regardless, it was a heavy-handed measure. Gaius, still tribune, made a show of strength by officially countering the senatorial edict, condemning the senate and promising his tribunician support to any allies in the city. It ended up being just that: a show. A test case arose when one of Fannius' lictors seized hold of a personal friend of Gaius and dragged him away out of the city. Gaius stood by and did nothing. Plutarch offers two possibilities about this incident. Either Gaius knew he lacked the power to protect the person, or he feared that acting then and there would spark a personal confrontation that could only give his enemies the pretext they needed to attack him decisively. So Gaius did nothing.[62] Non-citizens were expelled, roughly apparently, and the measure to extend the vote did not pass.

As the end-of-year elections for the tribunes of 121 loomed, Plutarch reports one final incident. Arrangements had been made for a gladiatorial show – where enslaved humans fought to the death to satisfy the Roman cravings for bloody entertainment – to be held in the Forum. Magistrates, tribunes included, Plutarch strongly implies, had paid for bleachers to be constructed around the impromptu arena so that they might rent these to the audience and turn a personal profit. In doing so they would prevent those who could not afford such seating from seeing the show. When Gaius found out, he went to the Forum and demanded the scaffolding be dismantled so the poor could see the spectacle for free. No one took any notice, so Gaius appeared at night with a posse of labourers and disassembled the seating. The next day there was plenty of free space for the poor. Needless to say, this endeared Gaius to them. Equally needless to say, it alienated those magistrates who saw nothing wrong in a little free enterprise and who had lost money paying for benches that had been destroyed. According to Plutarch, word on the street was that this fracas lost him election to a third tribunate. He won a majority of votes but his tribunicial colleagues fraudulently falsified the returns. Arguments broke out but Gaius was denied a legitimately won third tribunate.[63]

The Final Months

121 BCE found Gaius and Flaccus both private citizens and Opimius a consul with a taste for vengeance. Did Opimius seek to curb Gaius or crush him? Could Gaius let his legislation falter? Was there anything he could do without the formal powers of a tribune? Aspects of the final showdown suggest Opimius was most happy to destroy Gracchus, but that may have been a reaction to Gaius when he failed to accept the repeal of his programmes and the ebb of his influence and power. If that is how things played out, certainly the precipitating event to the veritable carnage was an assembly to repeal the law founding Junonia in Carthage. According to Appian, hot on the heels of Gaius' return from Carthage the senate proposed to repeal the law founding the colony there.[64] Appian seems to be mistaken, however, and this assembly happened some time after Gracchus had returned to Rome, moved to the Forum, annoyed his peers with the gladiator bench affair, and failed to secure a third tribunate. This error in chronology does not mean Appian preserved no accurate

details about the final assembly. And Appian or his sources attribute the spark for the final conflagration to Gaius. Opimius is not mentioned at this point in the account but he may have been, as Plutarch suggests, the magistrate who summoned the assembly to deliberate on the fate of the Junonia colony. The tiniest fragment of a speech Gaius delivered said to be against the tribune Minucius, who moved to repeal the law founding Junonia, may mean that Minucius was the one who had summoned the assembly, though alternatively he may simply have been the one against whom Gaius made his speech. In any event Opimius seems to have been on hand.[65]

The Fateful Assembly: Appian and Plutarch's Versions

Whoever summoned it, events in the assembly would seal the fate of Junonia and of Gaius Gracchus. As Appian relates, Gaius and Flaccus, along with their supporters, attended the assembly that day, carrying daggers no less. Fulvius arrived first and addressed the assembly. Then Gaius arrived with his supporters arrayed as bodyguards. Appian is clear that Gaius was bent on violence but had a moment of doubt and kept back from entering the assembly proper with his thugs. While waiting in a portico outside the assembly, watching to see what would happen, a chance event brought ruin to the second Gracchus tribune. A Roman named Quintus Antullius – the Greek writers Plutarch and Appian called him Antyllus – happened to be making a sacrifice nearby and saw Gaius' distress. He touched Gracchus and asked him to spare Rome from civil violence. Startled by the intrusion into his thoughts, Gracchus glared at Antullius. A supporter took the liberty to interpret this as a sign to strike, and murdered Antullius there and then. Cries broke out and some scrambled away to avoid harm. In this mess, Gaius worked his way into the assembly proper to explain the tragedy and avoid condemnation. He was ignored, and he and Flaccus were beside themselves as to what this tragic misstep would mean. They left the assembly, supporters following Flaccus and Gracchus to their respective homes. Crowds gathered in the Forum through the night, though to what purpose is not clear.[66]

Plutarch's version shares similarities but, overall, is far more sympathetic to Gaius. Opimius actively sought to repeal the colony at Carthage. Gaius remained in control of himself, but Flaccus and those like-minded pushed him to gather a force of supporters. No mention is made of secreting daggers; still, Plutarch may be referring to violent plans. A tidbit was preserved in his account that Gaius' mother, Cornelia, knew things would get rough and hired men from outside the city to enter Rome incognito, disguised as day-labourers. She then wrote to Gaius a coded letter informing him of the extra muscle. Other sources, Plutarch dutifully notes, rejected this and asserted that Cornelia opposed Gaius' plans. What plans? It seems Plutarch was well aware of the claim that Gaius and Flaccus went to the assembly that day with plans of disrupting it by force, even though he laboured to stamp out that rumour.[67] In Plutarch's version of the assembly, gathering procedures started early in the morning, and Opimius, Gracchus, and Flaccus were all present. In this version Quintus Antullius was one of Opimius' lictors and carried away the animal entrails from a sacrifice – presumably Antullius shouted some insult at Fulvius' crowd as he walked by – and may have made an obscene gesture in the process. A partisan stabbed him with a writing stylus. Death by the pen, though in this case, the pen was a long, sharpened bronze implement as good for stabbing as for writing. Fulvius, quite the erratic in Plutarch's account, was pleased, but Gaius was crushed for he knew it was an end to his hopes. Opimius seized the moment and egged on the assembly to avenge Antullius, but rain had scattered the assembly for the day. And certainly it seems more probable that Antullius was one of Opimius' lictors. This would provide Opimius with the proof to suggest that Gaius and Flaccus were revolutionaries, whose followers murdered a lictor performing his legal and sacred duties. This would presumably justify a stronger call to action – which is what happened – than a private murder in the crowd.[68]

The consul Opimius lost no time, in Plutarch's hinting, urging Romans at the assembly to avenge Antullius there and then.[69] He issued orders for an armed force – soldiers? citizens? – to gather on the Capitol and summoned the senate by messenger. Then he went to the Temple of Castor and Pollux in the Forum, the typical meeting spot for the Senate at that time, and waited, apparently through the night. Crowds gathered in the Forum until well after midnight, so disturbing had been the events of the assembly. Once the senators had gathered, presumably by the next morning, they ordered Gaius and Flaccus to appear and defend their actions.

The Senate's Final Decree and the Gracchans Slaughtered

Appian has it that the two rejected the summons. Instead Gaius and Flaccus trekked, armed and with supporters, to the Aventine hill, the ancestral stronghold of Rome's plebeians. Appian paints the two as the most sinister of rebels, suggesting that as they fled to the Aventine, they called out promising freedom to any enslaved person who chose to join them.[70] Perhaps, but it sounds suspiciously like the sort of claims the surviving aristocrats would make to justify Flaccus' and Gaius' end. Far more likely they made their way armed to the Aventine without running like firebrands through the city shouting for help; after all, they had thousands of friends and followers, judging from the great numbers of Romans who died the following day. Plutarch preserved a tender anecdote. Licinia, Gracchus' wife, embraced him and their young son, and noted bitterly that he went off without weapons or armour, effectively sacrificing himself to the murderers of his elder brother. Gaius said nothing, but gently disentangled himself from Licinia's embrace and made his way with his supporters to the Aventine.[71]

If they did fortify the Temple of Diana on the Aventine, they had selected a shrine built before the Republic and symbolically associated with Latins.[72] Apt, but it may simply have been the result of a tactical choice to secure some protection from whatever Opimius might muster. As Appian has it, Gaius and Flaccus essentially fomented rebellion since they offered freedom to the enslaved. Once they had fortified the temple, they sent Flaccus' son Quintus as their herald to the senate. The senate did not budge in its demands: they must relinquish their weapons, come to the senate, and plead their case. No more messengers. Quintus relayed the messages but was dispatched yet again to the senate, at which point Opimius arrested the youth. The time for negotiations was done. Opimius sent his armed forces to eliminate the insurrection's stronghold.[73]

Plutarch's account fills in important details Appian neglects and has the benefit that Livy's epitomator corroborates on a critical point. His account also provides more insight to Opimius' play. The day after Antullius' murder, Opimius summoned the senate to meet, presumably at the Temple to Castor and Pollux. He also arranged for mourners to carry Antullius' corpse on a couch by the meeting place, mourning loudly as they did – an effective touch of political theatre to lure more hesitant senators. The spectacle interrupted senate deliberations and pushed some senators to denounce the killing of Antullius. Plutarch also suggests some crowds present vented their rage on the oligarchy shouting that the aristocrats hated the Gracchi for the so-called crime of caring about the Roman commons.[74]

In this brittle air, the senate returned to deliberation. It issued a grim decree: the *senatus consultum ultimum*. It was, so far as we know, the first time the senate had ever issued this decree; it would not be the last. Cicero, writing three quarters of a century later, seems to have preserved the precise phrasing: 'The senate had once decreed that L. Opimius the consul was to see to it that the state took no harm.' Elsewhere he paraphrases the wording as did Plutarch and Livy's epitomator.[75]

Opimius was allowed to eliminate these 'tyrants' and their followers by any means available. On this point, the sources other than Appian are agreed: however much Opimius may have orchestrated the moment, the senate authorized Opimius to act.

And he did, efficiently and brutally. Opimius, a cold-blooded character who had once claimed a triumph for destroying a Latin city and would trumpet his victory over the Gracchans, swiftly took matters in hand. In a place and time long before civic police forces, a posse of sorts would be needed to inflict whatever its leaders saw as justice. Opimius instructed the senators to arm themselves and sent missives to the *equites* to gather in the morning, each with two armed enslaved servants for backup. In response Fulvius gathered a mob while Gaius wept as he passed his father's statue in the Forum and trudged back to his house. In Plutarch's version, no mob gathered around Gracchus; just a crowd of heartbroken supporters feeling guilty and sorry. And so while Flaccus and his followers drank the night away, Gracchus' supporters spent the night outside his house in a quiet vigil.[76]

Plutarch's tarring of Flaccus as a drunkard is a bit much; Flaccus gets all the blame and Gaius is the tragic hero. This continues into Plutarch's account of the morning. Flaccus' throng armed themselves with the spoils he had once stripped from defeated Gauls. They marched to the Aventine and shouted threats along the way. Gaius embraced his wife, Licinia, and young son to say goodbye while she bitterly predicted his fate. Then he set out quietly, armed only with a small dagger, and accompanied by his friends. He and Fulvius reunited on the Aventine Hill.[77]

Though there are discrepancies in our sources, the basic outline is clear. Once the assembly had dissolved in the rain, Opimius summoned the senate. The senate had issued its final emergency decree. Then after a night at home, Flaccus, Gaius, and their supporters fortified on the Aventine hill. There were negotiations of a sort, though bolstered by senatorial decree, and the gloves were off for Opimius. Flaccus sent his youngest son, Quintus, as an envoy down to the Forum to seek peaceful resolution. Opimius would have none of it: the two and their followers had to surrender in person, just as honest citizens should, if they wanted to ward off his wrath. Flaccus' son returned with the message. Opimius probably hoped that the two insurrectionists, as he had branded them, would refuse to surrender; the fact that he happened to have a contingent of Cretan archers that he could draw upon damningly suggests he had hoped matters would degrade to this point all along.[78]

What did the Gracchans' see as their options at this point once the son returned with the message? Would surrender bring safety? Hard to imagine they felt safe when Opimius had an armed guard and a contingent of Cretan archers to hand. It would have been naïve and astonishingly brave to trust to their innocence to shield them. And even if they were safe from mob justice, what then? Were they to subject themselves to the decrees of the senate, a senate packed with rivals and detractors? The sources say that Flaccus' son was dispatched a second time.[79] Were Flaccus and Gaius simply buying time, postponing the terrifying conclusion, an armed conflict? Surely they dared not hope that Opimius would relent upon reflection?

In the end, it was a bloodbath. Opimius dispatched his forces, with the murderous touch of promising their weight in gold if the heads of Flaccus and Gaius were brought to him. The Cretan archers showered the Aventine defenders with arrows. This must have seemed a disturbing use of foreigners to commit violence against citizens within the confines of the city. The Gracchans were not equipped to withstand an organized force, and they broke and fled for their lives. Then the massacre began in earnest. Opimius' forces occupied the hill. Flaccus fled with his eldest son and was caught and murdered in a bath house. Gaius meanwhile had avoided the fighting altogether and retreated to the Temple of Diana.[80] There he may have opted to take his own life, but later accounts suggest his comrades, Pomponius and Licinius, prevented him, snatching his sword and urging him to run. He crossed the Sublician bridge across the Tiber as two comrades died, slowing the avengers behind him. He fled outside the walls to a grove of trees sacred to the Furies. There, according to his wishes, the enslaved servant who had accompanied him in his flight, Philocrates, killed Gaius first and then himself.[81]

Three thousand Gracchan supporters lost their lives that day. Opimius got the heads of his foes and paid the gold.[82] The bodies of all were cast in the Tiber, and the property of the murdered Gracchan supporters was claimed by the state.

Final decree or no, it was far from clear that Opimius had acted lawfully. Without trial, thousands of citizens were executed, slaughtered really, by what was effectively an army, with a chief role played not by Roman soldiers but by foreign troops. In effect, as Plutarch noted, Opimius had effectively acted as dictator, though he was decidedly not a dictator but a consul who acted as a military commander within the city against citizens. But Opimius and his senatorial supporters doubled down. A purge afterwards led to the death of more suspected Gracchans.[83] And then they tripled down. A temple to Concord, to Harmony, was erected in the Forum, a slap in the face to those who believed the Gracchans had been summarily murdered by the senate and consul, citizens executed without trial. A nighttime scrawler added under the official inscription for the temple, 'This temple to Concord is the product of an act of insanity.'[84] Opimius, however, as Gracchans would have seen it, received his comeuppance. Caught some years later taking a bribe from Jugurtha, the usurper-king of Numidia, he was disgraced. And Rome became witness to his dubiously legal act. Statues of the Gracchi began to spring up and their names were included in the lists of prayers to the gods.[85]

Cornelia, two of her sons now murdered, retired to her estate at Misenum, on the Bay of Naples and continued to be known as a powerful and influential Roman, hosting scholars and diplomats and receiving goodwill gifts from kings. It is said that so strong, courageous and noble was Cornelia that she spoke without a quaver whenever asked about the greatness of her sons and the tragedy of their deaths.[86]

Just over a decade later, now the second Gracchus floated dead in the Tiber. His soul as the Romans reckoned it would receive no peace from death. And, like the first, the second Gracchus was slain as the result of a political rivalry. Violence as a solution for political differences, once unthinkable, seems in retrospect poised on the verge of a normal feature of late Republican politics. And the senate appeared to be an institution of the hyper-privileged that cared very little about groups outside their own ranks. This sense must have played a part in the sharp shocks of the next two decades as the Republic faced its first two civil wars: the first when Italy decided it would no longer tolerate serving Rome as subordinates. But this crisis, the Social War, as the Romans called it, came after the rise of a commander who would break all previous rules of holding consulships in the name of saving the Republic: Gaius Marius.

Chapter 5

The Noble, the New Man, and the Fallen Patrician: Metellus, Marius, and Sulla

He wept in frustration that day, the historian Sallust later asserted, and with good reason. Scion of an old and dignified family that had supplied the Republic with many consuls, Quintus Caecilius Metellus was an elite among the elite, a *nobilis*. The upstart Gaius Marius was not. A new man from an unremarkable equestrian family, he had no ancestry, no pedigree. So how was it that now, just as Metellus was finishing the job he had been sent to do – defeat and capture the rogue Numidian king Jugurtha – he received word that Marius had been elected consul – that most coveted honour – and assigned to relieve Metellus. Somehow he had manipulated the voters at Rome to believe the worst, believe that Metellus was losing the war against Jugurtha – when nothing could be further from the truth. Marius had won this round, Metellus had to concede, but what comfort would he have felt that day if he knew that Marius' victory would soon ring hollow? All too soon Marius would be the commander in Numidia while a subordinate stole his victory.

Numidia and the War against Jugurtha

Numidians were mostly known to third-century Romans for their amazing light cavalry. Reportedly the skilled Numidian riders manoeuvred with neither bridle nor saddle.[1] Hannibal knew their value and employed Numidian cavalry when he invaded Italy. They were part of the reason his army won the day at the Trebia and slaughtered the Romans at Cannae.[2] When the Republic regrouped and countered Hannibal's invasion with an African expedition, the king of Numidia allied with the Romans; and Numidian cavalry served ably at Zama under Scipio's command.[3] Since that time, Numidian cavalry had answered Rome's calls for allied troops and supplied auxiliary cavalry as the Romans battled the Gauls of northern Italy and the Hellenistic kingdoms of the east.[4]

Micipsa, king of Numidia, son of Masinissa, a staunch ally who had faithfully served the Romans, died around 118 BCE, and the inheritance struggle that erupted plunged Rome and Numidia into war. Micipsa intended his two biological sons, Hiempsal and Adherbal, to inherit Numidia. Jugurtha, his nephew, he raised as his own but initially left out of the royal settlement. Jugurtha, however, was a consummate politician. Through service to Rome as an auxiliary commander, he increased his reputation with the likes of Scipio Aemilianus and managed to secure a position as co-ruler with his foster brothers Hiempsal and Adherbal.[5] Jugurtha then reportedly arranged the murder of Hiempsal, placing royal control into his and Adherbal's hands and causing a great rift between them. Both rulers, hereditary and *de facto*, sought Rome's intervention. A ten-person committee, led by that Lucius Opimius who, as consul a few years before, crushed Gaius Gracchus and his followers, was established to divide Numidia between Jugurtha and Adherbal. Reportedly, Jugurtha bribed Opimius to gain a favourable division.[6] Civil war ultimately engulfed the country, during which Jugurtha managed to murder Adherbal and assume sole control over the kingdom. This violation of the Roman commission's dictates alone might have sufficed to pull the Romans deeper into the affairs of their Numidian clients, but when Jugurtha's soldiers slaughtered a group of Italian merchants who had sided with one of his rivals, there was no doubt. Prestige demanded that the Republic protect its own, and Rome declared war against Jugurtha in 111.[7]

A small-scale Roman invasion was followed by a quickly-negotiated peace treaty, possibly facilitated through bribery of the consul, Calpurnius Bestia.[8] It appeared the senate was not particularly interested in pursuing a more substantial campaign in Numidia. Then, scandal. Word spread on Roman streets, encouraged by tribune of 111, Gaius Memmius, that Jugurtha had bribed senators to look the other way and support peace. Memmius whipped up outrage among the citizenry to a peak and passed a law summoning Jugurtha to Rome on the promise of safe conduct as part of an investigation into the bribery charges. Before the Roman assembly, Memmius pushed Jugurtha to reveal who he had bribed, or risk disaster. Then the tribune Baebius inserted himself, insisting Jugurtha need not speak, essentially flouting the Roman assembly, much to the citizens' outrage. Jugurtha, a deadly foe, then found he had yet another potential rival for the Numidian throne in a certain Masinissa (no relation), currently in Rome. Jugurtha reportedly paid his lieutenant to murder the unfortunate pretender. He then returned home none the worse for wear, having been guaranteed safe conduct.[9]

And so what had looked like a short war lengthened, and the consul Albinus assumed command. When he left affairs to his brother and legate Aulus, Jugurtha countered, winning a smashing victory and compelling Aulus and his brother's army to evacuate Numidia and winter in the nearby Roman province of Africa.[10] At Rome, another tribune, Gaius Mamilius Limetanus, voiced the popular disgust over the whole affair with Jugurtha. At his proposal the assembly passed a bill that would investigate and prosecute a substantial list of Romans. Those Romans, the historian Sallust noted,

> at whose advice Jugurtha had disregarded decrees of the senate;
> … who had accepted money from him while serving as envoys or
> commanders; … who had handed back the elephants and deserters;
> … who had made terms of peace and war with the enemy.[11]

Sallust alleged, probably rightly, that more than a little of the support for this bill came from frustration with the senatorial class and its mismanagement of what had become a whole Numidian fiasco. So the Mamilian commission, a three person investigative body, dug deep and started to identify the corrupt senators Jugurtha had purchased.[12]

Metellus' Command against Jugurtha

Soon command of the war in Numidia fell to the consul of 109 BCE, Quintus Caecilius Metellus, a scion of the senatorial elite with consular ancestors stretching back almost two centuries. Metellus got down to business, seemingly determined to reverse the tide of Roman humiliation. His reputation as of yet was excellent, and when he levied substantial new troops with the senate's authorization, anticipation of a Roman victory mounted. There was much to be done. The demoralized mass of soldiers that had once been the Roman army in Numidia huddled in their unfortified camps in Africa. Metellus judged that training was necessary and began the exercises to slowly rehabilitate the soldiers. He marched them on long treks and reacquainted them to the rigorous Roman campaign protocols where a fortified camp was constructed every evening and struck every morning. He reportedly was to be found everywhere in the army, leading through example and building an effective fighting force. Jugurtha reportedly had no desire to tangle with this new commander and resurrected army. He sued for peace and offered a payoff. Unsuccessfully; Metellus stayed above the bribes and plied his own subterfuge, offering hefty bribes to the peace emissaries if they handed over the rogue king.[13]

Then came the time for Metellus to test his reforged army. They trekked to the leading market city of Vaga, and Metellus garrisoned it to serve as a supply base. Jugurtha, meanwhile, reportedly continued his efforts to bribe Metellus. They came to nothing. Battle it would be. It was a bloody affair. The Numidian forces, more nimble, feinted and harried. They disrupted the Roman formations and drew them out into so many separate masses unable to support one another effectively. Still the Romans fought back and Metellus did his level best to rally his troops and maintain order. The fighting was fierce and the possibility of disintegration and destruction high, but the Romans managed to fend off the Numidian attacks that day. Once the battlefield was secured, they constructed their usual fortified camp. The Romans had suffered considerably from the Numidian onslaught, however, and Metellus remained in camp for several days so that the wounded might be properly tended.[14]

Ultimately the battle decided nothing; it just made both leaders pause and take stock. Jugurtha remained in the fight and still had enough soldiers to follow his orders. Metellus, on the other hand, judged his army could not survive more costly clashes like that one, victorious or not. He adopted a new strategy, and his army began to roam the Numidian countryside, raiding and despoiling crops, destroying towns, and capturing forts to deny safe haven and supplies to Jugurtha and, perhaps, turn his subjects against him. Jugurtha, no poor strategist himself, countered by shadowing the Roman army with cavalry, waiting for opportunities, then pouncing on Roman stragglers, most likely the ever-present foragers that kept a large force supplied in hostile lands. Still, it appeared that Metellus had the upper hand. Reports reached Rome how he had disciplined the army and was now despoiling that rascal Jugurtha's kingdom. Indeed, the senate formally and officially recognized the achievements of Metellus and his soldiers by offering a public day of thanksgiving to the gods, sacrifices to thank the gods for their assistance on this campaign. Doubtless Metellus was pleased with the news honouring him, but he remained cautious.[15]

The Early Career of Gaius Marius

In describing Metellus' campaign, Sallust first mentions, briefly, that Gaius Marius served as Metellus' trusted legate.[16] In the initial battlefield clash against Jugurtha's forces, Metellus placed Marius in charge of the cavalry, an honourable posting. When he began his scorched-earth campaign, he placed Marius in command of half the army.[17] Metellus clearly trusted his subordinate. Plutarch extols Marius' virtues as a soldier: he undertook all tasks with energy and competence, endured all the toils alongside his soldiers, and showed sound military judgement.[18] It's worth noting, however, that Plutarch does not mention any specific thing that Marius did, so he may have just embellished Sallust's statements.

But Plutarch does help to fill in the details of his early career. Above all, Marius was a *novus homo*, a new man, one whose ancestors had never been in the Roman senate. Plutarch tries to insist that Marius was just a poor farmer from the town of Arpinum, whose inhabitants had enjoyed full Roman citizenship for decades before his birth.[19] Marius, however, was poor only when compared to the wealthiest in Roman society, for he was one of the *equites*, those who possessed the wealth necessary to serve as cavalry. He may even have been related to tax farmers.[20] What he decidedly was not, was what the Romans termed *nobilis*, a noble, one like Metellus whose ancestors had held the consulship and been one of the political elite. He made his way to political power through military service and a chance acquaintance. When Scipio Aemilianus commanded that brutal Roman siege of Spanish Numantia, Marius was there; in fact, he must have served alongside Tiberius Gracchus.[21] He stood out for his *virtus*, reportedly once killing an enemy in front of Scipio. Scipio favoured the young man, taking him into his close circle of officers and friends and, Plutarch reports, remarking at one dinner to these military companions that Marius had the spark of greatness.[22]

Encouraged to try his hand at public office, ironically enjoying the support of one of the many noble Metelli at Rome (not the Metellus who would command in Numidia) Marius won election as a tribune of the plebs for 119 BCE, a reasonable step for a one of his limited station and connections. His tribunate was noteworthy for the law he passed that would make it more difficult for voters to be intimidated as they cast their votes. Apparently when one cast a vote prior to this law, they had to journey across a walkway to submit the actual written vote. That walkway was broad enough to allow others to stand near the voter and, if they chose, intimidate him to vote this way or that. Marius' proposal narrowed the walkway so that bystanders could not congregate and intimidate the voters. It was exactly the sort of measure a tribune of the plebs might champion, and it passed. Not without a scuffle however. The consul Aurelius Cotta not only opposed the measure but passed a resolution blocking it and requiring Marius to defend himself to the senate. Marius stood firm, threatened to haul Cotta or any other opponent of the justly passed law off to jail, and forced Cotta to retract his resolution.[23]

Marius' career was hardly meteoric. He lost election to the aedileship on his first try and only just won election to the praetorship for 115.[24] Accusations of bribery in the election clung to him, and he barely escaped prosecution by a hung jury. With a praetorship to his name however, Marius had achieved significant political success for a new man. His stint in office left little impact, but he took advantage of his subsequent pro-praetorship and his assignment to govern Further Spain by systematically subduing bandits and outlaws in the rugged province. On returning to Rome he found his reputation and prospects sufficient to make a highly advantageous marriage. Julia, daughter of the somewhat eclipsed but still patrician Julii and aunt of the future dictator Gaius Julius Caesar, married Marius, further cementing his political foundation.[25]

That might have been the end of it. A distinguished career from a Roman with no family claims to political distinction and power. Except that Metellus had invited Marius to accompany him to Numidia as a legate, and, as we have seen, he had proven competent in that role.[26]

More Campaigning in 109

As the campaigning season stretched on, Jugurtha continued to play to his strengths. Defeating the Romans outright in a pitched battle was unlikely, so his skilled riders continued to harry the Roman army on the move, spoiling forage and tampering with a region's water supplies ahead of the Romans' arrival. The situation had shifted, and now Metellus sought a decisive battle. Changing strategies and hoping to force Jugurtha to commit to battle, he opted to besiege the fortified town of Zama. Marius again appears in the sources, this time in command of some foraging cohorts of soldiers.[27] When the Roman forces attempted to storm the city, the Numidians attacked their base camp, scattering all but a handful of soldiers who occupied high ground, and managed to fight off the deadly riders. Metellus and Marius reacted, following the cavalry sent back to camp with cohorts of allied infantry. Marius' detachment was brutally effective, killing a number of Numidians and securing the base camp.[28]

Time passed, but Zama held on and the summer of 109 concluded. Metellus had to prepare for winter quarters. He garrisoned those towns the army had seized, those with suitable defences. Then he marched the bulk of the army back to the Roman province of Africa for the winter. Metellus kept busy diplomatically that winter, however, reaching out to friends of Jugurtha that might yet be persuaded to turn on him.[29] Satisfied with his progress, the senate appointed Metellus proconsul and extended his Numidian command through 108. Sallust does not say how the Roman army occupied itself that year, but clearly nothing disastrous or triumphant occurred – at first. The next we hear, Marius, always ambitious, received a chance omen. A propitious looking mass of sacrificial entrails moved the attending priest to declare that he, Marius, would be successful in all bold undertakings. While this may not have been the triggering incident, there is no reason to be sceptical of Roman piety; Marius would have felt bolstered by this and perhaps other omens that did not make it into the historians' accounts. Marius decided to campaign for the consulship. He had served ably in the army for years and had, for a new man, done well in politics winning election as tribune of the plebs and, more recently praetor.[30]

Rivalry between Metellus and Marius

Sallust and Plutarch seem to differ on the origins and bitterness of Metellus and Marius' rivalry. Plutarch suggests Marius was a show-off, working to eclipse Metellus from the start, successfully endearing himself to the common soldiers, with the result that soldiers wrote home insisting that Marius should be consul, that he could win this war. But

Plutarch mentions this in a chapter with few specifics, and it seems that he got caught up in an anti-Marian source. Sallust provides a more comprehensible narrative: Marius served with distinction and there was no hint of trouble between him and Metellus until the matter of the consulship of 107 arose. Clearly whatever rivalry had simmered between Metellus and Marius now burst into a conflagration of enmity. Marius had served ably, of that there was no question. At some time during the year, Sallust reports, Marius approached Metellus and asked for official leave to return to Rome and be a candidate for the consulship of 107. Metellus was surprised. He was a skilful commander and knew Marius' martial mettle. But he was also a noble, a proud one at that. Marius had no lineage to speak of, no pedigree to commend him to the voters and win him the most coveted office in the Republic. He told Marius to back down. Worse, he mocked Marius' ambitions: why hurry? There would be time enough for Marius to run for consulship, Metellus gibed, when Metellus' own son was of age – in 20 years![31]

The insult stung. Proud Marius would hate Metellus to the end of his days, a hatred that bordered on the pathological. For the moment, he committed to making Metellus eat his own words. Now, following Sallust's order of events, Marius persuaded the Italian traders in Numidia and the *equites* in the army to write home, denouncing Metellus' leadership and encouraging all to elect Marius consul and place him in command at Numidia.[32] His timing was excellent. Frustration with the leadership of the senatorial nobility was at a peak, with the Mamilian commission at work in the City identifying corruption. The prospect of a new man serving as counter to the entrenched nobles was appealing.[33]

And then, disaster struck – or was it a miracle for Marius' ambitions? Jugurtha persuaded some inhabitants of Vaga to murder the officers of the Roman garrison and slaughter the soldiers throughout the town. Somehow the garrison commander, Titus Turpilius Silanus, alone survived the butchery. Metellus returned with the army and retook Vaga, but the slaughter of the Roman garrison cast suspicion and criticism on Turpilius. If he was not a traitor outright, fit only for scourging and beheading, was he not at least a coward who should have taken his own life after the debacle at Vaga?[34] Metellus summoned him to a court-martial.

Here our sources disagree on Marius' role. According to Sallust, Turpilius simply had no defence in his court-martial and Metellus sentenced him to death.[35] Plutarch, who used Sallust as a source, differs. Turpilius and Metellus were second generation friends, following their fathers' close bond. Marius took advantage of this bond to strike at Metellus. He served on the commission investigating Turpilius and went to great lengths to condemn him, unjustly says Plutarch. And when Turpilius ultimately was executed, Marius crowed about his victory to Metellus. Now in his narrative, Plutarch reports the insult Metellus gave Marius about waiting another two decades for the consulship.[36]

Plutarch's other source clearly had an axe to grind against Marius. According to this source, Marius strutted about proudly and insubordinately for his role in executing Metellus' friend. This event, added to Marius' general efforts to upstage Metellus, made the two open enemies. Only then did Metellus issue that stinging slight to Marius. The exact triggers of their rivalry are lost to the centuries and to hearsay. What is clear, however, is that Marius sought the consulship, and Metellus thought him unworthy. This would fuel the fire. Marius was determined to run for consul and Sallust asserts he nagged at Metellus until the commander approved his leave. Plutarch adds a bit of sabotage: Metellus only let Marius leave Numidia with a mere twelve days left before the elections.[37] Still, Marius had been successful in his letter writing campaigns and efforts to contrast himself with pedigreed nobles like Metellus by arguing that his *virtus* more than made up for his lack of distinguished family lineage. He raced to Rome and, once there, pledged to voters that he would bring Jugurtha to Roman justice, dead or alive.[38] His efforts paid off, particularly, Sallust asserts, with craftspeople and farmers, all those who made a living by their hands.[39] They were inspired by the sight of a consular candidate who, like they, only claimed what he had earned on his own. Enough voters were persuaded, and Marius won consulship for 107.[40]

Marius Succeeds Metellus

Though a magnificent achievement for a new man, that consulship did not automatically position Marius to command the army in Numidia. Initially, the senate exercised its power to extend Metellus' command for a second year, now his third in the province. Not for the last time, a tribune of the plebs decided to make short work of senatorial preference.

Titus Manlius Mancinus, certainly with Marius' approval, put a vote to the people. A large majority voted to assign the Numidian command to Marius.[41]

Meanwhile, Metellus ground his way towards a decisive victory in the province. Jugurtha was little more than a lone renegade at this point. He had killed many whom he suspected of treachery and driven many others from his side with his mercurial loyalties. Now Metellus manoeuvred him into a final pitched battle. The Roman army scattered the Numidians with ease and Jugurtha bolted to the desert town of Thala.[42] Metellus would not be denied however, and took pains to secure the water supplies necessary to sustain his army in the desert, conscripting local pack animals and shedding all unnecessary baggage to carry more water and food. When the avenging army appeared on the horizon, Jugurtha knew that there was no option left but to flee. So he assumed the life of a fugitive, staying no longer than a night in any place, always looking over his shoulder.[43]

Not for too long. Jugurtha soon persuaded his royal peer, King Bocchus of Mauretania, to shelter him and fight the Romans. Defeating the Romans in pitched battle remained unlikely however, and Bocchus and Jugurtha, who apparently had some soldiers left to add to Bocchus' army, targeted Roman baggage and loot at the depot town of Cirta. Metellus changed course to meet this new threat. Ever cautious, seeking information about this new Mauretanian foe, Metellus' army pitched camp near Cirta and waited.[44]

Only now word reached Metellus: his upstart lieutenant, Marius, had stolen his command through the machinations of a tribune, not only his command but his looming victory over Jugurtha. Metellus made no secret of his displeasure, his antipathy towards Marius, or his sense of injury. To no avail. Rather than risk his army and his reputation in battle against a new foe, Metellus sent envoys to Bocchus urging the king to resume his alliance with Rome and abandon this reckless course. Bocchus insisted that Jugurtha must have peace. Ultimately the negotiations stalled, which was fine by Metellus as he did not want to do anything that would aid Marius.[45]

Meanwhile, back at Rome, Marius launched a flurry of preparations. Doubling down on his strategy of antagonizing the Roman nobility, he insisted he would finish the job that they could not. He received senatorial approval to levy new troops and reinforce the legions in Numida. Sallust implies they did not dare cross him. He had little trouble finding willing recruits. He spoke publicly, disdaining the pedigrees of the nobles; their ancestors had secured their consulships through *virtus*, but these scions of valorous Romans had little themselves to offer when it came to winning Rome's wars. He emphasized his *virtus*, his military skill, and the spoils he had won through his abilities:

> I cannot, to justify your confidence, display family portraits or the triumphs and consulships of my forefathers; but if occasion requires, I can show spears, a banner, trappings and other military prizes, as well as scars on my breast. These are my portraits, these my patent of nobility, not left me by inheritance as [the nobles'] were, but won by my own innumerable efforts and perils.[46]

That was not all. He emphasized the loot to be won from Jugurtha and extended his recruitment drive so that even those without property could enrol. Encouraged by Marius and inspired by hopes of riches, many poorer Romans joined the expedition, and Marius' reinforcements swelled well past the figures authorized by the senate. When his preparations were complete, Marius sailed to Africa and assumed command of Metellus' army. Metellus himself could not stomach the transfer, and it fell to a subordinate to relinquish command to Marius.[47]

Marius had done it. A new man with a superb military reputation, he had risen up in the voters' estimation, and now he had a consulship and a ripe opportunity to gain glory by wrapping up the Numidian war. Metellus returned to Rome. As the target of so much of Marius' recent anti-noble polemic, he likely expected a rough reception, but the city embraced him, says Sallust.[48] There is even some evidence to suggest that he celebrated a triumph over Jugurtha.[49] It was the calm before the storm, however, for Metellus and Marius. Marius would simply not let his former commander be.

That was later. For now, Marius went to work. Winter over, the Roman army, augmented by Marius' new recruits, left Africa and invaded Numidia. Marius chose wealthy areas of the kingdom and set his soldiers to pillaging, stopping to take small towns and weak fortresses along the way. With each passing victory and with the plundered rewards, his new soldiers' morale increased, and veterans and recruits were welded into a single fighting army.[50] Jugurtha and Bocchus split their forces, Marius skilfully dogged Jugurtha, surprising his troops as they plundered Roman allies and inflicting casualties. Jugurtha and his forces fled and regrouped, as they had so often done. As Marius must have known, he could not bring Jugurtha down with these small-scale assaults. He needed to destroy Jugurtha's safe havens. And so Marius and the army methodically bribed or stormed town after town, fort after fort, whittling down Jugurtha's options for safety. Most notable on the list was Capsa, a large well-fortified town surrounded by desert.[51] Like Metellus before him, Marius overcame the logistical challenges of a desert campaign and reached the city. The inhabitants surrendered. Though nothing was certain in war, they could expect some leniency because they willingly yielded. But Marius was not interested in the niceties of war. He slaughtered every Numidian adult and burned the city, removing it permanently from Jugurtha's plans.[52]

Marius and his army continued on the offensive. The Romans suffered a few casualties but reaped a great deal of plunder. They cut a bloody, fiery swathe through Numidia, levelling towns and slaughtering inhabitants. If Marius could not capture Jugurtha, he could bring his kingdom down around him.[53] The pinnacle of his campaign: besieging the mighty, unnamed fortress perched atop a formidable rocky crest and harbouring Jugurtha's treasures. It was so well positioned that the Romans could not bring sufficient siege equipment up to the walls. Fortunately for them, a foraging Ligurian soldier in the Roman army with a taste for snails and a penchant for rock-climbing stumbled upon a treacherous but manageable route up to the citadel. Marius instructed him to make the climb again, accompanied by a small, hand-picked group of trumpeters. He renewed the main assault with little effect. Then the musical commandos sounded their horns from the opposite side of the fortress, panicking the Numidian defenders and allowing the Romans to overwhelm the city's defences.[54]

Sulla under Marius' Command

Now, when Marius was well on his way to fulfilling his pledge to the Roman voters and defeating Jugurtha, his new quaestor for 107, Lucius Cornelius Sulla, arrived with a newly-levied contingent of Latin and allied cavalry.[55] It may not have been their first meeting; it decidedly, much to the dismay of many Romans, would not be their last. Unlike the new man, Marius, Sulla descended from the patrician Cornelii. His branch had fallen on hard times: Sulla's father left him no inheritance, and he was forced to live below his station, renting lodgings in a poorer part of Rome. No elitist in his choice of friends, Sulla had a reputation for mixing it up with the outcasts of high Roman society – theatre folk. He began to earn the cognomen felix, 'lucky', when his love, a common but wealthy woman named Nicopolis, died and left her considerable property to him. That and a subsequent inheritance from his beloved stepmother righted Sulla's financial ship, enabling him to pursue political office at Rome.[56]

Now a quaestor, Sulla was at the very beginning of the Roman *cursus honorum*, the ladder of offices those eager to reach the heights of aristocratic power sought to hold. What evidence we have suggests he did not initially clash with Marius but simply sought to excel in his posting. Sulla was not one to avoid the work his subordinates carried out: he marched alongside them, shared guard duties with them, and showed his respect for the common soldier. Marius and the army loved him, and why not? Marius more than anyone could appreciate a devoted soldier, and the fact that Sulla avoided playing the insufferable aristocrat and instead threw himself into his military duties could only have helped him.[57]

Jugurtha, meanwhile, somehow persuaded the wavering King Bocchus to join forces again, this time reportedly by pledging to him a third of the kingdom of Numidia. This time they opted to surprise the Romans as Marius moved them into their winter quarters. The attack came late one evening and surprised the Roman soldiers, who were still in marching order, not ready for battle. Caught out of formation, the Romans did their best to fend off the attacking cavalry and infantry. Desperately the scattered troops formed a defensive circle to beat back the enemy. Marius kept his head on the chaotic battlefield and rode with his elite cavalry bodyguard to wherever he was needed most. The cacophony ensured that he could only communicate through hand gestures. Still, he rallied knots of soldiers who were flagging and panicked, charged those throngs where the enemy had massed, and managed to keep his soldiers in the battle.

As darkness approached Marius assessed the situation and gave the necessary orders. A nearby pair of hills would serve as the rallying point, one precipitous and easy to defend, the other with a life-giving spring. On his order Sulla and a cavalry force occupied the spring for the night, then Marius instructed his wide-ranging infantry to retreat to the hill more suitable for defence. They fought and marched and worked their way to the high ground. It proved an excellent position, and the Numidian and Mauretanian attacks were stopped cold. The Romans even managed to erect something resembling their daily camp fortifications. Danger abated, but only for a moment: the enemy army camped around the Roman position, encircling it with their greater numbers.[58] Marius crafted a plan. When the early morning light crept up, he gave the orders. Roman trumpets brayed, and the soldiers shouted, erupting from their camp and streaming into the enemy – apparently caught unawares. The reversal was devastating, enemy casualties substantial. The Romans drove off their foes, regrouped, then continued their march to winter quarters, with Sulla commanding the cavalry on the Roman right, an honourable position for a valued officer.[59]

As the Romans approached the important town of Cirta, a new attack brewed. Scouts reported clusters of enemy troops, but it was not entirely clear where they were massing in force. As it happened, Jugurtha had divided the Numidian forces into four contingents, hoping that the extra lines of attack would enable at least one to assault the Roman rear. Another battle erupted. Sulla distinguished himself commanding the cavalry. Meanwhile the Mauretanian infantry, commanded by Bocchus' son Volux, successfully attacked the Roman rear. Sowing lies that Volux had personally slain Marius, they did some harm to nearby soldiers' morale.[60] Sulla played the cavalry commander's part to perfection however, scattering his horsed foes then returning to drive off the infantry threat before the Roman formations broke. Marius' army had triumphed yet again.[61]

Bocchus, reading all-too-clear signs, petitioned Marius when the Romans arrived at Cirta. At his request, Marius sent two trusted officers, Sulla and Manlius, to parley with the king. Their initial talks proved favourable. As winter arrived, Bocchus sent five of his trusted officers to continue conversations with Marius.[62] They asked for peace with Marius and Rome. Marius sent three on their way to speak to the senate at Rome. The senate affirmed that Bocchus would be forgiven, but the Romans would not formally forge a treaty with him until he had truly earned it. Bocchus had grown to trust Sulla, and he continued to be the primary agent in the field negotiating with the Mauretanian king. Jugurtha did his best to derail the talks. Bocchus played a duplicitous game. Ostensibly he acted uncertain; secretly he and Sulla met with only interpreters and a single mediator, a sign of trust. Bocchus hoped that his turnabout would be sufficient to gain peace and an alliance with the Romans. Sulla, following the Roman line, disabused him of that notion. The Romans had already trounced Bocchus on several occasions. Why should they make peace with a beaten foe? No, Bocchus must do something to show his worth to Rome. Sulla proposed a deal: if Bocchus were to capture Jugurtha and deliver him to the Romans, they could then seriously talk of lasting peace and an alliance. Bocchus balked initially, but he had no room to squirm and soon took the deal. And that is how the lengthy trial by combat against Jugurtha and his Numidian forces ended: not by force, but by treachery and negotiation. Bocchus was as good as his word. Jugurtha was tricked, shackled, and delivered to Sulla, who took him to Marius.[63]

Sulla's covert negotiations would become a sore for Marius. Though Marius, as commander, celebrated the triumph for his victory in Numidia, Sulla claimed the credit for negotiating with Bocchus and for personally apprehending Jugurtha. Plutarch reports the detail that Sulla had a picture of Bocchus surrendering Jugurtha to him engraved on a signet ring that he used to seal correspondence.[64] A good way to tweak Marius' considerable ego.

The Cimbri and Teutones Threaten Rome

Marius and Sulla's rivalry would one day threaten to bring down the Republic. But for now a more immediate threat faced the Romans as the Numidian war concluded. The Cimbri, a migrating Germanic tribe, violently clashed with a series of Roman armies in the final decade-and-a-half of the second century. In the process, tens of thousands of Roman soldiers died, and fear gripped the city that the marauders would sack Rome itself. Where exactly the Cimbri came from and their movements through Gaul and the Iberian peninsula are difficult, at best, to track. In 114 they first appear in Roman sources plundering the lands of Illyricum on the Adriatic Sea. Since Rome had interests in the area, the senate tasked the consul of 113, Gnaeus Papirius Carbo, to locate and check the ravagers. In the second half of that year, Carbo and his force met the Cimbri. He played a duplicitous game, negotiating with the Cimbri envoys then treacherously attempting to ambush the tribal army. The Cimbri were not so easily defeated however, and a pitched battle ensued resulting in a terrible Roman defeat. Carbo later killed himself for orchestrating the Roman disaster. A few years later, in 108, the Cimbri defeated Metellus' consular colleague Marcus Junius Silanus, probably in Transalpine Gaul to the northwest of the Alps. Soon before or after this, the Cimbri sent envoys to the senate, requesting land to settle. The senate rejected their proposal, and the conflicts continued. Not immediately, and the quiet in the sources may suggest that the Cimbri settled down for a few years. In 105, however, a Cimbric army approached Arausio in Southern Gaul, the frontier of Roman control in the region. Two Roman armies were on scene, one commanded by the consul Gnaeus Mallius Maximus, the other commanded by the proconsul Quintus Servilius Caepio. Disagreement hobbled the commanders as Caepio resisted deferring to Mallius and the greater authority of his consular *imperium*. They failed to coordinate, and, as a result, the Cimbri slaughtered the armies, killing as many as 80,000 Roman soldiers. And so a powerful, unchecked army was close enough to Rome to terrify the citizenry. They responded by electing Marius consul for the second time, even though he was absent in Numidia and not a candidate, even though he had been consul a little over a year before and legally had to wait for ten years to pass between consulships.[65] Marius returned to Rome to celebrate a triumph and reap the prestige of a consul-elect. He entered office on the same day that he celebrated his triumph over Jugurtha.[66]

The Cimbri, as it turned out, did not invade Italy after their colossal victory at Arausio; instead the tribe migrated to the Iberian Peninsula for a brief period. Marius made good use of the time, training his soldiers, accustoming them to travelling lightly and carrying their own baggage to increase the army's manoeuvrability.[67] The Cimbri did not come that year and the electorate chose to make Marius consul again for 103 so that he could remain in command when the anticipated assault came. This was Marius' third consulship and his second consecutive consulship, both outside the laws regulating the office.[68] Still the enemy proved to be nowhere near Rome, and another consulship passed for Marius in preparations. Rumour of an impending attack in the spring won

Marius election to a fourth consulship, for 102.[69] The Roman electorate had essentially dispensed with the laws regulating office-holding, so persuaded were they that Marius was the general to properly defend them against the invaders.

Marius shared the consulship of 102 with Quintus Lutatius Catulus. Here, Sulla appears again in the evidence, as a legate in Catulus' army.[70] The Cimbri were on the move again and appeared ready to force their way into Italy and plunder the Roman heartland. Marius, accordingly, took a position on the Rhône river and had his soldiers build a fortified camp to defend the east bank from the invaders. Catulus, meanwhile, was tasked with defending northern Italy and the Alpine passes. The invading army of Cimbri, Teutones and Ambrones split into three large forces, the Cimbri to challenge Catulus in northern Italy, the others to clash with Marius.[71]

The army of Teutones and Ambrones was reportedly more than twice the size of Marius' forces.[72] When they approached Marius' army, he played a waiting game, keeping his soldiers within the fortifications of the camp. He made sure his soldiers, however, who knew nothing but terrifying rumours about the Germans, took turns along the fortifications watching the enemy, so that the exotic became ordinary. For their part, the Germans attempted to assault the camp once and had nothing to show for it but casualties. Since they could not compel the Romans to commit to battle, they marched past and continued along the coast towards the Alps and northern Italy. Once past, Marius ordered his army to strike their camp and followed the Teutones and Ambrones until they were at Aquae Sextiae.[73]

The Romans began to make camp. An unplanned skirmish along the river separating the Roman camp attendants from the Ambrones grew into a battle as more and more Romans entered the fray. The Ambrones got the worst of it, many dying in battle before night fell. The night passed, then a day and a second night before the Germans were ready to do battle. The Romans and their camp stood on hilly ground. The Teutonic army was positioned in a plain surrounded by forested ravines and valleys. Accordingly, Marius dispatched his subordinate, Claudius Marcellus, with a force of 3,000 soldiers to move to the enemy's rear undetected and ambush. The Teutones were eager for battle and attempted to climb the Roman hill and sweep the army away, but Marius ordered his soldiers to hold their ground and drive back their foe. Breaking the Teutonic momentum with *pila* volleys, the Roman infantry followed, employing sword- and shield-work from the advantageous high ground to force the Teutones back into the plain. When the enemy had been shoved back to the plain and reformed its line, Marcellus made his move. His detachment fell upon the enemy in the rear. Now attacked from front and rear, chaos radiated through the Teutones' ranks. They broke and fled with the Romans in pursuit. It was a smashing victory over a mighty foe.[74] To top things off, Marius soon received word he had been elected consul yet again, for 101, his fifth consulship and his fourth consecutive one, both of which placed him in an honourable position no Roman had ever occupied before.

Catulus and his forces, Sulla among them, did not fare nearly as well. Catulus decided not split his army to guard the Alpine passes. Instead he determined to face the Cimbri in the plains of North Italy. He fortified his position along the Atisio River, but his army fell back in panic at the approach of the Cimbri, who destroyed the Roman defences and raided the countryside unchecked.

Meanwhile, Marius and his army returned to Rome, fresh from the smashing victory at Aquae Sextiae. Soon they headed north to join Catulus and blunt the second enemy invasion. The two Roman armies, about 50,000 men, joined together to face a significantly larger Cimbric army. How much larger we cannot say; Plutarch estimates 180,000 warriors, but exaggerating the size of enemy invasions to add to the lustre of the defenders was a time honoured practice for ancient writers. Whatever the real numbers, the Romans won decisively that day. The sources for the battle, of course, varied in their takes. Sulla and Catulus himself left memoirs, though we no longer have them. They asserted that Catulus' forces, stationed in the centre of the battleline, handled the brunt of the fighting and were ultimately responsible for the victory, more than Marius and his troops.[75] Regardless of where the credit lay, Rome was now safe: tens of thousands of Cimbri had been slain, and tens of thousands captured for good measure.[76]

Marius in 101 BCE had reached the apex of his popularity, his dignity. Five times consul; triumphator over Numidians, Teutones, and Cimbri; defender of the Roman people. Yet Plutarch asserts he was at a loss when the wartime emergency had subsided. The daily life of Roman politics, the sharing of authority with other aristocrats, none of this was reportedly to Marius' liking after years as the highest elected magistrate empowered with *imperium*.

*   *   *

Progress in the war against Jugurtha was driven by competition between aristocrats, each seeking the *gloria* of conquering a foreign foe. Metellus, by all accounts, successfully commanded in North Africa the year of his consulship. Yet Marius managed to undermine his commander's achievements and cast himself, probably not unlike Cato decades before, as a virtuous Roman new man, one who lacked family but possessed all the necessary noble qualities to lead the Republic and its armies. In a rare case of Roman karma, the tables were soon reversed, and the patrician Sulla engineered a victory in Numidia that seriously undermined Marius' achievement. And Sulla milked that steal for all it was worth. Marius and Sulla would decidedly not be allies. Instead, their festering rivalry would erupt a bit more than a decade later into the first Civil War.

One might have thought that the competition in what was ultimately a small war in Africa would be curtailed during the threat to Rome posed by the Cimbri, Ambrones, and Teutones. And perhaps to some extent it was. The Roman voters rallied behind Marius with a conviction unmatched since the last threat to Rome of the war against Hannibal. For a moment, Marius had won all that he could hope for. He was the most powerful man in Rome, elected time after time to the consulship in disregard of custom and law, all because he had persuaded the voters that he alone could best meet the crisis. But the war had barely finished before the arguments began about who had served the best, who had contributed most to the defeat of the invaders. Competition as usual.

Marius soon found himself, when serving consul a sixth time after the invasion threat had ended, that he was in a most awkward position, clumsily navigating politics in the city and being forced to crush a wayward tribune who secretly was his ally. That story begins now.

Chapter 6

The Republic Devours Its Own:
Three Dead Tribunes and Two Civil Wars

His murder opened the floodgates, at least relatively speaking. Historians ancient and modern mark Tiberius Gracchus' brutal death at the hands of a senatorial mob as the start of steadily growing political violence at Rome. As we have seen, just over a decade later, Gaius was murdered for political conflicts stemming from his terms as tribune. More tribunes would die. In the three decades following Gaius' murder, three tribunes sparked political firestorms that resulted in their murder while in office. The murder of the first, Saturninus, came after citizens battled each other in the city streets. The murder of the second provoked the in-all-but-name civil war between Rome and its Italian allies. The last of this trio, Sulpicius, directly provoked consul Sulla to occupy the city with a citizen army, the start of Rome's first civil war (88–82 BCE). Sulpicius died in the aftermath.

That first civil war was, in many ways, the product of the rivalry between Marius and Sulla. With the outbreak of war came much murdering. Sulla thought he had crushed opposition when he occupied the city like a conqueror. He was mistaken. As Sulla subsequently led his army to the eastern Mediterranean, supporters of Marius occupied the city and purged it of Sullan supporters. Eventually, the tables turned again. Returning from the east, Sulla seized control of Rome for the second time (82 BCE). He had himself named dictator for restoring the laws and, as dictator, crafted a political system that he hoped would restore the proper functioning of the Republic under the legitimate authority of the senate. Viewing them together, the almost four decades from Gaius Gracchus' murder to Sulla's dictatorship (c. 121–82 BCE) saw increasingly intense political clashes ending in violence by Roman citizens against Roman citizens.

Compared with the well-documented activities of the Gracchi, evidence is relatively poor for these three doomed tribunes. We are at a disadvantage in large part because none of the trio made Plutarch's list of biographical subjects, and all belong to a period not covered by the surviving detailed narrative of first-century historian Livy. Working through the fragmentary accounts available, however, demonstrates these controversial figures were clearly at the epicentre of political rivalries in the years between the Gracchi and the Social War. It is difficult to fully illuminate the seismic clashes that ended in the murder of tribunes to one specific rivalry. Still, it remains clear enough that, at the heart of their murders, lay conflicts that went beyond the limits of ordinary political behaviour.

We are better informed, slightly, about the legislative topics that aristocrats at the start of the first century BCE clustered around as they attempted to build their political careers, increase their dignity and their ability to assist friends and thwart rivals. Three issues in particular were the prime political hotspots at the end of the second century and very beginning of the first BCE. First, the increasing demand many Italian allies of Rome had for full Roman citizenship. More and more, Italians felt due some reward commensurate with the blood and toil they had expended on the Romans. Citizenship fitted the bill for many.[1] A second charged issue: the juries for the permanent courts. Gaius Gracchus had passed a law requiring that the list of jurors for these courts consist of *equites* – wealthy non-senatorial members of the cavalry class – rather than senators. This continued to be a source of political struggle down to Sulla's time.[2] And finally: now that the hiatus on planting colonies had ended, which small farmers should get land, especially veterans from the continuing Roman campaigns; whose land they should be given; and which lawmaker should get the credit.

With this brief political overview in mind, it is time to investigate the short, violent career of the first in this trio of murdered tribunes: Lucius Appuleius Saturninus.

Murder and Mayhem: The Career and Death of Saturninus

It was a damnably hot day for autumn. And now the mob was coming for them. Saturninus, tribune of the plebs, would be murdered by the mob, along with his partner-in-provocation, Gaius Servilius Glaucia. Worse still, Gaius Marius, consul and, up till now, Saturninus' ally, had shown his true colours and led that mob, or, more precisely, that urban army. And so, the two ... murderers ... had fled from the Forum and occupied the Capitoline Hill, a makeshift fortress against the avenging nemeses of crowds and senate. What Saturninus hoped for was not at all clear. Absolution for his political murders? A return to the fold of senatorial politicians? He may well have had no plan, just knew that resistance was better than cowardly surrender. And perhaps that conniver Gaius Marius, now consul for the sixth time and behind-the-scenes backer of Saturninus' deadly mischief, would come through and save his and Glaucia's skins.

Marius had problems of his own. His star had risen steadily from the time he replaced Metellus in the war against Jugurtha to his recent victories over the invading Cimbri and Teutones. He had settled back into domestic politics halfway through his fifth consulship. He hankered after a sixth consulship. He also hoped to get land – small farms – for the soldiers who had loyally followed him and fought against the Republic's enemies. For these, or other reasons, he had formed an alliance of sorts with Saturninus and Glaucia. He had, if not actively supported, at least silently endorsed their cold-blooded murders of rival candidates for offices. In the rough-and-tumble of electoral politics, Marius had calculated that he would come away clean of the tribune's worst crimes. Now he was in the awkward position of consul, charged by the senate through its ultimate decree to handle the firebrand Saturninus, his associate. He could hardly disobey now; Saturninus had gone too far. More blood would be spilt.

Saturninus' Early Career

Lucius Appuleius Saturninus is a difficult figure to illuminate, but clearly had quite a short, disruptive, and violent career. The sources that remain are fragmentary and almost universally hostile. Appian gives the fullest account. For him the tale of Saturninus begins with Metellus – Quintus Caecilius Metellus Numidicus – the consul whose Numidian command had been reassigned to Marius in 107 BCE. Saturninus was first tribune in 103. In 102, Metellus was censor, and as censor exercised his lawful power to strip Saturninus and Glaucia of their senatorial rank, a mighty indignity.[3] Metellus' colleague in the censorship checked him. Still, the effort stung proud Saturninus. So he sought election to a second tribuneship, for the year 100, perhaps to defend himself from further political attacks, perhaps to seek vengeance against Metellus. For his candidacy, he may have had the help of his ally Glaucia, who served as tribune in 101 and may have presided over the elections.[4]

He and Glaucia also maintained a working relationship with Gaius Marius as the commander wrapped up his string of military victories. Marius seemed a natural ally. The old general had, on the strength of his military services alone, won a fifth consulship (fourth consecutive) for 101 BCE. He would attain a sixth consulship for 100. Land was what he needed most, land to give to his veterans for their service, or he would look weak and ineffectual. Probably the career commander felt genuine loyalty to 'Marius' mules' as some called them, the poor men turned stalwart soldiers under his leadership. Those common soldiers had helped check the Cimbri and Teutones when those tribes had sought to destroy the Romans. Marius also hated Metellus Numidicus. Really hated him. One might reasonably have thought that by this point Marius had given as good as he had got to Metellus. He did manage, after all, to appropriate his successful military command in Numidia. But Marius, like most of his aristocratic peers, was touchy about his honour. And Metellus had just a few years ago, when Marius aspired to the consulship, verbally spat upon his ambitions. Marius' rancour for Metellus may have drawn him to Servilius and Glaucia. In addition to rancour harboured for Metellus, Marius, despite his formidable string of consulships, seems to have had difficulty when it came to the compromises and subtlety of domestic politics. Energetic tribunes could help push laws that would benefit his veterans and strike at his enemies. So, whether Saturninus sought Marius' aid or vice-versa – the sources seem to disagree – the three allied.[5]

Saturninus did not win the election for 100 (held late in 101). Instead, says Appian, a plebeian named Nonius (Nunnius in other sources) was elected tribune. Why Nonius was the target is unclear, for there were nine other tribunes elected that day instead of Saturninus. Perhaps he was the target of opportunity – it all seems to have happened so quickly. It is also not clear whether Marius actively joined this plot.[6] Ultimately, however, tribune-elect for 100, Nonius, became Saturninus and Glaucia's prey. They followed him from the election grounds as he returned to the inn where he had stayed from the election assembly accompanied by armed thugs. As he walked to his lodgings, in the flush of victory, Nonius was murdered. The very next day, alleges Appian, tribune Glaucia and his followers gathered early to form a trumped up assembly before a more representative one could meet. This usurping assembly elected Saturninus tribune for 100 in December 101.[7]

Taking Down Metellus Numidicus

Saturninus would be a tribune in 100. He was effectively untouchable – though that chestnut of constitutional convention, that a tribune in office was inviolable, had rotted a bit since Tiberius Gracchus. He sought, so far as can be determined, to build a power base, to be a politician who had to be reckoned with by his rivals, through tribunal legislation. And he had a grudge against Metellus Numidicus. His position appeared strong. A generation later Cicero recalled that Saturninus was, of all the rabble-rousing speakers since Gaius Gracchus, the most capable orator. Cicero checks his limited praise swiftly however, noting that Saturninus moved the crowd more through his clothing, appearance, and gestures than through particularly skilful speech. This brings to mind Plutarch's observation that Gaius Gracchus was the first to incorporate violent gestures into his oratory. It seems that the popular orators of the late second century, at least according to their critics, had a more engaging, if not entertaining, method of talking to the people than previous orators.[8] Saturninus had that skill.

Topping the list of his legislation in 100, Saturninus proposed that the land the Romans had seized from the invading Cimbri in Gaul – the northern Italian Gaul, not the Transalpine Gaul – be divided and distributed to citizens desirous of a small-farming lifestyle. Marius' veterans, not least, would benefit. The proposed law would meet with resistance in the senate. Indeed it seems there were always senators to be found who objected to this or that law granting land to Romans and Italians. The example of Drusus, Gaius Gracchus' rival a couple of decades ago (see Chapter 4), illustrates that. Most land laws generated opposition because of two factors. The most substantial: the land usually belonged to someone else. The other: rivalries – a desire to prevent one's senatorial opponents from benefiting politically from a successful land grant. Saturninus anticipated resistance and added a provocative clause: if the law passed, each senator would be required to swear an oath to obey the law or be ejected from the senate and fined substantially.[9] A snub to the dignity of the senate anyway, this addition would likely trap the proud Metellus Numidicus: if he refused to swear the oath, Marius and Saturninus' rival would be exiled from Rome.

Apparently this particular agrarian law distributed more land to Italian allies than to Roman citizens, and, accordingly, upset voting citizens who lived in the city. They sought to reject the law in the assembly. Saturninus amassed a gang of peasants from the countryside – prime beneficiaries of the law – and attacked the assembly. A fight broke out. Saturninus and his mob cleared the assembly, formed their own replacement assembly, and passed the provocative land law.[10]

Saturninus had passed the law, violently all knew. Yet the law had the slight but critical veneer of legality because he was a tribune and he had convened an assembly, an action technically well within his authority. Now Marius, on his authority as consul, put the question to the senators. Would they swear the oath to preserve and obey this law? Metellus refused outright, and, with that, the first senate meeting dissolved in agitation.[11] What happened next is not entirely clear, insofar as Saturninus, Marius or both may have initiated it. But Plutarch and Appian agree that the senators were summoned publicly to swear obedience to the law. Marius was among them. Put on the spot – or perhaps prepared – Marius announced he would swear to obey the law, *if it were a law*. This chicanery apparently satisfied sufficient senators that Marius backed the law. And so other senators followed suit and swore the oath until it was Metellus' turn. He still would not yield, would not endorse this problematic law. His friends begged Metellus, fearing the punishments he might face. To no avail; he simply left the Forum.[12] There may have been a final showdown when Saturninus' lieutenant, presumably acting in the official role of the tribune's officer, attempted to arrest him in the senate house. Regardless, Saturninus nailed the coffin shut by passing a decree that Metellus be banished and offered no shelter by any Roman anywhere. Rather than challenge the decree, Metellus opted to retire peacefully and journeyed east to Rhodes to study Greek philosophy in its homeland.[13]

His rival exiled, and his power only increasing, Saturninus continued to benefit Marius. The tribune passed laws founding veterans' colonies in Sicily and the Balkans, perhaps even in Africa. The law also granted Marius the special honour of granting Roman citizenship to Italians of his choosing, three per colony.[14] This too would allow Marius to reward those who had served him loyally.

Other than these evidence scraps, the ancient narratives are compressed at this point; Saturninus' activities for most of 100 are shrouded. But he apparently desired a third tribunate. One for 99 BCE. He also supported his confederate Glaucia's bid for a consulship in that year. After all, consuls and tribunes made powerful partners, as this past year's events had shown.

The Death of Saturninus

A fight over the electoral results at the end of 100 led to the deaths of Saturninus and Glaucia. Appian provides a seemingly plain enough narrative. Saturninus had been elected tribune a third time (for 99 BCE). He hoped to get Glaucia elected consul. But the consular elections returned Marcus Antonius as the first consul. Glaucia competed for the second position against the popular Memmius. Fearing Glaucia would lose, and Saturninus would be left without a consular ally, the two dispatched thugs to dispense with Memmius. In the midst of the election, on the voting grounds themselves, the toughs publicly clubbed Memmius to death. Panic ensued, and the consular elections dissolved.[15]

But did Glaucia really fear losing to Memmius? Cicero, a child when these events occurred and thus positioned to later speak with eyewitnesses, disagreed. Glaucia, he remarks, in one of his forensic speeches, was actually an amazingly popular candidate for consul. Far from losing to Memmius, he surely would have been elected for 99 if he was not disqualified because of his current position as praetor.[16] In short, Glaucia had no reason to murder Memmius, or at least not the reason Appian gave.[17]

So what did move the two to murder Memmius, if not a seditious effort to neutralize him and put Glaucia in the consulship for 99? Here we have to draw from two centuries-later sources following now-lost parts of Livy's massive history: the fourth century CE summary of Livy called the *Periochae*, and the fifth century CE writer Paulus Orosius. Orosius lived long after the events. He was a young Christian presbyter who had the good fortune to associate with the early stars of the Roman church Augustine and Jerome. In response to critics who asserted that Rome adopting Christianity had brought disasters, Augustine tasked

Orosius to write a history. In it he attempted to demonstrate that disasters were a frequent part of Roman history centuries before the advent of Christianity.[18] Critical for us, he often followed Livy closely and provides a counter to Appian's selectively dramatized account. Neither Livy's summarizer nor Orosius suggest Memmius' murder took place in the *comitia* nor do either connect it with Saturninus' desire to make Glaucia consul. Rather they suggest that candidate Memmius had a sterling character and Saturninus feared he would thwart whatever he hoped to achieve that year.[19] But does this explain Glaucia's involvement?

In some sense, Saturninus and Glaucia's murky motives do not change the story awfully much. They murdered Memmius. More important is the difference in the two source traditions about what happened after the murder. These versions offer different pictures of the more-or-less venerable Marius, now finishing his sixth consulship. Appian asserts an impromptu urban plebeian mob coalesced to take street justice on Saturninus for the murder. Glaucia and he, however, had their own street gangs made up of rural plebs. They occupied and fortified a position on the Capitoline along with the quaestor Saufeius. At this point the Senate issued its *consultum ultimum*, that emergency decree seemingly first used during the violence that claimed Gaius Gracchus.

Marius seems to have been caught in a rather awkward position. An ally of Saturninus, he was hesitant to exterminate the tribune and his followers. Accordingly, Marius only trudged into action, slowly arming a group of citizens to take the rebels on the Capitoline. Meanwhile some enterprising engineering minds decided to cut off the water supply to the Capitoline, the better to force the parched rebels to come to terms on that unusually hot day.[20]

Orosius' version is significantly different from Appian's. Here a mob of plebeians still forms, but Marius has to speak to them to calm them down and win them over. In other words, the mob seems to *have leaned towards Saturninus!* Marius then, in siding with the senate and its supporters, had first to calm down those who might support the rebels. Whatever he said, Orosius qualified it as a 'soothing speech'. The angry Romans were mollified and Marius formed them into maniples, probably a loose use of the military term just to indicate that the people were mobilized to fight.[21] Cicero describes more fully what this citizen mobilization entailed in a legal defence he delivered years later:

A decree of the senate was passed that Gaius Marius and Lucius Valerius, consuls, summon the tribunes of the commoners and the praetors who seemed to them suitable, and give their attention that the sovereignty and majesty of the Roman people be preserved. They summon all the tribunes of the commoners except Saturninus, the [praetors] except Glaucia. They order whoever wishes the Republic to be safe to take up weapons and follow them. All obey. From the temple of Sancus and the public armouries, weapons are given to the Roman people, with Gaius Marius, consul, overseeing the distribution.[22]

So in Cicero's version, all Romans obeyed the call to arms, all knew the danger – which seems like an exaggeration given Saturninus and Glaucia did have supporters. But even aged senators, Cicero recalls for his audience, did their part:

when the consuls, in pursuance of the resolution of the senate, had summoned the citizens to arms; when Marcus Aemilius, the chief of the senate, stood in arms in the assembly; who, though he could scarcely walk, thought the lameness of his feet not an impediment to his pursuit of enemies, but only to his flight from them; when, lastly, Quintus Scaevola, worn out as he was with old age, enfeebled by disease, lame, and crippled, and powerless in all his limbs, leaning on his spear, displayed at the same time the vigour of his mind and the weakness of his body.[23]

Cicero could only stretch reality a certain amount in the trial at which he delivered this speech. So, while we can be sure on principle that all Romans did not condemn Saturninus, there probably was considerable consensus that the senate's ultimate decree was legitimate, that the Republic faced a serious enemy.[24]

This whole episode can only have embarrassed Marius. His known associates, Saturninus and Glaucia, were now enemies of the Republic. Plutarch elaborates on this embarrassment, suggesting that in the period before Memmius was slain, Marius was increasingly inconvenienced by Saturninus' tactics, and increasingly pulled between the rogue tribune and his senatorial and equestrian enemies. Plutarch probably goes too far supporting this thesis, reporting an incredible episode during which Marius simultaneously entertained Saturninus and his enemies at his house, surreptitiously alternating between each party by claiming bouts of diarrhoea.[25] This seems a stretch, but the tension Marius must have felt was real enough.

In the final analysis, Marius was no revolutionary, no incendiary. He craved pre-eminence in the Republic, not the supplanting of that very same Republic. He was consul, the decree had been given, the state was in peril. And so he eliminated the threat.[26]

Accounts differ how the final showdown transpired. Orosius gives some tactical details: Marius posted guards at the city gates and dispatched the other consul to guard an unspecified hill. Then Marius' militia engaged the rebels in the Forum. Saturninus, Glaucia, and their supporters were bested in the Forum and fell back towards the Capitoline hill, a serviceable fortress in this street action. Exploiting the hot day, Marius or his allies cut the pipes bringing water to the Capitol. Now forced to act, the rebels fought a desperate battle at the entrance to the Capitoline. The rebel forces were decimated, and Saturninus and confederate Saufeius – perhaps Glaucia had already died in the fighting – fled to the senate house in the Forum. The equestrians did not consider that a legitimate sanctuary however, broke open the doors, and killed the rebel leaders.[27] Alternatively, Plutarch and Appian suggest the rebels realized they could not last without water and surrendered themselves into Marius' safekeeping. Marius could not protect the rebels however, and they were slain as they made their way back to the Forum with Marius.[28] Whether lynched by the crowd after surrendering or dying in a street battle, Saturninus' end was grim enough; of that we can be reasonably certain.

So, Saturninus was the first tribune to die violently in office since Tiberius Gracchus. This after a contentious career that is difficult to fully comprehend but centres around political rivalries and the charged issue of land distribution. And Marius? Not satisfied with his unprecedented string of consulships, nor intimidated by his allies' deaths, he still had designs on future glories. But first, another tribune with controversial legislative proposals would be murdered, provoking a veritable civil war with Rome's Italian allies: Marcus Livius Drusus.

Marcus Livius Drusus and the Shoemaker Assassin

They were out to murder him. Marcus Livius Drusus, tribune of the plebs in 91, scion of a distinguished line, son of that Drusus who had challenged Gaius Gracchus for the voters' favour. Yet, for all that pedigree, they were out to murder him. Rumours flew through the streets. Unwilling to gamble with his life, Drusus shifted his tribune work to his townhouse, welcoming all who had business to conduct into its inner courtyard, the *atrium*. Here he could keep better watch on those who approached him, perhaps gaining security too from supporters who could stand guard. The atrium, however, was spacious and harboured dark corners, more than able to mask an evildoer or two in the crowd. And so the end of one business day became, for Drusus, the end of everything. As the crowds left the house, he shouted out that he had been wounded, then fell dead, a shoemaker's knife buried in his hip.[29] Or perhaps he died on the street; a variant tradition has the murderer hiding in a crowd outside his house and Drusus surviving a few painful hours before he died.[30] It may not have been the shoemakers of the city who had found fault with Drusus, but there were many candidates who may have taken the tool of that trade as a murder weapon.

When Drusus died, the last, best hope for the Italians to peacefully earn Roman citizenship died with him. Despair quickly fostered revolution as a number of former Italian allies joined forces to rebel against Roman rule and forced the Romans to grant them well-earned rights as full citizens. Old foes from the Apennines and beyond – Samnites, Apulians, Lucanians, and others – sought to shake off the chains of second class status. They sent envoys to negotiate with the senate: would Rome cease holding them at arm's length and grant them citizenship in return for their invaluable service in conquering an empire for Rome? But the Roman senate was intransigent: it would receive no ambassadors unless the Italians repented of their revolt and came in peace. With no acceptable options left, many Italians mobilized for war in 91 BCE.[31]

Though the murder and revolution that sprang from Drusus' securely dated tribunate are clear enough, Drusus himself, his ultimate motives, and even the exact form of his legislative proposals, are shrouded in mystery. The sources note his distinguished lineage and largely agree that he was motivated by a desire to buttress the prestige and authority of the senate.[32] He also seems to have closely associated with at least some leaders among the Italian allies. He had a reputation with some as a Roman of upstanding character; Velleius Paterculus calls him a most noble, most moral, and most eloquent man. He preserves the story that when Drusus' architect offered to build his Palatine house so that it would hide his activities, Drusus insisted instead that the house be built so he would always be subject to the public gaze.[33] Other sources, like Livy's summarizer and Florus, simply declared him to be a rabble-rouser, instigating the plebs with dangerous hopes of land grants and domination of their social superiors.[34] There is little about Drusus' activities and motives that is uncontested. What follows is an attempt to follow cautiously one path charted by historians.[35] It will not satisfy everyone.

Drusus' Legislation: Courts, Citizenship, and Colonies

Consider the legislative plan Drusus proposed. There appear to have been three parts, though the sources conflict on which took precedence. First, a judicial law that in some way restored senatorial control over the juries of the permanent courts. In 91 the equestrians were the sole jurors; Drusus sought to change that. Second, a law granting citizenship to the Italian allies. This seems to have been unconnected to the judicial law except in the general sense: passing these laws may have been intended to reduce resentment against the senate and thereby buttress its authority. A third was an agrarian law or laws planting colonies and assigning individuals public lands. Finally, another law further subsidized grain for Roman city-dwellers.[36]

Whatever their relative importance to Drusus, the proposal to grant Italians citizenship seems to have been his final legislative effort. This appears straightforward enough in its general content: give full Roman citizenship to the Italian allies. The agrarian laws are not nearly as straightforward. Appian suggests that colonies in Italy and Sicily had been approved by the assembly, and Drusus just took the necessary step of leading the colonists to actually plant the new towns.[37] Other sources suggest that Drusus actively worked on committees that granted individual Romans land.[38]

The judiciary law is a thicket of sources. Appian provides the fullest account. In his version, Drusus sought to smooth over conflicts with the senate through this judicial law. According to its terms, 300 meritorious *equites* would be recruited into the senate, increasing that body's size to about 600 members. That newly expanded body would regain the power and privilege of sitting as jurors in the courts – a loss to those who remained *equites*.[39] Appian's version of Drusus' judicial law has not persuaded many modern historians – small wonder: there are fragments – a sentence here and there – in other sources that seemingly contradict Appian's version, especially the part about doubling the size of the senate. Yet it seems risky to abandon Appian outright. His version is the most systematic and detailed by far, and it may well be that the other sources made errors or omissions in their brevity.[40] Velleius Paterculus, for example, at first seems contradictory because he makes no mention of the expanded senate: 'It was [Drusus'] aim to restore to the senate its ancient prestige, and again transfer the law courts to that order from the equites.'[41] Velleius may simply have neglected to mention that part, and, indeed, even when he refers to the dictator Sulla's court arrangements decades later, he neglects to mention that Sulla did, in fact, double the senate by adding *equites*. Another problem: the courts Gaius Gracchus' law established called for 450 jurors, so restoring the juries fully to the control of the senate – numbering some 300 members – would leave many juror's seats unfilled, again suggesting that perhaps Drusus did think that expanding the senate and returning the courts to its control was the best course. Livy's epitomator suggests what might be a middle ground: '[Drusus] put through a judicial law so that control of the courts would be shared equally by the senatorial and the equestrian orders.'[42] This solution would seem to solve the problem of how the law courts would still have 450 jurors to draw from. But then Cicero makes passing reference that Drusus' judicial law, whatever its content, was declared invalid by the senate in 91. It is difficult to understand why the senate would have annulled a law that restored to them partial control of the juries; it is far easier to explain why the senate would annul a law that added new members to its competitive and elitist ranks.[43] Truly a thicket of sources.

Drusus' Programme and Murder

Ancient sources, and modern historians, connect two or more of these issues – courts, land, Italian citizenship – depending on what they felt was Drusus' primary legislative concern. In essence we have these primary possibilities. First, following Appian, Italian envoys came to Drusus and sought citizenship. He agreed and sought to gain Roman voters' approval for a citizenship law by passing some popular agrarian laws. Then he attempted to heal the rift between senate and equestrians through the judicial legislation, but his legislation caused more problems than it solved. Finally, he proposed citizenship for the Italians. Some Italians were concerned, however, about the agrarian laws taking away public lands that they currently farmed, and Appian names Etruscans and Umbrians as particularly concerned.[44] Ultimately, opposition to the agrarian laws, Appian suggests, is what earned Drusus a shoemaker's knife in the side.[45] According to this hypothesis, a disgruntled Etruscan or Umbrian would most likely have wielded the knife.

On the other hand, Velleius Paterculus suggests that reforming the law courts and buttressing the senate's authority through a judiciary law were Drusus' main concerns. And so Drusus proposed agrarian laws to win over the voters to his judicial law. Those agrarian laws generated friction within the senate, and his measures were not supported. Only then, frustrated in his efforts to bring the agrarian and judicial laws to pass, did Drusus attempt to grant citizenship to the Italian allies. His murder ended that.[46] He was in the Forum seeking support for this citizenship proposal when he was stabbed by somebody in the crowd outside his house. According to this hypothesis, it is anyone's guess who ultimately sanctioned the murder. There could have been a large list of possibilities.

Another possibility? Drusus sought to grant land to the veterans of recent commanders who were his political allies. Knowing this would upset the Italian allies, he proposed the grant of citizenship as compensation. The judicial law then is either not fully connected or perhaps a way to win over senatorial support to the citizenship grants.[47] And again, the list of possible murders is unknown, but it is long.

Regardless of the motives, the murder of Drusus sparked the Italian allies' revolt, asserts Appian. This seems plausible enough. Drusus had supported the push for allied citizenship; his murder dashed whatever hopes the allies had pinned to him. The eruption of hostilities, the flames of revolt, happened, the sources suggest, something like this. The first and second century CE poet Florus attributes murderous motives to the Italian rebels. They conspired to assassinate the Roman consuls of the year, Lucius Marcius Philippus and Sextus Julius Caesar, while the two were busy sacrificing to the gods during the yearly Latin festival. Their plans were discovered and came to nothing.[48] Perhaps only the plot to murder the consuls came to light, not the whole revolution-under-wraps, because the thread then trails to Asculum, a prominent town in Picenum, northeast of Rome on the shores of the Adriatic. Here, Appian adds details. He asserts the Romans suspected revolutionary mischief in Italy and kept a stable of informants to apprise them of trouble. The praetor, Servilius, assigned to manage Rome's interests in the Picenum, got a hint of trouble and less-than-delicately threatened the people of Asculum as they were celebrating a festival. They assumed their plot had been revealed. Seeing nothing to lose, the plotters at Asculum murdered Servilius and his legate. For good measure, they slaughtered all Roman citizens at Asculum too.[49] The Picenes declared war against the Romans and were joined by many – though not all – of the regions of Italy.[50]

The rebel Italians – Samnites, Picenes, Apulians, Campanians and more – formed an independent political league they named Italia. Their forces scored early victories against Roman armies, unsurprising since they had supplied the larger part of Rome's soldiers for some time now. Ultimately, the loyalty of the Latin colonies and the unwillingness of powerful regions like Etruria and Umbria to join the revolt made it most likely that Italia would ultimately be defeated. Also in the hopes of preserving loyalty, the Republic offered citizenship to existing allies and those who ceased rebelling. Still the war would continue into 88 BCE.[51]

At the end of this civil-war-in-all-but-name, the third of the murdered tribunes, Publius Sulpicius Rufus met his end. He had provoked the wrong Roman, consul Lucius Cornelius Sulla. And he would pay for that mistake with his life.

Sulpicius, Marius, and Sulla: The First Civil War

Publius Sulpicius Rufus fled the city, but he could not escape Sulla. The consul had done the unthinkable. He occupied Rome with citizen soldiers and drove the tribune, Marius, and their supporters from the city. All the tribune's measures were abolished, and the senate, following Sulla's lead, declared Sulpicius and Marius enemies of the state. Sulpicius hoped to escape Sulla's agents by hiding in an Italian villa whose location has been lost to time. Sulpicius' enslaved servant willingly sold his enslaver's hiding place out for a reward. Sulla's agents dragged Sulpicius into the open and murdered him. Though he did not live to see it, many more murders would follow that decade as control of the city lurched back and forth between Sulla, Marius, and their various associates.

The Social War had strained Rome's military power to breaking point, but the Republic prevailed. The conflagration of war and revolt, however, was not over. Italy was not yet pacified when Lucius Cornelius Sulla, consul of 88, marched with his army against Rome, occupied the city, and ushered in the First Civil War. The rivalry between Marius and Sulla exploded, when the tribune Sulpicius took sides and passed a law Sulla could not accept. The evidence for Sulpicius, as it was for Saturninus and Drusus, is problematic and fragmentary. Still, any investigation of the origins of the first Roman civil war must include a visit to the Pontic King who would prove a thorn in the Republic's side for decades: Mithridates VI.

Mithridates and the War against Rome

Mithridates VI Eupator, king of Pontus, a region in Asia Minor on the shores of the Black Sea, was nothing if not ambitious. He sought to expand his regional power, and the kingdom of Cappadocia to the south particularly enticed him. Around 100 BCE, Mithridates installed his son, Ariarathes Eusebes, on the Cappadocian throne. The Romans had had an interest in the balance of power in the region for decades, especially after the King of Pergamum bequeathed his kingdom in western Asia Minor to the people of Rome. Rome did not officially respond at first to Mithridates' political puppeteering in Cappadocia. Eventually the senate dispatched Sulla to Cappadocia after his praetorship (perhaps held in 97) to handle the situation. Sulla deposed Mithridates' son and, in response to the Cappadocian request for a king of their own, installed Ariobarzanes sometime around 96 or 95 BCE.[52]

Mithridates must have rankled at the setback but bided his time. When he saw the Romans fully occupied by the Social War, he made his move to further consolidate Pontic power. He deposed young Nicomedes IV, king of neighbouring Bithynia to the west, and removed Ariobarzanes from Cappadocia. The senate had its hands full but sent Manius

Aquillius (consul in 101) on a diplomatic mission to restore the displaced rulers. Aquillius demanded Mithridates cease his political stratagems, and cease he did, even executing his Bithynian puppet-ruler for good measure.[53] Aquillius and the ambassadors, however, hankered for war, as many Roman aristocrats did, and did their level best to goad Nicomedes and Ariobarzanes into invading Pontus. Ariobarzanes demurred, but Nicomedes, as it happened, owed money to the Roman ambassadors. The ambassadors leveraged this debt to provoke a war. Mithridates was stuck. Fighting Nicomedes would give the Romans a desirable pretext to attack Pontus, and he surely knew the disaster that would result from that. So he simply allowed Nicomedes to invade and raid Pontus, then complained to the Roman ambassadors. They were maddeningly unhelpful, and just warned Mithridates not to war against Nicomedes – or else. Mithridates was caught between the metaphorical rock and hard place with few alternatives. So the belligerent Romans got their wish: Mithridates fought back.

The Roman ambassadors and their allies were caught off guard. Mithridates first drove Ariobarzanes from the Cappadocian throne. He did not stop there, however, but scattered the small Roman force in the region and occupied the Roman province of Asia. He slaughtered the Romans and Italians he captured in Asia Minor, some 80,000, and captured Aquillius in the process. For that Roman's greed, the king reserved a special revenge, pouring molten gold down his throat. Effectively, Mithridates now controlled most of Asia Minor. The threat to Roman interests in the region was real enough, and the senate opted to assign a consul against Mithridates for 88.[54]

Consul Sulla and the War against Mithridates

Sulla's motives and actions up to the start of the civil war in 88 BCE are perhaps the least mysterious of the four principal actors, so only a brief pause is needed now. Sulla himself had put Ariobarzanes on the Cappadocian throne a few years before and understood the situation in Asia Minor with Mithridates as well as, if not better than, Marius. Sulla's career after his praetorship is more than a bit puzzling. He was eligible for the consulship in 96, but he did not win election to the office, nor seemingly did he even run for it, until 89. Arguably the soon-to-be-famous Sulla had few allies of influence in Rome, and consequently no real chance of winning the consulship, that pinnacle of an aristocratic political career. It seems, however, that the Social War provided Sulla with a golden opportunity to relaunch his stalled political climb. He served with distinction as a legate of consul Lucius Julius Caesar in 90 and again under Lucius Porcius Cato in 89. Through 89 the war raged on, and when Sulla won election to the consulship of 88, it appeared he would command legions in Italy. Sulla, at 50, was certainly behind the fastest office-climbing aristocrats and had an unusual eight-year gap between praetorship and consulship. He planned to continue fighting the remaining rebel Italians. In 88, however, matters in Asia had deteriorated sufficiently that the senate designated Asia as a consular province, and Sulla won the command by lot.[55] Shortly, as Sulla would see it, that command was stolen.

Marius in the 90s

Marius had secured an unprecedented string of consulships but wanted more. A bit over a decade earlier, he managed to play both sides in the conflict between Saturninus and the senate, though ultimately he came down hard on that rogue tribune. His activities in the 90s are somewhat difficult to trace. Marius travelled to the Roman province of Asia at the end of 99. Metellus Numidicus, whom Saturninus had worked with Marius to exile, had the support needed to return home. Time for Marius to travel: beyond his lack of enthusiasm to see his enemy, Marius too may have felt an absence warranted by his connections to Saturninus. Time to let matters settle down. Still, even if Marius had suffered a setback when the senate restored Metellus, he clearly had influence still at Rome even after the Saturninus affair. After all, in 98 that college of priests who observed the skies for signs from the gods, the augurs, selected him to join their ranks.[56] While in Asia Minor, Marius met with Mithridates. Plutarch preserves the tradition that Marius sought to goad Mithridates into war, hoping to gain an important military command as consul or proconsul and reassert his influence at Rome.[57] It is a recurring problem to be aware of; the main sources that form the basis of Roman accounts of Marius in this period were all substantially biased against Marius. Most of all, the memoirs of Sulla, which Plutarch explicitly cites several times, did not give Marius the benefit of any doubt.[58]

Marius was in Rome when the Social War erupted and participated in the Roman war effort. In 90 he had a successful stint in command, proving effective enough to be assigned to an army in northern Italy. Somewhat puzzlingly, the senate assigned him no command in 89. Why? Plutarch, again likely drawing from a hostile Sullan tradition, says that Marius made the case himself that old age and ill health made him unfit for command. Given his subsequent bid to go to war against Mithridates, this seems unlikely. More likely his publicly trumpeted ambitions to hold a seventh consulship made his rivals and enemies in the senate loath to provide him with opportunity through a continuous military command.[59] Yet Marius craved new military challenges and honours. When it was decided Mithridates would provide the opportunity is not clear, but decide he did.

Ultimately, it was Marius' determination to command against Mithridates that drove Rome into a civil war. Marius, as we have seen, made the ambitions of the average Roman aristocrat seem tepid. Here he was, 70 and distinguished by a string of consulships unmatched in the history of the Republic, yet he craved the command against Mithridates, a chance to shine once more, to capture the Romans' fast-fading attentions. He was hardly the obvious choice.[60] There were more vigorous leaders to be found, like, for two examples, the duly elected Sulla and Pompeius.

How could Marius engineer this transfer of command? Marius understood more than most the power of the tribunate to upset the machinery of state and to aid those who could appeal to the people. Accordingly, he allied with Publius Sulpicius Rufus, a tribune of the plebs for 88. Sulpicius would play a central role in the violence to follow.

Publius Sulpicius Rufus

The main narratives of Plutarch, Appian, and Velleius Paterculus, all relying to some extent on Sulla's memoirs or other pro-Sulla accounts, dismiss the tribune Publius Sulpicius Rufus as a mere cipher, a tool for Marius' ambitions. Fortunately for historians the events of 88 belong to the period when that most prolific of Roman senators, Marcus Tullius Cicero, lived; he was in his late teens at the time. Comments he made later about Sulpicius give a glimpse of this critical figure's political origins. Says Cicero:

- Sulpicius associated with Livius Drusus, just recently murdered, and it seems that he shared Drusus' interest in reinforcing the power and prestige of the senate.
- Sulpicius was a close friend of Quintus Pompeius, one of the consuls of 88 and a colleague of Sulla.

Certainly, his first political action accorded firmly with the interests of the senatorial elite. In 95 he prosecuted Gaius Norbanus. As a tribune in 103, Norbanus had prosecuted Quintus Servilius Caepio for losing his army to the Cimbri and Teutones in 105. Some tribunes attempted to veto the prosecution and were forcefully driven off. In the process, someone struck the elder statesman and bastion of senatorial privilege Marcus Aemilius Scaurus (cos. 115) on the head with a rock. On these grounds, Sulpicius tried Norbanus for treason. Norbanus was acquitted, but the incident seems to demonstrate Sulpicius' initial attachment to the senatorial oligarchy. Nothing suggests that attachment had dissolved when he began his tribunate in December 89.[61]

Something certainly changed before the end of his tribunate and his life in 88. He had recruited a band of 3,000 swordsmen for controlling the streets and amassed 300 *equites* as an entourage he called his 'anti-senate'. He passed laws that probably did not appeal to many senators, one in particular providing greater voting power to new citizens and freedmen. Unsurprisingly given his turnabout, the ancient sources did not know quite what to make of him. Velleius Paterculus suggests he was ambitious, eloquent, and energetic, known for his honourable behaviour before his association with Marius and the turbulent days that sparked the civil war.[62] Plutarch differs: Sulpicius was rotten to the core, second to none when immorality was the standard.[63] An aspiring Saturninus some labelled him, which may be no more than the easy observation that Sulpicius too would use the tribunate and the muscle of thugs to pursue his agenda.

Though the three main narrative sources remembered Sulpicius most for obtaining Marius the command against Mithridates and in doing so contributing to the outbreak of civil war, Sulpicius clearly was his own agent with his own plans for influence. The exact details of his legislation are unclear, but he did more than just seize the Mithridatic command for Marius. He also passed a law prohibiting senators from acquiring excessive debt and a law that would distribute the new Italian citizens evenly among the voting tribes of the tribal assembly.[64] But why had he stopped supporting senatorial authority and moved instead into populist politics? The best guess is that Sulpicius had some unrecorded falling out with leading senators. Some scraps of evidence, barely noted by most of the sources, suggest Sulpicius locked horns with the senate at the start of his tribunate over Gaius Julius Caesar Strabo. Caesar Strabo's bid for the consulship appealed to many of the senatorial oligarchy, but he was precluded by law from running for the consulship of 88 because he had held no office higher than aedile.[65] Sulpicius, Cicero mentions in passing, joined with his tribune-colleague Antistius to oppose Caesar Strabo's candidacy for the consulship of 87. It is possible that the senate squashed Sulpicius' protests by granting Caesar Strabo a special exemption, not an uncommon thing for the senate to do. Cicero certainly seems to suggest that this incident was the turning point that drove Sulpicius in populist politics. The reasoning would have been, 'the senate stonewalled me in my open-and-shut case; I will seek other means to make my mark while tribune.'[66]

Perhaps. No better explanation is apparent. Nor is much light shed on Sulpicius' political actions at this point other than that he challenged the senatorial oligarchy with his measures, which seems clear enough from their content. First, consider his law redistributing the newly enfranchised Italian citizens throughout the 35 voting tribes. A brief explanation: the tribal assembly in the Republic was, alongside the centuriate assembly, one of the two main voting and electoral assemblies.[67] Unlike the centuriate assembly, which was organized so that the wealthy had a greater amount of voting power, the tribal assembly, because its voting blocks were the male members of each tribe, with no wealth distinctions, was more democratic.[68] It appears that when the Italians were first granted citizenship after the outbreak of the Social War, they were distributed among a limited number of tribes. This meant all the new Italian citizens together, even though in actual numbers they outnumbered existing Roman citizens, could only influence four of the 35 votes. Sulpicius proposed a law to change this. If the newly enfranchised citizens were distributed more evenly among the 35 tribes, the Italians would gain greater influence in the laws and elections decided by the tribal assembly. There were those in the senatorial oligarchy who opposed such a law, presumably because of the disruption to traditional voting patterns and power blocs.[69]

Exactly when in the year Sulpicius proposed this is not clear, but there is a good case to be made that it was not at the start of the consular year. Sulla ultimately received the command against Mithridates, yet at the beginning of the year his army was occupied in besieging the rebel Italian stronghold of Nola. In other words, the Social War had not been wrapped up and Sulla's army was still involved in important operations. This detail suggests the senate had assigned both consuls to Italy at the start of their term.[70]

Sulpicius, Marius, and Sulla: Descent into Civil War

As is so often the case, the final events leading to the first civil war vary depending on the source followed. For Plutarch, Sulpicius' proposal to transfer the Mithridatic command to Marius was the only proposal that mattered: Plutarch ignores the other legislation. When Sulpicius proposed the law shifting the command to Marius, Sulla and his colleague, Pompeius, were both in the city. They used their authority to suspend public business – if no laws could be passed, no command could be transferred to Marius.[71] Street violence followed, perhaps at the assembly where the consuls suspended public business. Sulpicius and his gang murdered the son of his former friend, the consul Pompeius. At this point Pompeius disappears from Plutarch's narrative. Sulla, however, is forced to hide in Marius' house and subsequently forced to end the suspension of business. Then Sulla disappears, dropping out of Plutarch's account while Sulpicius passes the law. Sulpicius and Marius send military tribunes to take command of Sulla's army at Nola. Sulla happens to be there, however, and successfully appeals to his soldiers. They murder Marius' lieutenants and follow Sulla to occupy Rome, starting the First Civil War.[72]

Appian, however, provides the more likely account. Where Plutarch is vague and essentially ignores the other laws, Appian connects the citizenship law and law about the Mithridatic command into a more detailed, lucid account.[73] He links the street violence to Sulpicius' proposal to redistribute the new Italian citizens among the voting tribes. In his version, Sulpicius does not foment the violence; rather, old citizens and new citizens began to brawl of their own accord in the streets with stones and improvised clubs. In response, the consuls declared a holiday from voting, creating space and time for tempers to cool. Sulpicius and his gang, however, confronted the consuls publicly and demanded that they rescind the holiday. The consuls stood firm. Sulpicius' gang had brought daggers to the mix, however, and the confrontation degraded to violence quickly enough. In the melee the consuls escaped, but Sulpicius' gang murdered the consul Pompeius' son.[74] When Sulla escaped the city he went to his army, planning to depart for Asia and his war against Mithridates. While Sulla was gone from the city, however, Sulpicius passed the law stripping the Mithridatic command from Sulla and assigning it to Marius. When Sulla heard this, he appealed to his soldiers, at first referring only to the slander and abuse he had suffered, not the martial remedy he sought.[75] His soldiers knew the score, however, and at least some were concerned that the transfer of command to Marius might leave them out of the campaign and all the wealth it promised. Accordingly, they encouraged Sulla to lead them against Rome, against those who had stolen his command. And Sulla did.[76]

Still, there are problems. Why did Sulla leave Rome after the riot with Sulpicius exploded? Surely he must have known that Marius sought the Mithridatic command and that leaving the city would allow Sulpicius to pass a law bringing that to pass? Sulla was now 50: a teenager when the senate led by Opimius issued its final decree (senatus consultum ultimum) and destroyed Gaius Gracchus, a young adult during the Saturninus affair. He had sufficient precedent guiding him to summon the senate and push for a decree to put Sulpicius down. Knowing this, it becomes reasonable to suppose that Sulla intended to march on Rome as he left the city.[77] The other obvious possibility is that Sulla did not know that Sulpicius would act to transfer his command to Marius, in which case Sulla simply had washed his hands of the city and decided to set out to Asia.[78] Marius' attempt to win over his soldiers perhaps convinced Sulla that he needed to act.

Sulla Marches against Rome

Sulla and his soldiers were determined. Presumably the army marched along the Via Latina, the most direct route from Nola to Rome, merging with the Via Labicana outside the city and entering Rome through the Esquiline gate. Before it set out, two praetors dispatched by Marius ordered the army to halt its march. The soldiers broke their fasces along with their authority, sending the praetors packing. Sulla would not be denied his justice, his revenge.[79]

Meanwhile at Rome, Marius scrambled to meet Sulla's invasion. This may have involved murdering some of Sulla's allies in the city, but it certainly involved rallying at least a makeshift force.[80] Arms, no doubt, were seized from the public armouries. It must have seemed all too familiar to Marius: twelve years before, he had armed citizens and formed a corps to battle Saturninus. Sulla, however, was no Saturninus. His army was real enough and full of veteran soldiers, not a mass of street-fighters. Marius may well have had some veterans available in the city, but it cannot have amounted to much compared to Sulla's six legions of battle-tested troops.

Before reaching the City, Sulla checked the omens and sacrificed to the gods, a necessary precaution for such a monumental undertaking: he was the first to lead an army of citizens against Rome itself. The priest on hand, Postumius, reviewed the divine signs and staked his life that Sulla's invasion would succeed. The tale attached itself that Sulla saw a goddess in his dreams who armed him with a thunderbolt and called him to destroy his enemies.[81] About twelve miles from the city, Sulla met with more ambassadors from Rome and agreed to pitch camp and wait. It was a ruse to buy time; he was too close to be deterred now.[82] When they reached Rome, Sulla's soldiers went to work to secure their entry and, if need be, escape. One legion of veteran soldiers occupied the Esquiline gate, controlling the easternmost point of the ancient Servian walls. Pompeius took a second legion to seize the Colline Gate less than a mile to the north. A third legion covered the wooden Pons Sublicius, the oldest bridge across the Tiber. Its exact location is now lost but it seems to have been connected to the *Forum Boarium*, the cattle market, deeper in the city near the Tiber. A fourth legion stood watch outside the Servian walls. When they had all taken their positions, Sulla entered the city with the remaining two legions, presumably at the Esquiline Gate.[83]

They met a hail of resistance as nearby inhabitants pelted the soldiers with rocks and roof tiles. The resistance proved fierce enough that the soldiers fell back initially. Sulla took command of the situation and, in Appian's more charitable version, cowed the house-dwellers by threatening to set fire to the houses.[84] More likely, since at this point he was a veteran commander faced with the military operation of occupying a city, he torched the houses outright, as Plutarch asserts.[85]

Now Marius brought his improvised army together, and the forces clashed in the local forum near the gate. Citizen fought citizen in a deadly struggle to control the streets. Sulla had the advantage of numbers and reserves, outmanoeuvred the Marian forces, and drove them off.[86] Marius made a temporary stand at the temple of Tellus, and there, reportedly, offered to free any enslaved people who joined him. Perhaps an exaggeration by pro-Sullan writers, but still, Marius must have been truly desperate at this point. His efforts to check his enemy failed, and he became a foe in an increasingly hostile city. He may well have tried to bargain with nearby enslaved people to gain more soldiers.

After his clash with Marius, Sulla moved to the Via Sacra in the Forum, positioned guards at various points in the city, and camped his troops. We will consider the remainder of this war and Sulla's dictatorship in the next chapter. At the moment, fresh from defeating Marius' makeshift army, Sulla and Pompeius, the duly elected consuls for the year, had restored Rome to their form of order. They declared Sulpicius and Marius, along with twelve other ringleaders, enemies of the Republic, subject to summary execution. As an extra enticement, a reward was put on Marius' head. For good measure they annulled all of Sulpicius' legislation.[87]

And what about the now-renegade tribune, Sulpicius? He, along with Marius and their remaining allies had fled the city, doubtless with some degree of terror. Sulla was not one to leave foes a moment's peace however, and dispatched agents to pursue the newly declared public enemies. Marius managed to escape their murderous grasp and escape Italy. Sulpicius was not so lucky. One of his enslaved servants informed on him and Sulla's agents murdered him.[88] In a grim display of his literal sense of justice, Sulla freed the enslaved servant as reward for the information, then had him hurled from the Tarpeian rock for betraying his enslaver.[89]

* * *

In the span of a dozen years, from 100 to 88 BCE, the tally of murdered tribunes in office more than doubled to five, Saturninus, Drusus, and

Sulpicius joining the ranks of Tiberius Gracchus. To this death count we should probably add Gaius Gracchus since his activities as a tribune indirectly served to get him declared an outlaw and killed. They differed in origins and motives; they differed in their plans. Still, a common thread runs through all five of their incendiary terms of office. All had offered some form of economic support to those with less means, whether landless farmers or the urban plebs who needed affordable grain. With the exception of Tiberius, all had proposed laws designed to appeal to those who were not inherently part of the senatorial oligarchy, the office-holding elite that controlled the Republic. All had taken advantage of their power to legislate directly through proposals to the assembly rather than submit bills for the senate to approve first. And all had sparked intense rivalries within the ruling class that had led to their deaths and perpetuated the sense that many Romans new and old must have had: the senatorial class was more interested in its rivalries and competitions for power and influence than it was in concerns outside the senatorial class. Violence had grown, slowly but surely, in Republican politics until the unthinkable happened. A Roman consul led a Roman army to attack the City. It was only a hint of the violence yet to come in the First Civil War.

Chapter 7

Bloody Masters of Rome:
Marius, Cinna, Carbo, and Sulla

Marius hurried from haven to haven after he fled the city, looking over his shoulder for Sulla's henchman. Plutarch gives an elaborate account of near misses as Sulla's riders ranged through Italy looking for the six-time consul on the wrong end of a rivalry.[1] Eventually Marius found a ship and set sail for Africa. As soon as he stepped ashore, however, the Roman governor's agent halted his flight, offering him a simple choice: get back on the boat and leave Africa or be treated as a public enemy according to the senatorial decree Sulla had passed. The six-times consul, victor over Numidians and Cimbri, now could find no grateful place within the Roman Empire for shelter. He returned to his craft and sailed west to Numidia. There he anchored his ship offshore and spent the winter.[2] At some point, his son, Gaius Marius, and several other comrades joined his exile.[3]

While Marius sought asylum, Sulla was busy. When he had occupied the city and driven off the Marians, he had the senate decree Marius, Sulpicius, and a handful of other associates enemies of the Republic, sentenced to death. Did Sulla do more than this? Some ancient sources suggest that he made some adjustments to the Roman constitution at this time – the oral body of rules and customs regulating politics. When Sulla returned to Rome about five years later, however, he had himself named 'dictator for making laws and preserving the Republic' (*dictator legibus faciendis et reipublicae constituendae*) and used that position to impose changes to the government – revolutionary changes. So, it is possible some ancient sources were confused and that Sulla did not tinker with the Roman government until he returned from the East.[4] Rather, he seized control of the city, outlawed Marius, and restored a semblance of public order before heading east to campaign.

Whatever policies he might have instituted, Sulla decided to fully restore Rome to the senate and magistrates' control and soon sent his army south to Capua to await him. He knew how unpopular his actions were with a significant percentage of the population. Many viewed his march on Rome as the most vile rebellion and his outlawing of Marius and his associates as nothing more than the violent partisan actions of a military despot.[5] Sulla remained at Rome at least long enough to hold elections for the magistracies of 87. They did not go as he had planned: Sulla's preferred candidates did not meet the voters' approval. Nowhere was their dissatisfaction with Sulla made more manifest than in their choice of his political rival Lucius Cornelius Cinna to be consul for 87 alongside Gnaeus Octavius.[6] Cinna apparently swore an oath upon election that he would support Sulla's policies. He would not keep that oath long.

The Problem of Pompeius Strabo

A threatening wildcard in Sulla's seizure of power was Pompeius Strabo (here referred to as Strabo), consul of the previous year, and now proconsul in command of an army still battling Italians in the Social War. No news leaked of Strabo's leanings; he had not declared for Marius or Sulla. Perhaps aiming for, though not necessarily settling upon, the least provocative reaction to Strabo's command of a potentially problematic army, the consul Quintus Pompeius was authorized – presumably by the senate under Sulla's direction – to relieve Strabo and take command of his army. Pompeius went to Strabo's camp, and Strabo ostensibly complied with the order to surrender his command. His soldiers decidedly did not. The morning after his arrival, they crowded around Pompeius, pretending they were listening to his dictates, then murdered him. Strabo resumed command of his army. Appian asserts he was displeased to have to do so; not everyone is so certain that Strabo had not planned it all.[7] Sulla must have been a little jumpy about the debacle. There was little he could do, however, about Strabo – and, after all, Strabo still refrained from siding openly with Sulla's enemies. Sulla let the matter drop.

Probably more troubling than Strabo, Cinna soon challenged Sulla's arrangements, such as they were, immediately upon his inauguration at the start of 87, by attempting to prosecute Sulla in collaboration with the tribune Virginius. The situation in Asia was too serious, however, and Mithridates was growing too powerful, for Sulla to wait any longer. Doubtless he hoped the consul Octavius, who had proven himself a supporter, would check Cinna. Sulla essentially ignored Cinna's indictment, returned to his army and deployed in the East in the campaign season of 87.[8]

The Domination of Cinna

Since Cinna had begun his year in office by swiping at Sulla, it is not surprising that he continued to endorse Marius' cause. His next target: the newest Roman citizens. Before he was driven out of the city and murdered, Sulpicius had passed a law distributing the newly enfranchised Italians among the voting tribes, necessary for them so that they could vote. Sulla and Pompeius nullified his acts. So Cinna took up the cause again, seemingly in Marius' name. Octavius countered by rallying the older citizens to resist Cinna's proposal. Clearly, few thought it was an opportunity for civil debate. Cinna's supporters allegedly came to the Forum assembly, with daggers strapped on. Octavius' supporters brought their own blades to the vote. When several tribunes formally blocked Cinna's proposal, the new citizens rioted, some going so far as to assault the tribunes on the Rostra, tribune sacrosanctity be damned![9]

Octavius seems to have had a bit more concern for the health of the Republic than Cinna, for Appian asserts he came to the Forum with his own henchmen – perhaps his lictors – and broke apart the rioters. It provided only a moment's pause. Octavius pursued Cinna to the temple of Castor and Pollux in the Forum and drove his colleague from the city. Some of Octavius' partisans, however, reportedly without orders, returned to the brawl. They murdered a number of new citizens and drove the rest from the city.[10]

Cinna had seen his street force melt away and left the city. He may have offered freedom to any enslaved people who joined his cause; it is hard to know because Roman sources loved to throw that accusation around. The claim is made several times, however, and certainly seems to fit with Cinna's goals. He made a tour of towns nearby that had recently received the vote, collecting supporters and funds. It is important to remember, at this point, Cinna was one of the chief executives of the Republic, a consul. He was not a lone fanatic, however much his enemies wished to paint him so. Indeed some of his supporters from the senate joined him as he made the rounds, Romans like Quintus Sertorius and Marius' son, Gaius Marius the younger.[11]

The senate in Rome, if not controlled by supporters of Sulla, was at least governed by enemies of Cinna and Marius. The senators stripped Cinna of his consulship and his citizenship for good measure. They selected Lucius Cornelius Merula to replace him as consul. The news did not slow Cinna in the least. Now he aimed for the loyalty of the Roman army stationed at Capua. Appian attributes to Cinna a not-unsophisticated populist argument delivered to the troops. The citizen-soldiers had voted him the consulship, so the senate had unlawfully stripped the people's choice of office. If the soldiers did nothing to check this crime, the senate would continue to dominate the popular assemblies.[12] It was a strong argument in favour of the rights and power of the common voter. Cinna could have meant it sincerely, regardless of his self-interest. He arguably did not see himself as a rebel but a legitimate consul fighting for the legitimate rights of the people against the tyranny of a partisan senate.

Cinna closed his appeal to the Capuan army with an extra bit of political theatre. He tore his clothing, leapt from the speaker's platform, and cast himself in the dirt, abject, pitiful. The soldiers knew their part. They picked him up and brushed him off, put him back in his curule chair, his official chair of office, and implored him not to despair. They would follow him as consul wherever he might lead. The military tribunes seized on the rising good will of the soldiers, all taking an oath of loyalty to Cinna – so Appian tells it – and inducing the common soldiers to do the same. Velleius Paterculus, however, would have none of that. In his account, Cinna simply bribed the centurions and tribunes first, who in turn induced the soldiers with the help of bribes.[13] The two versions and two methods – dramatic political theatre and bribery – are hardly mutually exclusive, nor are they incompatible with a sincerely believed argument by Cinna. The most sincere political beliefs, at least in Roman politics, could be made more palatable through cash. Ultimately, Cinna got his army.

Bolstered, Cinna continued his rounds to newly-enfranchised towns and insisted that all he suffered, he did on behalf of equal voting rights for the new citizens. He had been cast out for them and deserved their support. With the Social War not completely extinguished, there was a fair amount of hostility to the senate and Republic in Italy and this found expression in the money and soldiers that communities provided Cinna.[14]

Octavius and Merula, equally convinced of their legitimacy it seems, made plans to resist a new march on Rome, this time by Cinna. Fortification trenches were dug, walls repaired, and artillery positioned. The consuls requested troops from those towns in the vicinity that remained loyal, and from Cisalpine Gaul, on the Roman side of the Alps. They also summoned – perhaps begged – Strabo to aid them.[15] Strabo did march to Rome after all and camped near the Colline Gate. Cinna approached with his own army and camped nearby. Neither seemed willing to provoke the other to a battle without cause. No doubt rumours ran rampant through the city about Strabo's motives. Whom would he support?[16]

The Return of Marius

87 BCE had been a busy year for civil warriors and was still far from over. Now Marius returned to Italy. Energized by the reports of Cinna's loyalty and opposition to pro-Sullan forces, he landed in Etruria along with his comrades-in-exile. Starting a recruiting drive of his own there, he capitalized on the pity his unshorn hair and unwashed road-filthy body sparked. Like Cinna, Marius continued to stress the cause of voting equity, promising to secure the new Italian citizens equal political rights. For his efforts, Marius recruited 6,000 Etruscans, a personal legion that he marched to Rome, where all the armies seemed to be massing. Marius and Cinna joined forces and divided their combined army into thirds commanded by loyal Marians: Cinna and Gnaeus Papirius Carbo; Quintus Sertorius; and, of course, Marius. Each third occupied a position outside the city. They systematically severed Rome's grain supply from nearby towns and the port of Ostia. For good measure, Cinna captured the town of Ariminum, strategically blocking the route for any troops from Cisalpine Gaul that had heeded recruiting calls from Octavius and the senate.[17]

That meant Octavius and Merula, still in the city, still essentially lacked armies. Sulla and his army were already in the East, too far away to recall. Wildcard Strabo, it seems, did nothing to counter the Marian forces and remained silent, biding his time and seeing how events played out.[18] The one unaccounted-for army in the field served under Caecilius Metellus, still fighting the recalcitrant Samnites in the south, Rome's centuries-old foes who had not given up on the Social War. Octavius and Merula commanded Metellus to make the best peace deal he could leverage, but in any event, to make peace and come with his army to

Rome. The Samnites learned of their suddenly strong bargaining position and made demands that Metellus found intolerable. Marius grasped the opportunity and reached out to the Samnites, promising that he would honour their demands should they support his righteous effort to restore him to the Republic's good graces.[19]

Meanwhile at Rome, Marius had severed the Roman grain supply. He and Cinna attempted to occupy the city, taking advantage of a military tribune in the city who owed Marius a favour. The tribune left a city gate open. Octavius drove the Marians from the city. Now Strabo acted, assisting Octavius in repulsing Marius and Cinna – perhaps Strabo simply wanted to preserve a balance?[20] Velleius suggests a major battle erupted and agrees the Marians were driven out. As fate would have it, Strabo was struck down by plague, though word on the street suggested he had been slain by a lightning bolt.[21] Neither Appian nor Velleius say what happened to his army. Perhaps the plague? It had been making its deadly rounds that year. Ultimately, the city remained in Octavius and Merula's control with Marius and his allies outside the walls.

Marius had methodically strangled Rome's supply lines, however, and matters in the city became desperate. The senate was on its own resisting the armies outside its wall; the consuls and their army had headed south to check Cinna. Nervously the senate sent envoys to Cinna. Could there be peace? Cinna, a proud Roman aristocrat like his rivals, asked if the senate sent messengers to him as consul or as a private citizen. The envoys sensed the danger of the moment. They lacked instructions for how to respond and returned to the senate for clarification. Meanwhile, citizens practically streamed from the city to join Cinna. His cause looked to be the stronger, and many Romans were betting their lives on the outcome of this duel between senate and Cinna.[22]

The senate was trapped and knew it. They simply lacked the forces to resist. Octavius – who at some point, apparently, had escaped the city to join Metellus – would not engage with his army, fearing Cinna's strength.[23] Options vanished. The senate sent envoys back to Cinna, as consul. Realizing they could ask for little more in the way of terms, the senatorial envoys begged Cinna to swear an oath that he would shed no blood in the city. No oaths, retorted Cinna, but he promised he would not intentionally cause anyone's death. At some point in all of this, Octavius – perplexing this author as much as the readers – had returned to the city. Cinna pointedly instructed the senate to keep Octavius away from the Forum, lest something evil befall him in the inevitably approaching violence.[24]

Marius' Retribution

With that, Cinna, Marius, and their soldiers entered the city. That much is certain. Pretty much everything else is up for grabs, given the conflicting sources and the efforts to praise or slander Marius and Cinna. Marius, despite his renegade status, entered the city too. Appian asserts everyone essentially knew that allowing Cinna into the city meant that Marius was also allowed back in the city. Velleius Paterculus says that Cinna entered first alone, then passed a law recalling Marius, a law to nullify his current outlaw status. Plutarch sort of combines the possibilities. In his version, Marius peevishly said he would not set foot in the city until Cinna summoned the assembly and passed a law negating his exile and inviting him back, but impatiently entered the city after only a handful of the 35 tribes had voted. The kernel of Plutarch and Velleius' versions seems the most likely, especially since Appian's version does not strictly contradict them: Marius, who had never shied from leveraging the legitimacy of a hastily-passed law, agreed or encouraged some law of welcome to be passed, and Appian either did not see it in his sources or thought it not important enough to mention.[25]

Regardless of the precise legal details, Cinna and Marius now had the authority in Rome of conquerors at the head of an army. And so the murders began as Marius and Cinna reckoned with their enemies, real, potential, and imagined. Murder and looting were the fates for those they labelled foes.[26]

Here the sources again diverge significantly, reflecting the accusations, hearsay, and hopefully at least some solid truths of the sources all mixed together. This was a public and *ad hoc* purge of enemies. The city was in a fair amount of chaos. How did the consul Octavius die that terrible day? Not by the conquerors' hands, says Appian. Cinna and Marius had promised Octavius he would not be harmed, but insisted he leave the Forum for his own safety. When the occupiers took the Forum he reluctantly withdrew to the Janiculum, the hill named for the god Janus, with his aristocratic supporters and the few loyal remnants of his army.

Wearing his toga of office, he sat in his consular chair with fasces-bearing lictors in attendance. Censorinus – whoever that was; Appian does not say – attacked the consul with a squad of horsemen. Octavius' friends begged him yet again to flee the city, but he sat with dignity and awaited the equestrian murderers. Censorinus severed Octavius' head. It had the dubious honour to be the first head of a consul suspended in front of the Rostra, there in the Forum for all to see.[27] Not so, Plutarch suggested. Marius dispatched men to kill the consul before he and Cinna even entered the city. They found Octavius still in the Forum, hauled him off the Rostra and carved him like so much meat.[28] Velleius tersely dissents from both sources: Cinna sent the man who slew Octavius, how and where he does not say.[29]

But Octavius did die, probably horribly. So did many others, ultimately at Marius' and Cinna's command. Some were ostensibly charged with crimes and summoned to improvised courts; others just slaughtered. Merula, the senatorial appointee to replace Cinna as consul, cut his veins, and, as befitted a priest of Jupiter, died bleeding on the altars, calling upon the gods to punish Cinna.[30] Plutarch adds the pious detail that Merula removed his priest's cap before he did, because dying with the cap on was deemed a sin.[31] Lutatius Catulus, Marius' co-commander in the smashing victory at Vercellae in 101 BCE, was accused of crimes, but opted to end his own life by suffocation. He filled a freshly plastered room with charcoal smoke.[32] Catulus' friends had begged Marius to spare him. Marius only responded, 'HE must die.'[33] Marcus Antonius, accounted one of the finest orators, also had a death warrant that day. The soldiers sent to do the deed were charmed by his affability and eloquence, however, and it fell to a military tribune, who checked on the soldiers' progress, to murder Antonius and bring his head to Marius.[34] These were just the most prominent victims. Many died from trumped up charges or even more wanton murder as soldiers ran riot through the city.

Marius and Cinna had purged Rome of their enemies. Now they would claim the highest office as their prize. Cinna and Marius were elected to the consulships for 86. This was Cinna's second; it was Marius seventh. Though he had seized it by force, the ancient sources counted it as a seventh, and it placed Marius in a unique position not matched until the Republic had fallen and the autocrat Augustus would hold almost double the number. But Marius would not enjoy the office for long. He died from an undetermined illness a few weeks into his term in 86 BCE.[35] With Cinna's approval, Valerius Flaccus was appointed as the replacement consul for Marius. All the while, aristocrats steadily flowed from the city to travel east and join Sulla's camp.

The senate – assuredly with Cinna supervising – next dispatched consul Flaccus east along with the legate Gaius Flavius Fimbria and an army to deal with Mithridates. Appian suggests that Sulla had been declared a public enemy and Flaccus was tasked with curbing him. In the second century CE Memnon's version, which exists in fragments, the senate treated Sulla carefully. Flaccus should share the campaign with Sulla if he agreed to work together, or attack him if he did not.[36] Which is more likely depends on how strong Cinna and his supporters perceived their positions to be. Certainly, giving Sulla the option to collaborate was strategically wiser. Sulla's army had soundly defeated Mithridates' armies and allies in Greece more than once; Flaccus' force would not defeat it easily if the civil war continued.[37]

Sulla in the East and the Short Command of Fimbria

What happened to Flaccus' expedition is not exactly clear, since Appian and Memnon tell it somewhat differently. Neither's version would mean an auspicious outcome for the campaign. According to Appian, Flaccus' force suffered the worst luck from the start, a tempest drowning some in the crossing to Greece, and an attack on the vanguard that had crossed to Thessaly slaughtering more. To make matters worse, the soldiers resented Flaccus' harsh discipline, acceptable, perhaps, from a skilled commander but not from an incompetent one. Some soldiers deserted to Sulla. Flaccus' legate Fimbria, a far more skilled commander and with the soldiers' support, kept most loyal – loyal long enough for the expedition to reach the Roman province of Asia. Then Flaccus and Fimbria fell out when Flaccus sided with his quaestor over Fimbria in an argument. The slight stung, and so when Flaccus was away on a mission, Fimbria stole control of the army away from the assigned subordinate. When Flaccus returned, Fimbria forced him into hiding. Only for a short while: Fimbria hunted the consul down, cast his severed head in the sea and left his headless corpse unburied.[38] Memnon agrees that Flaccus' army suffered setbacks, but they were minor and the expedition made its way to Asia. The army clearly preferred legate Fimbria to consul Flaccus, however, and this rankled Flaccus. On one occasion Flaccus chastised Fimbria in public, and two of the more independently-minded soldiers murdered their commander outright. Word reached the senate. They were decidedly not happy but, with little option, confirmed Fimbria as the new commander of the Roman expeditionary force.[39] Judging whether Fimbria revolted or some soldiers did the murderous deed is a matter for an ancient law court. The practical outcome was the same: Flaccus had been murdered, and now Fimbria commanded the Roman army sent to engage Sulla.

Appian and Plutarch narrate the rest of Sulla's war against Mithridates, and the details need not detain us here.[40] Suffice to say, Sulla forced Mithridates to return to Pontus and make peace, but the residents of Asia were most perplexed by two Roman armies, those of Sulla and Fimbria, roaming the lands yet working against one another. Sulla was not one to leave a potential enemy in the field, however, and when he had curbed Mithridates, he turned his attention to Fimbria's forces.

Sulla closed with Fimbria's army near Pergamum and gave Fimbria a simple order: yield his illegal command and surrender his forces to Sulla. Fimbria cast the order back in his teeth: Sulla was the illegitimate proconsul, not he. When words failed, a siege forced the issue. Sulla's soldiers hemmed in Fimbria's army. Given a stark choice between being the besieger or the besieged, most soldiers deserted to Sulla. Those who remained refused Fimbria's pleas to fight: not for duty, not for money. Ruin awaited Fimbria. Stealing away to a temple of Aesculapius, he stabbed himself. The wound was not deep enough to do the job, however, and it fell upon an enslaved attendant to end his suffering.[41] Sulla now not only had successfully pacified Mithridates – only for the moment as it turned out, but for now, pacified – he had essentially doubled the size of his army should civil war continue. Sulla was coming to Rome for a reckoning.

The Road to a Reckoning

Sulla was coming.

By some accounts, Sulla never shied from his clear purpose to punish Cinna and the Marianists for wronging him during his years in the East.[42] Lest there be any uncertainty, Sulla wrote letters to the Senate crystalizing his intentions. He recounted his considerable résumé gained while serving the Republic: Numidia, the Cimbri, the Social War, and now, Mithridates. And what thanks had he received from Rome? His property destroyed and his friends murdered; his wife and children barely able to flee to him safely. The senate had declared him a public enemy, a menace to the Republic. But soon, very soon, Sulla would return, and he would punish those who wronged him. No one else need fear him.[43]

Cinna and Carbo had no doubt where they stood with Sulla. Appian declared them terrified, and with good reason. Sulla was a skilled commander. He and his cause were popular with the soldiers, as evidenced by the Fimbrian forces that defected to him. His soldiers were veterans. What could his foes do? If they chose to remain in Italy and hold onto their consular powers – however frail they might have been in practice – there was nothing to do but raise armies of their own and hope to contest Sulla's return. And so, Cinna and Carbo scoured Italy for funds, troops, and supplies. They made overtures to influential senators and noted to the newest citizens that they were in danger for their sakes, attempting to rekindle the issue of voting rights for the newly enfranchised. The senate had its own plans. They sent messengers on a peaceful mission to Sulla and ordered the consuls to cease their martial efforts and await Sulla peaceably. While Cinna and Carbo might have agreed outwardly, they continued their recruitment drive in Italy. For good measure, they proclaimed themselves consuls again for 84, without holding elections and without returning to Rome.[44]

Sulla was coming.

Cinna and Carbo shipped their new recruits to Liburnia, in the Balkan Peninsula just across the Adriatic from Picenum, to stage their defence there. The citizen-soldiers they recruited had their own ideas. After some capsized transport ships portended future doom, the soldiers grew reluctant. A death-struggle with the fellow citizens in Sulla's army had little appeal. Deserters streamed from Cinna's Liburnian camp. Matters came to a head when some recruits finally refused to cross to Liburnia at all. Cinna badly misread his soldiers and called them together for a brow-beating. They would have none of it. One of Cinna's lictors struck a soldier to make way for the consul. Another soldier in turn struck back at the lictor for good measure, not caring that he was challenging the consul's authority. Cinna demanded the arrest of the impertinent soldier.

Nearby recruits snapped at the order. Some hurled stones at Cinna. Others expressed their grim disapproval more decisively, stabbing the consul to death with their military daggers. Cinna died at the hands of his own army.[45]

Carbo could read these signs clearly enough and recalled the troops from Liburnia. He kept away from Rome at first, likely fearing its streets as a place where anyone, not least Sulla, could readily trap and kill him. Then some tribunes of the plebs issued an ultimatum: they would strip him of his rank if he did not return to hold consular elections for Cinna's replacement. Bad omens, however, including a lightning strike on the temples of Luna and Ceres, caused the elections to be postponed till later in the year, and Carbo remained sole consul in 84 BCE.[46]

And Sulla was coming.

In response to the senate's peace overtures, Sulla noted that he would not stop the city from forgiving the Marianists. He would never forgive. Nor would he disband his army.[47] Learning about the turmoil in Italy and Cinna's death, Sulla landed his army at Brundisium, the busy port in the heel of Italy, in 83. The Brundisians sensibly allowed him to land without interference.[48] Plutarch adds an anecdote. The soldiers knew Sulla's concerns that they might, as not untypically happened, disband upon reaching Italian soil. Instead they took a voluntary oath to stay under his command and do no harm to Italy unless ordered. They even went so far as to donate money to his expedition, but Sulla thanked them and declined the funds.[49] He did, of course, keep his soldiers in arms.

Here's how matters stood in 83 BCE. Carbo was proconsul of Italy and the Italian side of Gaul. Sertorius, another loyal Marian and a talented general for good measure, was propraetor of Spain but still actually in Italy. The two probably had some allied governors who commanded armies in Transalpine Gaul, Further Spain, Africa, and Sicily. They also enjoyed the loyalty of the two consuls for 83, Gaius Norbanus and Lucius Cornelius Scipio. The death of their most charismatic politicians, Marius and Cinna, certainly blunted somewhat their recruiting successes, but overall they were in a strong position. They had a fair amount of Italian support. Gaius Marius, son of the elder Marius and in his 20s, helped gain the support of Marius' former associates and clients. In addition, Carbo and Sertorius enjoyed the veneer of legitimacy as the seemingly lawful representatives of the Republic. For 83 they leveraged these advantages and recruited an army – perhaps 100,000, maybe more – to check Sulla. Sulla, on the other hand, had his five veteran legions and cavalry, some 40,000 soldiers, and some forces brought to him from Africa by the proconsul Metellus Pius – son of that Metellus Numidicus who found Marius an implacable foe. What his forces lacked in numbers they amply made up for with experience. These were no raw recruits; they were veterans tempered by the eastern wars. Determined to prevail, Sulla and his army made their way from Brundisium to Campania. [50]

Sulla was coming.

His forces marched without incident. He kept his troops under tight control, hoping thereby to win more support for his cause: Only his enemies need fear him, he had said. When he reached Campania, the consuls Norbanus and Scipio challenged him, each with a substantial army. Sulla and Norbanus' forces clashed near Casilinum and, though the details are mostly lost, Sulla seems to have killed 6,000 of Norbanus' soldiers and forced the rest of the army to hole up in Capua. Then Sulla moved to a position near Teanum to face Scipio's army. He sent peace overtures to Scipio's troops. Ultimately these overtures persuaded, and Scipio's legions joined Sulla. Once again, Sulla had acquired an army without striking a blow. For the remainder of 82, however, Sulla and Norbanus were in something of a standoff. Though defeated once, Norbanus' army was clearly still a force to be reckoned with, and the two armies dogged each other in Campania, attempting to subvert or destroy each other's allies in the region. Meanwhile more senators reportedly joined Sulla's cause, though many still hoped for a peace between Sulla and the Marians. With support wavering, Carbo returned to Rome to stiffen his faction's resolve. The assembly passed a law declaring all of Sulla's supporters enemies of the Republic. Carbo's efforts to shore up support seemed to succeed and clearly the war would last into the next year.[51] Still, Rome must have been a pretty joyless place. To make matters worse, a new calamity struck the city: the Capitoline hill burned along with all of its ancient temples, including some that had survived the Gallic sack three centuries before. It took no imagination to see the conflagration as a sign of the gods' displeasure, though some attributed it to Marian or Sullan sabotage. The signs were foreboding, whoever was responsible.

While these events transpired in Rome and Campania, a new player joined the fray in the north: young Gnaeus Pompey – later to be called

Pompey the Great. He was the son of that near-universally disliked Strabo, the commander of 88 who succumbed to plague or lightning. Pompey had drawn upon his family connections in Picenum to raise at least one legion of Strabo's veterans. Fresh from recruiting, young Pompey captured the pro-Marian city of Auximum, then worked his way south. The Marians sent three small forces against the upstart. Pompeius defeated them all handily, and then in the second half of 83 BCE made his way south and joined Sulla's forces. Sulla was pragmatic. Though in his early 20s, far too young even to have started the *cursus honorum*, let alone hold an office with *imperium*, Pompey had raised an army and defeated all comers. Sulla hailed him as *imperator* and kept him close at hand as a legate.[52] Marcus Licinius Crassus too raised some forces and allied with Sulla, just a few years older than Pompeius and, one day soon, a rival. Sulla accepted Crassus' contributions but did not seem to trust him with important commands as he did Pompey, surely a source of friction between the two aristocrats.[53]

At the end of 83, the civil war had not been settled. Sulla had grown more powerful, but Italy still seemed to support the Marian cause overall. Carbo chose to take the consulship personally for 82, his third in four years. This time he held office with yet another precocious youth, Gaius Marius, still in his mid 20s. The consuls levied new armies for the forthcoming year's campaign. 82 saw a handful of battles in Italy between forces commanded by Sulla, Metellus, and Pompeius against the consular armies of Carbo and Marius. Both Pompeius and Metellus apparently trounced Carbo, and a number of his troops switched to the Sullan side. Then Sulla defeated Marius soundly, and trapped the young consul and the remnants of his army in the Latin town of Praeneste. Nearby Rome was now vulnerable to Sulla. Reports of Sullan victories reached the city and the urban praetor, Lucius Junius Brutus Damasippus, arranged the mass murder of those senators who still maintained a show of neutrality in this polarized Republic. The atrocity did nothing to check Sulla's progress, and he seized the city gates then entered the city, with urban praetor Brutus and the forces he could muster fleeing before him.[54]

Sulla, Master of Rome

Sulla, at long last, had arrived. It was the second time in a decade that he had occupied Rome with an army. He stayed just long enough to sell off the property of his Marian rivals and, perhaps, to repeal his own enemy-of-the-Republic status. There were still Marian forces in Italy, however, so he kept moving. More battles followed between Sullan and Marian forces. The campaigns culminated in the decisive battle of the Colline Gate where Sulla defended Rome and defeated a Samnite army that, still resentful of Roman rule over the past two centuries, had joined the Marian cause. Word of the smashing victory reached Marius' army at Praeneste swiftly. Marius' forces soon surrendered and an enslaved person ended Marius' life. At the end of 82, Sulla had control of Rome and Italy. Though almost a decade of battles with Marian supporters in different parts of the Empire followed – most notably the formidable Sertorius in Spain – Sulla was now effectively master of Rome.[55]

His generals, especially the so-called 'Young Butcher', Pompey, pursued and slaughtered the remaining Marians in their seats of power over the next decade: Carbo in Africa, his allies in Sicily, and Sertorius in Spain. But Sulla was master in Rome. He called the people of the city together. A speech followed, and Sulla trumpeted his achievements, mollified the obedient, and terrified his enemies. Then he followed up his threat with action. Sulla had the grim honour in Republican history to be the first to launch an official proscription.[56] It worked like this. A list of enemies of the Republic – effectively Sulla's enemies – was drawn up. Any who killed one of these public enemies would earn a handsome reward. The property of the proscribed was seized by the state, which at this moment was synonymous with Sulla. The first draft of the list, according to Appian, included, 1,600 *equites* and forty senators. More were added. Appian offers a chilling description.

> Some of these, taken unawares, were killed wherever they were caught, in their houses, in the streets, or in the temples. Others were hurled through mid-air and thrown at Sulla's feet. Others were dragged through the city and trampled on, none of the spectators daring to utter a word of remonstrance against these horrors. Banishment was inflicted on some and confiscation on others. Spies were searching everywhere for those who had fled from the city, and those whom they caught, they killed.[57]

Sulla's slaughter extended outside the city, for he ensured that Italians who had supported the Marians tasted his vengeance too. Sometimes whole communities faced his wrath and citadels and walls were razed. He planted colonies of his soldiers in Italy onto land seized from those he had marked as enemies.[58]

Plutarch asserts that Sulla then simply made himself dictator. The nuance of Appian's account, however, provides a credible analysis of the details, especially since Sulla was very interested in the legality of things.[59] Constitutionally, there were no consuls alive to run the electoral assemblies that would elect their successors. Commonly this situation called for an interrex, a 'king between', a special five-day ruler whose essential task was to provide symbolic continuity in office – no leaderless savages were they, self-satisfied Romans told themselves – and assemble the centuriate assembly to elect consuls. Valerius Flaccus was the interrex, but instead of holding elections, another constitutional mechanism sprang into action, the dictatorship. Interrex Flaccus at Sulla's 'request' put a motion to the assembly to declare Sulla dictator. Appian hyperbolizes that no one had held this supreme executive office in four hundred years. Really it had been more like 130 years, the time of the great war against Hannibal. Still, quite a while ago.[60]

Sulla innovated here. Ordinarily a dictator held power for no longer than six months. Sulla's appointment ostensibly would last until he could re-establish the city, its laws, and the peace that had been torn apart by the civil wars of the past seven years. At least initially Sulla had little interest in breaking with established Republican custom any more than necessary. So consuls Marcus Tullius Decula and Gnaeus Cornelius Dolabella were elected for 81 BCE even though they would be subordinate to the dictator.[61]

Most importantly, during this dictatorship, Sulla to a large extent transformed the Roman Republic. He seems to have started from scratch, replacing any initial settlements he may have made in 87 before the war with Mithridates. Recently, a persuasive argument reassessing Sulla's arrangements suggests he imposed revolutionary changes to the Republic of Fabius Maximus, Cato, and even the Gracchi brothers. In short he created a new Roman political commonwealth. It maintained associations with the past through titles of offices and political concepts, but was fundamentally new. And so, in an odd way, the patrician dictator Sulla proved to be a more successful revolutionary reformer than the Gracchi or Drusus.[62]

The senate, 300 members on paper but depleted by the civil wars, Sulla enlarged, doubling it to 600. The new recruits were equestrians and municipal leaders from the Italian formerly-allies-now-citizens. Most would never hold any office at all since the rules for office-holding became, as we shall see, stricter. Primarily they would serve to staff the courts with juries, juries that Sulla transferred completely to this new senate. In effect, Sulla created a new multi-tiered status hierarchy, the majority – which included many new to senatorial status – holding few or no high political offices, and the inner circle of the nobles and high office holders. As for magistracies, Sulla systematized the rules. Each year 20 quaestors, 4 aediles, 8 praetors and 2 consuls were elected by the assemblies. Rather than depending on censors to enrol new senators, the 20 quaestors were automatically awarded senatorial status when their year in office was up. The office of the censor he eliminated, as well as the divisive title of *princeps senatus* that the censors traditionally granted. Minimum ages were imposed on the offices, with the quaestor open only to Romans aged 30 or more. No one could hold the same office until ten years had passed – a check to a future Marius.[63]

The way Sulla handled the tribunes of the plebs shows how he judged their role in the political violence of the past decades. He muzzled the office. No longer could a tribune propose and pass laws in the tribal assembly – though how Sulla envisioned the everyday legal needs of the Republic to be handled is not clear. A severely limited veto power. Most limiting of all, Sulla made the office a political dead-end by legislating that no tribune of the plebs was eligible for higher offices ever.[64]

There were other arrangements. Perhaps most striking for any potential rivals of Sulla, the dictator freed 10,000 enslaved people seized from the proscribed. Adopting their final enslaver's name, a Roman custom, meant there were 10,000 freedmen with the name of Cornelius in the city, Sulla's eyes and ears.[65]

All in all, however, the traditional Republic had ended. 'The new system,' notes historian Harriet Flower,

> relied almost entirely on the rule of law and on norms and guidelines that had been clearly encoded in Sulla's legislation. In other words, lex was to replace mos maiorum. The basic foundation of Sulla's republic was new, therefore, even to the extent of being a revolutionary

change in political life at Rome. At about the age of 60, Sulla the dictator effectively declared that a traditional republican system led by nobiles had failed within his own lifetime.[66]

For a moment, there would be a respite from the political chaos that had marked the system for much of the past five decades.[67]

Only for a moment. Some features of Sulla's system persisted. Others, like the tribunate and the censorship were restored after the dictator retired and soon died. Ultimately, the political rivalries that plagued the Republic did not end. It was, in many ways, simply the passing of generations. The Sullans and Marians gave way to what is sometimes called 'The Last Generation of the Roman Republic'.[68] And it is to this final generation of aristocrats in the Republic that we now turn.

Chapter 8

The Butcher and the Financier:
The Early Careers of Pompey and Crassus

B itter rivals were Pompey and Crassus, many sources say, each
rankling the other as far back as their first arrival on the political
scene during Sulla's second march on Rome. Crassus had pursued
a traditional aristocratic career. He had followed the rules. And yet
Pompey, some years younger, seemed to eclipse him with extra-legal
commands and honours. So Crassus looked for opportunities to thwart
his rival. As for Pompey, he was willing to scrap with Crassus too when it
suited him, going so far as to steal the latter's victory over the rebel army
of Spartacus. And so, when the two held the consulship of 70 together,
Plutarch asserts, 'As a matter of fact ... after they had been elected consuls,
they quarrelled and disagreed over everything.'[1] It is a convenient story
that has been circulated over the millennia: the grand rivalry of Pompey
and Crassus. But as so often is the case, the convenient story does not
hold up to investigation.

The 'Young Butcher', Pompey

Adulescens Carnifex – the Young Butcher – one source asserts that some
enemies called Pompey.[2] Certainly his early career was steeped in the
deaths of his enemies. Pompey, or Gnaeus Pompeius, as the Romans
knew him, was the son of the infamous Pompey Strabo, a man whose
corpse the public dragged through the streets of Rome, as sure a mark
of unpopularity then as ever. We know little about Pompey Strabo's
career beyond his military success at the start of the Social War and his
election to the consulship for 89. His achievements in the war were solid
but far from spectacular. He avoided losing the army of clients he had
raised in his homeland of Picenum by bursting free from the besieged
city of Firmum. This was his initial claim to fame. Still, in the desperate

early days of the Social War, avoiding disaster was success. As consul in 89, Strabo besieged the Italian rebel stronghold of Asculum. Pompey seemed to have had a role on his father's military council – his group of camp advisors that weighed in on military matters – but whether he was actually at Asculum is unclear. Either way, Strabo successfully captured Asculum and remained in command of his army as proconsul for 88 BCE.[3]

This was, of course, the year when all hell broke loose over the command against Mithridates, king of Pontus. The consul Sulla, as we saw in the last chapter, was assigned the command. Marius found a willing tribune and instigated a law to appropriate the Mithridatic command, instigating bloody riots in the process. Sulla fled to his army, persuaded them that his cause was theirs, and occupied Rome, crushing Marian opposition – for a moment. Strabo remained in the field in command of his army, and this posed a problem for Sulla. He distrusted Strabo; that much is clear because he ordered Strabo, no doubt with senatorial approval, to relinquish high military command. Strabo countered, finding a convenient tribune to block the recall. Sulla upped his game, again probably with senatorial support, and dispatched the consul Pompey Rufus (no relation or only slightly related to Strabo) to relieve Strabo of command. Rufus botched the transfer or, more precisely, Strabo's soldiers would have none of it. They murdered the consul less than a day after he assumed command while he set about performing the morning sacrifices. Strabo, perhaps the orchestrator, but regardless the prime beneficiary of the mutiny, resumed control of his army, and there was nothing Sulla or the senate could do to shake him loose of his loyal soldiers.[4]

And so, as we have seen, Sulla and his army left for the East, and Marius, lurking in wait, moved to seize Rome. Strabo soon departed the mix; he died from the plague that was making its grim round of the armies. Or perhaps he died from a stroke of lightning; this is also attested.[5] Soon after, in any event, the Marians occupied Rome. Strabo had few friends in death. Someone plunged a hook in his corpse and a crowd dragged it through the city. Some tribunes managed to stop this desecration, but they could not stop the public's hatred for Strabo.[6]

With his father dead, young Pompey was in a tough spot. Cinna pillaged his house at Rome, newly inherited from his father.[7] Yet somehow Pompey avoided making it onto the list of the proscribed and so avoided being slaughtered for his property. He successfully escaped conviction for extortion with the help of some powerful friends, engaged himself to the daughter of the praetor who presided over the trial, Antistia, and disappeared from the historical record for three years, presumably lying low in the turmoil of the Cinna years.[8]

Precocious Pompey Raises an Army

When Sulla began the march home from the east, and Cinna was murdered by his own troops (84 BCE), Pompey made a critical gamble: he began to levy troops of his own from his ancestral homeland of Picenum. The consul Carbo attempted to outbid his recruiting offers, unsuccessfully. Pompey levied an army, perhaps as large as three legions; though the only primary source, Cicero, felt no need to specify exact numbers.[9] Pompey also allied with some Romans who would be critical to him in later years: Titus Labienus and Lucius Afranius. Then he journeyed south, presumably to join forces with Sulla, though what the avenging patrician would make of this young upstart was anybody's guess. Carbo, dead Cinna's Marian colleague, sent armies – three, to be exact – to curb the audacious young Pompey. Pompey defeated the first in pitched battle, personally leading a magnificent cavalry charge to slay an allied Gallic commander and his troopers. The remaining two armies were insufficient to check Pompey's movements.[10]

Sulla's army, meanwhile, wended its way towards Rome. He made short work of one Marian army poised to check him at the Volturnus River. The second army defected to Sulla quickly enough, and Sulla was now positioned to move against Rome. Still, significant Marian forces remained in play and controlled much of Italy. The exception was Picenum in the north where Pompey's soldiers had carved a place for him at the bargaining table. For his victories against Marian armies, his soldiers had declared him 'Imperator', the formal term for an independent and victorious Roman general, one worthy of celebrating a triumph. When Pompey and his army reached Sulla, the veteran proconsul approached the youth on foot and honoured him greatly by repeating the title the soldiers had bestowed: Imperator![11] Pompey was not only far too young to be a consul and thus hailed as imperator, he had held no Roman public office to date. He was no more than an aristocratic youth with some pedigree, a status many in the ruling class could claim. Still, he had personally raised and commanded an army to victory. The audacious lad may well have felt he had earned that precocious salute given by his soldiers: Imperator![12]

As the Civil War continued, Pompey fought with Sulla's blessing as a legate.[13] After Sulla occupied Rome, Carbo fled to Africa while the Marian partisan Sertorius journeyed to Spain, both raising armies and continuing resistance from these regions. As we saw in the last chapter, in Rome Sulla claimed the dictatorship for re-establishing the Republic with all that entailed.

Pompey flourished under Sulla. He divorced Antistia and married Aemilia, Sulla's stepdaughter and the daughter of a consul, strengthening his standing in the aristocracy and with Sulla.

Antistia, about whom we know almost nothing, deserves a moment's recognition. She was divorced through no fault of her own, a casualty of political manoeuvres. But aristocratic marriages were political as much as anything else and she suffered the stigma of divorce simply because her name offered less to Pompey than Aemilia's.[14]

Aemilia was pregnant with her child from her first marriage when she was compelled to marry Pompey. The dictator demanded she and her husband Glabrio divorced. But neither seem to have welcomed the union, and it did not last. Poor Aemilia died giving birth shortly after marrying Pompey.

Pompey and the Marian Rebels

Fortunately for Pompey, civil wars remained to be fought and he, though very young, excelled at this. Sulla initially dispatched Metellus to counter Sertorius in Spain.[15] He needed Pompey to crush Marian resistance in Sicily. To do so with a semblance of proper legality, Sulla required the senate to give Pompey the powers of a propraetor. Pompey thus had a legal command – if one ignored the fact that he had never been a praetor and thus really should not have propraetorian powers. The Marian in command, Perperna, did not contest Sicily, fleeing instead. Carbo paused on the island momentarily then attempted to flee himself. Pompey's soldiers captured him in the act though, and he was humiliated in death, begging to be spared from Pompey's executioner. Carbo had defended Pompey when on trial for embezzlement several years earlier, but that did not persuade the Young Butcher to allow the miserable man an honourable suicide.[16]

After Sicily, came Africa. The senate under Sulla's thumb decreed the command in Africa to the extra-legal commander, and Pompey set off to slaughter more Marians. Marian rebels in Africa – or more precisely, Sulla's enemies – in Africa, like Domitius Ahenobarbus, were defeated. Pompey went a step further and operated independently of his assigned province, campaigning in Numidia and even installing a king. All was done in the name of Rome, but none of the arrangements were referred to the senate, as convention dictated. Through it all though, Pompeius' soldiers loyally followed him, saluting him as Imperator and bestowing on him the nickname Magnus, 'the Great'.[17]

It does not require particularly deep assessment to estimate the effects of all this success on young Pompey's psyche. He got his way. Soldiers followed him loyally. Honours and offices came to him early. He acted as the sole Roman authority in the field. He was the exception to the rule. He was Magnus. Nor was Pompey's run even close to complete after pacifying northwest Africa. In a moment of heightened tension Sulla wanted to relieve imperator Pompey of his command now that Africa was under control. Pompey informed his troops of Sulla's order and its natural consequence: if he did not return to Rome while still in command of his troops, he could not triumph. His soldiers, outraged, declared they would not abandon him and would instead follow him against Rome itself. Pompey begged them to stop short of rebellion. It was all quite dramatic, and Sulla got the message: Pompey was loyal, he was no revolutionary; but he would have the honours he believed he had earned.[18]

The Civil War in Spain

Sulla returned from his dictatorship in 79 BCE and soon died of an illness. But the shockwaves of the civil war continued. Meanwhile, Marius' partisan, Sertorius, had initially seized control of the province with an army of Romans, dislodging the elected praetors when they resisted. He then built a larger army with the addition of Spanish troops. Appian says he went so far as to create a 'senate' of 300 friends.[19] Considering he seems to have seen himself as a representative of legitimate Roman government, perhaps this detail is true. Metellus Pius had battled him for years but was no closer to pacifying the skilled general, in part because Sertorius relied on guerilla tactics to keep Metellus Pius off balance.[20] At some point Sertorius siphoned Perperna's troops when Perperna fled from Sicily to Spain. So in 76 the Roman ruling class, continuing Sulla's employment of the Young Butcher, dispatched Pompey to handle the matter.[21]

The general outline of Pompey's time in Spain matches in Plutarch and Appian's accounts. He began by trekking his army overland to counter Sertorius. He had a rough start: Sertorius' army slaughtered a whole legion out foraging. While Pompey could do nothing but watch, Sertorius' army went on to take at least one Roman city, Lauron, while Pompey watched, outmanoeuvred. Pompey and Metellus joined forces however, and continued the fight. Over time there may have been friction, says Appian, between Sertorius' Roman and Spanish troops, and Sertorius may have come to prefer the latter, sparking further resentment.[22] It is certainly plausible since Spanish troops were available and Roman troops in short supply. Still Sertorius fought on, and still Pompey and Metellus were not able to win a decisive victory. In the end Sertorius did not actually lose a battle. Rather Perperna and a conspiracy ring got him drunk at a banquet and murdered him.[23] Perperna tried to threaten and bribe Sertorius' soldiers now under his command. To say there was a morale problem in what was once Sertorius' army, however, is to put it mildly. And so in a final encounter – Metellus had left the matter in Pompey's hands – Pompey's troops mopped up Perperna's demoralized army. Reputedly poor general Perperna offered little help, hiding in a thicket before the battle was over. Pompey's cavalry apprehended him. Perperna tried to prolong his life by hinting at all the secrets he could reveal to Pompey through surrendering Sertorius' letters from secret allies in Italy. Pompey declared he did not want the burden of that knowledge, put Perperna to death and, so he said, burned the letters.[24] One cannot help but wonder if he kept them for future leverage or at least read them.

Marcus Licinius Crassus' Early Career

Unlike Strabo, Crassus' father and brother died in Cinna and Marius' bloodbath. How exactly is not clear. Plutarch intimates they were slain in the city by the Marians, and Diodorus Siculus says the father was slain in the senate chamber. Appian asserts the two initially escaped the Marians and the father slew the son as an act of mercy but was captured before he could kill himself.[25] Cicero, who lived through the proscriptions and was in the best place to know, indicated the two took their own lives to avoid falling prey to the Marians.[26] In any event, Crassus, shorn of protection, had to flee. He reportedly went to Spain to hide for a time, and then when Cinna died joined Metellus Pius in Africa, but after a falling out made his way to Sulla.[27] Sulla must have trusted him to some extent for Crassus was dispatched to raise troops when Sulla had reached Italy.

Plutarch suggests that the rivalry between Crassus and Pompey arose from Sulla's treatment of the two. The younger Pompey had honours and commands heaped upon him while the elder Crassus did not. This seems not to be the whole truth however, for Appian notes that Pompey and Crassus commanded together at Spoletium in 82, suggesting they could at least work together.[28] Plutarch reports too that Crassus commanded Sulla's right wing to victory at the decisive battle of the Colline Gate – though Appian makes no mention of this.[29] True, Pompey's rise was precocious and unmatched, a potential source of envy, but Crassus hardly withered in Sulla's regime. Quite the contrary: his contemporaries and later sources knew well that he had acquired a fortune during the proscriptions. So had many.[30] But Roman writers tended to moralize more explicitly about Crassus' gains. Cicero notes explicitly that Crassus along with Sulla profited, shamelessly in his opinion, by auctioning off property, seizing it from legitimate owners, and transferring it to strangers who could pay the price. Plutarch goes on to accuse Crassus of opportunistic, if not extortionate, real estate deals: when a house was on fire he would offer to purchase both the burning house and the ones adjacent to it for a pittance; the latter owners would be more likely to sell because they feared their property would be part of the general conflagration. Then Crassus extinguished the houses as needed with a force of skilled enslaved labourers.[31] And of course there were always the rumours that floated about: Pliny, that first-century CE encyclopedist, alleged Crassus had a pair of astronomically expensive and beautiful goblets, but 'he was too ashamed to ever use them', by implication because of the way he had obtained them.[32]

Crassus was more than a mere profiteer however. He used his wealth to build connections, lending rather generously without interest to his friends, though insisting that repayment be on the exact due date.[33] He had a reputation for generosity that extended to strangers. His house, reports Plutarch, was open to anyone who might visit.[34] He also used his skill as an orator to serve as a legal advocate widely, building networks within the Roman elite and commoners.[35] If one reads past the insults, Cicero grudgingly acknowledged his competent oratory:

> He had moderate theoretical training and even less natural talent, but by toiling diligently and using his dedication and influence to defend cases successfully, he stood for some years among the foremost advocates. He used proper Latin in his oratory and diction that was not commonplace, and his organization was carefully considered, but there was nothing decorative or brilliant, and the intensity of his feeling was not matched by his delivery: virtually everything was spoken in a monotone.[36]

And Plutarch notes that he was always ready to speak on behalf of a client. Further, where Pompey had a level of condescension in his conversations with social unequals, Crassus reportedly put on no airs and treated all with a degree of kindness.[37] Thus he built a wide network of friends and allies. So, while Pompey was off doing the military work of Sulla's regime and murdering Marians, Crassus took advantage of his time in the city to build his political networks and financial resources. This helped him rise to the praetorship in 73 BCE.

The Spartacus Revolt

Soon an opportunity for glory presented itself to Crassus, who had had to be content with building a political network while his rival Pompey was off accruing still more military victories. Spartacus and his army of the formerly enslaved had rebelled, providing the opportunity. Plutarch and Appian recount the episode and a number of other sources mention the rebels, notably because they proved so difficult to crush. Essentially Spartacus, an enslaved gladiator of Thracian origin, and a group of comrades at the gladiatorial school in Capua (interestingly enough the Latin word for a school for children and a collective of enslaved gladiators, *ludus*, was the same) overthrew their enslavers and gained freedom. They were initially based at Mount Vesuvius and were joined over time by other enslaved fugitives and perhaps even, says Appian, by free Italians.[38] The growing rebel army defeated two praetors, Clodius Glaber and Publius Varinius, seized weapons and armour from the defeated soldiers, and grew stronger as tens of thousands flocked to Spartacus.[39] What had seemed a minor disturbance had grown into a significant threat, and, in 72 BCE, the senate dispatched the consuls Lucius Gellius and Gnaeus Cornelius Lentulus to deal with the growing menace of Spartacus' rebel army. Gellius snared a detachment of the rebel army and crushed it, but simultaneously Spartacus' main force defeated Lentulus' army.[40] Then for good measure the rebel army made its way northwards – perhaps to leave Italy via the Alps – and defeated the forces of Cassius, the governor of Cisalpine Gaul.[41] Yet, for some reason, Spartacus' army did not leave Italy.

And so an opportunity for Crassus presented itself. He acquired a command against the rebel army. The technical details are a bit puzzling. Appian states no one was willing to run for the office of praetor for 72, fearing Spartacus' army, so Crassus volunteered to be elected praetor, but Appian seems to have been confused.[42]

1. Crassus had just been a praetor in 73, and probably did not hold the office twice;
2. The consuls had failed to defeat Spartacus and his army, so there is little reason to suppose that they would opt to dispatch a praetor next, who typically commanded fewer legions than a consul;
3. Provinces for praetors were generally chosen by lot, and Appian suggests Crassus specifically volunteered to be sent against Spartacus.

This final detail may be the key. Plutarch also specifically states the senate chose Crassus, and this may mean he held a special command granted to him while he was a *privatus*, a private citizen.[43] The detail that he commanded an army of six legions, much larger than those ordinarily commanded by a praetor, and that his army would include the armies of the two consuls, also suggests this was a special command.[44]

Why did the senate choose him for this task? Well, the current consuls had proved ineffective and the go-to commanders Pompey and Lucullus were already abroad on military campaigns. Perhaps, as Appian seems to suggest, though in a confused manner, the senate sought volunteers, and Crassus was the only one. Or it is possible that Crassus offered to fund the six legions out of his own pocket, and that tipped the balance in his favour.[45]

Crassus certainly did not lack audacity, in that he accepted a special command against an army that had killed thousands of Romans and defeated a handful of praetors and two consuls. Despite some differences in the details, the general outline of Plutarch and Appian's accounts is not too problematic. Early in Crassus' command, both sources agree, he punished some of his soldiers for their defeat using the brutal disciplinary technique known as decimation: every tenth soldier was beaten to death by the other nine. The sources, however, do not agree at all which units he decimated. Appian offers two versions: Crassus decimated the defeated soldiers who had fought under the consuls, or he decimated his own army after losing its first engagement against Spartacus, an engagement that he does not otherwise refer to.[46] Plutarch differs, suggesting Crassus decimated a group of 500 soldiers who had fled in a minor battle while his legate, Mummius, was in command. Perhaps this is the engagement Appian cursorily mentions. In any event, Spartacus and his army headed south and attempted to cross from the toe of Italy, the region of Lucania, into Sicily.[47] Plutarch provides the detail that Spartacus attempted to negotiate passage across the strait with Cilician pirates; the pirates betrayed his army, however, leaving it stranded on the Italian shore at Rhegium.[48] Crassus' army then built a siege wall on the landward side trapping Spartacus' army on the shore.

At this point, Pompey seems to have returned from Spain with his army to Italy, ready to celebrate a triumph over Sertorius. Plutarch suggests Crassus wrote to the senate at about this point, asking them to recall Pompey from Spain and Lucullus from his war against Mithridates so that they could aid the effort against Spartacus.[49] Appian vaguely suggests that 'the Romans' decided to send Pompey and his recently arrived army south. Both agree, however, that Crassus was eager to conclude the campaign without Pompey's assistance. Here the accounts differ more but they agree that Spartacus' army broke free of its pinned position in Rhegium, marched either towards Mount Petelia in Lucania or Brundisium, but ultimately turned and faced Crassus' forces in a pitched battle.[50] Crassus' troops won decisively, and only a few thousand rebels survived.[51] Appian asserts that Crassus pursued the remnants piecemeal and in the process crucified 6,000 rebels on the road from Capua to Rome, brutal even for a Roman and perhaps an indication of how much they feared revolts of those they had enslaved. Appian does not mention any actual involvement of Pompey and his army.[52] Plutarch, however, suggests that several thousand of the defeated rebels were caught escaping by Pompey's army, which crushed them and the final embers of the revolt. Ampelius, the third century CE author who wrote a summary of world history as he knew it, sometime after the reign of Emperor Trajan, agrees with Plutarch: Pompey mopped up.[53] As a result, Pompey, says Plutarch, wrote a letter to the senate snatching some of Crassus' glory, claiming that Crassus may have won a pitched battle but he, Pompey, actually extinguished the revolt.[54]

Did Pompey claim the credit? Possibly, and it certainly fits the conventional understanding that the two were bitter rivals. Still, it is not certain Pompey ever made this claim, but even if he did, it did not mark any serious effort to steal Crassus' glory.[55] Ultimately, Pompey claimed his second triumph for the wars in Spain, not for any action against enslaved rebels. So either he did not make the claim or was largely unsuccessful in his attempt.

As for Crassus, the senate granted him a considerable honour by allowing him to celebrate an ovation, a sort of junior triumph. It was a highly appropriate honour for a victory against enslaved foes, which for the Romans was more than a bit ignominious. The senate paid Crassus a considerable honour even allowing the ovation, but they went one step further and authorized him to wear a crown of laurel leaves, normally only worn in a triumph, instead of the normal myrtle leaves of an ovation. Considering this was all in war against rebelling slaves, the senate essentially paid Crassus considerable honour in these celebrations.[56] Again there is no substantial evidence that Pompey seized credit in the aftermath.

Late in 71 BCE, then, when Spartacus' revolt had been extirpated, both Crassus and Pompey were in Italy and in command of armies. Both would seek the consulship for 70. Presumably both would need permission to run *in absentia*. They remained in command of their armies, and a proconsul's *imperium*, the power to command, ended when they crossed the sacred boundary into Rome. Crassus had the better claim to the office. The law Sulla had established, based on the much earlier Lex Villia Annalis

(c. 180 BCE), formalized the *cursus honorum*: to run for office, a consul had to have served as praetor and be at least the minimum age, 42. Crassus fitted both these criteria. Pompey, on the other hand, had neither qualification. He was in the anomalous position of having prosecuted two wars and sought two triumphs – the second sometime at the end of that very year – without ever having held an elected office, or at least not the ones required by Sulla's *cursus*.[57]

So Pompey was the wild card, and Plutarch suggests there was more than a little concern at Rome when Pompey did not immediately disband his army. Some spread rumours that Pompey would use that army to occupy Rome and seize power, just as Sulla had – for the second time – a bit over a decade before.[58] Pompey seems to have been clear from the beginning, however, that he kept his soldiers in arms because he sought to celebrate a triumph. This certainly is consistent with what we know about triumphal procedures: the army participated in the general's triumph. And, as it turned out, Pompey did triumph over Spain on the last day of the year, entering his consulship of 70 the very next day.[59] His army is never mentioned again, so Pompey, true to his word, had disbanded it. The suggestion Appian makes that he kept his Spanish army encamped near the city even while serving as consul would be revolutionary in itself and need strong corroboration for us to entertain it. There is none.[60]

Still, Pompey did have an army close at hand when he ran for consul. Did he essentially coerce the senate into allowing him to run for the office? For the candidacy to work, legally, the senate ultimately did excuse Pompey from Sulla's law on officeholding – Pompey had never been praetor, and he was still too young.[61] Did the senate do so because it feared Pompey would occupy the city with his army and force through his consulship? Plutarch certainly seems to suggest people feared this. But a reasonable case has been made that Pompey had other political options at his disposal and was not even remotely in the desperate sort of position that would necessitate an act of rebellion. Fresh from a victorious war and about to head into a triumph, he could persuade his allies to stall elections, for example, and wait for popular sentiment to carry his claim.[62] Was there any armed standoff? Appian suggests that at the end of 71 Crassus kept his soldiers in arms simply because Pompey would not dismiss his.[63] This is certainly possible, but it is surprising that no other source mentions it, when effectively it was an armed impasse of the type common in the civil wars. It also makes a bit puzzling Plutarch's insistence that Crassus sought and gained Pompey's express approval – even eager support – to run for the consulship of 70 himself.[64] So, probably, Appian is mistaken here. And, indeed, throughout his career, Pompey seems to have consistently refrained from seizing control of offices and honours through his legions, preferring to be granted them by senate and people.

Pompey and Crassus: Consuls of 70

Pompey and Crassus were elected consuls for 70 BCE and took up their offices at the start of the year. It was a momentous year, not least because of the consuls. They took several steps to dismantle some of Sulla's arrangements. They held the first election for censors since 86. There must have been support for the restoration of the censors, but the consuls, as the presidents for the electoral assembly, had decisive influence over whether elections were held at all.

As the newly-elected censors drafted the list of citizens and their wealth ratings, an exceedingly rare circumstance arose. Part of completing the census required officially discharging any member of the cavalry class who had completed their required years of military service with a state-supplied warhorse, the *equites equo publico*. The Roman rider in question would publicly testify to his service record on the occasion. On the day of the review, Pompey seized the opportunity for a little self-aggrandizement. He came unexpectedly up to the censors' stand with his horse. Everyone watching, it seemed, was delighted. Then one of the censors asked Pompey whether he had, in fact, performed his required military service. Pompey was in the rather unique position of answering not only **had** he performed his required ten years of service, he had done so **under his own command** as imperator. The crowd reportedly gave a shout and they and the censors escorted Pompey home in an impromptu parade.[65] It was the kind of accolade Pompey loved.

More momentous than restoring the censors, Pompey and Crassus also restored the powers of the plebeian tribunes that Sulla had stripped: the right to veto and the right to introduce legislation directly to the assembly.[66] A considerable amount of popular support for this had been brewing over the last few years. In 75 the consul Gaius Aurelius Cotta 'with the great eagerness of the people and the nobility unwilling' removed the Sullan arrangement that tribunes could hold no higher office, making the office politically viable once again for a young Roman aristocrat with political ambitions.[67] The next year, the tribune Lucius Quinctius pressed to restore to the tribunes their pre-Sullan powers.[68] In 73 the tribune Macer continued the pressure to restore the office to its full powers. He may even, if a speech fragment from Sallust's partially preserved *Histories* can be trusted to this extent, have called on Pompey to make it happen. Indeed, by the end of 71, Pompey as consul-elect announced his intent to do just this. All that was left, then, was to officially restore the office's powers. It is an action whose significance can hardly be overemphasized. In the years ahead Pompey would personally and politically benefit from tribunes proposing laws directly to the assembly on his behalf. Then, too, powerful tribunes intent on legislating without the support of the senate would continue to be a force in the final decades of the Republic.[69]

Less significantly, but worth mentioning, the praetor Marcus Aurelius Cotta, doubtless with Pompey and Crassus' approval, shifted the juries of the public courts yet again from the exclusive preserve of the senate – Sulla's arrangement – to a combination of senators and *equites*.[70]

At this point it is reasonably clear that Plutarch's assertion, 'As a matter of fact ... after they had been elected consuls, they quarrelled and disagreed over everything,' simply does not hold up. We have seen several important issues upon which Pompey and Crassus agreed. Plutarch, indeed, does not provide even a single example of the two consuls conflicting.[71] The bitterness of their rivalry seems overstated at the least.

Pompey in the 60s: Pirates and Potentates

Pompey and Crassus expressly did not take provinces at the end of their consulship and went politically quiet for a while. The decade had approximately begun with the dictatorship of Sulla and ended with Pompey and Crassus repealing some critical parts of the dictator's programme. Over the course of that decade-or-so, Crassus seems to have pursued a traditional yet highly distinguished political path, exercising influence among his peers. Pompey, however, went on to even greater military exploits, success that earned him the jealousy, if not hostility, of many senators at Rome. It is also in this period that the careers began of

Gaius Julius Caesar and Marcus Porcius Cato – two who would have a great deal of impact on the political landscape.

In the summer or autumn of 60 BCE, Crassus, Pompey, and Caesar, in part because of their rivalry with Cato, would form a political pact to gain Caesar the coveted consulship. And the dissolution of that pact led about a decade later in 49 to the second civil war and the effective end of the Republic. So, the rising politicians of the 70s and 60s are what one historian dubbed 'The Last Generation of the Roman Republic'.[72] And so with one contingency causing another and ending in civil war, it is important to investigate what can be said about Pompey and Crassus in the decade before the formation of that pact called the First Triumvirate. We shall see a bit more of Cato in the next chapter.

Pompey's exploits in the 60s are the best documented, for he assumed two very important, prestigious and powerful commands that brought him great wealth and distinction, though not without accompanying political headaches. After his consulship, he seems to have been quiet for a couple of years. The next opportunity for military distinction came in 67 BCE. The problem of piracy had peaked in the Mediterranean, and Roman efforts to deal with the problem, such as they were, had not made the sea any safer. So in 67 the tribune Gabinius – since tribunes now could pass legislation directly through the assembly again – proposed that a special command be granted to a Roman senator of consular rank: a charge to eliminate the pirate menace. To that end, the chosen commander would have access to considerable resources: two hundred warships, troops as required, and funds from the public treasury. The commander would also have extensive *imperium* across the entire Mediterranean sea and all its islands and coastline up to a distance of 50 miles inland from the shore. When one looks at a map and remembers that most of the Roman empire lay within 50 miles of some Mediterranean shores, the massivity of this command becomes clear. Pompey was not explicitly named as the recipient of this special and sweeping command, but word on the street was that the people would assuredly vote him to fill the post if the law passed. And so, despite significant opposition from leading senators, the law passed, soon followed by the expected law granting Pompey this special command.[73]

Pompey fulfilled his charge swiftly and effectively, sweeping along the pirates before his forces so that they ultimately gathered in their home territory of Cilicia. Pompey crushed the pirates and captured their base, Coracesium. In victory he showed mercy; instead of crucifying or scourging to death the pirates, he deported them to various inland territories and set them to farming. The whole thing took only a few months and earned Pompey some extra hostility from those whose *imperium* he had encroached upon in the process.[74] But what a glorious operation!

Now, his work essentially done, Pompey managed, again with the help of another recently-empowered tribune, to seize another prestigious military command. This time a tribune persuaded the assembly to replace Lucius Licinius Lucullus as commander in the new war against Mithridates. A little background should help here. In 74 BCE king Nicomedes IV of Bithynia died, willing his kingdom to the Roman people. The Romans lost little time in occupying the province, putting them into conflict again with Mithridates who had his own interests in the region. Lucullus had been assigned the command against Mithridates in 74, when Pompey was still in Spain hunting Marians. Lucullus swiftly defeated Mithridates in Asia. The king fled and gained asylum with his son-in-law, king Tigranes of Armenia. By 70, Lucullus had gained control of Mithridates' entire kingdom of Pontus. Lucullus thought the war was over; he held a victory celebration at Ephesus and notified the senate of his achievement. All that remained was to extract Mithridates from his refuge in Armenia. The senate confirmed this understanding, sending the customary ten-person commission to aid Lucullus in making peace settlements in Pontus. By 69, however, diplomatic efforts to apprehend Mithridates had failed; Lucullus prepared to invade Armenia. This segment of the war had not concluded by 66 when the tribune Manilius, with considerable senatorial support and an enthusiastic populace, passed a law transferring the war to Pompey's command.[75]

And so, Pompey began what would become his legendary eastern campaigns of the 60s. He defeated Mithridates, who had again raised an army in Asia Minor, and went on to invade Armenia and force Tigranes to terms that included the surrender of all the territories he had conquered. But Pompey was not finished; he then led his armies into the territories of Syria and Mesopotamia formerly controlled by Tigranes and seized control of them in the name of the Republic. He even worked his way down to Palestine, intervened in Judaean politics, and captured Jerusalem. By 62 he had finished the campaigns ostensibly linked to the

Mithridatic War, and many others in addition, and reported his victory to the senate. The senate in turn declared ten days of thanksgiving.[76]

We will come back to Pompey and his return to Rome from his eastern campaigns at the end of the next chapter. Now it is time to see a bit more of Crassus' activities in the City and investigate a case of rivalry turned into conspiracy in Rome while Pompey was away: the conspiracy of Lucius Sergius Catilina to seize power at Rome.

Chapter 9

The Orator and the Conspirator: Cicero and Catiline

It was the last straw. Lucius Sergius Catilina, Catiline as moderns call him, had run yet again for the consulship and lost yet again. His noble patrician ancestry demanded that he make his way up the *cursus honorum*, but the voters continued to support less worthy candidates like that new man Marcus Tullius Cicero. It was time for fire and blood, for revolution. So he sent his co-conspirator Gaius Manlius to Faesulae in Etruria to muster revolutionaries and others to Picenum and Apulia. He planned arson and plotted to murder the consul Cicero, who had stolen the office that was rightfully his. But his plans proved too slow in execution, so he planned some more, summoning his chief conspirators, agents he had cultivated, like Publius Cornelius Lentulus Sura and Gaius Cornelius Cethegus. They met in the dead of night at the house of ally Marcus Porcius Laeca.

Strikingly, a rarity that merits pause, the first-century historian Sallust notes a woman among the chief conspirators at these nocturnal meetings: Sempronia. If only we could know more about this clearly formidable agent and not be limited to Sallust's prejudices against a capable woman.

Amongst [the conspirators] was Sempronia, who had often performed many deeds of manly daring. This woman was quite fortunate in her lineage and appearance, and in her husband and children besides; learned in Greek and Latin literature, she played the lyre and danced more elegantly than is necessary for a virtuous woman; and there were many of the other things which abet luxury. Yet, to her, everything was always dearer than respectability and chastity. Whether she was less sparing of her money or her reputation, you could not have easily decided: her lust was so inflamed that she more often sought men than was sought by them;

but often before now she had betrayed her trust, abjured credit, been an accessory to murder. Through luxury and indigence she had fallen headlong. Still, she was in no way intellectually inept: she could write verse, produce a joke, and indulge in conversation which was either restrained or tender or provocative; in fact, she had considerable wit and considerable charm.[1]

Sallust's is a textbook hatchet job condemning Sempronia with grudging praise for not conforming to the gender expectations of male Roman writers. Clearly, though lost to us, the measured praise between the criticism indicates there was so much more to Sempronia.[2]

Catiline chided them all for insufficient resolve, laid bare his master plan for revolution and sought two assassins who would eliminate the chief obstacle to his plans: Cicero. The murder of a consul shocked the sensibilities of many present, but two, the senator Lucius Vargunteius and the equestrian Gaius Cornelius, did not shy from the gruesome task.[3] So Sallust reports in his account *On the Catiline Conspiracy* written a couple of decades after the events.[4]

But Cicero, consul in 63 BCE, was not without his own spies. One plant, Curius, witnessed the night meeting of the conspirators at Laeca's house. He reported it to his lover (Fulvia) who dutifully passed the information on to the consul. So when the assassins appeared at Cicero's door the next day, he forbade them entry.[5] Either later that day or the next, Cicero convened the senate. It is not at all clear that he knew whether Catiline would attend, but he did. It is not at all clear today what his motives were with his speech.[6] Whatever the intention, Cicero denounced Catiline in shockingly strong language, the first of four speeches he would deliver against Catiline over the course of the month.[7] The barbed claims made in that first verbal foray:

- Catiline had plotted to murder many, perhaps all of the senators, along with the consul Cicero.
- The armed rebel force in Etruria that the senate had recently become aware of, under the command of Manlius, was Catiline's doing.
- Catiline had planned to murder the nobles of the senate a couple of weeks before but had been thwarted by the constant watch of Cicero's vigilant guards.

- During the secret nocturnal meeting at Laeca's house, the conspirators designated the various areas of Italy they would raise in rebellion, and the various places in the city they would torch, in addition to renewing their commitment to kill Cicero.

But Cicero knew, he crowed at Catiline. He had his informants. He knew the whole grand plan of destruction, fire, murder, and revolution. Indeed Cicero knew, he announced in the senate, that Catiline had plotted to murder him several times this past year, not including yesterday's attempt that he had thwarted.[8] As a result of this speech, Catiline fled the city and went to join Manlius and the army he had raised. It looked as if another civil war had come.

Here is the problem for modern historians. There is little doubt Catiline conspired in some manner to secure political power for his own benefit and the benefit of his allies. This conspiracy may stretch back as far as the consular elections of 64 BCE.[9] And there is no reason to doubt that Catiline's focus on cancelling debts was appealing to many in his circle. Whether that conspiracy mostly focused on the not-uncommon practice of bribing Catiline into the consulship, however, or was something truly incendiary is not clear. Surely Plutarch's claim that the lead conspirators sealed their oaths with the blood of a sacrificed child is a bit of an exaggeration? Nor does the assertion that Catiline planned to systematically destroy the City and the Republic, central to Cicero's claims, hold up well to scrutiny.[10]

It is more certain, however, that Catiline left the city after Cicero's speech, and he died at the head of a rebel army in Etruria early in 62 BCE.[11] More than our usual assortment of only secondary accounts, when it comes to Catiline's conspiracy we have the testimony of two Romans who were there, a bounty of primary sources the likes of which one almost never finds for earlier periods in the Republic. The first, Gaius Sallustius Crispus, or Sallust as moderns call him, wrote several histories in the middle of the first century. One short text was devoted wholly to Catiline's conspiracy. Sallust was in his early twenties when Catiline's conspiracy, whatever exactly it was, was hatched, and he certainly should have had access to credible accounts. But he was a moralizer whose subject was an enemy of the state, and he went out of his way to demonize Catiline.[12] His take is riddled with internal inconsistencies, and there are clearly cases where he took datable events and rearranged them out of chronological order to serve his purposes.[13] Our other witness is perhaps even more problematic: that consul of 63, Cicero. Cicero's speeches against Catiline are rhetorical edifices designed to persuade the senate and the people of Rome that Catiline was the most foul of miscreants and that he and his co-conspirators deserved death. Some might suggest he made up most of the details to fabricate a single grand plot with Catiline as the mastermind. This seems excessively sceptical. Still, Cicero clearly benefitted from Catiline's condemnation. The more evil Catiline appeared to the Romans, the grander his conspiracy, the greater Cicero's accomplishment appeared as consul in thwarting him. And Cicero, like every Roman aristocrat, was particularly attentive to situations that would make him look good.[14] So it is not beyond possibility that Cicero fabricated some of the charges in his first speech against Catiline.

And so, much modern discussion has ensued. Did Catiline actually plot to murder Cicero, or plot anything revolutionary for that matter, before the fateful day that Cicero verbally attacked him in the senate? On that note, had Catiline truly orchestrated the revolutionary army Manlius had recruited in Etruria, the army Catiline seems to have joined after he quit the city? And finally, did Catiline direct the incendiary and murderous plots of the conspirators who remained in the city after he left? Cicero connects this all into a grand tapestry of mayhem, as does Sallust. Whether one accepts it as such really comes down to whether one believes Cicero's claims had to have a core of truth to fit the sensibilities of his audience in the senate and Forum. Not every historian does; one historian declared that Cicero was either 'guilty of gross exaggeration at least', or 'guilty of fabrication on a grand scale', and others have expressed doubts.[15] Nor is Cicero's credibility the only problem facing those who want to reasonably reconstruct Catiline's activities. For Plutarch, Appian, and Dio Cassius also give accounts of one conspiracy or another involving Catiline, and their details are not always consistent, nor is it always clear whether they date Catiline's conspiracy to his run for the consulship in 64 or to his run in 63 – he ran for the office at least twice. Some, like Sallust, allege that Catiline plotted consistently through both elections. Plutarch and Dio assert that Catiline tried to have Cicero assassinated during the consular elections of 63.[16]

So what can be said with any confidence? First, it is simply unprovable that Catiline plotted a destructive revolution as early as 65 and continued to plot until his open break with the Republic in November 63. Catiline, judging by his public actions, was trying to play the game of Republican politics, not end the Republic. We can be confident of this, not least because he tried to run for the consulship in 65 and did run for the consulship in 64 and 63. He was unsuccessful every time. The salient point, however, is that he tried to win election, hardly the move of a true revolutionary.

The election held in July 63 for the consulships of 62 seems the most crucial. During this bid, Catiline first associated, so far as we can determine, with Gaius Manlius who would lead the revolutionary army in Etruria at the end of the year. Manlius was the leader of a group of disgruntled veterans of Sulla.[17] The failed effort to secure the consulship yet again seems to be a significant factor that set Catiline on a revolutionary bent.[18] Connected or not, Manlius' activities forming a revolutionary army from a band of dissatisfied Sullan colonists arose a few months after the election, towards the end of October 63.

From that point we get into the period covered by Cicero. So this is what seems can reasonably be said from the time of Cicero's delivery of the first Catilinarian speech in early November 63 BCE. Catiline sat and listened to Cicero's blistering tirade, then implored the senate not to let this new man, this 'resident alien' as he scornfully labelled Cicero, sully his patrician name. The senate reportedly shouted him down. And so Catiline left the senate and the city to join the rebel army with Manlius in Etruria. Sallust says it was in part because Catiline now knew the City was too vigilant to fall prey to arson. At least one historian has noted that devastating accidental fires were a common plague on Roman city life, so it seems probable that even an unskilled arsonist could easily have torched large sections of the city if he had wished.[19] Be that as it may, Catiline made his way to Manlius and the rebel army in Etruria.[20] Probably. There was some rumour that Catiline had not gone to Etruria but instead had taken a longer journey to Massilia. Cicero explicitly noted the strength of this rumour and challenged it in the speech he delivered to the crowds in the Forum.

Over the next few weeks in late November 63, a second conspiracy developed that seems to be connected with Catiline.[21] Two of the chief conspirators still in the city when Catiline had left, Gaius Cornelius Cethegus and the praetor Cornelius Lentulus Sura, sought allies for their revolution among the Allobroges. These Gallic people, living in what is now southeastern France, had grown increasingly unhappy with how Roman magistrates treated them and with the crushing debts their people faced. Accordingly they had sent an embassy to Rome to seek some measure of justice. The senate refused to entertain their concerns. Knowing this, Lentulus sent a messenger to the Allobroges promising to aid them if they joined in revolt. The envoys jumped at the chance to improve their situation, especially in light of the senate's intransigence. A bit more reflection, however, brought ambivalence. True, they felt mistreated by their Roman rulers, but they also feared the inevitable Roman reprisal should the revolt fail. Ultimately the Allobrogic ambassadors spilled the secret plot to their Roman patron, Quintus Fabius Sanga.[22] As consul, Cicero then arranged for two of the praetors to catch some of the plotters in the act, exchanging letters and oaths about the plot with the Allobrogic envoys late one night on the Milvian Bridge across the Tiber. A conspirator caught in the net, Volturcius, turned witness for the senate in return for a pardon, and the leading conspirators, Lentulus, Cethegus, Statilius and Gabinius were seized. Lentulus was forced to relinquish his praetorship and the four were placed under house arrest while the senate further investigated the conspiracy. [23]

The next day, 3 December 63 BCE, Cicero addressed the Roman crowd, a crowd doubtless eager for news of the nighttime arrests on the Milvian Bridge. Now Cicero delivered what came to be known as his *Third Catilinarian Oration*. In this speech he described the capture of the conspirators and made sure to emphasize his role in the sting operation. Letters they carried linked them to Catiline as did letters petitioning the Allobrogic people to revolt against Rome. The four ringleaders confessed to the letters bearing their seals, letters designed to foment Allobrogic rebellion. They also confessed to plans to slaughter citizens, Cicero thundered, and join forces with Catiline's army.[24]

Over the next few days, the senate investigated the roots of the conspiracy, with Cicero guiding. Lucius Tarquinius testified; he had been apprehended on his way to Catiline. His version corroborated that of the informant Volturcius, but with one critical detail added. He claimed to bear a message of collaboration from Crassus himself to Catiline![25] Cicero rejected the testimony – either on principle because he felt some obligation to spare Crassus, or, as Sallust had it, he secretly put Tarquinius to it, wishing to scare Crassus back into the Republican fold. Still, in later years Sallust insisted he spoke with Crassus and Crassus bluntly asserted he blamed Cicero for the charges laid against him.[26] Some senators too, namely Catulus and Piso, reportedly tried to ensnare Caesar in the plot with the Allobroges, but Cicero refused to consider their accusations, and the matter dropped.[27]

Another day or two passed. Catiline, Manlius and their army were still out there, somewhere to the north. The conspirators in the city, the ringleaders at least, were safely in custody. The senate rewarded the Allobrogic envoys and Volturcius, and the state enjoyed a brief respite. How long would that last? Gangs of Cethegus and Lentulus' enslaved and freed were scouring the city looking for their patrons, planning to break them free. Cicero received reports and, says Sallust, 'deployed guards as the situation and moment suggested' and convened the senate on 5 December 63.[28] He posed what would be a fateful question in more ways than one: what should be done with these conspirators under house arrest? Death by strangulation was one grim option, common for traitors to the Republic. But these conspirators had not received the benefit of a trial and Roman law gave all citizens the right to a trial and to appeal.[29] Yet tensions were high. Many senators feared, and Cicero certainly stressed, that Catiline was out there somewhere in Italy with an army. The consul-elect, Decimus Junius Silanus, offered his opinion first, thanks to his rank. Execute the traitors. Others concurred as their turns came to offer an opinion. Most seemingly agreed with Silanus at the start, though according to Appian, Tiberius Claudius Nero urged keeping the conspirators alive and detained until more was known about the plot and Catiline's army found and defeated.[30]

Then it was Gaius Julius Caesar's turn, the master-of-the-Roman-Empire to be, now a praetor-elect. Sallust writes a lengthy speech for him. While Caesar's precise words assuredly differed from Sallust's account, his point is well established in the sources. As Sallust has it, he spoke for a while, noting that execution was not cruel for such immoral firebrands, but the laws were clear that accused citizens must receive the benefit of a trial before the people, especially in capital offences, and convicted felons could opt for exile rather than death. Violating these laws, even with good intention, might set a precedent that less moral senators some future day might follow to everyone's harm. And so, Caesar urged, seize all the conspirators' wealth and possessions and imprison them forever in secure towns throughout Italy.[31] It cannot have helped his argument that some believed him to be a conspirator.[32]

Notably, Sallust gave a long speech to Caesar in his account, but chose not to mention Cicero's speech, the so-called *Fourth Oration against Catiline*. To be fair, however, Cicero and Sallust were contemporaries, and Cicero had publicized the conspiracy in numerous accounts, including the speech he ostensibly delivered. He had even asked others to write on the topic. In short, Sallust quite likely saw no reason to reproduce another valorization of Cicero.[33] Cicero's speech is still extant, however, and reveals, if there was any doubt, Cicero's stance. He emphasized the danger the Republic faced and the monstrosity of the conspirators' plot. These captive traitors were not noble Gracchi.[34] They had plotted no less, Cicero thundered, than to burn Rome, murder the senators, and open the city gates to welcome Catiline and his revolutionary army. The senate had letters with the conspirators' seals and handwriting. The senate had their confessions. The plot was already underway and needed to be eradicated before ruin befell the senate and Republic. The speech also indicates that while Cicero strenuously disagreed with Caesar, he took pains not to denigrate him personally, criticizing only his proposal. The unlucky Italian towns and leading citizens who were stuck with the task of imprisoning the conspirators would be unduly burdened by Caesar's plan. What's more, imprisonment without hope of parole was, in its way, far crueller than simply ending the traitors' lives. In short, death was the solution. The popular repercussions to senatorial heavy-handedness might be serious, but Cicero, as consul, was prepared to execute the senate's decree: he would not shy from this grim task.[35]

Sallust does provide a speech for Marcus Porcius Cato, however, the tribune elect, introducing us in the process to another key player in the rivalries at the end of the Republic. Called Cato the Younger to distinguish him from his great-grandfather Cato the Elder (Chapter 2), Cato was orphaned at a young age along with his half-brother Servilius Caepio and his sister Porcia. The three grew up in the household of Marcus Livius Drusus, that Drusus who proposed citizenship to the Italians and was murdered with a shoemaker's knife (Chapter 6). Plutarch characterizes him as serious, stubborn, and fond of Stoic philosophy, and it seems at least in part he wished to model himself on his famous great-grandfather.[36]

He was a child, perhaps 7 years old, when Sulla first marched on Rome, and barely a teenager when he did it for the second time. He had a distinguished career as a soldier after a rocky start with the consuls Gellius and Lentulus prosecuting the war against Spartacus and then as a military tribune.[37] After a tour of duty as a tribune in Macedonia, he took a tour around Asia, and met the famous Pompey busy executing his own plans at Ephesus; Plutarch even says that Pompey honoured him.[38] He had no qualms about quarrelling with his seniors. His quaestorship provides an example. He read up on the laws governing the quaestorship and set out to reform sloppy practices at the treasury. This led him to expel one fellow quaestor from the treasury for shady practices and prosecute another for outright fraud. The defrauding quaestor's case was taken up by none other than one of the censors that year (65 BCE), Catulus Lutatius. Others might have yielded when so senior a magistrate intervened, but Cato stood firm, even boldly criticizing Catulus in public for siding with a clear criminal.[39] Priding himself on his virtue, when Cato was certain he was in the right – and he was often certain – he was a righteous and implacable opponent. And Cato was certain he was right as he forcefully reiterated the arguments for executing the captive conspirators. The conspirators had been caught in the act. They deserved death. Keeping them alive simply to honour a point of law was not worth the risk to the Republic, a risk that Caesar insufficiently feared.[40] His oration moved the senate, who in the majority ignored Caesar's proposition. They decreed the plotters should die.[41]

And so those captives met their end without trial. Sallust reports the ending, and though it is grim reading, it provides insight into Roman methods of justice:

After the senate (as I have said) had divided in favour of Cato's proposal, the consul, deeming that the best thing to do was to forestall the impending night to prevent any revolutionary move during the course of it, ordered the triumvirs to prepare what the punishment demanded. After the deployment of guards, he personally escorted Lentulus to the jail; the same was done for the others by the praetors. There is in the jail a place called the Tullianum, on the left when you have gone up a short way, and sunk into the ground about twelve feet. It is fortified on all sides by walls, and the roof above is spanned by stone vaulting; but neglect, gloom and stench give it a foul and terrifying appearance. That was the place to which Lentulus was taken down, whereupon the executioners of capital cases, whose commission it was, broke his neck with a noose. So it was that a patrician from the most distinguished clan of the Cornelii, who had held consular command at Rome, met the end which his behaviour and deeds deserved. From Cethegus, Statilius, Gabinius and Caeparius, punishment was exacted in the same way.[42]

And so the senate and Cicero extirpated the conspiracy in the city. Cicero's role in executing the conspirators without trial, however, would come back to plague him before long.

Meanwhile, of course, Catiline had joined the small rebel army that Manlius had cobbled together. Sallust numbers the soldiers at two legions; Appian suggests a slightly larger force of 20,000. Regardless, they were in a rough state. There were recently demobilized soldiers and centurions among them, but arms and armour were scarce: only a quarter of the force bore what Sallust termed 'military arms' – presumably helmet, sword, and shield, possibly mail of some sort. The rest carried whatever they had scrounged: hunting javelins, light spears, or simply stakes they had sharpened. Though Catiline and Manlius kept the army on the move, before long the consul Antonius and his army were on its trail. Sallust asserts that many enslaved people attempted to swell the rebel ranks but Catiline rejected them, insisting that they could not share in this just rebellion of free citizens.[43] Report of the executions of the leading conspirators finally reached Catiline's army. Not a few lost their nerve and deserted the rebel force. The rest Catiline led north towards the mountains, presumably planning to escape to Transalpine Gaul. Alerted to the rebel movements, however, Quintus Metellus Celer's three legions from Pisa headed them off.[44]

Fate had caught up with Catiline, or more precisely Celer's troops to the front and Antonius' closing behind. Sallust narrated the final hours of Catiline's army in respectful tones that no doubt would have satisfied the renegade. He did not describe the rebels as a mass or mob, but described their deployment almost as if they were a regular army. Catiline sent away all the horses, his own included, so that all would meet their fate on foot together and none could easily flee. The former centurions and recent veterans he stationed in the front along with the best armed of his forces. Manlius commanded the right side of the battle line, and a man of Faesulae whom Sallust could not or did not care to name commanded the left. Catiline had pride of place in the centre, surrounded by his freedman and attendants. They carried a legionary standard – the eagle – reportedly borne by Marius' own soldiers as they battled the Cimbri decades before.[45]

Appian and Livy's summarizer both provide cursory details and note that Antonius' army fought the rebels.[46] Sallust provides the extra detail that Antonius was overcome by his gout on the day of battle and it fell to his legate, Marcus Petreius, to command the Roman force. Sallust gives him no speech, just the reminders he gave his troops that they faced nothing but weaponless bandits out to destroy the Republic. The armies closed to sword range quickly and clashed. The rebels resisted bravely, though the outcome probably was never in doubt. Catiline and his associates in the centre made a most determined defence, but Petreius' elite praetorian soldiers carved their way to Catiline then cut him down. Manlius and the Faesulan both died at their posts too. Sallust testified to the rebel army's bravery:

> But it was only when the battle was over that you could have perceived properly what daring and what strength of purpose there had been in Catiline's army. Almost everyone, after gasping his last, protected with his body the place which he had taken by fighting when alive. Nevertheless a few, whom the praetorian cohort had scattered from the centre, had fallen over a somewhat wider area, yet all of them with frontal wounds.

They had died facing their foes.[47] Catiline not least of all: they found him close to uttering his death rattle, far ahead of his men and surrounded by the corpses of enemies, his expression still defiant to the very end.[48]

And so ended Catiline's conspiracy.

In the aftermath of the plot, responses to Cicero's extreme exercise of executive power varied. Some – Caesar chief among them says Plutarch, but far from alone – continued to criticize Cicero. Others supported him, like Cato who successfully moved that Cicero had saved the Republic and should be saluted as *pater patriae*, 'father of the fatherland,' *i.e.* saviour of the Republic.[49] As the year 63 closed, Cicero's consulship also came to an end. On his last day in office, in December 63, he sought to mount the Rostra and deliver what would have been a lengthy speech extolling his deeds on behalf of the Republic. Metellus Nepos, however, one of the newly inaugurated tribunes for the forthcoming year, blocked him from giving the speech. He would be allowed no public speaking opportunity other than to swear the customary oath that he had discharged his duties faithfully. Seizing a minor victory from the jaws of defeat, Cicero, instead of that customary oath, swore that he had saved the Republic. According to Plutarch the crowd approved and confirmed his oath. Dio noted that his trick just made Caesar and other detractors more angry.[50] They would find a champion in the person of the tribune Clodius in a few years' time.

Epilogue: Pompey's Return and Cato's Intransigence

With Cicero's turbulent consulship at a close, Pompey's inevitable return from the East loomed large. He journeyed with his army to Brundisium late in 62. As he approached Italy, he decided to divorce his wife, Mucia. He did so in a letter, reportedly with no reasons given, even though they had three children together and had been married for 18 years. It was not least a political decision, judging from Pompey's efforts to quickly secure an advantageous new marriage, as we will see shortly. The rumour mill suggested, however, that she had been engaged in extra-marital affairs. On the other hand Cicero, who was a contemporary of them both, seems to indicate that these accusations were fabricated. What Mucia thought of all this, if it was recorded at the time, has not reached us. She seems to have fared reasonably well, at least publicly. She married Aemilius Scaurus soon after her divorce and had a son with him. She proved a politically important diplomatic tie for her son with Pompey during the triumvirate of Octavian decades later, suggesting she maintained a degree of political influence and respect.[51]

When Pompey reached Brundisium, Plutarch suggests, some feared Pompey might 'pull a Sulla', as it were, and occupy Rome with his army. Plutarch also adds the detail that Crassus, either because he was simply afraid, or because he wanted to stir the pot and inspire anti-Pompey sentiment, left Rome with his money and his children, but it is hard to know whether to believe this.[52] As soon as Pompey arrived in Italy, in any event, he disbanded his army after reminding them to return when called to celebrate his triumph.[53] He hoped to make his peaceful intentions clear beyond any shadow of a doubt. Whatever else his goals may have been, there were two political issues that he must have anticipated. First, he wanted – expected, it seems – the senate to approve all of his settlements in the East. This consisted of the whole corpus of administrative decisions Pompey made in the name of the Republic in the eastern Mediterranean: supporting some people in positions of power and deposing others, the whole of his diplomatic, military, and political arrangements. Second, he wanted farmland awarded to his veteran soldiers as just compensation for their years of service expanding the empire. Having a supporter in the consulship would make it considerably easier for Pompey to secure these two goals. So he sent ahead to Rome Marcus Pupius Piso to run for office. He also wrote to the senate asking them to delay the consular elections a bit so that he could personally campaign for Piso. The senate apparently agreed with the proposal until the tribune Cato vetoed the measure: there would be no extension for Pompey.[54]

When Cato vetoed the measure to postpone the consular elections, it was a foreshadowing of the rocky relationship he and Pompey would have. But Pompey still seemed hopeful to win the young senator over. He proposed to marry one of Cato's nieces and have his eldest son marry the other. Marriage with Pompey and his son was a prestigious offer, and, reportedly, Cato's sister and mother both approved of the match. Not Cato. He saw the overture as an effort to control him, corrupt him really, and refused the proposals.[55] The year was not entirely a political loss for Pompey however. In late September, planned to land on his 45th birthday, Pompey celebrated a magnificent triumph, his third, for two days. He left an inscription on the temple of Minerva he had built with some of the proceeds, and the first century CE encyclopaedist, Pliny, later quoted it. The statistics were quite astonishing.

[Gnaeus] Pompey Magnus, Imperator, having brought to an end a war of thirty years' duration, and having defeated, routed, put to the sword, or received the submission of, twelve millions two hundred and seventy-eight thousand men, having sunk or captured eight hundred and forty-six vessels, having received as allies one thousand five hundred and thirty-eight cities and fortresses, and having conquered all the country from the Mæotis to the Red Sea, dedicates this shrine as a votive offering due to Minerva.[56]

Pompey's eastern campaigns greatly benefitted the Republic: in addition to the thousands of talents of precious metal he had deposited in the treasury, he had doubled the income Rome would derive in the future from its provinces, a point he advertised in his triumph.[57]

The triumphal procession was a spectacle for the Romans and doubtless very satisfying for Pompey's ego.[58] For most triumphs, the victorious imperator claimed to have overcome one nation or people. Pompey, however, claimed a triumph over many: Asia, Pontus, Armenia, Paphlagonia, Cappadocia, Civilicia, Syria, Judaea, the Albanian and Scythian peoples, Iberia, Crete, and the Basterni.[59] Plutarch too gives a sense of the extraordinary scope of this triumph:

> As for the prisoners who were displayed in the procession, apart from the pirate leaders, there were the son of Tigranes of Armenia, along with his wife and daughter; Zosime, the wife of King Tigranes himself; Aristobulus, the king of Judaea; Mithridates' sister, five children of his, and some of his Scythian women; and hostages given by the Albanians, the Iberians, and the king of Commagene. Then there was a huge number of trophies, one for every battle in which he had been victorious, either in person or through the agency of his commanding officers. But the major boost to his prestige was provided by the fact that, for the first time in Roman history, not only was this the third triumph he had gained, but he had gained each of them in a different one of the three continents. He was not the first to have celebrated three triumphs, but he brought the first one back from Africa, the second from Europe, and this last one from Asia, so that in a sense it seemed as though the whole world had been subdued by his three triumphs.[60]

Pompey advertised this last part with a trophy that was labelled to indicate it represented all of the known world over which Pompeius had triumphed.[61]

But spectacular triumph complete, Pompey still made no political headway arranging land for his veterans, and less than he hoped ratifying his eastern settlements. Pompey's allies in 60, the consul Lucius Afranius and tribune Lucius Flavius, certainly sought to pass his legislative agenda. It has been argued at times that ratification of the whole of Pompey's eastern settlement was blocked by the senate. A careful examination of the evidence for Rome's provincial dealings in the eastern Mediterranean in 61 and 60, however, demonstrates that at least some of Pompey's arrangements were put into practice immediately.[62] The sticking point seems to have been those settlements Pompeius forged that would, if approved, replace ones Lucullus had previously made before he was replaced in command. When the issue of approving Pompey's eastern settlements in a single block was raised in the senate, it was challenged by Metellus Creticus and Cato. In what must have seemed a divinely inspired moment of revenge, Lucullus, from whom Pompey had essentially usurped the Mithridatic war, came out of retirement and argued that the senate should scrutinize each and every act in Pompey settlements, compare them to the acts Lucullus had crafted before Pompey took over, and determine which they preferred. Pompey was stymied and dropped the matter. The tribune Flavius proposed a land law for Pompey's veterans that also made some provision for the urban plebs. Consul Metellus Celer blocked consideration of the bill. Frustrated, Flavius had the consul thrown into prison for obstructing the legal process. Celer, imperturbable, summoned the senate to attend him in prison and they dutifully went. Doubling down, Flavius positioned himself in front of the prison entrance using his sacrosanct tribune's body to block contact with Celer. Celer called his move by ordering the prison wall torn down so that he could meet with the senate that way. It was all quite embarrassing for Pompey to say the least, and he told Flavius to let the matter drop. So when the summer of 60 arrived, Pompey and his allies had made little progress, and if anything Magnus Pompey looked rather impotent when it came to senatorial politics.[63]

Crassus in the 60s BCE

And what about Crassus during this decade? Like Pompey, Crassus did not take a province in 69 after his consulship and, based on the paltry evidence available, went about his political business. In 65 he was elected censor alongside Lutatius Catulus. The two apparently quarrelled about whether to make Egypt a Roman province and whether to grant Roman citizenship to Italian Gauls north of the Po River. These, and perhaps other disagreements set the two at odds to such an extent that they were unable to work together and laid down their office before their term was up.[64] There are various references to his activities, and historians have tried to make overall sense of Crassus' career in the 60s by allying him with this or that group or cause.[65] Of course, he seems to have been momentarily implicated in Catiline's conspiracy, though that was likely just talk. Overall, Plutarch points out that Crassus was exceedingly good at building his own political capital. He was a competent orator and served as an advocate to many in need, and also lent money to colleagues and friends putting many in his debt.[66]

Not least, Crassus formed a connection with Gaius Julius Caesar. Caesar had incurred an epic debt financing his early political career.[67] When he had completed his praetorship in 62 and was about to set out for his province of Spain in 61, his creditors blocked him from leaving Rome. At this point, Crassus stepped in, taking responsibility for Caesar's debts.[68] And so the pieces fell into place for that threesome – Crassus, Pompey, and Caesar – whose alliance and its subsequent collapse would be so catastrophic to Sulla's Republic. The so-called 'First Triumvirate'.

Chapter 10

Sky-watching and Law-making:
Bibulus and Caesar

Any consul could veto their colleague's actions. This was a time-honoured convention of Roman politics, a critical check on the otherwise frightening magnitude of power each consul wielded, including the power of life and death over citizens outside the city. True, the veto had not been exercised much over the centuries; it was not until Sulla that both consuls were even regularly in the city at the same time. But in theory it worked. And so Marcus Calpurnius Bibulus planned to shut Caesar's agrarian legislation down. Caesar had gone to the senate initially, properly respecting that august body up to a point, but probably also laying the groundwork for his ultimate appeal to the popular assembly. Some senators supported his motion – there were always some that would support popular agrarian laws – but the dominant voices in the senate ultimately opposed Caesar's proposal, an agrarian law to provide citizens with land. If not explicitly stipulated, the point that the primary beneficiaries would be Pompey's veterans from the wars in the East was clear enough. Caesar's opponents disapproved – awkwardly since Caesar's bill had no visible problems – and Caesar refused to yield to the senate's authority. This surprised no one less than Bibulus, who had served as Caesar's colleague as aedile and praetor and knew him well. And so when Caesar stood on the Rostra and addressed the citizens of the Forum, extolling the benefits of yet another agrarian law, Bibulus took lawful action to shut the whole matter down. He announced that the omens from the gods were unfavourable. He had the authority to make such a claim, as consul, and those omens meant that no political business could be conducted, certainly not the passage of a law in the assembly. The matter, as far as Bibulus was concerned, was finished.[1]

In a different time, perhaps, Bibulus' action might have stymied his opponent. But Caesar did not miss a beat. Instead, Caesar's followers

– ignoring Bibulus' office, his lictors, their fasces – assaulted the consul and his associates and drove them from the Forum.[2] Someone fetched Cato, who tried next to speak against Caesar's land proposal. He was no more successful than Bibulus. Caesar's allies lifted Cato up and summarily carried him from the Rostra. His further efforts to block Caesar proved impotent, and Caesar passed the land law through the assembly.[3] Bibulus decided that Caesar's thugs ruled the Forum and it was too risky to challenge him physically, and so stayed home for the remainder of the year – a long period – issuing regular notices that the gods were sending ill omens that prohibited any legislative business.[4] A joke made the rounds: instead of the normal practice of identifying the year by the consuls, hence 'the consulship of Bibulus and Caesar', some wits called it 'the consulship of Julius and Caesar'.[5] How had the political process come to this?

Caesar's Early Career

As a rising politician, Caesar showed particular skill in courting the average citizen. As aedile in 65 he spent enormous sums entertaining the populace with games, plays, and public works, the time-honoured methods of an aedile hoping for higher office. Spectacles were expensive however, and Caesar had incurred mighty debts. So much so that, after his praetorship in 63, his creditors prevented his departure to a governorship in Further Spain. The sources say that Caesar had to negotiate terms for repayment. Plutarch offers the detail that Crassus intervened, standing surety for Caesar's debts. This seems credible enough, for otherwise it is not clear how Caesar, with no money at his disposal, could placate his creditors.[6]

In Spain, the sources disagree about the civil side of Caesar's governorship. Plutarch reports he soothed troubled relations between various cities and resolved tensions between debtors and creditors.[7] Appian contradicts: Caesar ignored public business and judicial matters altogether. Both agree, however, that Caesar warred against the Lusitani and other Spanish peoples whom the Romans had not yet subjugated.[8] 'Restoring order', Suetonius termed it, but ultimately these were wars of choice, prosecuted so that Caesar could gain glory and, equally important given his financial straits, funds.[9] His strategy succeeded up to the required point; when the year had passed, he claimed sufficient Spanish victories to merit a triumph.

So, Caesar returned from his Spanish governorship in 60 ready to celebrate a triumph. That put him in something of a legal quandary however, because the day of the consular elections for 59 was fast approaching, and Caesar also aimed to win that office. To seek and celebrate a triumph, a spectacle that required planning, Caesar had to remain outside the city walls until the moment of the triumph to legally retain his *imperium*, his right to command. To run for the consulship, however, he and all candidates had to appear personally in the Forum and announce their candidacies to the Roman voters. The final day to announce candidacy for the consular elections was fast approaching and now Caesar would have to choose: triumph or consulship. Unless there was another option? Caesar petitioned the senate to grant him an exception, to allow him to run for the consulship *in absentia*, without entering the city. This would allow him to keep his *imperium* long enough to hold the triumph and still hold the consulship. He seemed to have sufficient support in the senate to get this request granted. Cato, however, would have none of it, and shut the request down by means of a filibuster. On the last possible day for the senate to grant this exception to Caesar, Cato delivered a speech without interruption, as was his right as a senator, until the sun had set and the senate had to disperse. Thwarted, Caesar gave up the triumph and focused on running for the consulship.[10]

The almost-legendary pact between Caesar, Pompey, and Crassus came soon, though the order of events is not entirely clear. The first century Roman grammarian Varro wrote about the pact in a book titled *The Three-Headed Monster*, and it certainly was a cause for concern for those who did not trust Caesar, his ambitions, and his willingness to court the average Roman.[11] Roman historians have tended to refer to this group as the First Triumvirate. Accounts vary concerning who initiated the arrangement: most say Caesar; Appian says Pompey.[12] Certainty on this point eludes. Pompey and Caesar both had political goals with which the other could assist. Pompey needed land for his veterans and, possibly, passage of any remaining settlements from the eastern campaigns. Caesar craved the consulship and the consequent consular province that would allow him to achieve greater *gloria* and acquire more wealth. The weight of the testimony, though it all comes second hand from writers who lived a century or more – sometimes a lot more – after the events, is that Caesar went into this political alliance before the elections. This is perfectly reasonable, of course, since Caesar was short on money and would need funds to win election, which Crassus and Pompey could give.[13]

The early second century historian and imperial bureaucrat Suetonius, however, offers an intriguingly different scenario. In his account, Caesar ran against Lucius Lucceius and Marcus Calpurnius Bibulus. Bibulus he could count as a rival; Lucceius possessed enough wealth to ingratiate himself and Caesar with the voters, not necessarily through entirely legal means. In response to the news of his candidacy, Caesar's senatorial rivals splurged on a bribery campaign for Bibulus so that he might win and check Caesar's ambitions; even that self-proclaimed bastion of moral rectitude, Cato, reckoned bribery was acceptable when the Republic was at stake.[14] Caesar and Bibulus won the consulship for 59, and the senate, or rather some dominating part of the senate, assigned the consular provinces for 58 as Forests and Hills. Essentially this meant that neither Caesar nor Bibulus would have a territory to govern – which also meant to economically exploit – in the year after their consulship. Caesar, determined to govern a proper Roman province, then turned to Pompey and Crassus, forming an alliance. There are problems with Suetonius' account however. Most importantly, the *Lex Sempronia* of Gaius Gracchus required the senate to set the consular provinces before, not after, the consular election.[15] He may simply have had that detail wrong. But it is highly likely that Caesar banded with Pompey and Crassus because he knew he would need more political clout to get what he wanted: a serious military province after his consulship.[16] Caesar, no political fool and certainly well aware of his opposition in the senate, had planned carefully where to find senatorial support, before or while he journeyed from Spain.[17]

They were not the only aristocrats Caesar hoped to ally with. In a letter to his friend Atticus dated to the very start of 59, before the temporary alliance later called the triumvirate was revealed, Cicero relates a conversation he recently had with one of Caesar's associates, Cornelius Balbus, about Caesar's planned agrarian law.[18]

> For I must either firmly oppose the agrarian law – which will involve a certain struggle, but a struggle full of glory – or I must remain altogether passive, which is about equivalent to retiring to Solonium or Antium; or, lastly, I must actually assist the bill, which I am told Caesar fully expects from me without any doubt. For Cornelius has

been with me (I mean Cornelius Balbus, Caesar's intimate), and solemnly assured me that he meant to avail himself of my advice and Pompey's in everything, and intended to endeavour to reconcile Crassus with Pompey. In this last course there are the following advantages: a very close union with Pompey, and, if I choose, with Caesar also; a reconciliation with my political enemies, peace with the common herd, ease for my old age.

And yet, Cicero could not bring himself to join with Caesar, Pompey, and Crassus on this or much else. He seems to have sincerely believed that tradition, especially the tradition of senatorial power and prerogative guiding the Republic was the right path. Hence Caesar, Pompey, and Crassus, who set personal goals before the dignity and power of the senate, were on the wrong path.[19]

So, what can be said with reasonable certainty about the campaigns for consul for 59:

- more than two men ran for the consulship;
- Caesar's opponents trusted Bibulus, his former colleague as aedile and praetor, to check Caesar;
- Caesar looked for political and financial support in his campaign, possibly from Lucius Lucceius, and certainly from Pompey and Crassus, and, it seems, Cicero, though Cicero resisted his overtures.[20]

Furthermore, before Caesar and Bibulus took office on 1 January 59, Caesar had reached some form of political understanding with Pompey and Crassus.

The short-term goals of Caesar and Pompey seem clear enough, and the ancient sources tend to agree. Caesar, of course, wanted the consulship, wanted it so badly that he had just foregone a triumph, a rare award. Pompey wanted land for his veteran soldiers. No more than a few months had passed since the embarrassing affair with tribune Flavius arresting the consul Metellus in a ploy to get land for Pompey's veterans. What Crassus gained is not entirely clear. One possibility historians have noted is that Crassus had colleagues among the equestrian *publicani* – the tax farmers. When the Romans wished to collect provincial taxes, companies offered bids on how much revenue they projected to gather for the state treasuries. Then it was up to the company to collect more than that amount in taxes in order to turn a profit from the contract. Recently the tax collectors of Asia, with whom Crassus associated, had bid too much for the contract and faced ruin if they could not get the senate to lower the amount they must pay. Perhaps a lower sum is what Crassus hoped to get from a friendly consul in 59.[21]

It may not have been Caesar's first legislative act as consul, but his agrarian law was certainly one of the most controversial.[22] Reading the abbreviated ancient secondary accounts it is easy to mistakenly assume that Caesar rushed into this legislation. On the contrary, he planned for some time. That previously-mentioned letter from Cicero to friend Atticus in December 60 makes clear that Caesar somewhat openly determined to pass an agrarian law. He was working with Pompey, planned to work with Crassus, and even sought Cicero's support on the issue before he entered office (January 1st, 59).[23] But he needed to move swiftly because of some details of political procedure: he was the first consul for 59 and January was an important month. During the Republic the first consul, the one who first received a majority of voting centuries during the election, had some precedence over the second. When their consulship was referred to for official purposes, the first consul's name was listed first. In January and the other odd months of the year, the first consul's twelve lictors were said to hold the fasces, and the first consul summoned and directed senatorial discussions.[24]

Legal procedure dictated that Caesar announce the bill several weeks – at least 17 days – before he convened the tribal assembly to vote. That meant he would need to get the bill approved by the senate early in January.[25] And by bringing the proposal to the senate first, Caesar certainly made a public effort to win over *optimates* in the senate. Cynical sources suggest it was little more than a ruse for the radical populist, Caesar: he knew they would reject his land law and provide him the useful excuse for legislating through the assembly and ignoring the senate.[26] But Caesar's interactions with Cicero suggest that, regardless of how likely it was, Caesar was determined to at least try to follow the traditional legislative path. Dio stresses Caesar's proposed law was unobjectionable. Public land would only be purchased from those who desired to sell it and at legitimate rates established by tax assessments. The funds for the whole administration would come from the sizeable monies that Pompey had deposited in the treasury from his eastern campaigns. The board of commissioners executing the land law would be limited to a few agreed upon members, and Caesar fully excluded himself from consideration as a commissioner.

However palatable the proposal, the optimates still opposed it. Cato, the one named opponent, reportedly found no specific fault with the law but objected on principle that no new laws on this subject should be made.[27] He may have sought to initiate another filibuster at this point, for Dio asserts that Caesar prepared to haul him off to prison, a plausible action to counter delaying tactics perhaps, but not for simply announcing one's opposition. Caesar's tough stance with Cato backfired. As soon as he threatened him, Cato indicated he was more than ready to go and indeed had supporters willing to follow him, preferring, as one senator reportedly said to Caesar, 'to be in prison with Cato rather than here with you'.[28] Caesar adjourned the meeting and abandoned any hope of senatorial approval for his land bill.

Caesar the consul, as many tribunes that past century had done, pivoted and proposed his land law directly to the tribal assembly. Since sufficient time had to pass before the assembly could vote, he held *contiones*, informational meetings where he and others could address the Roman voters. During one he called upon his consular colleague Bibulus and put the question to him: was there anything about the land proposal that he disagreed with? Bibulus stonewalled, simply declaring that he would not allow any innovations, i.e. new laws, to be made during his year of office.[29] Caesar excited listeners to collectively entreat Bibulus to yield. Considering the number of people who would benefit from this distribution of land, it was probably not difficult to goad them. But Bibulus stood his ground.

During the assemblies before the vote, Caesar also, as was often done, called leading senators to speak in favour of the land law, in this case Pompey and Crassus. When he asked if they approved of the land law, they averred. Pompey noted that the law would give land not only to his veterans but to Metellus' deserving veterans from the recent pirate wars and campaign to annex Crete. He also noted that the monies he had won for the treasury would fully fund administering the law. Then he added a simple threat: should anyone challenge this legislation with a sword, he would meet them with not only a sword, but a shield for good measure, a clear reference to Pompey's substantial number of obliging veterans residing in Italy.[30]

Bibulus may have gathered some tribunes to veto the law, but if so their delay was not decisive, and it is hard to say why that would have been; perhaps those tribunes yielded once they saw the great popularity of the bill?[31] He also may have declared sacred holidays on all the remaining days in the year when assemblies could legally meet, a sweeping tactic that would theoretically block all legislation for the remainder of the year. Caesar was not dissuaded from his course. Bibulus even announced ill omens from the gods, but Caesar ignored him. The night before the tribal assembly would vote, supporters of the land bill occupied the Forum, probably to make sure they were not prevented from meeting the next day. Caesar arrived and, when the new day officially came, addressed the assembling Romans from the tribunal on the stairs of the Temple of Castor and Pollux. And so, his constitutional options for stopping the popular land bill almost exhausted, Bibulus went to the Forum to use a less delicate but perfectly constitutional solution: a veto.[32] When Bibulus arrived, the people had occupied the space in front of the temple stairs and must not yet have formed into tribes for the vote. Time still for him to intercede. Bibulus attempted to climb the steps above Caesar accompanied by his allies and lictors, shout him down, and interpose his veto. Violence broke out, however, and consul Bibulus was, at the very least, roughed up. Caesar's armed supporters not only ignored Bibulus' constitutional authority, they assaulted him and his lictors, seizing their fasces and breaking them into kindling, even dumping a basket of manure over the consul's head for good measure.[33]

Driven from the Forum, Bibulus convened the senate, with the hopes of countering Caesar, perhaps harbouring hope to declare him an enemy of the state. The senate did not oblige. The popularity of Caesar's land law to the Roman people was only too apparent, as was Caesar's own popularity. Lacking support, Bibulus, therefore, spent the remainder of his consular year at home. His final official response was a blanket effort to block Caesar's legislation, all of it, on religious grounds since he had been unable to do so by other means. Legislation, according to the Roman system, could only be passed by the appropriate assembly on a 'comitial' day, a day on which it was lawful for the *comitia*, the assembly, to meet. There were a number of movable feast days and other holidays in the Roman calendar that could be set according to the consul's discretion; for example, days of thanksgiving for military victories. Bibulus now arranged it so he had placed a sacred day of some sort on every remaining assembly day in the year – it was January! – so that, theoretically, Caesar could not lawfully summon the tribal assembly to vote. Caesar simply ignored these arrangements and proceeded to legislate directly through the assembly. To provide extra sanction against Caesar's laws, Bibulus also officially dispatched word to Caesar, every day that he proposed legislation, noting that he had seen evil omens and that no legislative business could be held that day. Caesar essentially ignored this too.[34]

Caesar continued to ignore Bibulus' decrees and passed a considerable number of laws, though the order and timing of them are not certain. His initial land law exempted the incomparably fertile – for Roman Italy – Campanian land, but he passed a second land law that distributed Campanian land to farmers with at least three children.[35] He also passed a law intended to more closely monitor Roman provincial governors and limit their all-too-common mistreatment of provincials.[36] He ratified whatever was left of Pompey's eastern campaign settlements and passed a law granting some adjustment of the Asian tax-collector's bid, which seems to have met with Crassus' approval.[37]

In 59 Caesar married Calpurnia, daughter of one of the favourites to win the consulship for 58, Lucius Calpurnius Piso, presumably a means of securing his good will and protecting Caesar's legislation when Caesar left office.[38] Of greater impact, Caesar's daughter Julia married Pompey. It was Pompey's fourth marriage. Recall that Pompey had divorced Antistia back in 82 according to Sulla's wishes. In 79, as we have seen, Mucia married Pompey and became his third wife. They divorced in 62. Julia was already engaged to Caepio. Caesar broke the engagement and offered Julia to his new political ally, Pompey. He was 23 years her senior – 47 to her 24. Her thoughts about marrying Caepio and being required to marry Pompey instead may never have been recorded; they certainly did not survive. But according to the reports, something quite rare happened. Not only did Pompey seem to love Julia very much, she seemed to love him, and theirs was a happy marriage, for the few years it lasted.[39]

Regardless of the happy contingency that the couple actually loved each other, the political ramifications were clear. Pompey and Caesar cemented their alliance. Cicero remarked, prematurely, but perhaps not completely melodramatically, '[Caesar] is preparing a despotism and no mistake about it: for what else is the meaning of that sudden marriage union, the Campanian land affair, the lavish expenditure of money?'[40]

Most importantly for his future, Caesar circumvented the optimates' efforts to limit his province to the woods and hills of Italy. A law assigned him the provinces of Cisalpine and Transalpine Gaul for five years, the work of the tribune Publius Vatinius. Vatinius also legislated a command for Caesar in Illyricum, that eastern stretch of the Adriatic coast. The senate subsequently added Gallia Comata to his provinces – Gaul north and west of the Alps. Apparently Metellus Celer, the currently assigned governor of Transalpine Gaul, had died before even reaching his province, so a new governor was needed. The senate, Suetonius asserts, felt Caesar would probably get the province anyway through another bill before the people. They cut to the chase and simply granted it to him. These commands brought along with them the control of four Roman legions.[41]

* * *

And so Bibulus had proved an ineffective rival and Caesar had a momentous consulship. He had accomplished the political goals of his triumvirate and secured a grand province for his martial ambitions. As Caesar prepared to leave Italy, it came time for a new rivalry to explode, between Cicero and a tribune name Publius Clodius.

Chapter 11

The Patrician Populist and the Statesman: Clodius and Cicero

Cicero wrote – and his assistant, the once-enslaved Tiro, published posthumously – a great number of letters to friends, colleagues and associates. One friend, the equestrian Titus Pomponius Atticus, received books of correspondence – or, more precisely, handwritten copies of copies of copies – which survive today. They offer one of the very few primary sources for the decades before the dictatorship and murder of Caesar, as good a place to mark the end of the Republic as any. At the end of one brief letter discussing other political news with Atticus, in January 61 BCE, Cicero dropped this intriguing nugget of news:

> I suppose you have heard that P. Clodius, son of Appius, was caught in woman's clothes at Gaius Caesar's house, while the state function was going on, and that he was saved and got out by means of a maid-servant: and that the affair is causing immense scandal. I feel sure you will be sorry for it. I have nothing else to tell you.[1]

But there is much more to say about this intriguing act of religious gate-crashing that ultimately fostered the bitter rivalry of Clodius and Cicero and resulted in Cicero's exile.[2]

To understand the conflict between Clodius and Cicero, we need to step back a few years before Caesar and Bibulus' consulship, investigated in the last chapter, to the winter of 62 BCE. The ancient sources report that the scandal, the break-in to Caesar's house during religious rituals, came about like this. One of Rome's divinities, whom the Romans called Bona Dea, 'The Good Goddess', enjoyed a series of sacred rituals traditionally performed in December by a select group of noble women. Males were forbidden. On the evening of the sacred day, the rites were held by a woman whose husband was a magistrate with *imperium*. This year it was

Pompeia, wife of the praetor and *pontifex maximus* Julius Caesar and granddaughter of Sulla.[3] As evening came, all the males left Pompeia and Caesar's house. The imperative that no males be present at the sacred rites extended even to removing male animals and artistic depictions of males from the house. Then Pompeia, as host, decorated the house with flora, including little enclosures made up of grape vines. Bona Dea, the cult image of the goddess was brought to the hall where the festival would take place and placed near a couch and a table from which her meal would be served. Then a sacrifice for the sake of the Roman people, a sow followed by Pompeia performing a libation – a drink offered to the Goddess by pouring the liquid on the ground. The Vestal Virgins stood witness to the ritual. These sacred ceremonies were followed by a party, complete with feasting, drinking, music, and, no doubt, laughter.[4]

Clodius crashed this ceremony and thereby tainted the important religious rites – no small matter. Cicero makes no mention of motives in his earliest references to Clodius' impropriety.[5] Later came the charge Cicero hurled in his diatribes and preserved in Plutarch: Clodius longed for an affair with Caesar's wife, Pompeia.[6] The evidence to suggest she was involved, however, is not compelling. Caesar famously divorced Pompeia on the grounds that she might well be innocent but that the wife of the *pontifex maximus* must be above any suspicion of misconduct.[7] Unfortunately, we know little more about Pompeia.

So Clodius apparently judged that this night of religiously-inspired merrymaking unburdened of males at the house of the woman he desired was a perfect opportunity for a late night adventure. The plan: dress as a woman, possibly as one of the lute-players who would entertain the Roman ladies, gain access to the house with the help of a maidservant, and then ... do whatever it was he hoped to do. He made it into the house thanks to an associate on the inside. Apparently he grew bored or nervous waiting for this confederate to bring Pompeia to him, and so he began to stroll about the house. At this point one of Aurelia's servants – Aurelia was Caesar's mother and present for the rites – found him wandering about. She asked this lute-player where she was heading and recognized Clodius' male voice when he was compelled to speak. Aurelia's servant shouted an alarm, the women interrupted their sacred celebration, hunted for the sacrilegious intruder, and drove him out of the house. The Vestal Virgins, since the ceremony appeared tainted, performed the rituals again.[8]

A scandal to be sure and one that risked damaging the *pax deorum*, the proper relationship between the Romans and their gods. This sacred relationship was sincerely important to many Romans and fastidiously maintained as a civic duty even by the less devout. Then too there was the dignity of the matrons who were without male chaperones and reportedly under the influence of alcohol – no doubt a horror to the sensibilities of the Roman patriarchy. Clodius had played havoc with Roman standards of propriety by any measure. And yet, the initial response to the break-in by priests and senators alike seems to have been ... nothing. In no small part this may have been because of Clodius' standing and his connections. On top of an ancient family line, he had reasonably important family members – his brothers Metellus Nepos (cos. 57) and Appius Claudius (cos. 54) – and friends, like Gaius Scribonius Curio the elder (cos. 76) – some would not have wanted to anger. He had won election to the quaestorship for 61, evidence of his political popularity. Indeed he counted among his friends the consul of 61, Pupius Piso, who presided over the senate meeting that January and did nothing to call attention to Clodius' controversial impropriety the month before. Caesar, at whose house the misconduct occurred, kept silent about the matter and proclaimed ignorance when questioned at Clodius' later trial, even after Caesar's own mother had testified that Clodius had infiltrated the house. In early January 61 it appeared that all the most powerful senators were content, if not eager, to delicately pass by the whole affair.[9]

So Cicero said in a letter: the nobles said nothing about the Bona Dea business. And so it might have ended if not for the religious sensibilities of senator Quintus Cornificius. Not a leader of the senate by any means, but a Roman of dignity – both wealthy and a former praetor. Once he had brought up the matter, one so clearly religiously problematic to say the least, it would not do for the nobles to let it drop. And so, at his urging the senate put the issue of the Bona Dea break-in to the pontifices, the priests. They in turn, predictably, declared that a religious misconduct had occurred. Clodius had been caught in a place at a time sacred law prohibited. Still, this finding did not mean that Clodius was in any legal trouble. The pontifices declared that the ceremony simply needed to be repeated.[10] The Vestal Virgins had, apparently, already done this at the time of the break-in. But the opportunity for political wrangling had appeared, and while Clodius had many powerful friends, he clearly had many powerful enemies. Those enemies moved the senate to, through a bill proposed by the consuls, set up a special court to investigate Clodius on the charge of *incestum*.[11]

Cicero resisted this heavy-handed approach, thinking it better for Clodius to live legally unconvicted for the scandal rather than tried in a court and potentially acquitted for the whole affair.[12] But a trial did take place after some political wranglings.[13] It promised to be a public spectacle, as many court cases between aristocrats were in these decades. Clodius was known by the optimates, by everyone, to be very popular with the common citizens of Rome. Supporters were at the trial – supporters the nobles classified as common – and apparently boisterously supported Clodius, eyewitness Cicero told Atticus in a letter that year.[14] Indeed Caesar himself seems to have calculated that charging this young man with sacrilege, who had made advances or more to his wife Pompeia in his own house, would produce nothing useful because of Clodius' popular support. But Caesar went further than simply refusing to prosecute Clodius. In the trial, when questioned, he simply stated that he knew nothing about the events inspiring Clodius' indictment.[15] Regardless of Caesar's politic silence on the issue, other senators willingly took the stand as character witnesses and excoriated the young patrician mischief-maker. Accusations flew from these witnesses. Clodius reportedly had committed a number of immoral deeds, not least, they had heard, adultery and incest with his sister, Clodia, at that time married to Lucullus.[16]

The casting about of scandalous accusations and the animated support of Clodius' allies surrounding the court unnerved the jurors. They demanded guards be stationed at the court to protect them from the people's anger. Clodius, notes Cicero, had no real defence against the charges of breaking-and-entering the house of the women's sacred ceremonies except for this: he claimed that he was not even in Rome at the time of the break-in. A lie: we learn from Cicero that he had visited Cicero in his house at Rome for some consultation or other on the day in question. Cicero was called on to testify. As he recollected it to Atticus – with his usual effort to appear the distinguished man of developed political instincts – Cicero sized up the jury. Many of the jurors selected by the defendant Clodius, Cicero judged to be marked by 'poverty and low character'. In other words, Cicero claimed he knew Clodius was likely to bribe them.[17] And so, as Cicero related it, he limited his testimony, suspecting it to be of no use, 'and gave no evidence beyond what was so notorious and well-attested that I could not omit it,' namely, that Clodius had in fact visited him in Rome when he claimed to be out of the city. Cicero sank his alibi: Clodius was clearly available for the nocturnal escapade at Caesar's house.[18]

Cicero may not have relished the prospect of giving evidence at Clodius' trial, despite his certainty – everyone's certainty – that caught-in-the-act Clodius was guilty. Still, he did appear to move decisively from a relationship without any particular friendship or enmity with Clodius, to a bitter hatred. Why? Elsewhere in the sources lies a possibility. About a decade earlier, in 73, Clodius had publicly accused Catiline of sleeping with the Vestal Virgin Fabia, the crime of *incestum* as the Romans called it. Such a charge, of course, damaged Fabia's reputation, and her ability to be a sacred Vestal Virgin, just as much as it harmed Catiline. But Fabia, it happened, was the half-sister of Terentia, Cicero's wife. And though Catiline and, by implication, Fabia were acquitted of the charge, the accusation and the infamy – the whiff of scandal – stuck. A remark in Plutarch's biography of Cicero suggests, perhaps, that Terentia harboured animosity to Clodius ever since. Cicero himself well documented how seriously he took Terentia's advice throughout their marriage, and Terentia certainly had motive to dislike Clodius.[19] This does still leave us, however, to deal with Plutarch's suggestion that Cicero and Clodius were friends up to this point. Perhaps that was simply a conclusion the biographer drew based on the fact that the two both worked against Catiline: the enemy of my enemy is my friend.[20] There seems to be little other evidence of it.

Cicero testified. Yet, as he feared, the jury acquitted Clodius. If the facts are as we have received them, they received lavish bribes from Clodius and his supporters to acquit him, for he certainly had no substantive defence; after all, he had been caught in the act. Probably, despite Valerius Maximus' later moralistic charge that Clodius bribed the jury with prostitutes, he paid them in money, the standard for bribing juries in the Republic.[21] At the time of the trial, the senator Catulus reportedly noted the inconsistency that the jury bribed by Clodius demanded protection from the pro-Clodius crowd. He quipped to one juror, 'Why did you ask us for a guard? Did you fear being robbed of the money?' – the money Clodius had paid the jurors to acquit him.[22]

Cicero reported subsequent sparring in the senate to Atticus. Of course, when recalling a verbal joust, Cicero not infrequently portrayed himself as the wittier and more successful combatant; he was by no means immune to self-praise. Still it is illuminating to see the kinds of jousts he reported to Atticus, if for no other reason than to illuminate the rather rowdy parliamentary-style debates that could take place in the senate. Cicero launched into a prepared speech denouncing Clodius in the senate, associating his degenerate nature to that of Catiline and his conspirators and stating that with Clodius, 'a third such criminal has now been let loose by jurors upon the Republic.' He showily bid the senators to take courage, and chastised Clodius, calling him out, 'You are mistaken, Clodius: it is not for the city but for the prison that the jurors have reserved you, and their intention was not to retain you in the state, but to deprive you of the privilege of exile.' Clodius, 'the dandified young gentleman', as Cicero labelled him, fought back, and there was, in Cicero's estimation, a duel of words. Barbs that are difficult to fully understand by modern readers apparently flew back and forth. Here are a few zingers. Clodius thought to accuse him of undignified spending by asserting 'you have bought a house'. Cicero retorted 'you have bought a jury'. The jury 'did not trust you on your oath,' Clodius parried. 'Yes,' said Cicero, 'twenty-five jurors did trust me,' (i.e the ones who voted to convict Clodius), 'thirty-one did not trust you, for they took care to get their money beforehand!' In Cicero's recount at this moment, '[Clodius] was overpowered by a burst of applause and broke down without a word to say.'[23]

Clodius had escaped conviction by the court, but the blow to his dignity was considerable. Enemies like Cicero (as he truly was now, it appears), Catulus, and Cato hounded him. Cicero openly declared both privately and publicly that Clodius had disgracefully bribed the jurors. In a speech, Cato moved the senate to promote a bill punishing jurors – non-senatorial jurors – who took bribes, certainly a swipe at Clodius. Cicero persuaded the senate to cancel the consul Pupius Piso's forthcoming governorship in Syria, and this seems to have dashed Clodius' hopes to serve as his quaestor in that lucrative province. Clodius punched back, holding his own *contiones* in 61 in which he attacked Cicero both directly and by verbally assaulting Terentia's half-sister, the Vestal Virgin Fabia.[24]

Then Clodius went to Sicily, to serve as quaestor for the propraetor C. Vergilius Balbus in 61 BCE. It was a quiet term of office as far as the sources' silence suggests, By June 60 he had returned to Rome. Cicero and his animosity do not appear to have abated in the least. Cicero reported an early encounter with Clodius about that time to Atticus. The two exchanged barbs yet again. Clodius suggested he might become the new patron of Sicily, implying he would replace Cicero.[25] Cicero picked at the low-hanging fruit, joking about Clodius' incest with his sister Clodia. Cicero noted in his letter that the swipe was probably beneath him, but he simply detested her.[26]

And now, in the second half of 60, if not before, Clodius worked to transition from patrician to plebeian status, a *transitio ad plebem*, which would allow the patrician scion to hold a tribunate of the plebs. It is not clear when Clodius first hatched this plan, but he seems to have mentioned the matter even before his term as quaestor in Sicily. One of the tribunes of 60, Herennius, was willing to propose a bill to – this is a little technical – authorize a magistrate with *imperium* to summon the centuriate assembly and hold a vote authorizing Clodius' transition. These arrangements happened before Clodius had returned from the island. Herennius, mostly an enigma to us, persisted in his attempt but was vetoed by his colleagues in the tribunate, as Cicero mentions in passing in a letter to Atticus. Other efforts seemed to have fizzled including one obstructed by his own relative, the consul Quintus Caecilius Metellus Celer. [27]

Things would change. In 60 Pompey still sought political allies to secure his land law for veterans and, Plutarch suggests, cultivated a relationship with the seemingly-down-and-out Clodius.[28] Certainly this relationship would be cemented, as mercurial as it would prove to be, when the consulship of Caesar and Bibulus began in 59. For Caesar engineered, apparently effortlessly, what Clodius could not achieve, no matter how hard he struggled: his transition to plebeian status.[29] What had changed? Why did Caesar, and presumably Pompey, support this?

In a word, Cicero. As we have seen, Cicero was not happy with the power of Caesar, Pompey, and Crassus combined. In addition to grumblings he made privately, he took an opportunity that year to vent when defending his former consular colleague Antonius in the courts, prosecuted for some aspect of his Macedonian governorship. Rather than deal with the question of Antonius' guilt, Cicero lamented the deplorable state of the Republic with the triumvirs now established. It was too bold a critique for the triumvirs' taste. Immediately after this diatribe – a few hours apparently – Caesar arranged the transition through an adoption. As consul he summoned the curiate assembly, the one empowered to approve such transitions, and as *pontifex maximus* he sanctioned the adoption of Clodius to the plebeian P. Fonteius. It did not escape notice that Fonteius was in his twenties and so significantly younger than his new son Clodius.[30]

Cicero launched several diatribes, privately and publicly, against Clodius' adoption after-the-fact. In April of 59, south of Rome, he dispatched a letter to Atticus noting his feelings about the matter: 'Are they going to deny that Publius has been made a plebeian? This is indeed playing the king, and is utterly intolerable.'[31] His most articulate attack on the adoption, however, comes in a later speech from 57, *De Domo Sua*, 'About His Home'. Here Cicero railed against the illegal adoption. And while Cicero had a substantial axe to grind at this point and hoped to nullify Clodius' entire tribunate, the irregularities of Clodius' adoption must have been a source of derision in at least some quarters. For, among other objections,

- Clodius was older than his adoptive father;
- Clodius did not become his heir, the normal reason for adoption in the Republic; and
- Clodius was legally emancipated immediately and so not under the legal authority of his plebeian father.

Cicero excoriates Clodius for the illegitimacy of this adoption, despite Cicero's objections, objections apparent to anyone in 59 when the adoption took place. The adoption, in any event, was acceptable enough to the voters. The tribal assembly elected Clodius as a tribune of the plebeians for 58.[32]

And then a shocking bit of political theatre shook things up, and probably drove a wedge between Cicero and his protector Pompey. This is the account Cicero gave Atticus at the time: 'As far as I can make out,' he wrote, Vettius (his informant during the business with Catiline) promised Caesar to implicate the younger Gaius Scribonius Curio in some misdeed. He insinuated himself into Curio's confidence and told the young aristocrat that he, Vettius, planned to murder Pompey. Curio dutifully told his dad, who told Pompey, who brought the matter to the senate.

Hauled before the senate, Vettius agreed to reveal the plot if the senate protected him. They agreed. The account he gave the senate: Curio and other aristocratic youth – he named some – planned to murder Pompey in the Forum with the support of the consul Bibulus. The senate imprisoned Vettius afterwards for, by his own confession, carrying a dagger in the city. The next day, however, Caesar brought Vettius to the Rostra and the tribune Vatinius compelled him to speak.[33] The story had changed. The conspirators had changed from youthful aristocrats to ranking senators like Lucullus, Fannius, and Domitius Ahenobarbus. Vettius did not explicitly name Cicero but strongly implicated him nonetheless. Cicero claimed not to be worried, but even so, this event sowed the seeds of mistrust and likely drove Pompey to stop protecting Cicero. The purpose the powerful wished him to serve having been fulfilled, Vettius did not last; he was strangled by an unknown assailant in the prison.[34]

Though Caesar seemed interested in curbing Cicero, Clodius' run for the tribunate of 58 was apparently against Caesar's wishes. It would appear Clodius and Caesar's relationship had ruptured in only a few months. Clodius had transitioned to the plebs by April 59, according to Cicero's letters, and was at odds with Caesar by July.[35] Now Clodius proclaimed himself Caesar's mortal enemy and announced his run for tribune. He declared he would cancel all of Caesar's legislation this year. Cicero was justifiably alarmed at the thought of his rival Clodius wielding the powers of a tribune. In letters to Atticus, however, Cicero reiterates that Pompey had previously checked Clodius and he had faith Pompey would protect him still.[36] Truly, there was little he could do, other than cultivate his close acquaintance with Pompey as he usually did. Clodius was elected tribune, and in a letter to his brother Quintus in October 59, Cicero floated this assessment to Quintus, then propraetor in Asia:

If Clodius gives notice of an action against me, the whole of Italy will rush to my support, so that I shall come off with many times greater glory than before; but if he attempts the use of violence, I hope, by the zeal not only of friends but also of opponents, to be able to meet force with force. All promise me the aid of themselves, their friends, clients, freedmen, slaves, and, finally, of their money. Our old regiment of loyalists is warm in its zeal and attachment to me. If there were any who had formerly been comparatively hostile or lukewarm, they are now uniting themselves with the loyalists from hatred to these despots. Pompey makes every sort of promise, and so does Caesar: but my confidence in them is not enough to induce me to drop any of my preparations. The tribunes-designate are friendly to us. The consuls-designate make excellent professions. Some of the new praetors are very friendly and very brave citizens – Domitius, Nigidius, Memmius, Lentulus – the others are loyalists also, but these are eminently so. Wherefore keep a good heart and high hopes. [37]

For anyone who harbours sympathy for Cicero, it is tragic to know with hindsight that Cicero was flat-out wrong about his chances against Clodius the tribune, and wrong about Pompey's protection.[38] Did he know his hopes were in vain?

Clodius was elected tribune in December 59 BCE. He had plans other than simply harming Cicero however. He proposed four laws at the very start of his tribunate. These were clearly the product of considered thought, and would aid the people, as a *popularis* was expected to do; some would benefit the higher classes. These measures stood to gain Clodius a great deal more political support.[39]

The first was a law aimed at reviving and empowering the *collegia* of Rome.[40] We know very little about these as our sources were concerned with the top of the social, political, and economic ladder. Collegia were social and religious groups for ordinary Romans. Some were based on occupations, like the collegia of craftspeople. Others were based on neighbourhoods in Rome. Some of the more important for ordinary Romans were the neighbourhood groups that were responsible for tending to the local gods of each neighbourhood, the *Lares Compitales*. The size of collegia ranged from one hundred to more than one thousand members. They met regularly and apparently often held suppers for members. In this way the collegia provided social interaction, food, status, and a sense of belonging to ordinary Romans.[41] The senate was sometimes hostile to the collegia – perhaps an extension of the disdain senators generally seemed to have had for those who laboured for a living and the destitute – groups that often overlapped. In 64 the senate clamped down and outlawed any collegia that might have been hostile to the Republic. They also prohibited the celebration of the Compitalia, the games for the neighbourhood gods that provided so much purpose for the collegia.⁴² Clodius' law apparently reversed the prohibitions allowing certain collegia to reform. It also seems to have allowed new collegia to form. Since collegia membership and rank brought a measure of status to ordinary Romans in addition to social support, enabling new collegia to form expanded these ordinary Romans' opportunities for distinction and support. This was a measure that should have been very pleasing to the urban inhabitants of Rome, from whom Clodius gained much political power.⁴³

The next law, also surely popular with the ordinary inhabitants of Rome, expanded the city's grain subsidies.⁴⁴ The availability and market price of grain was critical to thousands of Romans who relied on bread and other grain staples for most of their daily calories. If prices rose beyond what a person could pay, they and their family could very well starve. Aediles often interacted with the grain market in *ad hoc* ways, subsidizing lower prices at times and arranging extra shipments of grain. Gaius Gracchus had passed a law fixing monthly sales of grain to citizens at a low fixed price.⁴⁵ It appears the amount supplied by Gracchus' law was not sufficient to feed a family, however, and even the poorest Romans would still need to purchase some grain at market prices to survive. The exact details of grain subsidies varied over the decades. Sulla eliminated the practice for a time. Mostly the aristocracy seems to have seen it as a necessary obligation, either for ethical reasons or, equally likely, a base fear of angry and starving crowds. Even Cato, that self-proclaimed bastion of the optimates, passed a law as tribune in 62 increasing the amount of state-subsidized grain.⁴⁶ Now Clodius' law did even more, seemingly providing all Roman citizens a free living ration of grain every month. He undoubtedly lifted thousands out of destitution and food insecurity. But not without great expense to the state: clearly the new subsidies required even greater expenditures than Cato's expansion. Special coinage had to be minted in 58 to cover the costs. It was an expense, however, that the Republic could certainly cover from the immense wealth brought in by its Mediterranean empire.⁴⁷

The other two laws targeted issues other than the concerns of the average citizens. The effects of the law about *obnuntio* – reporting bad omens from the gods – are not clear. It seems, however that the law abolished magistrates and priests watching for omens on days when legislative assemblies were scheduled to be called, effectively taking the religious veto out of political opponents' arsenals.[48] The other law dealt with the censors' selection of senators. Before this, censors could strike a Roman off the list of senators without any opportunity for the demoted to challenge the claim. Now the procedures were changed so that anyone the censors wished to strike from the lists could mount a defence.[49]

Judging from these laws, Clodius was not a one-note populist but rather a serious political competitor who appealed to various classes of society. Of course the plebs came first, as was expected from a tribune. But his measures were broadly appealing enough that the leading senators did not oppose them. Except for Cicero, but he achieved nothing other than fanning the flames of his rivalry with Clodius. The laws all passed.[50]

Then, trouble; a direct clash. The hostilities between Cicero and Clodius had simmered while Clodius enacted his legislative programme. By January, however, he had completed these four laws. Now Clodius targeted his rival Cicero directly. Was he taking advantage of his tribune's position to harm Cicero simply for the joy it would bring him? Was it just a matter of bitter rivalry? Yes and no. The case has been reasonably made that, while Clodius, like any Roman aristocrat, saw revenging himself on a political and personal enemy as an act of power consistent with his dignity, he also had grown to realize the power his *popularis* stances gave him. And Cicero was, in every sense, not a *popularis*. So when Clodius attacked Cicero, he not only harmed his foe but further cemented his stance as a populist tribune, and bonded with his supporters. In short, attacking Cicero was personally and politically good practice.[51]

It would require careful planning to strike a politically lethal blow. He needed the consuls' good will, or at least indifference. The triumvirs too needed to acquiesce, or his political assault would be countered swiftly. And so Clodius went to work. To secure the consuls' approval, he gave them potentially lucrative provincial governorships after their year in office. He passed a law assigning Macedonia to Piso and Cilicia (later Syria) for Gabinius. This got them into an agreeable mood.[52] Then he announced a bill that reiterated the time-honoured right of every Roman citizen to appeal to the people, to receive a trial by jury before being punished for a capital crime. The bill stipulated that exile would befall anyone who had executed a Roman citizen without trial.[53] This would be the mechanism for removing Cicero, and, despite the fact that his name was not in the bill, everyone knew he was the target. Yet the bill was certain to receive wide support, even among those optimates that would rather not see Cicero harmed. Reaffirming the centuries-old right to appeal to the people was not only perfectly acceptable behaviour for a *popularis* tribune, it was a traditional right endorsed by all levels of society. And so, even though it was crystal clear who had executed citizens without a trial very recently, the optimates could not counter such a fundamental expression of cherished legal principle. As for the triumvirs, when asked about the law, Pompey gave one of his non-answer answers – made famous to us by Cicero's piqued letters; he would not object, it appeared. Pompey did note that he would consult with his father-in-law, Caesar. Caesar, when asked, publicly praised the principles of the law. Privately he invited Cicero to join his command staff in Gaul.[54]

Cicero was not idle in the interval before the vote on this law. He wore mourning garb and publicly petitioned passers-by to save him.[55] Many among the equestrian class, the Italian gentry, came to his defence clothed for mourning in their own public displays at Rome. Supporters in the senate also attempted to don mourning clothes, but the consuls forbade it. Still, a handful of senior senators spoke in support of Cicero, including Hortensius, Lucullus, and the Elder Curio.[56] Even Crassus' son, Plutarch notes, supported and eventually reconciled his father to Cicero. Clodius steadily pressured Cicero and his supporters, however, by dispatching gangs to harass them; sometimes verbally, some were even assaulted. Clodius also continued to work the optimates, especially Cato. For it surely occurred to Cato that he too, as tribune elect in 63, had been instrumental in summarily executing the conspirators. To separate Cato from Cicero, Clodius announced a special bill that would grant Cato the *imperium* to organize the island of Cyprus as a Roman province, a prestigious and likely lucrative post.[57] Cato did not protest.

Left without options and unwilling to become an adherent of Caesar, Cicero left the city that he loved in self-imposed but soon-to-be-ordained exile.[58] Clodius was hardly done with his rival however. He swiftly followed Cicero's exodus with a second law. This one targeted Cicero by name for executing Catiline's supporters and sentenced him to permanent exile. Cicero had to remain at least 500 miles away from Italy on pain of execution. The law also stipulated that those who dared shelter him faced execution.[59] As for his property, the Republic would seize and sell it, including his Tusculan villa and domus on the Palatine. Cicero would declare with a flourish a few years later, his enemies 'flew to drink my blood, and, while the republic was still breathing, to carry off and divide my spoils'.[60] Clodius saw to it that Cicero's beloved grand *domus* on the aristocratic Palatine hill, the most expensive and visible monument of his status, was levelled. To wipe the land clean, as it were, and prevent Cicero from ever rebuilding if he somehow managed to come back, Clodius had the land designated as sacred, and commenced plans to build a shrine to divine Liberty.[61]

For Cicero, it may have felt that his enemy's vengeance was complete. Broken in spirit, he headed south to Brundisium then made his way to Greece.[62] He continued to correspond with Atticus and wrote some letters to his wife, Terentia, while abroad. Though the wait felt interminable, Cicero's exile would end; he would return, for Clodius, flush with his power as a tribune and a gang leader, began to burn some important bridges he had built with powerful Romans. He pivoted on Pompey. Clodius moved to repeal some of Pompey's eastern settlements and, perhaps, prosecute some of Pompey's friends.[63] He went further. Pompey after his return from the East kept as a guest-hostage the prince of Armenia, Tigranes. The prince lived under house arrest of Pompey's ally Lucius Flavius, a praetor in 58 BCE. Clodius, reportedly for a bribe, openly abducted Tigranes from Flavius, using his tribunician immunity as protection. A brawl then erupted on the Appian Way between Clodius' gang escorting Tigranes to freedom and Flavius' men attempting to recover the prince. In the altercation, Pompey's friend Marcus Papirius was killed.[64]

Violence begat violence. The incident along the Appian Way and the clear threat of Clodius' gangs in the city moved the consul Gabinius to form his own street gang. Clodius' forces proved stronger in the ensuing brawls however, and his agents attacked Gabinius in Rome, shattering the fasces of his lictors for good measure. That is worth a pause. One of the lawful consuls of Rome, in his exercise of office, was manhandled and humiliated by the street fighters of the tribune. But Clodius did not stop there. In the aftermath of the brawl he devoted Gabinius' *domus* at Rome to the plebeian patroness Ceres. Between legislative power and the strength of his gangs, the power of Clodius at this point early in 58 was stunning.[65]

Clodius' heavy handedness, however, inspired enough enmity from Pompey and resolve from other senators that the desire to recall Cicero grew more open. In June the tribune Ninnius made a proposal about Cicero's recall but it was vetoed.[66] Eventually the senate refused to discuss any business at all until the consuls Gabinius and Piso moved to recall Cicero. Clodius posted a public reminder about the terms of his exile law, the part about not discussing any recall.[67] Talk about a recall hushed, but only momentarily. Pompey came to see the value of restoring Cicero as a check against Clodius. He made clear that he would communicate with his father-in-law, Caesar, on the matter.[68] Still, it did not seem that anything could be achieved decisively for the recall of Cicero that year, and in the summer the elections for the consuls of 57 BCE were held. Publius Lentulus Spinther and Metellus Nepos were elected. How the two would affect Cicero's recall was unclear, for Lentulus seemed allied with Pompey but Metellus was related to Clodius and no friend to Cicero.[69]

And then, another man with another dagger. In August 58 Gabinius interrogated one of Clodius' enslaved servants who had been spied with a dagger near a senate meeting. When questioned the enslaved man averred that his charge, from Clodius himself, was to murder Pompey.[70] Whether this was a genuine murder plot or a calculated show, the impact was significant: Pompey fortified himself in his domus for the remainder of the year, and became for a moment a political non-entity. Clodius doubled-down on Pompey's fears and dispatched gangs to watch Pompey's house without interruption and keep him bottled up, seemingly powerless, at home. But others still worked to recall Cicero. In October eight of Clodius' fellow tribunes, Ninnius among them, moved to recall Cicero with the consul-elect Lentulus' support. The measure was vetoed, but the pressure to bring Cicero home grew.[71]

Cicero provides us with an account of the efforts to restore him to Rome that year in a speech he delivered (in 56) defending Publius Sestius, a tribune of 57. On 1 January 57 BCE the new first consul Lentulus convened the senate and brought up the matter of Cicero's exile. His colleague Metellus noted that though he personally disagreed with Cicero, he agreed the matter was critical and needed to be discussed in the senate. Senator Lucius Aurelius Cotta spoke first. He opined that Cicero's exile had been unlawful, noting that Cicero quite ironically had been exiled without trial for executing citizens without trial. Cotta proceeded to dismantle Clodius' law against Cicero in a withering legal analysis: the law was so flawed, it was functionally invalid. Therefore there were no legal obstacles to Cicero's return. Pompey spoke next, approving of Cotta's opinion. He added, though, that it would be best for Cicero's safety and to avoid confusion, if both the senate decreed he could return and the assembly approved a law to that effect. The senate unanimously agreed, says Cicero; it is clear, at least, that they decisively agreed. Before a senatorial decree could be issued, the tribune Atilius Gavinius interrupted. He did not impose his veto; Cicero implies he would have regretted that when the senate was ready to act. He did however ask for a day's recess, and through some legal manoeuvres managed to keep the senate from meeting for the rest of the month. Late January arrived, and the scheduled day for an assembly vote on Cicero's recall. A crowd of supporters occupied the assembly-grounds before dawn, including the tribune Quintus Fabricius, other supporting tribunes like Sestius, and senators such as Cicero's brother Quintus. Clodius, however, had anticipated that move and assembled a gang that included gladiators his brother had conveniently hired for some funeral games. Violence erupted in the Forum and a number of Fabricius' supporters were wounded or killed. Whether it was true that the Tiber was 'filled with the corpses of the citizens, that the sewers were choked up; that blood was wiped up out of the Forum with sponges' as Cicero asserted in his speech, the fact remained that Clodius, though no longer tribune, wielded considerable power through his gangs on the streets of Rome.[72]

Now Titus Annius Milo appears in the sources, an important aristocrat in these struggles. A tribune of the plebs for 57 with no love for Clodius, Milo investigated the Forum riot and charged Clodius with illegal violence. Clodius still had powerful friends even after his substantial forays into street wars, however, and the case was never heard in court. But in the process Clodius' gangs harrassed Milo in the streets and attacked his house. Soon enough, Milo recognized that legal attacks would not curb Clodius. Accordingly, Milo created his own gang to contest the streets. And so the street violence continued. Clodian gangs assaulted the tribune Publius Sestius who was attempting to block a legislative assembly with an unclear (to us) purpose. On that occasion the theoretically inviolable tribune Sestius was well and truly roughed up by the gang, barely escaping death. Not a slow learner, Sestius followed suit with Clodius and Milo, gathering his own entourage of street brawlers. It probably started to seem like everybody was doing it. Soon Pompey joined the trio, employing men from his Italian estates to brawl as needed on the streets of Rome. Ultimately Clodius was out-ruffianed in what was a tumult on the Roman streets.[73]

At this point too, Pompey kicked his campaign into high gear to recall Cicero. Touring Italy, he persuaded the municipal elites to publicly call for Cicero's return. Support grew in the senate. On the first of January in the temple of Virtus that Marius had built, the consul Lentulus Spinther moved, and the senate decreed that all citizens who cared about the Republic should gather in Rome in support of Cicero's recall.[74] The political winds were shifting. At the same time increasing numbers, not least the powerful tax collectors and the scribes' guild, added to the voices calling for Cicero.[75] In July the senate met again, this time to move decisively and recall Cicero. Clodius stood alone, the sole senator voting against the orator's return.[76] The next day, a dignified bunch consisting of no less than the consul Spinther, Pompey, and the collective senators of consular and praetorian rank, held an assembly to speak for Cicero. A day further and the senate decreed it unlawful for anyone to block the recall of Cicero and that anyone opposing legislation on this point would be an outlaw. Clodius persisted against the shifting tide. Finally, in early August, a crowd gathered in the Forum before the forthcoming recall vote of the centuriate assembly. Clodius' gangs attacked the crowd. Pompey's thugs were up to the task, however, and booted Clodius from the Forum. The vote passed.[77]

And so Cicero triumphantly returned to Italy in September of 57 BCE.[78] He wrote to Atticus that his homecoming was 'like the beginning of a second life'.[79] Plutarch put the restoration like this:

Thus Cicero came home in the sixteenth month after his exile; and so great was the joy of the cities and the eagerness of men to meet him that what was said by Cicero afterwards fell short of the truth. He said, namely, that Italy had taken him on her shoulders and carried him into Rome. And there Crassus also, who was his enemy before his exile, now readily met him and was reconciled with him, to gratify his son Publius, as he said, who was an ardent admirer of Cicero.[80]

Over the next year, Cicero recovered much of his property and successfully moved to have the temple of Libertas and the sacred status of the site removed so that he could rebuild his Palatine house.[81]

* * *

Clodius' impassioned attack on Cicero had been reversed, but Clodius was still a force to be reckoned with when it came to controlling the streets of Rome. And the triumvirs, though seemingly at least a bit shaky in the aftermath of Cicero's return, would soon reforge their understanding – at least for a time. Hindsight is a misleading nuisance for the historian, but for the storyteller it can be a great asset. For our story now must move into the final few years of the Republic. Soon the rivalry of Caesar and Pompey would end in civil war, a civil war that would effectively end the Republic.

Chapter 12

The Triumvirate Disintegrates: Pompey, Crassus, and Caesar

It had come to this. About a decade ago, Caesar had secured, with the help of Pompey and Crassus, the consulship in 59 BCE. Then, with assistance from a tribune, he engineered a military command in Gaul, first for five years, and then for an additional five. Caesar took full advantage of that time. Under his command legions had subjected the whole of Gaul to Roman authority, defeated incursions across the Rhine from fierce Germanic tribes, and even launched prestigious expeditions to Britain. Year after year, Caesar commanded his legions – for the battles for Gaul had certainly forged them into his legions – through near-catastrophes, spectacular victories, and everything in between. By the end of 51 BCE, Caesar's army had essentially pacified the warrior tribes of Gaul. Things had changed. In 59 Caesar was, by any stretch of the imagination, the junior partner in a political cabal with Crassus and Pompey. In 49 he was a powerful aristocrat of consequence with a string of exceptional military victories that had elicited many official public prayers of thanksgiving from the senate. The spoils of victories in Gaul had made Caesar the wealthiest Roman of his day, save for the fantastically wealthy Pompey. Now the time had come for him to seal those victories and his glory for his Gallic conquests. A second consulship and a spectacular triumph for the conquest of Gaul: these were to be his earned prizes. The Roman assembly, through the Law of the Ten Tribunes, had granted him in 52 the right to run for the consulship *in absentia*. When the time was right, Caesar could submit his candidacy without the required return to Rome, even if he were, say, still in command of legions in Gaul.

But things had taken an ominous turn for Caesar at Rome. His future in Gaul had grown tenuous as rivals, like those in the Marcellus clan, sought to replace him prematurely as proconsul in Gaul. His very acts as governor of Gaul were challenged, in spectacularly blunt ways. So, for example, the consul of 51, Marcus Claudius Marcellus, publicly flogged a resident of the Gallic Latin colony of Novum Comum to demonstrate that Caesar had illegally granted citizenship to the inhabitants of the region. Citizens could not be flogged; subjects could, and Marcellus sought to impress Caesar's humiliation into the flesh of the poor notable.

By 51 BCE, Caesar's rivals at Rome had made the end of his Gallic command a regular conversation in political circles. Talk also hinted that perhaps Caesar's frequently trumpeted right to campaign for the consulship *in absentia* had been nullified by a law of Pompey's. Without that right, Caesar would have to return to the city in person, a private citizen no longer in command of troops, to campaign for the consulship. This Caesar would simply not do; there was no question in his mind that all ten tribunes of 52 had passed a law granting him the right to run for consul *in absentia*, when he chose. To come to Rome in person violated his earned legal privilege and insulted his dignity in the process. And Caesar cared mightily about his dignity. But this, in the end, seems to have been the position of Caesar's rivals who had chosen Pompey, proconsul of Spain and the leading Roman of the day, as their leader. Tensions had escalated, for Caesar and Pompey both commanded considerable armies. Eventually, an alternative to the deadlock was proposed by the tribune Curio. Let Caesar and Pompey resign their proconsulships and become private citizens. Let them make the same sacrifices – loss of the proconsulships and the armies they commanded – so that the Republic could persist.

As for Pompey, he continued to see himself as THE pre-eminent Roman. His treatment at Rome bore this out, which included prestigious and uniquely powerful military commands awarded to him alone, time and time again. He also had the wealth. Through his command of legions in the provinces of Spain, he had the army. Should Caesar decide to march on Rome with his Gallic legions, Pompey offered the only plausible defence for the city and senate. And so, Caesar's rivals in the aristocracy – Romans like the Marcelli and Scipio – sought Pompey's approval as they backed Caesar into a corner. And Pompey was persuaded to represent them and persuaded not to grant Caesar all of what he wanted.

By the start of 49 it was clear that his rivals, with Pompey as their rallying point, were determined to humble him. The senate, or as Caesar saw it, the rival faction that dominated the senate, had issued the final decree, the *senatus consultum ultimum*. The magistrates of the state should take all necessary steps to protect the Republic from harm. It was a moment of crisis that would lead the Roman Republic into a terminal series of civil wars from which it would never recover. Long-term political order and stability would only be reimposed decades later by the creation of a new Roman monarchy, the Principate, crafted by Caesar's adopted son, Augustus. Ancient authors, drawn to the drama and aware of the historical import of Caesar's standoff with his enemies and Pompey, tried to make the story even more dramatic. Plutarch, citing Asinius Pollio, a member of Caesar's command staff in 49, provides this famous account of the decisive moment, the plunge into civil war:

> Withdrawn and silent, [Caesar] spent a long time mentally torn between the two alternatives, and even at this late stage his intentions fluctuated wildly to and fro. Then he spent an equally long time voicing his doubts to those of his friends who were with him (who included Asinius Pollio), with a tally of all the troubles that their crossing of the river would initiate for the whole world, and with reflections on how the great tale of it would be their legacy to subsequent generations. Eventually, however, in a burst of intense emotion, as if thrusting aside rational considerations and abandoning himself to whatever the future held, he turned to the river, prefacing the crossing with the usual words spoken by people before embarking on hazardous and uncertain enterprises: 'Let the die be cast!' There were no further delays to his rapid advance.[1]

There must be some truth to this account, but it is caked with rhetorical additions. Caesar was a product of his day. He knew well the results of the civil wars of his lifetime. When Sulla returned from his war on Mithridates nearly thirty years ago, he battled his way to Rome and seized power as dictator for restoring the Republic. Lists of state enemies, which largely meant enemies of Sulla, followed. Emboldened and authorized by those lists, hundreds, if not a few thousand, Roman aristocrats and some commoners were slaughtered, their property confiscated, with impunity. Wars with Marian forces in Spain continued through much of the seventies. When Catiline failed in his attempts at revolution in the mid 60s, he fell with an army of rebellious Romans. If Caesar crossed into Italy from his province of Cisalpine Gaul at the head of a mobilized legion and marched on Rome, Romans would die. Even if in his eyes he opposed, not Rome, but a clique of personal enemies, many Romans would die and not just his enemies. Was this what Pompey truly wanted? Is this what Caesar wanted?

What had brought Caesar and Pompey to this standoff? The two most powerful people in the Republic, once politically close associates, became the ultimate rivals of the Republic in a long line of political rivalries. What persuaded these Romans, who had already experienced the horrors of civil war, to initiate another?[2]

Caesar and the Start of The Gallic Wars

When Caesar left Italy in 58 BCE, as noted in the previous chapter, Cicero had been freshly exiled from Rome and the tribune Clodius dominated the politics of the Republic. At this point, though Caesar absolutely kept an eye on Rome, he was highly engaged with problems of his own governing Gaul. Or, more accurately, highly engaged with finding suitable wars in Gaul so he could seek greater *gloria* and enrichment, just as he had in Spain a few years before. At the time he left Italy, Caesar's official provinces included Illyricum along the Adriatic, but his focus, as it happened, became Transalpine Gaul.

The term 'Gaul', a Roman label, implies a unity that did not exist at the time. Caesar famously divides Gaul into three main groups and regions: Belgae, Aquitani, and Gauls.[3] Even this division masks the linguistic variety of the peoples there, though most spoke languages in the Celtic family. These many peoples of Gaul were organized politically into various forms of kinship groups. Caesar would call these groups *civitates*, the Latin word both for city and civilization, but modern historians often call them tribes for lack of a better word. Some groups were ruled by kings, some by councils of elders, some had elected magistrates, some all three. Some allied with their neighbours; some fought with them for dominance; some varied in their practices.[4] Politically, Gaul was a big place with many peoples.

The Republic had encountered Gallic peoples regularly throughout its history. The infamous Roman defeat at the Allia River in 390 BCE allowed the Gallic Senones to seize and sack Rome.[5] Almost two

centuries later, after many conflicts with various Gallic peoples of
north Italy, like the Boii, many tribes allied with Hannibal when the
Carthaginian ranged northern and southern Italy. Following their victory
against the Carthaginians in 202 BCE, the Romans continued to battle all
sorts of Gauls, extending their power over northern Italy on their side of
the Alps, and eventually naming it Cisalpine Gaul. They also steadily
increased their control over the coastal route through Southern Gaul,
from north Italy over the Alps to their provinces in Spain, essential for
marching soldiers to and from these important territories.[6] By the end of
the second century, Romans had planted the colony of Narbo along the
coast (modern Narbonne, France) and established a permanent presence
in Transalpine Gaul. When in 59 BCE the tribune Vatinius legislated to
gain Caesar the proconsulship of Transalpine Gaul (along with Cisalpine
Gaul, and Illyricum across the Adriatic Sea), that Roman province was
relatively small: the land from the Alps to the Mediterranean and south
and east of the Rhône river.[7] The increased regularity and magnitude of
Roman involvement brought with it a fair amount of trade – especially in
Roman wine – and diplomatic ties with many Gallic peoples of southern
and Central Gaul. In turn this economic activity seems to have played a
role in urbanizing the southern Gauls, spurring them to develop larger
fortified towns.[8]

But the entire land of the Gauls was still a large territory containing many
peoples, mostly independent of Roman authority and mostly satisfied with
that arrangement. It was a perfect setting for an enterprising proconsul,
one who had already demonstrated while governor in Spain that he was
talented at justifying – and profiting from – Roman military expeditions.

Though governing his provinces in the modern sense – interpreting
and executing laws, taxation, and so on – was part of Caesar's position,
he focused mostly on military operations, part and parcel of most
proconsulships. Initially Caesar's military expeditions in Gaul began,
ostensibly, as a response to news that the Helvetii, a large tribe with
significant military resources, desired to leave their current homelands
near Lake Geneva and migrate to the western Atlantic coastal region of
Gaul. Such a migration would inevitably, from the Roman perspective,
disrupt the political and military relationships that kept the Gallic
province safe. And so, Caesar's first major campaign in Gaul was to
check the Helvetii migration. Caesar raised and trained his first new

legions, a process he continued during his time in Gaul. Doing so went beyond his formal powers, beyond senatorial authority, so he developed a workaround. It appears that a large percentage of the soldiers in his new legions were, in fact, not citizens. They lived in the highly Romanized, but not yet enfranchised province of Cisalpine Gaul, often called Gallia Togata, because those Romanized residents had adopted toga wearing. Since these cultural Romans were not Roman citizens, the legions Caesar formed with them were not technically legions. They would need pay and provision however, and since again the senate had not authorized any additional funds or troops, Caesar relied on funds he obtained from his campaigns to pay and supply them. Militarily, these units were very much legionaries, armed and equipped as legionaries and quite able to fight as legionaries.[9] By the end of Caesar's command, all accounted them as Roman legions in fact.

Despite successfully provoking and fighting wars in Spain a few years before, Caesar was very much still learning to command in Gaul and he certainly made mistakes during the campaign against the Helvetii. But he honed his skills. Equally important, he demonstrated to his soldiers time and again that he valued them and was willing to share their risks, exhorting and rewarding his soldiers when there was need or merit, fighting in the front lines to stiffen resolve. Caesar even went the extraordinary extra step of learning the names of each of his over-300 centurions, the sergeants that kept the soldiers in line and fighting. Indeed, when Caesar addressed his troops he referred to them as comrades – not as subordinates, though of course they were that. These efforts had just started in the initial successful campaign against the Helvetii. But even at the start of what would become his iron-forged relationship with his soldiers, the legionaries proved highly effective. They crushed the Helvetian forces in their first pitched battle near the town of Bibracte and forced the tribe to return to its homes near Lake Geneva.[10] This was Caesar's first summer in command.

Caesar still had most of his five-year command ahead of him. Checking the Helvetii was not nearly a significant enough victory for him. As part of his efforts to gain the utmost prestige from his exploits, he wrote a series of commentaries on his command in Gaul known as the *Gallic Wars*. According to the perspective he advanced in that text, the next legitimate opportunity for the legions in Gaul to act came swiftly.[11]

A mass of tribes in Central Gaul, Caesar claimed afterwards, sought protection against the continuing excursions of hostile Germanic tribes across the Rhine River. King Ariovistus led those invading German tribes and had established control over some territory west of the Rhine – Gallic lands as Caesar reckoned them. Caesar demanded Ariovistus yield the territories he had dominated and return across the Rhine with his warriors. Ariovistus saw himself as a conqueror occupying these lands by right of might. There would be war. At the end of the campaigning season of 58, Caesar managed a decisive battle against Ariovistus' army. The king and forces melted away, lost to the Roman sources. In the winter of 58 Caesar conscripted another two legions, bringing his total up to six, double what he had been assigned by the senate.[12] In 58/7 Caesar spent the winter as he often did, in Cisalpine Gaul away from the legions and closer to Rome.

The justification for war in 57 BCE: the Belgae. This group of northern Gallic tribes was concerned, to say the least, with growing Roman diplomatic and military sway in Central Gaul. Thus, they formed an army. So again, Caesar and his legions campaigned, building their skills, increasing their deadly effectiveness, strengthening their cohesion. The decisive battle of 57 was at the Sambre river against a Belgic tribe known as the Nervii. The legion smashed the Nervii's army at the Sambre. Minor Roman operations followed. Altogether it was sufficient to get the senate, as Caesar proudly noted in his commentaries, to grant fifteen days of public thanksgiving to the gods for his victories. This was the end of the campaign season of 57. Caesar again wintered in Cisalpine Gaul.[13] We'll return to Caesar in the early spring of 56. For he would essentially campaign against some people – whether Gauls, Germans, or Britons – every season until Gaul was fully pacified in 51 BCE.

Cicero's Return to Rome

Cicero had left Rome in 58 BCE heartbroken, exiled from the city and the political life he loved so much. Through a considerable legal process – accompanied by organized street violence engineered by aristocrats like Clodius, Milo, Sestius, and even Pompey – Cicero's return was accomplished. By September of 57 – sometime close to the battle of the Sambre in Gaul – Cicero had triumphantly returned home.[14] He had much to keep him busy, from recovering his lost property to making a full senatorial comeback. He began the latter task by delivering a speech, a version of which we still have, naming and praising his supporters and castigating those who had abandoned him – like the consuls of 58, Gabinius and Piso. Cicero seems to have felt most obligated to Pompey for his rescue – indeed he stated so in the speech he delivered upon returning to the senate.[15] And so he worked assiduously to ally himself more closely to Pompey on his return.[16] He hoped doing so would detach Pompey from Caesar and Crassus. In 57, this may well not have been a fool's errand. There is no reason to suppose the triumvirate of Caesar, Pompey, and Crassus was designed for permanence. Certainly strains in the three aristocrats' association were appearing in 57 and 56.[17] Cicero's first major political move to ingratiate himself more with Pompey, just a few days after his return, was to propose a special five-year commission for Pompey to supervise the city's grain supply. Rome faced yet another devastating shortage of grain, perhaps exacerbated by Clodius' significant expansion of grain subsidies. Effectively Pompey was made proconsul in- and outside Italy with extensive authority over harbours, shipping, and farming – a considerable chunk of Mediterranean economic affairs. He also had access to a fleet and soldiers to secure grain in sufficient quantities at favourable prices.[18] Authorized to appoint fifteen legates to carry out the job, Cicero was, unsurprisingly, first on the list.[19] This was a unique and prestigious position granted to the Roman of his generation who had held other unique commands – one against pirates and another that resulted in Roman domination of the eastern Mediterranean.[20] It cannot have done anything to mitigate his vanity. After creating this prize for Pompey, Cicero turned to the practical problem of regaining his property, especially the cherished spot on the Palatine where his destroyed townhouse had been replaced by a temple to Liberty.[21]

56 saw strains in the triumvirate, particularly between Crassus and Pompey, and saw Cicero associating more closely with Pompey. It was also clear that Pompey and Clodius were completely at odds. The main issue seems to have been the problem of restoring the deposed king of Egypt, Ptolemy Auletes, to his throne. Which Roman would undertake this assuredly lucrative mission in Egypt to restore Ptolemy? Both Pompey and Crassus seem to have wanted the position.[22] Clodius, knowing this, saw an opportunity to humiliate Pompey. Clodius had been elected aedile

for 56, saving himself from prosecution for street violence and giving him a political platform to attack his rival Milo for his own use of gang violence. The trial of Milo was as large and showy as any with crowds inflated by the presence of Clodius and Milo's supporters and gangs. Notably Pompey spoke in defence of Milo, despite the disruptions of Cato's followers. Then Clodius took the floor and began playing directly to his crowd. As Cicero described it to his brother Quintus, Clodius raged, in the very midst of the shouting, putting questions to his claque: 'Who was it who was starving the commons to death?' His ruffians answered, 'Pompey'. 'Who wanted to be sent to Alexandria?' They answered, 'Pompey'. 'Who did they wish to go?' They answered, 'Crassus'.[23] His incited gang began spitting at Milo's supporters and fighting erupted. Clodius got himself thrown from the Rostra in the brawl. So, Clodius and Pompey were certainly not on good terms, but it also seems quite likely that Crassus allowed and perhaps actively encouraged this stunt at the trial, designed to embarrass Pompey.[24]

Criticism of Caesar had gained a foothold in the city by late 57 or early 56. Cicero delivered a defence for Sestius, who as tribune along with Milo in 57 had used street gangs to counter Clodius and restore Cicero. Charged with inciting violence, a grateful Cicero came to his legal defence. During the trial Cicero attacked the former tribune Vatinius, the one who in 59 had secured Caesar's command in Gaul. Cicero ostentatiously worked to separate Vatinius from Caesar, to lessen the risk of collateral offence, but his words still appeared to be a criticism of the Proconsul of Gaul. A more concrete challenge to Caesar, Cicero scheduled a senatorial debate in early spring of 55 on the Campanian land law Caesar had passed – a debate that threatened to secure its repeal.[25] Then too, Lucius Domitius Ahenobarbus let it be known that he would run for the consulship of 55 and, if elected, relieve Caesar of his legions.[26]

Caesar, Pompey, and Crassus Meet at Luca

Whatever Cicero's hopes were for winning Pompey away from Crassus and Caesar in 56 and early 55, they were dashed when the triumvirs patched up their differences in April of 55 and opted to renew their alliance. In April 56 BCE Caesar was finishing his winter at a town in the southern part of Cisalpine Gaul called Luca, a bit to the northeast of Pisa. Plutarch and Appian give a similar account: a flood of senators visited the increasingly influential and wealthy Caesar. The fact that both sources give the same numbers – 200 senators and 120 lictors – suggests, however, that they drew from the same source or Appian copied Plutarch. Still, Caesar had apparently been busy funding politicians. The operative visitors in all of this, however, were Pompey and Crassus. The operative non-visitors were Cicero and Cato. At Luca the three triumvirs crafted a working agreement. Pompey and Crassus would run for the consulship with Caesar's support. With their influence in office the senate would be persuaded to vote Caesar funds for his wars in Gaul and extend his provincial command for another five years.[27]

Crassus and Pompey's Second Consulship, 55 BCE

The sources are a bit chaotic in their picture of the consular elections for 55. Plutarch and Appian, for example, capture some of the details of the election process and actors, but do not give an overall clear picture. Dio seems a bit better here in technical details but still needs elaboration to make a sensible account.[28] Combining them yields something like this. It seems Pompey and Crassus were fairly confident that they could not win the consulship for 55 in a normal open election. Not least because Cato had returned from Cyprus. He resumed staunchly opposing the triumvirs and backed their rival, Lucius Domitius Ahenobarbus, for the consulship.[29] And so their ultimate strategy was to delay the elections until the consuls of 56 had to step down, at the end of the calendar year. This is a bit of a technicality to decipher. With no new consuls elected to take office and no old consuls still in power, an *interrex*, an 'in-between king' (in between two pairs of consuls) had to be appointed. The interrex, by ancient custom, presented only two candidates for the consulship, and the centuriate assembly simply met to affirm the presented pair. Accordingly, the trick then was to get a favourable interrex to name Pompey and Crassus as the consular pair, which apparently was not very difficult for them to achieve. So, if that indeed were the underlying plan, Pompey and Crassus had to stall the elections. Part of that required not openly declaring their candidacy. At some point one of the year's consuls, Marcellinus called upon Pompey and Crassus to announce their candidacy, and both refused to commit definitively. Part of their 'electoral' strategy – if one can call it that – also seems to have revolved around using street toughs[30] to prevent the centuriate assembly from meeting to hold an election in the Campus Martius.[31] It also involved dissuading rival candidates, namely Domitius. Before one scheduled election when he journeyed to the Campus Martius in the grey hours of the morning, Domitius and the enslaved servant bearing his torch were attacked. The servant was murdered and Domitius scared off from future attempts to win election.[32] Ultimately, the year closed without consuls, a sympathetic interrex was appointed, and Pompey and Crassus were brought forward as the only candidates. Thus confirmed, the centuriate assembly confirmed them. They were the consuls for 55.[33]

A few salient details about their year as consuls are preserved by the sources. Upon their inauguration at the start of 55, Cato decided to run for the forthcoming praetorship of that year and position himself to check their activities in office. To no avail; he did not win the office. The lengths to which Pompey and Crassus went to secure this were rather striking. According to Plutarch, the consuls laid the groundwork against Cato by quickly pushing through the senate a decree that elected praetors would take office immediately. Normally they were not inaugurated immediately so that any allegations of electoral bribery could be resolved. This shift in practice enabled bribery against Cato on a massive scale with effectively no accountability. Even so, Cato was still a forerunner for the office. So, when the assembly gathered to vote and the publicly announced first votes were for Cato, Pompey, the president of the assembly, claimed to have heard thunder – a bad omen from the gods – and dissolved the assembly. More bribery followed, Plutarch reports, and some street-violence to keep Cato's supporters, the 'best citizens' as Plutarch termed them, from reaching the voting grounds. Cato could not compete with this array of pressures and was not elected. He had failed twice in relatively rapid succession to thwart Pompey and Crassus. Vatinius, an associate of the triumvirs who as tribune had secured Caesar's provincial command in Gaul, on the other hand, easily became a praetor for 55.[34]

Whether Cato as praetor could have decisively blocked Pompey and Crassus' aims is not clear, but now he lacked the magistracy that would have strengthened any opposition. Two items on the triumvirs' agenda for 55 survive in the sources, both the result of legislation passed by the cooperative tribune Gaius Trebonius. The first law assigned five-year provinces to the two consuls: Syria and Egypt for one, Nearer and Further Spain for the other.[35] Pompey and Crassus would control legions and provinces on a scope comparable with Caesar's command in Gaul and Illyricum.[36] Cato, even without public office seems to have done his best to block passage of the bill by speaking against it at length in the assembly – for two hours Plutarch and Dio suggest – but, again, to no avail.[37] He may have been arrested in the process of obstructing the law's passage.[38] Trebonius' second law extended Caesar's command. For how many years is not exactly clear and it has been a source of considerable debate since the official end of Caesar's command seems to have been a major point of contention in the months leading up to his invasion of Italy. Dio asserts that Caesar's command was extended for three years, giving an end date of sometime in 52 BCE. Plutarch, Suetonius, and Appian, however, all assert that Caesar's command was extended an additional five years, giving an official end to Caesar's command sometime in 49 BCE.[39] An extension of five years, however, makes much better sense of the debates about the end of Caesar's proconsulship in 52 and 51.

Cicero, Clodius and the Triumvirs after Luca

When Cicero learned of the renewed association of the triumvirs in 56, he executed a whiplash-inducing turnaround. Early in the year he had opposed Caesar's Gallic command altogether. By June he was defending Caesar's position publicly.[40] Soon he began to defend agents of the triumvirs in court, like Caesar's loyalist Balbus, and by the middle of 54 he reported essentially being swamped in defence cases.[41] Like a loyal ally, he even attended the bloody games dedicating Pompey's theatre, though he had no taste for that type of entertainment as he complained on at least one occasion.[42] He cultivated a friendship – perhaps it was sincere – with Caesar, with whom he shared an interest in good writing. The demands for legal support for those the triumvirs picked, however, were demoralizing. So Cicero devoted a considerable amount of energy to working on his philosophical works in the period through 53, including a treatise on good oratory and the start of his great philosophical discussion of the Roman state, *The Republic*.[43]

Clodius continued to play a role in politics, as aedile in 56, but does not appear often in the sources for a bit after that. His brother, Appius

Claudius, was one of the many who visited Caesar, Pompey, and Crassus at Luca. Clodius seems to have followed Appius' lead in supporting the triumvirs. He even publicly made amends with Pompey. Clodius arguably remained an important player in the city even when not in office. And in 55 when the tribune Gaius Cato had vetoed elections as part of Pompey and Crassus' electoral manoeuvres, Clodius supported Gaius, his friend, and supported the veto in the face of considerable senatorial opposition. He certainly could have been involved in the electoral violence of that year but there is no mention of him in the sources. Indeed we hear little about Clodius in 55; he seems to have focused on more obscure matters, like perhaps securing a lucrative embassy mission somewhere in the eastern Mediterranean. When he resurfaces in the sources it is to seek election in 53 for a praetorship in 52.[44] In 52, however, he would die violently, as we will see.

Rome Descends into Disorder (54 BCE)

When his consulship ended, Crassus departed for Syria, eager it seems, to undertake a campaign that would bring military glory, command of armies, and further riches.[45] Allies like Pompey and Caesar had grand military accomplishments to their name, but Crassus, though a competent commander, only had to his credit the crushing of a rebellion of enslaved gladiators. As Crassus sought military distinction in Mesopotamia, Pompey remained near Rome. In hindsight that seems a poor choice for him; who knows what military and strategic advantages Pompey might have had a few years later when civil war broke out if he had travelled in 54 to Spain to take command personally of his legions and develop stronger bonds with a veteran army. But that truly is hindsight. Living forward as all people must, Pompey still had extensive powers and responsibilities supervising the Roman grain supply, one of the reasons he remained in Rome. Also he was about to dedicate a magnificent stone theatre funded from his provincial adventures, an edifice that survives today in the modern city.[46] This entailed a spectacular array of gladiatorial shows, which Dio describes:

> In [the theatre, Pompey] provided entertainment consisting of music and gymnastic contests, and in the Circus a horse-race and the

slaughter of many wild-beasts of all kinds. Indeed, 500 lions were used up in five days, and eighteen elephants fought against men in heavy armour. Some of the beasts were killed at the time and others a little later.[47]

Dio finishes with a sympathy-invoking description of the sufferings of the poor elephants. This was how the Romans celebrated.

As for other compelling reasons to stay in Italy, Pompey loved his wife, Julia, dearly and she him. She was, recall, the daughter of Caesar and a critical political tie between the two aristocrats. Despite this, they had, it seems, a happy marriage. So the claim some sources made that staying in Italy allowed he and Julia to spend more time together seems correct.[48] Sadly, Julia died in childbirth towards the end of the year 54, a not uncommon tragedy for mothers in the medical landscape of the ancient world. She seems to have captured the popular imagination at Rome, however, and the loss of Julia in childbirth was a tragedy that sparked a public response. Plutarch, Livy's summarizer, and Dio assert the crowds opted to honour her publicly with burial in the Campus Martius.[49]

The remainder of 54 and the whole of 53 was a decidedly bad period for the Roman political class, not to mention a bad year for anyone caught in their manoeuvres. Street violence – and murder – bribery, and other illegal behaviours derailed the elections in 54 for the magistrates of 53.[50] Added to this mix, the tribune Gaius Cato apparently vetoed the consular elections, ensuring there would be no chief magistrates at the start of 53. Pompey's role in the electoral violence and mischief is not entirely clear. According to Appian, Pompey secretly wanted to be named dictator and encouraged violence through his own street agents to amplify the need for a dictatorship.[51] Plutarch similarly reports that Pompey supported regular candidates for the elections, but when bribery favoured less desirable candidates, Pompey 'allowed a condition of lawlessness to arise in the city, and before long Rome was filled with talk about the necessity of having a dictator'.[52] Dio differs on Pompey's ulterior motives, but all agree Pompey was offered the office.[53] Resistance flared. Cato the Younger, now praetor, may have publicly condemned the proposal; that would not be surprising.[54] Reactionary riots sparked from the very suggestion of a dictatorship. In response to the city's agitation, Pompey himself, reportedly, declared he had no intention of becoming dictator. But this seems to have been a pattern for Pompey – get other people to demand offices and honours for him so that ostensibly he just acquiesced to people's wishes, rather than manoeuvring for self-interested power. Eventually sufficient order was achieved for consuls to be elected for 53, at least seven months into that year. Gnaeus Domitius Calvinius and Marcus Valerius Messalla took office for a short stint.[55] Within a few months, disorder in the city, however, would lead many Romans to demand Pompey's authority again.

Crassus and the Parthian Campaign

As political violence wracked the streets of Rome, Caesar conducted his second invasion of Britain, and Cicero learned to live with the shame of assisting the triumvirs. Meanwhile, Crassus determined to invade the Mesopotamian territory of the Parthians, the Persian dynasts that ruled the Central Asian empire to the east of Syria. The trek into the rival's empire began in 54. Crassus, accompanied by his son, Publius Crassus, fresh from Caesar's legions in Gaul, commanded a massive Roman army of seven legions. They marched east towards the Euphrates river, seeking a Parthian army to battle. Eventually one rose to meet them, commanded by a powerful subordinate of the Parthian king known as Surenas. The armies clashed near Carrhae, a town fifty miles east of the Upper Euphrates.[56] Today the Battle of Carrhae is remembered as something of classic match-up of different military systems. The Romans' excellent heavy infantry clashed with the Parthians' exceptional heavy cavalry and mounted archers. The Parthians won the battle, Publius Crassus died in the conflict, and the elder Crassus attempted to lead his defeated legions back to Roman Syria. Agile Parthian horse-archers, however, harried their retreat, whittling down the remaining Roman army to remnants. Out of options, Crassus arranged to parley with Surenas. In the process he was ambushed and slain while attempting to avoid capture. His head was presented as a trophy, along with the Roman legionary standards, to the Parthian King.[57]

By the end of 53, the triumvirate was disintegrating. It was shorn of the ties Julia provided for Caesar and Pompey, and stripped of its third member, Crassus, who may also have been an agent of balance between the two egos. Caesar and Pompey's rivalry would spark into flames soon enough.

Chapter 13

Deadlock and War: Pompey and Caesar

The years from 52 through 50 BCE were notable for disruptions in Rome and disruptions in the province of Transalpine Gaul. While a semblance of Roman order was imposed in the city, and to a much greater extent in the province, the growing break between Pompey and Caesar, the fundamental rivalry over who was the pre-eminent Roman, would lead to a deadlock and then to a civil war that would usher in the dictatorship of Julius Caesar and the fall of the Republic.

Clodius Murdered

The election of the consuls in the second half of 53 BCE did little to moderate the violence in the city. Those epic rivals, Milo and Clodius, both campaigned in 53 for offices of 52. Milo sought the consulship and Clodius the praetorship. Their followers, as was becoming customary, were not above brawling in the Roman streets. They still detested one another, and the electoral violence and bribery – rampant even by Roman standards – continued to delay the elections of the consuls, and thus the praetors. When the year 52 began, there simply were no magistrates. With the exception of the ten tribunes – and perhaps minor offices that left no record in the sources – the election systems of the Republic provided no leaders. The state was failing.[1]

So, the Republic was already struggling at the start of 52. Within a couple of weeks, however, matters got decidedly worse. Milo and Clodius clashed violently outside Rome. Milo's band – perhaps under his direct orders – murdered that charismatic and incendiary leader of the urban plebs, Clodius. The political impact was explosive. Cicero's defence speech for Milo – as one would have hoped from a competent Roman defence lawyer – provides a clever rhetorical, selective, and embellished account of events. It is not a particularly reliable source for the fatal brawl. Fortunately we have another excellent source for the murder. Asconius, a first-century CE scholar, wrote a series of commentaries on some of Cicero's speeches to help educate his children. His notes on Cicero's defence speech for Milo provide the fullest account of the fatal encounter between Clodius and Milo and how that brawl sparked a radical political innovation.

As Asconius tells it, on 17 or 18 January, 52 BCE, Milo travelled southeast from Rome along the Appian Way to his nearby hometown of Lanuvium. He travelled with his wife, Fausta; she was a granddaughter of Sulla, as it happened with a name that spoke of joy and good fortune – we know nothing else about her.[2] Travelling by carriage, the two were accompanied by a sizeable band of enslaved servants. Some gladiators rounded out the gang – extra muscle should the need arise. The arrangement does beg the question: what on Earth did Milo envision happening to him on his short trip? Meanwhile, Clodius rode northwest on horseback from the town of Aricia to Rome. His entourage drew less comment – thirty enslaved servants each armed with a sword was a normal retinue for the time, says Asconius. Clodius was also accompanied by three friends, though what happened to them in the subsequent mayhem is not clear. The parties passed on the road. Perhaps the two enemies might have simply scowled at each other and continued their journeys uninterrupted. As it happened, however, two particularly well known gladiators, Eudamos and Birria, dawdled at the back of Milo's entourage. For whatever reason, they decided to rough up some of Clodius' enslaved attendants. When Clodius saw this, he rode towards the scuffle, with a look suggesting he was likely to reproach them all. Clodius' countenance, apparently, was all Birria required to stab him with a javelin.[3]

Seriously wounded in his shoulder, Clodius was carried to the nearby tavern, presumably by his enslaved servants. Meanwhile Milo heard word of the encounter: Birria had egregiously assaulted Clodius. Milo would almost certainly feel the legal consequences, not to mention the political and social sting of a further antagonized Clodius. Milo quickly calculated: the penalty for finishing the job – if he was convicted – would probably be less severe than the danger a wounded and wronged Clodius posed. So Milo dispatched servants, who dragged the helpless Clodius from the tavern, stabbed him to death and left him by the side of the road like so much refuse. It is not clear what happened to Clodius' enslaved servants, though a number were killed and seriously injured in the episode, it seems.

Of Clodius' three notable travel companions, we hear nothing. Later that day, a travelling senator found Clodius' body beside the road. The senator must have recognized Clodius' corpse despite its mauling, for he ordered it to be carried back to Rome in his personal litter.[4]

Clodius' murder provoked an uproar in the city, to say the least. Supporters carried his corpse to his house. A 'great crowd', Asconius says, of plebeians and enslaved people gathered to grieve around his lifeless body. Clodius' wife, Fulvia, fanned the flames of rage by pointing to the various wounds her husband had suffered. The large crowd had grown even larger by the next morning and now 'notable people' attended the scene at the house on the Palatine. Two tribunes of the plebs were there, Titus Minucius Plancus and Quintus Pompeius Rufus. They persuaded the crowd to bear the body as it was – stripped down and stabbed – to the Rostra in the Forum.[5]

Unsurprisingly, for they were friends of Clodius, tribunes Plancus and Pompeius stirred up the mourners. Clodius' corpse was carried from its grim viewing on the Rostra to the nearby senate house. Matters were getting out of hand. In the senate house a pyre was improvised using the benches and books of the senatorial scribes. Clodius was cremated on the spot. As his body burned, the flames spread out of control – or maybe were intentionally fanned – and the whole of the senate house burned to the ground. The crowd's anger was fired along with the senate house as they vandalized the home of the current interrex, Marcus Aemilius Lepidus (no consuls had been elected yet for 52). The crowd also attacked Milo's house. Milo was still away from the city but a retinue of archers guarded the house and drove off the enraged crowd. Finally the crowd nabbed some *fasces* from a shrine in the city, the symbols of a Roman magistrate's *imperium*. It delivered these insignia to Pompey's urban gardens and shouted for Pompey to be named consul or dictator.[6] Whichever he wanted; just put him in charge!

Pompey is Named Sole Consul for 52

Turmoil surged through the city in these first weeks of 52. Clodius' followers had torched the senate house along with one of the city's major market buildings, the Porcian Basilica. The Clodian crowd demanded justice – vengeance against Milo. Milo, however, inspired by news of the adverse reaction to Clodius' vengeful crowds, returned to the city and resumed campaigning for the consulship. These days that meant he was also accompanied by a formidable gang.[7] This just enraged Romans on the streets and among the aristocrats who wanted Milo prosecuted. Clodius' kin and friends in the senate demanded a senatorial investigation of the murder. Seize Milo's enslaved servants and force them to testify! Seize Fausta's servants; seize those of Clodius; of Clodius' friends! Rumours spread about that fatal clash on the Appian Way. Some said Milo had plotted murder all along, his gang of 300 enslaved enforcers jumping Clodius at the first opportunity. And with agitation in the city growing, still the Republic had no consuls, no chief magistrates to lead the state. The steady spate of violence in the city at the start of 52 had made it impossible to convene the centuriate assembly for the election of consuls. In this air of violent instability, the senate, as it had in the past, issued its ultimate decree, a sign of how far the situation had deteriorated. This was the same decree used against Gaius Gracchus, Saturninus, and Catiline. Since the state had no elected magistrates with *imperium*, the decree authorized the interrex, Lepidus, the tribunes, and the Spanish proconsul Pompey, to take any steps needed to protect the Republic. One of those steps was to levy troops as needed from Italy to restore order to the city.[8]

Let's pause a moment on the choice of Pompey in the senate's ultimate decree. He had lived outside the city itself for some time at this point, for the *imperium* he held as proconsul of Spain would lapse if he entered the city. And while proconsul of Spain was an appointment by the state, he was not an elected magistrate, a consul or praetor. Elected magistrates by time-honoured custom enforced the senate's decrees. In the City, however, the practicality of his proximity drove the senate. There really was no-one else: interreges and tribunes did not command armies, proconsuls did, and the ultimate decree authorized the use of troops to restore order in the city.

On the tail end of this decree came the unusual decision to appoint Pompey sole consul for 52. Some crowds, recall, had recently demanded that Pompey be made dictator or consul. Now this possibility was bandied about in the senate. At some point in the deliberations, an alternative to dictatorship was proposed: have the interrex appoint Pompey sole consul. Fate is not, it seems, without a sense of irony; Marcus Bibulus, Asconius reports – the same Bibulus whom Caesar had essentially ignored during their nominally shared consulship in 59 – proposed Pompey be given the solitary office.[9] Even Cato, to the surprise of many, agreed, a sign of the state he thought the Republic was in.[10] The point of a sole consulship rather than dictatorship was to avoid the bloody precedent of Sulla. Pompey would not be a dictator. There may well have been an assumption too that he would pick a consular colleague once order was restored. That is what Pompey ultimately did.[11] Distinctions like these, between dictators and solo consuls, though they may seem like mere technicalities to us, were important to many Romans. A solitary consul was not a dictator, and nor was a *rex*, a king, the political title most detested by the Roman aristocracy. Even when the Republic was no more, replaced by a monarch in the form of Caesar's adopted son Augustus, the label 'king' was never used – not openly at least.

Pompey's Sole Consulship and the Trial of Milo (52 BCE)

Pompey, who at this point in his life had refined strategic political indecision to an art, was decisive enough as sole consul. He crafted two proposals that made their way through the senate and passed into law. The first was a law against violence that specifically targeted Milo's murder of Clodius, the conflagration that destroyed the senate house, and the assault on the interrex Lepidus' house. The second was a tighter bribery law. The puzzling detail here: it was made retroactive to 70 BCE. Accordingly, it did not apply to Pompey and Crassus' consulship but it certainly applied to Caesar's elections to praetor and consul. What was Pompey playing at here? It is not clear. But both laws streamlined the trial process with new special courts and increased penalties on conviction. Milo's allies in the senate, seeing a trial under these laws in their friend's future, protested. Pompey made himself clearer than usual: if force was needed to defend the Republic – in this case by convicting Milo – Pompey would indeed use force. Whatever use Pompey had for Milo as a foil to Clodius, he clearly no longer had it.[12]

With the enabling laws in place, Clodius' nephews indicted Milo. A special court was summoned in April of 52 BCE, complete with the stipulated jury handpicked by Pompey.[13] Cicero led the defence. He was in a tough spot. Milo surely counted as a friend: he had closely supported Milo in the past and was assuredly ever-grateful that Milo had freed him from the oppressive thumb of Clodius. Pompey and the optimates, however, clearly expected a conviction. The air around the public trial was charged, to say the least. Supporters of Clodius hounded the court, threatening to disrupt its proceedings. Pompey responded with troops dispatched to impose order around the trial. So passed the first three days of the trial. The fourth and final day loomed with rumours of still more agitation to come. Pompey tightened his grip with more active military policing. As a precaution, though it must have been unpopular, wineshops in the city were closed that day. For good measure, Pompey and his soldiers guarded the Treasury, and soldiers occupied the Forum and streets in and out of it. Cicero, whatever courage he may have had, buckled between the threats of Clodius' enraged supporters and the presence of troops everywhere. They were intended to secure Milo's conviction as much as to quiet Clodius' supporters. Hopelessly condemned, Milo chose exile in the coastal city of Massilia.[14]

Pompey's Legislation as Sole Consul

A number of important events followed the trial of Milo in 52. Sometime after Julia died, Caesar had tried to marry Pompey to his sister's granddaughter – even though she was currently married to a Marcellus (probably not one of those who hated Caesar). Pompey declined.[15] At some point then, or perhaps earlier in the year, Pompey decided to marry again, this time Cornelia, the daughter of Metellus Scipio.[16] Thanks to Plutarch, we know a bit about her. In addition to praising her beauty, a perennial focus of male Roman writers, and stereotyping and moralizing Roman women in the process, Plutarch asserts,

> She was well versed in literature, in playing the lyre, and in geometry, and had been accustomed to listen to philosophical discourses with profit. In addition to this, she had a nature which was free from that unpleasant officiousness which such accomplishments are apt to impart to young women; and her father's lineage and reputation were above reproach.[17]

Sifting out the patriarchal tone – Cornelia seems quite remarkable. She was dramatically younger than Pompey, the appropriate age to marry his son really, and contemporaries pointed this out. However successful their marriage was, as it turned out, it would not last long. Indeed Pompey would not last long.

The political intentions this marriage signalled seem clear enough. Certainly a closer relationship with her *optimate* father, Metellus Scipio. 'The noblest man in Rome', one modern historian aptly called him, noble both through his biological father Scipio and adoptive father Metellus.[18] But Metellus Scipio was no friend of Caesar. It has been suggested that perhaps Pompey planned to simultaneously aid himself and Caesar by extending their aristocratic connections. Not impossible; but it still rather looked like Pompey was distancing himself from Caesar with this marriage, and it seems likely that Caesar felt that way too.[19] Certainly Pompey did not stop here when allying with his new father-in-law. He defended Metellus Scipio from a bribery conviction in 52 BCE. The best guess is that he invited all 360 jurors to his house and spoke to them before the trial. His tack was not subtle; he may also have worn mourning clothes publicly to show his loyalty to his father-in-law.[20] Metellus Scipio, of course, was acquitted. And when it came time to select a consular colleague for the remainder of 52, Pompey chose him.[21] At face value, Pompey was firmly attaching himself to *optimate* leaders of the senate, opponents of Caesar.

Still, Pompey did address Caesar's main concern: a second consulship. The so-called Law of the Ten Tribunes in 52 assured this – or at least so it seemed. Initially all ten tribunes agreed to propose recalling Caesar early from Gaul and appointing him as Pompey's consular colleague for 52, an honour. But Caesar still had his hands full – Gaul was in open rebellion under Vercingetorix's leadership – and induced the tribunes to pass a different, but still favourable law. It explicitly stipulated Caesar had the legal right to run for the consulship *in absentia* when he chose.[22] In other words, he could remain a commander of legions in Gaul yet still be elected consul in Rome – and his popularity made it virtually certain that he would be elected. Pompey seems to have supported this, Cicero reported.[23]

Two important laws Pompey passed this year need only divert us for a moment. One was to be expected: he extended his proconsulship in Spain by five years.[24] A second seems reasonably pro-active: it stipulated that, from this point forward, all provincial governors had to wait five years between holding a magistracy and serving as a provincial governor. Ostensibly this law would cut down on bribery and violence. No longer could aristocrats afford to overextend themselves to win elections, because there would be no quick provincial payoff.[25]

But the law that snubbed Caesar directly was this. Now all candidates, Pompey legislated, had to come to Rome in person to declare their candidacy. Legally, this negated Caesar's recent privilege to run *in absentia* granted by the tribunes. Pompey could hardly have forgotten this law; it had passed only a few months before at most. Just in case, however, Caesar's supporters noted this new law directly conflicted with the law of the ten tribunes. Pompey's response was illuminating in its lack of clarity: he had never meant to negate Caesar's exemption. Accordingly, Pompey added a note to the bronze tablet on which the new law had already been engraved, stating that Caesar was exempted. But as everyone knew, not least Pompey, the exemption had not been ratified by the assembly; it had not been voted on at all. The text of the law that was passed was clear: all candidates had to campaign in person. The most charitable interpretation of this has Pompey supporting Caesar while demonstrating that he held more of the power in the relationship.[26] In this light he wanted Caesar reassured, but fully aware that he depended on Pompey's favour to achieve his political aims. At best. To many then and now, however, Pompey simply seems to have been double-dealing.

Caesar in Gaul 55–52 BCE

Caesar campaigned most of the time after Luca (56 BCE), increasing Roman authority from the Atlantic to the Rhine. In the winter of 56/55 BCE he decided to invade Britain, as much for the prestige that it would gain him and Rome as for any substantive military goals. That same winter, however, two German tribes crossed the Rhine into Gaul – the Usipetes and the Tencteri. In doing so they violated Caesar's policy, if they were even aware of it, that the Rhine was to be a firm, fixed boundary for the Germanic peoples. Caesar's legions crushed the warriors of those tribes with relative ease. To emphasize Roman control and authority on the frontier, Caesar followed up by carrying the fight across the Rhine to the Germanic tribes. Ten days of hard, skilled work and the legions had bridged the Rhine with a substantial stone span that included forts on each end to protect the structure. Then the legions crossed. None of the tribes in that region wanted to clash with the legions. They abandoned nearby villages and homes and retreated into the thick and defensible woods. So the first expedition across the Rhine resulted only in a spree of destruction of crops, homes, and villages. The legions had made their point: the Romans could invade Germania at any time. Caesar and the legions returned to Gaul and destroyed the mighty bridge they had constructed. They had shown how little the mighty Rhine had slowed their movements.[27]

This still left Caesar time in 55 BCE to invade Britain. The first invasion was close to a disaster for the Roman expedition and achieved nothing substantial. The very spectacle of the invasion, however, was rewarding. When Romans heard news that legions spread Roman authority at the edge of the known world, they were excited and proud. Indeed, in response to that first crossing, the senate authorized twenty days of thanksgiving to the gods for Caesar's victories. Caesar crossed again to Britain in 54. The legions met with some more success but still achieved nothing of any practical consequence other than a boost in imperial morale at home. After the legions left Britannia in 54, the island would enjoy almost a complete century of freedom from Roman legions and governors.[28]

Another Gallic rebellion in the winter of 54/53 was crushed through the efforts of the legions. It was serious enough that Caesar stayed in Transalpine Gaul that winter rather than travelling to his usual quarters closer to Italy in Cisalpine Gaul. Caesar levied more legions to further secure Roman control over their northernmost province. The revolt was largely crushed by the start of 53. The legions spent the rest of the year devastating the territory of rebellious Gallic tribes, especially in the northeast.[29]

In 52 however, the year when the ten tribunes sought to recall him to Rome to share Pompey's consulship, Caesar's legions faced perhaps their greatest challenges in Gaul. Now that Caesar and the legions had been in Gaul for over five years, it was clear to most Gauls that the Romans had no intention of leaving the region. And so, many Gauls launched a final effort to shake off Roman control. This time tribes rebelled that had remained peaceful the whole of Caesar's governorship. This time, even chiefs who had fared well under Roman influence rebelled. The Gallic aristocrat Vercingetorix, charismatic and capable, rallied the rebels into a formidable force. The warriors of rebelling tribes flocked to him and together posed a serious threat to Roman control in the region. The legions had their work cut out for them. After a hard, dangerous campaign, however, they pacified the Gauls yet again. Vercingetorix and his army were forced to surrender after a grand siege of the Gallic town and hillfort of Alesia. The smashing victory at Alesia in late 52 turned the tide decisively. Indeed the senate, led by Pompey back in Rome, declared even more days of public thanksgiving.[30] The hardest work behind them, the legions continued to extinguish smaller pockets of resistance into 51. Caesar and his legions had essentially conquered Transalpine Gaul. The remainder of Caesar's time in the province was spent in diplomacy, Caesar applying clemency and rewards to illustrate the advantages of Roman authority.[31] As the end of his provincial command seemed to be approaching and his province had been pacified, Caesar could focus his attention on Italian politics and a second consulship.

The Consulship of Marcus Claudius Marcellus (51 BCE)

When Marcus Claudius Marcellus entered the consulship at the start of 51, he ratcheted up the political pressure to end Caesar's command in Gaul. What moved him? Unfortunately we are in the dark. Three members of the Marcellus family, two brothers and a cousin, held three successive consulships, in 51, 50, and 49, the period immediately before the civil war. All sought to check Caesar. But of these three, the consul of 51 was the most antagonistic. Perhaps he was a true *inimici*, a declared political enemy of Caesar? We have seen time and again that Roman political culture and systems encouraged rivalries and allowed for enemies. By most standards, Marcellus, consul of 51, surely qualified as one.[32] The consul was determined to humiliate Caesar, to thwart him, and to force the end of his Gallic command. Marcellus brought the issue to the senate for deliberation early in his term.[33] His position was simple: Caesar's proconsulship should end immediately, and a successor should replace him in Gaul. At a quick glance, the argument had some heft: Caesar had essentially pacified Gaul for the Romans by early 51 – indeed Vercingetorix was in chains, and the senate had approved days of thanksgiving for Caesar's victories. Why then, argued Marcellus, should Caesar remain in Gaul now that he had subjugated the province?[34] But

Trebonius' law of 55, facilitated by Pompey and Crassus, was clear: Caesar's command legally would last at least until sometime in the year 50.[35] Marcellus' motion was dead in the water. Not only did his colleague Sulpicius oppose any senatorial debate or decree on the matter, but some tribunes also added their vetoes for good measure.[36]

Pompey may have avoided commenting on Marcellus' proposal initially in 51, since the law of 55 extending Caesar's time in Gaul was clear enough and magistrates had vetoed deliberation. Soon, however, he went on record and declared that Caesar had done nothing to warrant being recalled from his province ahead of the time allotted by law.[37] Still, Marcellus hoped to bring the matter up again that year. But it seems the majority of the senate moved to let the matter drop.[38] The respite would not last long.

Marcellus' inability to move the senate must have been frustrating. That may explain why he vented his anger on a bystander, a client of Caesar's outside the senatorial elite. The circumstances are lost but the act itself is well documented. Marcellus publicly flogged a local magistrate from the Latin colony of Novum Comum in Transpadane Gaul to dishonour Caesar.

We need to unpack this. Back in 59 BCE, in addition to his other legislation, consul Caesar had assigned 5,000 new colonists to the Latin colony of Novum Comum in Transalpine Gaul.[39] Marcellus whipped one of those new colonists, who also happened to be a magistrate of the colony.[40] If Caesar's law sending colonists in 59 was legitimate and this person was a magistrate, by law they held full Roman citizenship. This meant, among other things, that they could not be subjected to corporal punishment without a conviction by jury-trial. Marcellus aimed to deny the legality of that magistrate's citizenship by publicly whipping him, brutally denying the legality of Caesar's law in 59 in the process.[41] It was a shocking object lesson inflicted on a bystander's body: all Caesar's laws were illegitimate, Marcellus underscored with a whip. Cicero expressed the disgust at the time many must have felt: 'Marcellus' action in the case of the man of Comum was disgraceful. Even if he were not a magistrate, he was yet an inhabitant of Gallia Transpadana.'[42] Several years in the future when Caesar had won the civil war, he pardoned many formal enemies and rivals. It took him longer to do so for Marcellus however, quite probably because of this outrage, the sort of extreme a formal enemy might reach. It is reasonable to suppose Marcellus counted himself a formal enemy of Caesar; why, we do not know.[43]

In September 51 the senate moved to require Caesar's replacement. Pompey, once again, opposed discussing the early termination of Caesar's command. But his father-in-law Metellus Scipio moved, and the senate decreed that the end of Caesar's proconsulship be the only item for discussion on 1 March 50. As with the hostile consuls named Marcellus, it is entirely unclear why Metellus Scipio opposed Caesar. He certainly did not share the vitriol of the consul of 51, but, as events will show, he was no friend of Caesar.

At his insistence Pompey acquiesced to his new father-in-law and senatorial supporters; the deliberations would take place.[44] Pompey's position on debate seems to have been based on a consistent principle, one that would ultimately trouble Caesar. Arguably, any debate leading to replacing Caesar as proconsul in Gaul in 51 would violate the term of his command legislated by Trebonius. A discussion in March 50, however, even if it resulted in Caesar's immediate replacement, would fall after the expiration of Caesar's Gallic command specified by Trebonius' law. In short, Pompey was prepared to deliver on precisely what he felt he owed Caesar and the law. That obligation did not include extending Caesar's command past what Pompey saw as the formal expiration date. Indeed, just days later, Pompey made clear that Caesar could legally be replaced in Gaul on or after 1 March 50 BCE.[45] The line in the sand had been drawn.

After August 51, when Cicero happened to be abroad governing the province of Cilicia, his young aristocratic friend Marcus Caelius kept him informed about politics at Rome. He included in one letter to Cicero the exact words of two senatorial decrees, just issued in September, on the matter of Caesar's command. The first decreed, as we have seen, that Aemilius Paullus and Marcellus (consuls of 50) would 'bring the matter of the consular provinces before the senate' on 1 March. In other words, Gaul **would** be designated as a consular province, so Caesar would have to end his proconsulship and yield his *imperium* to a successor. Caesar would be replaced.[46] Pompey's position in all this was crucially important to all at Rome who hoped to replace Caesar. After all, Pompey was the only one with sufficient rank and sufficient legions to challenge Caesar, should it come to that.[47] Pompey's position seems to have been that Caesar could not use his rights to run for the consulship while still commanding in Gaul – 1 March coming several months before the consular elections of the summer. And so, as Caelius dutifully reports to Cicero, some senator asked Pompey what would happen if someone vetoed the deliberations of the senate on that day? Pompey remarked that a veto of the meeting by anyone would be tantamount to Caesar refusing to obey the senate. Clear enough. Someone, however, sought more clarity, as Caelius reported:

'What if,' said someone else, '[Caesar] shall determine both to be consul and to keep his army?' To which [Pompey] answered – with what mildness ! – 'What if my son should choose to strike me with his stick?'[48]

Here we have Pompey's sense of the situation. Caesar was younger, had held far fewer offices than Pompey, and had not even triumphed once. Pompey was the Roman conqueror of the known world; he had triumphed an extraordinary three times over three continents; he had been consul three times including once without a colleague. He was the father in this analogy, Caesar the son. They were still close; Pompey's familial metaphor indicated closeness – closeness that neither may have really felt at this time. But Caesar was the subordinate.[49] Pompey expressed all of this 'mildly', Caelius pointedly noted. He neither expected Caesar to challenge him, nor did he feel it would be particularly daunting if he did.

We have been considering events in this chapter mostly from the perspective of Pompey and the senate. It is time to pause and consider: What did Caesar want in all of this debate?[50] For centuries, many historians ancient and modern have argued what Caesar feared most of all as his command in Gaul came to a close was prosecution and conviction for crimes he had committed during his tumultuous consulship of 59. According to this interpretation, Caesar insisted on his right to run *in absentia* as a protection; he did not want to return to Rome as a private citizen and risk a major prosecution. Suetonius seems to provide the clearest expression of this possibility and he runs through a list of several:[51]

Others say that [Caesar] dreaded the necessity of rendering an account for what he had done in his first consulship contrary to the auspices and the laws, and regardless of vetoes; for Marcus Cato often declared, and took oath too, that he would impeach Caesar the moment he had disbanded his army.[52]

Here Suetonius suggests Caesar wanted to stay in Gaul, safely in command of his army and so legally untouchable until he entered his consulship on the first day of the year and, again, became legally untouchable. But the serious proposal that Caesar most of all feared a prosecution for the events of 59 does not hold up well. Many in Rome, including Pompey himself, benefitted from Caesar's legislation in 59, so a conviction that overturned his laws would be undesirable to many in power. It is also noteworthy that when Cicero lists Caesar's options exhaustively in a letter at the end of 50, prosecution is not even mentioned.[53] Even more striking: when Caesar ultimately invaded Italy, he quickly offered a peace proposal that included yielding his right to run for consulship *in absentia*.[54]

So, what did Caesar want and what did Caesar fear in the time leading to the civil war? Clearly he wanted to hold a second consulship – and his popularity pretty much ensured he would win election – and celebrate a triumph. At the end of his governorship in Spain (60 BCE), he had sought from the senate the right to run for the consulship *in absentia*. Permission would have allowed him to remain outside the city, keep his *imperium*, and celebrate a triumph immediately before entering the office of consul. Cato had stymied his efforts; Caesar had been forced to run for consul in person, and that required entering the city, losing his *imperium* and giving up his triumph. It is reasonable to suppose this was on his mind in 50.[55] To these concerns about offices and glory, we should add that Caesar wanted dignified treatment. He wanted recognition that he was now as distinguished and accomplished a Roman as even Pompey the Great. He was not Pompey's junior. He was not willing to concede to the senate's authority – or rather to his rivals in the senate – unless Pompey also conceded something. One without the other would mark Caesar as lower status. Our investigation of Roman aristocrats has regularly indicated that they cared deeply about their status among peers, rivals, and subordinates. None cared more than Caesar. He had an ease in his dealings with all manner of social subordinates, whether soldiers or members of the urban plebs. But he would not take second place to any aristocrat; certainly not to Pompey.

The Elections for 50 and the Tribunate of Curio

Tensions were rising about the end of Caesar's governorship, now that the date of 1 March had been set and Pompey's position was reasonably clear. 'Reasonably clear' because no one yet knew how far Caesar, Pompey, or Caesar's rivals were willing to go to uphold their political positions and their pride. And so, as so often in the past, there was considerable focus on the elections for 50. The consular elections returned Gaius Claudius Marcellus, yet another opponent of Caesar, and Lucius Aemilius Lepidus. Among the tribunes for the year, one demands special attention for his role in encouraging a genuine crisis between Caesar and Pompey: Gaius Scribonius Curio. Initially the sense among senators was that Curio would staunchly oppose Caesar's objectives. Caelius says as much in a letter to Cicero.[56] Appian suggests Curio began as a bitter enemy of Caesar's, but that may be taking matters too far.[57] Ultimately, however, Curio decidedly did not become a bulwark against Caesar. For he was deep in debt and Caesar agreed to get him out of it in return for political support.[58] So, as an agent of Caesar, Curio played a clever, but very dangerous, game.

The senate meeting of 1 March 50 came, and consul Marcellus proposed a specific end date for Caesar's Gallic province. Aemilius kept quiet, arguably moved by Caesar's recent substantial bribe. Curio vetoed the deliberation. He had been leaning this way despite *optimate* hopes for his support.[59] Swiftly, however, Curio took a course that arguably ensured Pompey and Caesar would be truly deadlocked. Curio proposed that Pompey should yield his proconsulship of Spain – along with command of the legions there went without saying – and Caesar should yield his Gallic command. The two should simultaneously and immediately end their proconsulships. This proposal radically changed the nature of the debate. Caesar had been blamed as the stubborn one, the one who must concede his ambitions for the good of the Republic. Now that responsibility to concede was not on Caesar alone: Pompey was cast as one of the stubborn participants causing the growing standoff. Now Pompey could also be criticized for failing to do what was best for the Republic: giving up his proconsulship so that Caesar would give up his own and there would be peace.[60] Both should yield; neither should surrender any more dignity than the other.

Pompey resisted. At some point later that spring, he proposed an alternative: Caesar must be replaced in his province by 13 November 50. This alternative proposal would seemingly allow Caesar to

- run for the consulship of 49 in the summer of 50;
- remain proconsul of the two Gauls while running for office;
- presumably get elected consul – everyone was clear Caesar was almost certain to win election;
- surrender his armies and command in Gaul to a successor in November as consul-elect;
- spend the remaining few weeks till the end of December waiting outside the city so that he could arrange a triumph right before taking office as consul on 1 January.

Why did Pompey offer this? It certainly seems to have given Caesar what he wanted? Decades ago, historian Robin Seager suggested that there was a critical aspect to this counter-offering to Curio and Caesar that may not be immediately apparent. Most importantly, this was Pompey's offer, not Curio's, and so Caesar's safe transition from Gallic commander to consul and the opportunity to win approval for and celebrate a triumph for Gaul would be owed to Pompey. Accepting this offer essentially meant acknowledging that Pompey truly was the leading citizen in the Republic, as he certainly claimed to be, and that he condescended to charitably allow subordinate Caesar to get his consulship. The fact that Caesar would be forced by the senate to yield his command while Pompey retained his Spanish command and legions would only drive the intended humiliation deeper. Curio, acting for Caesar, vetoed Pompey's offer. It had been a moment of truth, and that truth was that Pompey would not acknowledge Caesar as an equal in *dignitas* and Caesar refused to recognize Pompey as a superior.[61] Here the political rivalry endemic in the Republic split the two most powerful Romans of the day, the two with large armies under their command, the two willing to use them to defend their pride and honour.

And so by spring 50 BCE a political deadlock trapped Caesar, Pompey, their adherents, rivals and enemies. Perhaps, though, Parthia, and its threat of the Roman province of Syria, might provide a way to break the standoff. The Parthian Empire, agitated by Crassus' disastrous campaign, now threatened Roman Syria. Perhaps a command against Parthians might draw one of the two commanders away, probably Pompey so that his presence in Italy would not continue to provoke Caesar. Seemingly to that end and to defend Syria, in the summer of 50 the senate decreed that Pompey and Caesar should each supply one legion for the war effort against Parthia. Pompey picked this moment to publicly remind Caesar that, for some time now, Caesar had commanded a legion that was raised on Pompey's authority, a legion Pompey had technically 'loaned' to Caesar. Therefore Caesar needed to give up two legions, one of his own and the one Pompey had loaned him, while Pompey surrendered nothing. Caesar was stuck; he gave up the two legions.

Then, still in the summer of 50 BCE, Pompey grew very sick at Naples. There was concern that he would not survive. But when he recovered later that year, the resulting expressions of gratitude from Romans across the peninsula were epic. Countless voices cheered for Pompey and thanked the gods that he had survived this illness. It is not unlikely that Pompey took all these supporters and well-wishers too much for granted; that he considered that all the celebrations for his recovery meant these people would also willingly serve as soldiers, should Pompey need to levy them against Caesar.[62]

The Final Countdown

The 1 December meeting of the senate in 50 did nothing to resolve the impasse. Again Curo, as tribune, proposed that both Pompey and Caesar resign their commands. The senate seemed agreeable. Then the consul Marcellus attempted to outmanoeuvre Curio and manipulate the wavering senate. He split Curio's proposed motion into two separate items for voting by the senate. And so the senate voted yes to the proposal that Caesar should resign and no to the proposal that Pompey should resign. But Curio persisted and proposed once more: should both proconsuls resign their commands? The vote of the senate was reportedly 370 in favour of both consuls resigning their proconsulships, 22 opposed. Clearly the senate for the most part wanted both Romans to yield for the good of the Republic. Consul Marcellus simply adjourned the senate meeting, and thus the chance of any senatorial decree that might calm the crisis.[63]

A few days later consul Marcellus got an opportunity to stir the pot and charge the political atmosphere that much more. Appian reports what seems a sound enough story. Rumour had spread to Rome that Caesar was on the march against Rome (he was not; not yet). Marcellus wished the senate to declare Caesar an enemy of the state but Curio blocked the proposal. And so Marcellus left the senate with some supporters, including the consuls elect for 49: Gaius Marcellus (this one the brother of the consul of 51) and Lucius Cornelius Lentulus Crus. They took the short trek outside the formal city boundaries to meet Pompey. He handed Pompey a sword and authorized him to levy troops, take command of the two legions currently in Capua, and march against Caesar. This was not the sort of thing a consul could authorize, no matter how many consuls-designate agreed. It was for the senate to authorize troops. Marcellus, however, wished to force the issue after the majority of the senate had just voted for both Pompey and Caesar to resign their commands. At the same time, he would force Pompey's hand. Would Pompey take the sword that Marcellus offered and wield it for the Republic?

Pompey accepted the position, arguably because he saw little else that could be done.[64] He accepted command of the two legions in Campania and agreed to levy more troops. Even at this point it did not seem that Pompey wanted war. Rather Pompey was willing to go to war if peace and his position as the leading citizen of Rome was recognized. In other words, it seems entirely likely that Pompey still thought Caesar would come to his senses, as he saw it, and lay down his command.[65] A particularly dangerous tactic. Curio countered, insisting that Pompey's illegitimate levy efforts be ignored, but no one in Rome was listening to Curio anymore. Soon he would leave the city to join Caesar.[66]

On 1 January 49 BCE, a letter from Caesar reached Rome.[67] Through considerable effort the tribunes Marcus Antonius and Gaius Cassius moved to have the letter read aloud in the senate. So Caesar himself tells us at the start of his *Civil War* commentary – which frustratingly is missing the original first chapters. Caesar does not tell us what the letter said. Soon after, Cicero described the letter as 'menacing and offensive' in a note to his freed scribe Tiro.[68] For more details, we must reconstruct from later accounts. Though they vary in this or that detail, there are two salient points in the letter. Caesar complained it was an unacceptable affront to his dignity to concede everything while Pompey conceded nothing. So Caesar offered this: he and Pompey should resign their proconsulships and dismiss their armies. Both would become private citizens and return to Rome.[69] It seems that many in the senate agreed that this was the escape from war they must seize. No vote seems to have been taken.[70] Indeed the consul Lentulus declared that if the senate sought reconciliation with Caesar, he would override them. Antonius and Cassius were unable to persuade the other magistrate to have the senate vote on the topics presented in the letter.[71]

There were more last-minute letters, and perhaps suggestions of deals, but the deadlock persisted. Pompey would not budge; nor would Caesar. Pompey and other agents had been working on levying troops, and on 7 January the senate passed the *senatus consultum ultimum*, or rather the optimates dominating the senate got the motion passed. As a further step, the consuls warned Antonius, Cassius and two other Caesarian tribunes explicitly: if they attempted to block anything about or involving the decree, their personal safety was at risk. Understanding the threat, these tribunes left along with Curio and joined Caesar in Cisalpine Gaul.[72]

After six months of travel and a year as a reluctant governor, Cicero returned to Italy to find Rome in this state. There was little he could do: war was coming. His report to Tyro after the senate's ultimate decree on 7 January:

> I arrived at the city walls on 4 January. Nothing could be more complimentary than the procession that came out to meet me; but I found things in a blaze of civil discord, or rather civil war. I desired to find a cure for this, and, as I think, could have done so; but I was hindered by the passions of particular persons, for on both sides there are those who desire to fight. The long and short of it is that Caesar himself – once our friend – has sent the senate a menacing and offensive despatch, and is so insolent as to retain his army and province in spite of the senate, and my old friend Curio is backing him up. Furthermore, our friend Antonius and Q. Cassius, having been expelled from the house, though without any violence, left town with Curio to join Caesar, directly the senate had passed the decree ordering 'consuls, praetors, tribunes, and us proconsuls to see that the Republic received no damage'. Never has the state been in greater danger : never have disloyal citizens had a better prepared

leader. On the whole, however, preparations are being pushed on with very great activity on our side also. This is being done by the influence and energy of our friend Pompey, who now, when it is too late, begins to fear Caesar. [73]

It would be war.

And so, in January 49 BCE, Caesar, declared an enemy of the state, crossed the Rubicon with his 13th Legion, effectively invading Italy, effectively igniting the military conflagration of the second Roman civil war. Political rivalries had ripped apart the Roman Republic again. It would never recover.

Conclusion

The Death Throes of the Republic

The Civil Wars, 49–45 BCE

The ousted tribunes, Marcus Antonius and Quintus Cassius Longinus, reached Caesar's camp. Soon after, Caesar crossed the Rubicon with his 13th Legion – his remaining eight positioned around Northern and Central Gaul.[1] Importantly, at least two more of Caesar's remaining legions subsequently joined him in a span of only a few weeks – so swiftly that they cannot have been positioned on the other side of the Alps. In other words, Caesar's careful military preparations and swift strike belied his claims to appear purely peaceful, forced into war by his opponents. Caesar had prepared for the possibility of war well before taking the final steps in January.[2] Now his forces marched speedily down the Adriatic side of northern Italy, accepting many cities' surrenders as they went.

When Pompey and his allies learned of Caesar's advance, Pompey seems to have seriously considered defending Rome. But Pompey had trouble shifting his allies from political diatribes to sound military strategy. Unlike Caesar, he was not the sole commander of the Pompeian efforts. The consuls of 49, in particular, continued to interject their own strategic plans, and this seems to have hampered Pompey more than a little.[3] On top of it all, Caesar and his forces, of unclear size but growing in strength, were marching incredibly fast – too fast. Pompey decided that his current forces, the two legions taken from Caesar the year before, simply could not defend Rome. So he withdrew from the city and headed south. In some senses this could be seen as a grave propaganda error – abandoning the heart of the Republic. Cicero certainly complained bitterly about the decision.[4] But Sulla had set the strategic precedent: a Roman commander could recapture Italy after a sojourn east. So, too, Pompey sought to gather a large invasion force from his extensive connections in the eastern empire.[5]

However prepared for war Caesar might have been, he actively sought peace. Strikingly, Caesar offered well-documented peace terms to Pompey regularly and repeatedly in the first months of 49. The core terms Caesar offered remained the same:

- Both he and Pompey would disarm, disbanding their armies;
- Caesar would relinquish his right to run *in absentia* for the consulship.

These overtures underscore that Caesar's core motivation was to protect his *dignitas*. And, for Caesar, that *dignitas* hinged on a point of justice. It was simply unjust to strip Caesar's proconsulship away while Pompey retained his. These overtures included sustained efforts to meet with Pompey face to face. Caesar would continue into March to seek a personal meeting with Pompey to talk terms as Pompey and his allies and troops left Italy. Pompey, assuredly with some influence from his allies, steadfastly ignored these overtures.[6]

Caesar and his forces sped along while Pompey withdrew, ultimately heading to the southeastern port of Brundisium. Against Pompey's wishes and efforts, Lucius Domitius Ahenobarbus and some senatorial-rank enemies of Caesar decided to make a stand at the town of Corfinium, east of Rome.[7] Caesar reached the town in February, besieged the Pompeian defenders, and accepted their surrender by 21 February. Here Caesar famously began a formal policy of *clementia*, forgiving his enemies and allowing them to return fully to Republican life. It was a policy he would pursue through his remaining years of life.[8] Throughout the civil war campaigns, Caesar steadily practised this policy of clemency established at Corfinium, forgiving his enemies, whether common soldiers or aristocrats, and restoring them to political society. He clearly hoped to avoid Sulla's bloody precedents and worked to recover some sense of legitimating normalcy in the Republic. It was not easy. Historians have debated how Caesar's clemency was received. Looking back from Rome under the emperors in the first century CE, some Romans associated clemency with despotism. In other words, only one who ruled unilaterally and held all the power could forgive another, a *de facto* inferior. Following this line of reasoning, many aristocrats must have found Caesar's clemency a slap in the face. But there is little evidence that Caesar's contemporaries actually felt this way, though some thought him insincere in his offers of reconciliation. His actions, however, underlined his sincerity: the dictatorship of Caesar brought with it no proscriptions.[9]

Caesar pursued Pompey's small army as it retreated to the southeastern Italian port of Brundisium in March. Meanwhile, he continued to seek a face-to-face meeting with Pompey. Pompey continued to ignore that request and Caesar's terms.[10] At Brundisium, Caesar hoped to block the port and prevent the escape of Pompey's forces. He lacked a sufficient navy, however, and Pompey's forces embarked on 17 March and sailed to Macedonia to gather strength. Caesar returned to the vicinity of Rome. Notably, he did not occupy the city. He did not even enter the city; his claim to be a legitimate proconsul with *imperium* prevented him. Strikingly, as noted above, no proscriptions followed. Instead his friendly tribunes, Antonius and Cassius, summoned a meeting on 1 April of senators who remained in the region. Caesar explained to them his sense of the legal wrongs inflicted on him and Roman voters by his enemies and his goal to restore balance. He also encouraged the senate to send peace overtures, again, to Pompey.[11]

Even though Pompey would grow slowly stronger in Macedonia, the seven Pompeian legions in Spain posed a more pressing threat to Caesar. They could march overland if their commanders chose to contest control of Italy with Caesar. And so Caesar and his legions marched to Spain and outmanoeuvred and besieged the Pompeian legions – who were ineffective in part because their three commanding legates could not work particularly well together. At Llerda they surrendered. With the Spanish campaign finished for a time, Caesar returned home in the summer of 49 BCE.[12]

Back in Rome, most senators preferred neutrality, and most magistrates were absent. Some sketchier-than-usual technicalities were required, therefore, to get Caesar appointed dictator so that he could then hold elections to become consul for 48. Publius Isauricus was chosen as his colleague. With this questionably legitimate office, Caesar chased Pompey to Macedonia at the start of 48. There, Caesar and Pompey's armies manoeuvred for some time to secure an advantage. Pompey hoped to strategically defeat Caesar rather than commit everything to a single pitched battle. His colleagues disagreed and won out. The two armies finally met in pitched battle at Pharsalus. Pompey, in an uncharacteristic display for such a skilful commander, abandoned his soldiers while they were still locked in combat with Caesar's legions. Caesar's legions won decisively; Pompey's legions surrendered.[13]

As for Pompey, he reunited on-the-run with his wife Cornelia. Officers and friends sailed with them to Egypt where Pompey sought asylum with the teenage King Ptolemy Auletes. Pompey had been friends with his father. Egypt was spectacularly wealthy, and Ptolemy had provided Egyptian auxiliary soldiers to Pompey's army. All good reasons for Pompey to regroup there. Young King Ptolemy, however, had other plans. At the urging of chief advisors, Ptolemy welcomed Pompey and dispatched a small boat to bring him to an audience onshore. Pompey seems to have been suspicious, but perhaps too exhausted to care. His plans and hopes had been dashed. Pompey boarded the boat. It headed to shore, and, while Cornelia and his friends watched from the bay, Ptolemy's agents murdered Pompey. Ptolemy ordered Pompey's head and signet ring removed. His corpse was left on an Egyptian beach until eventually buried by some of Pompey's freedmen. So ended Pompey the Great.[14]

When Caesar arrived, King Ptolemy's messenger gave him Pompey's ring – and his head. Reportedly, Caesar wept. Certainly, Pompey's assassination was hardly good news. Despite their differences, there is no reason to think Caesar personally hated Pompey, and his policy of clemency would most probably have applied to his former ally Pompey; he forgave far more bitter foes. That opportunity was lost forever. Caesar continued to Egypt and became involved in the political intrigues between sibling monarchs, Ptolemy and the famously brilliant Cleopatra Philopator. Cleopatra manoeuvred diplomatically and secured Caesar's support to restore her to the throne alongside her brother. This involved committing himself and the legions with him to a civil war known as the Alexandrian War. Upon victory, both Cleopatra and Ptolemy were restored to the throne, though Cleopatra was clearly the superior of the pair.[15]

Famously, Caesar delayed some months with Cleopatra in Egypt – certainly longer than the military and political position of the Mediterranean seemed to require. A lightning-fast campaign in Asia Minor followed, against the militarily minor inconvenience of King Pharnaces of Bosporus. Then, like Scipio some 150 years before, he staged an invasion of Africa from Sicily with six legions – five of which were likely composed of Pompeian soldiers who had surrendered.[16] The African campaign included some close calls for Caesar's army, but it decisively defeated Metellus Scipio and King Juba of Numidia's forces at the Battle of Thapsus.[17]

Though also in North Africa, Cato was not at Thapsus and did not participate significantly in defending the province against Caesar. Rather, he remained at his post defending Utica. Whatever else he was, Cato's final days only cemented his legacy as a Roman of conviction. He famously read Plato's *Phaedo*, a philosophical treatise extolling the virtues of death for a true philosopher.[18] His first stab pierced his stomach but was insufficient. Cato's son caught his father in the act of suicide and fetched a doctor to treat and bind the wound. When Cato recovered a bit and saw his plans were being thwarted, he finished his job.[19]

And so, in July of 46, with Pompeians soundly defeated around the Mediterranean, Caesar returned to Rome. He had only grown stronger, defeating all of his rivals in the civil war and building new legions from the Pompeian soldiers who surrendered. Surviving senators knew all too well that Caesar was functionally a monarch at this point, regardless of his official office. No doubt this helped move the senate to vote him forty days of thanksgiving – his greatest number yet – for his victories. Caesar followed up the thanksgiving with four successive triumphs stretched out to create a weeks-long festival: Gaul, Egypt, Asia, and Africa. Then, in November 46, Caesar returned to Spain again. His ally, former tribune Cassius, had proved to be a terrible governor of Spain. The troops under his command mutinied, and many now claimed they were Pompeians. Hearing the reports, Pompey's sons journeyed to Spain and headed this new rebellion. And so Caesar and an army journeyed back to Spain. After a decisive battle at Munda (45), the civil war was truly won, and Caesar commanded a formidable army of veteran legions.[20]

Caesar's plans, both when he chose to invade Italy in 49, and even more so when he essentially controlled the Republic, have exercised historians for centuries. Some have seen Caesar as a visionary: he realized that the political institutions of the Republic simply could not handle the administrative needs of the now-massive Roman empire. Clearly Caesar knew that only some form of monarchy could effectively manage this Mediterranean empire. Others have seen him as a typical Roman aristocrat – albeit an incredibly successful one – competing with rival aristocrats. In this light he did not have a vision to transform the government of Rome; he simply defended his dignity in a series of battles. In the end, he happened upon power by the contingency – for he had many close calls – that he had defeated his enemies in the civil war.

Regardless of which interpretation is more likely, or some other explanation altogether, Caesar was a legislative and political whirlwind in the period 46–44 BCE. He increased the senate by hundreds, rewarding *equites*, Italian aristocrats, and perhaps even some loyal centurions, with distinguished positions. He settled tens of thousands of Roman soldiers and civilians in colonies. He conducted a careful census of the City's population and adjusted grain subsidies to fit the new data – always a very expensive cost to the state. He even fixed the Roman calendar, which was out of synch with the solar seasonal year by about three months. He engaged in massive building programmes in the City, most notably his new Julian Forum complex and the Saepta Julia building that would house the centuriate assembly on the Campus Martius. And amid all this work, he planned a campaign against the Parthians.[21]

Murder cut short whatever other plans Caesar had. Effectively, Caesar was a monarch; this escaped no one's notice. He had held the position of dictator and consul for much of the time since 49 BCE. In 45 he extended his dictatorship from five to ten years. This already placed him in an unprecedented category for Roman officials. Sulla retired from dictatorship after only three years because he felt he had restored the Republic to a sound footing. In contrast, by early 44 BCE Caesar decided to have himself named *dictator perpetuo*, dictator for life. It proved to be a short life. Within a few months of that declaration, Marcus Junius Brutus and Gaius Cassius Longinus led a conspiracy of senators to murder Caesar in the senate.[22] It was death by daggers for Caesar.

The Second Triumvirate and the Rise of Augustus

Caesar's assassination in 44 BCE ushered in another, longer, period of intermittent civil war between his assassins and his potential successors. Chief among these successors were Caesar's posthumously adopted son Gaius Julius Caesar Octavianus, and his loyal lieutenants, Marcus Antonius and Marcus Aemilius Lepidus.[23] These three each claimed the loyalty of some of Caesar's veteran soldiers, and were ready to fight one another for power. When Caesar's veterans refused to slaughter each other, the three reluctantly joined forces late in 43. The helpless senate – with no army of its own – was forced to create an entirely new political position. Called the 'Triumvirate for Restoring the Republic', the office essentially conferred on each triumvir dictatorial powers to rule, tax, and, most importantly, levy and command armies in their assigned region of the Empire. A most un-Republican set of officials were now officially in charge of the Republic, appointed by a senate that had little choice in the matter. Indeed for some historians, the creation of the Triumvirate, such an aberration from Republican politics of the previous centuries, marks the true end of the Republic.[24]

The powerful new triumvirs consolidated their position and thinned the ranks of the Roman elite by decreeing a proscription almost immediately. Octavian, Antonius, and Lepidus condemned hundreds of senators and a couple of thousand *equites* for the crime of being personal enemies. Most of those branded enemies of the Republic – the Republic controlled by three dictators – were hunted down and murdered. The murderers and triumvirs acquired their wealth. This is the moment when poor Cicero died in 43, for he had earned the ill will of Antonius with a famous set of diatribes, the *Philippics*. An assassin took his head and hands and brought them to Antonius. In 42 BCE Octavian and Antonius transported their armies east to war against Caesar's assassins, most importantly Brutus and Cassius, in battle at Philippi. Octavian was ill during the battle – though later he claimed otherwise. Antonius did the job – barely. There were two days and two battles. Cassius was defeated and killed the first day. Brutus despaired and took his own life on the second. The leading assassins of Caesar were dead.

With no significant enemies left, Octavian, Antonius, and Lepidus fell out. Lepidus, whose place at the triumvirs' table had shrunk steadily, was forcibly retired in 36. Octavian and Antonius' relations – never great – grew more strained. Antonius famously allied with, loved, and married Cleopatra, the brilliant queen of Egypt. Octavian, a masterful propagandist whatever else he was, used this to his advantage. He cast Antonius as an un-Roman foreigner, one who had abandoned the Republic for the bed of Cleopatra. Open civil war broke out again and essentially ended in 31 BCE at the Battle of Actium. Octavian's navy – ostensibly the navy of the Roman Republic, commanded by his skilled general Marcus Agrippa – decisively defeated Antonius and Cleopatra's combined navies. Cleopatra and Antonius fled back to Egypt where both committed suicide rather than die as prisoners displayed in one of Octavian's triumphs.

The Roman Republic, if that is what it can be called in this period, had suffered a series of civil wars and – effectively – dictatorships in the almost-twenty years after Caesar crossed the Rubicon. Caesarians fought Pompeians, then, after Caesar's murder they fought Caesar's assassins. Octavian's adherents fought Antonians – and even some resurgent Pompeians. The soldiers of these factions fought each other and died: thousands had died in the wars and proscriptions. Octavian's bloody achievement of being the last triumvir standing made him the *de facto* winner. By 27 BCE Octavian controlled much of the Roman state. Several hundreds of thousands of soldiers, the combination of his armies and those of Antonius, were now his to command. Indeed he demobilized thousands and still commanded massive armies. He controlled all the provinces where the vast majority of legions were stationed; a paltry few legions were still assigned to a few senators as provincial governors. And so when the senate met one day in 27 BCE, packed with supporters and with those who knew better than to protest, Octavian 'restored the Republic'. He announced that all the state's enemies had been defeated and he could now retire from commanding legions and heading the state. A number of senators, in an epic performance of political theatre, objected, begging him not to abandon the Republic or his custodian's position over armies and provinces. For the good of the Republic, Octavian agreed; he would keep his position as commander of most legions and many provinces. He still called the Roman state 'The Republic', as did his contemporaries. After all *res publica* simply meant 'the state' or 'the public affairs', and a Roman state persisted. In that slight sense the Republic did not die. But there was a decisive shift to a government led by a *princeps*, a 'first citizen'. This novel position, created over time by Octavian, included the powers of a consul, tribune, and censor, one that, in Roman terms, effectively amounted to a dictatorship. The title granted to him by the senate of Augustus, 'holy revered one', captured his superiority to other Romans. For centuries Augustus and his successors, usually one monarch at a time, ruled the Roman Empire, which is why we commonly refer to Augustus and his successors as emperors. But the Republic as a government led by more-or-less independent aristocrats competing for offices, honours, and legislation formally approved by assemblies, was finished. Now aristocrats gained their offices and honours from the Emperor. Now assemblies were only summoned to vote – when they were summoned at all – when the outcome was assured, or irrelevant.

In reality, however, most citizens, especially after citizenship was extended to all of Italy in the late 90s BCE, and then later to thousands across the Mediterranean, could never practically vote in citizen assemblies anyway, even when the Republic still functioned. And exceedingly few Roman citizens possessed the wealth necessary to be senators and hold elected office. Which is why, in the end, the Republic that collapsed was really in large part the Republic of the free independent aristocrats. They were the ones that lost the most politically to an emperor in terms of freedoms, privileges and offices. So the fall of the Roman Republic, in many ways, is very much the story of how competitive aristocrats ripped their political system apart, returning the state to a monarchy that the system was designed to avoid.

The Fall of the Roman Republic

Still the question fascinates: why did a Republic that had functioned for centuries – since its creation in 509 BCE – collapse into civil wars and dictatorships that only ended when the new monarchy of Augustus imposed itself? How did a functioning political system – one that gave at least some voice to average citizens, allowed super-competitive aristocrats to share power mostly peacefully, and conquered most of the Mediterranean – fail so spectacularly that it was replaced by dictatorship ultimately based on military power, however discreetly exercised?

Clearly, any explanation offered for the fall of the Roman Republic must consider not only the intensely competitive aristocracy, but also the various limits on competition the Roman political system imposed on its aristocrats. Annual offices with new office-holders who had new opportunities to seek glory and fame; religious objections to limit extreme political behaviours; the ability of each magistrate to check their rivals; the tradition of the senate as a guiding body of experience. These limits provided checks to the acquisition of excessive power for centuries. But why did these limits fail in the end? Long before Cato the Elder's many prosecutions, and the debates between Scipio and Fabius, Roman aristocrats competed for offices and honours intensely, sometimes even challenging conventional behaviours. But the system of the Republic seems to have functioned all those centuries, until the period starting with Tiberius Gracchus and ending with Augustus.

So what had changed? Why could conventional limits to power contain a Scipio Africanus but not a Caesar? For that matter why did powerful Pompey not subvert the state, but Caesar did? In closing, let us consider some of the explanations historians have given for the fall of the Republic.

Some Theories to Explain the Fall of the Republic

Is it the case that the groups that had supported the growth of the empire and enabled the competitive Republic to function over centuries – small farmers, wealthy and privileged *equites*, Italian allies (and eventually new citizens) – simply grew disenchanted with the Republic? In the end did they come to see the Republic as a system of senatorial domination where a small group of competitive aristocrats squabbled, caring little about the people and concerns outside their clique? Did wave after crashing wave of violence and civil war overwhelm Romans to the point where the Republic was not even seen as worth saving?[25] In that case, was the fundamental choice for most outside the senatorial elite in these wars not who authentically represented the Republic, but who was likely to win the next struggle? And in a world like this, did a Caesar and then, more permanently, an Augustus come out on top because they gained enough support from enough people who had little stake in preserving the traditional Republic – *equites*, new Italian citizens, and veteran soldiers?[26]

Or was the Republic not by any means destined to collapse and possessed no systemic flaws that doomed it? It has been argued that the Roman aristocrats of the so-called 'Last Generation', the generation that came to political adulthood under Sulla, behaved in ways fundamentally similar to their aristocratic ancestors. Cicero, Caesar, Crassus, Pompey, Cato, the Marcellus consuls, Metellus Scipio and many others competed, often very intensely and in ways that could be called hostile, just as Fabius, Scipio, Cato the Elder, and Flamininus had. Roman aristocrats had competed intensely and often bitterly for centuries. Thus, this argument goes, the appearance of identifiable systemic flaws in the Republic is a trick of hindsight: we know the civil wars ended the Republic, so they must have been, we mistakenly assume, inevitable? But really was it the contingent, unpredictable victory of Octavian after decades of civil war and thousands of deaths, that happened to be the end of the Republic?[27] It would seem that the case studies in this book do not support this thesis as well. The increase in political violence, excessive competition for office, and vying for extraordinarily lucrative commands in the period from Tiberius Gracchus to Caesar seem distinct from the earlier Republic. Perhaps.

Or is it the case that we are simply not looking at this the right way? Perhaps the very idea of a single monolithic Republic lasting centuries from 509 BCE to its collapse somewhere between 44 and 27 BCE is a modern construction, obscuring the more complicated reality? Recently it has been argued that, in fact, at least six Republics stretched across the period from 509–33 BCE, and later Republics differed radically from earlier ones. And so there were many substantially different political systems, different Republics, that the Romans experimented with throughout the period that we identify – unhelpfully – as a single Roman Republic. And so the aristocratic Republics of the third and second centuries of Fabius, Scipio Africanus and Cato the Elder were not only different than earlier Republics, they came to a collapse in the violence and upheaval of the period, not in the period 44–27, but really in the fifty years from the murder of Tiberius Gracchus to the civil wars of Sulla and the Marians. In this light, Sulla's system was substantively different and an end to the traditional nobles-led Republics, and it was only Sulla's Republic that collapsed in the civil wars of Caesar's day and beyond.[28] Perhaps the case studies in this book, though not fully organized according to such a thesis, complement such an interpretation.

No solution is without its problems: understanding humans and human politics is complicated. But this book's examination of aristocratic politics and competition in the centuries from Fabius Maximus and Scipio Africanus to Pompey and Caesar suggests there was much about the Republic that was fundamentally volatile. Even though things could have turned out differently, the seeds of the Republic's collapse seemed to lie in its extremely competitive nature.

In this light, the real question is not, Why did the Republic collapse? It seems to have collapsed underneath increasingly intense competitions for superiority that led over time to a whole set of violent precedents for resolving political conflicts: murder, street violence, and civil war most of all. But Roman aristocrats were intensely competitive for centuries and yet the system persisted.

So maybe the real question is just the old one turned on its head. **Why did the Republic function for as long as it did?** Why was it able to fulfil the basic functions of an ancient state and provide a political arena in which aristocrats could compete intensely for offices and honours? Why did it survive such a fractious group of political squabbles for so long? One reason seems to be that, even though aristocrats competed intensely, they fundamentally supported the system of senatorial oligarchy leading the state.[29] And so with the rhetoric of service to the Republic from the powerful senatorial class motivating its members, political differences, for centuries, did not reach the point where the system itself fractured. When it ultimately did, the senatorial political leadership based on independent election to office was replaced with an imperial monarchy with a senate that competed for imperial favours and served as the court of a monarch. But until then, the senatorial class had found ways to get its members to behave, in the grand scheme, to compete with one another for pre-eminence while not challenging the oligarchic system. As one historian put it, for senatorial politics and conflict 'solutions had usually been found through a combination of informal negotiation and peer pressure (and a certain willingness to defer to superiors)'. In the period from Tiberius Gracchus to Julius Caesar, however, the willingness of individual politicians to ignore the centuries-long purview of the senate to moderate and mitigate disruptions that would overthrow its system of government steadily increased. Aristocrats more freely disregarded the conventional rules and practices as they introduced more volatile disruption into the political mix through civil and military violence.[30] While the question is still open and perhaps a mix of factors was involved, this interpretation seems to be best supported by the case studies in this book. But it still leaves other questions unanswered. Why were certain aristocrats less willing to conform and more willing to act in ways that challenged the claim of the aristocracy to effective rule? The influx of extreme amounts of wealth into Italy? The challenges and rewards of administering an empire? Even the answers lead to more questions.

This book provides no simple solution to any of these questions. Rather, I hope it offers an interesting and somewhat detailed means for readers to grapple with the evidence of the aristocratic Republic and the competition that drove it. For only through a close reading of these rivalries and struggles and the cohesion they upset can a deeper understanding of the dangers inherent in the political competition of the Roman state come to light. And that topic, politicians pursuing self-interest ruthlessly and causing the disintegration of political order, is something worth understanding for us all.

Appendix A

Glossary

Aedile – one of two junior magistrates elected yearly to maintain the infrastructure of Rome including roads, temples, and other public buildings. Aediles also held public games and played a role in managing the grain market at Rome.

Censor – one of two magistrates elected every five years whose primary task was to revise the list of Roman citizens, including those who had the status of senator.

Centuriate assembly (*comitia centuriata*) – The assembly of Roman citizens organized so that the wealthier citizens had more voting power than the poorer citizens. The centuriate assembly elected consuls and praetors, and declared wars, among other functions.

Civitas sine suffragio – conquered people of Italy to whom Rome granted citizenship without voting or other political rights.

Consul – One of the two most powerful yearly magistrates. Consuls were the chief executive officials of the Republic and the chief commanders of the Roman armies.

Contio – Assemblies held by Roman magistrates to disseminate information and to debate potential laws. No voting was conducted in a *contio*.

Cursus Honorum – The 'course of honours' or 'course of offices'; the traditional hierarchy of offices the most successful Roman aristocrats would hold during their political careers: aedile, praetor, consul.

Dictator – A special magistrate selected by a consul to serve as supreme commander during a military crisis, or to hold elections when the consuls could not. A dictator had no colleague in office and, by convention, had to step down from office after six months.

Fasces – An axe tied together with a bundle of rods symbolizing *imperium* and carried by the lictors who accompanied consuls, praetors, and dictators in public.

Fetiales – Ancient Roman priests whose responsibilities centred on declaring religiously correct, and thus just, wars against Rome's enemies.

Imperator – The title a victorious army could choose to address its commander. In the late Republic being declared imperator by one's troops was considered a prerequisite for celebrating a triumph.

Imperium – The formal power consuls, praetors and dictators possessed to have their decrees executed and the power to levy and command armies.

Interrex – a special magistrate selected to hold elections when normal consular elections did not take place within the normal time frame.

Iugera – A Roman unit of land measurement. One *iugerum* was a bit over half an acre.

Latin colonies – Colonies of Romans and Latin citizens planted by Rome to extend Roman power and to provide land for citizens and allies. The inhabitants of Latin colonies possessed Latin rights.

Latin rights – The core rights for those Italians that had Latin status: the legal right to trade and intermarry with Roman citizens and the right to move to Rome and adopt full Roman citizenship.

Mos maiorum – The customs of the ancestors, to whom Romans attributed traditional practices when justifying them.

Optimates – Those allegedly considered the defenders of aristocratic privilege and the leading role of the senate in the Republic. The term was often thrown about.

Patrician – the original Roman nobility, traditionally the descendants of the 100 Romans the first king, Romulus, chose as senators.

Pax deorum – The 'peace of the gods', the desired status when the Republic was in religious good standing with the gods. Violating the *pax deorum* risked the anger of the gods.

Plebeians – Essentially those Roman citizens who were not patricians.

Popularis – Those reportedly seeking to champion the will of the people, i.e. common Romans, and seeking to legislate through the popular assembly. The term was often thrown about.

Praetor – A magistrate second in power to the consuls. Praetors served as judges, as lesser military commanders, and, in time, as governors of provinces. Their number increased over time from one praetor in 367 to eight praetors by the end of the Republic.

Princeps senatus – An honorary title, 'First man of the Senate' granted traditionally, but not always, to the oldest living former censor. The *princeps senatus* had the privilege of offering their opinion in the senate on any issue first.

Proconsul – the commander of an army or governor of a province whose term of command was set by the senate and who had the military authority outside Italy of a full consul.

Propraetor – the commander of an army or governor of a province whose command was set by the senate and who had the military authority outside Italy of a full praetor.

Quaestor – the lowest major elected official, a junior magistrate who commonly served as a treasurer to a consul.

Sacrosanctity – the characteristic sacredness of a tribune in office. Because they were sacrosanct, tribunes could not theoretically be harmed while in office. As readers of the book know, this sacrosanctity was violated often in the late Republic.

Senatus consultum ultimum – The 'final decree of the senate', a term used in the later Republic when the senate declared a state of emergency and ordered the magistrates to take any steps necessary to protect the Republic.

Sponsio – A judicial wager. Two parties bet money that they were in the legal right on some contested issue. After the bet had been made, both spoke to an arbiter who decided whose case was the stronger, who won the bet.

Tribal assembly (*comitia tributa*) – The assembly of Roman citizens organized so that wealthier and poorer citizens had equivalent voting power. The tribal assembly elected tribunes and ratified laws, among other functions.

Triumph – The quintessential Roman victory parade. Granted to commanders who were deemed worthy by the senate and soldiers, triumphs were large-scale parades and celebrations where the imperator's victory over an enemy of Rome was celebrated.

Virtus – literally 'manly qualities' which for Roman aristocrats of the Republic centred on courage and resilience in battle.

Appendix B

List of Ancient Authors and Available Online Translations

Happily for those who want to read the ancient sources in English, the Perseus Digital Library (www.perseus.tufts.edu/hopper/) and the Lacus Curtius Project (chnm.gmu.edu/worldhistorysources/r/208/whm.html) are home to most of the sources cited in this book, which are listed in the table below. This is also a good place to remind the reader that attalus. org is a fantastic collection of references to ancient sources organized into years and topics. Combining the three allows the reader to access almost every ancient source used.

Abbreviation in the Notes	Full
App. *B Civ.*	Appian, *Civil War*
App. *Hisp.*	Appian, *Spanish War*
App. Mith	Appian, *Mithridatic War*
Asc. Mil	Asconius, Commentary on Cicero's Pro Milo
Caes *BGall.*	Caesar, *Bellum Gallicum*
Cass. Dio	Cassius Dio
Cic. *Amic.*	Cicero, *Laelius On Friendship*
Cic. *Att.*	Cicero, *Letters to Atticus*
Cic. *Brut.*	Cicero, *Brutus*
Cic. *Cat.*	Cicero, *Against Catiline*
Cic. *Cat. Mai.*	Cicero, *Cato the Elder*
Cic. *Dom.*	Cicero, *On His House*
Cic. Fam	Cicero, *Letters to Family and Friends*
Cic. Leg	Cicero, *On the Laws*
Cic. Man.	Cicero, *On the Manilian Law*
Cic. Mil.	Cicero, *On Behalf of Milo*
Cic. Pis.	Cicero, *Against Piso*
Cic. QFr.	Cicero, *Letters to his Brother Quintus*
Cic. Rab Post	Cicero, *On Behalf of Rabirius Postumius*
Cic. Red sen.	Cicero, *On his Return to the Senate*
Cic. *Verr.*	Cicero, *Against Verres*
De Vir. Ill.	Author Unknown, *About Famous Men*
Diod. Sic.	Diodorus Siculus

Dion. Hal. *Ant. Rom.*	Dionysius of Halicarnassus, *Antiquitates Romanae*
Flor.	L. Annaeus Florus
Front. *Strat.*	Frontinus, Strategemata
Gell. N.A	Aulus Gellius, *Attic Nights*
Hor. Carm.	Horace, *Carmina or Odes*
Liv.	Livy, *Ab Urbe Condita*
Liv. *Per.*	Livy, *Periochae*
Nep. Cat.	Cornelius Nepos, *Life of Cato the Elder*
Ov. *Fast.*	Ovid, *Fasti*
Plin. *H.N.*	Pliny, *Naturalis historia*
Plut. *Caes.*	Plutarch, *Life of Caesar*
Plut. *Cat Mai.*	Plutarch, *Life of Cato the Elder*
Plut. *Cat Min.*	Plutarch, *Life of Cato the Younger*
Plut. Cic.	
Plut. *C. Gracch.*	Plutarch, *Life of Caius Gracchus*
Plut. *Crass.*	Plutarch, *Life of Crassus*
Plut. *Fab.*	Plutarch, *Life of Fabius*
Plut. *Luc.*	Plutarch, *Life of Lucullus*
Plut. *Mar.*	Plutarch, *Life of Marius*
Plut. *Pomp.*	Plutarch, *Life of Pompey*
Plut. *Sull.*	Plutarch, *Life of Sulla*
Plut. *Ti. Gracch.*	Plutarch, *Life of Tiberius Gracchus*
Polyb.	Polybius
Sall. *Cat.*	Sallust, *The Conspiracy of Catiline*
Sall. *Iug.*	Sallust, *The Jugurthine War*
Sen. Ep.	Seneca, *Letters*
Sil. *Pun.*	Silius Italicus, *Punica*
Suet. *Jul.*	Suetonius, *Life of Julius Caesar*
Suet. *Tib.*	Suetonius, *Life of Tiberius*
Tac. *Hist.*	Tacitus, *Historiae*
Val. Max.	Valerius Maximus
Vell. Pat.	Velleius Paterculus
Zon.	Zonaras

Notes

Introduction

1. And, as I hope will become clear throughout this book, this is all debatable and subject to interpretation and revision, not least because of the fragmentary state of our evidence for the Roman Republic.
2. Polyb 6.53 (Shuckburgh trans.).
3. Polyb. 6.53 (Shuckburgh trans., which I very lightly edited).
4. Polyb. 6.54 (Shuckburg trans.).
5. With the exception of the period in which Cicero and Caesar flourished (say 70–43 BCE) for which we do have many documents they and others wrote at the time. 'Many' is relative, of course: the majority of the evidence from the ancient world is mostly lost to us even in these better documented periods.

Chapter 1

1. Scipio's (consul 205) early career: Military tribune at the disastrous battle of Cannae: Liv. 22.53, Val. Max. 5.6.7, Oros. 4.16.6; Aedile in 213: Liv. 25.2. See T.R.S. Broughton, *The Magistrates of the Roman Republic*, (American Philological Association), 1.251, 263.
2. In 216 a dictator, Marcus Fabius Buteo, was appointed to fill the large number of vacancies in the senate due to the war: Liv. 23.22–23. Scipio probably was not old enough to be selected at the time even though he had served as a military tribune.
3. Liv. 26.18–19. For the Second Punic War in Spain through 211, see D. Hoyos, *Mastering the West*, (Oxford, 2015), 164–71.
4. Scipio (consul 205) in Spain: Hoyos, *Mastering the West*, 172–185.
5. Liv. 28.38.
6. Liv. 28.45.
7. Liv. 28.38–9.
8. See J. McCall, *Clan Fabius, Defenders of Rome: A History of the Republic's Most Illustrious Family* (Pen & Sword, 2018), 86–148; Livy, books 22–30 and Polybius, books 3 and 8 refer regularly to Fabius Maximus.
9. Fabius' speech in the senate: Liv. 28.41–42.
10. Ibid.
11. Liv. 28.43.
12. Scipio as aedile in 213: Liv. 25.2. See Broughton, *MRR*, 1.263.
13. Scipio's speech: Liv. 28.43–45.
14. Liv. 28.45.
15. Liv. 28.45.

16. Liv. 28.45.
17. Liv. 28.45–46.
18. Liv. 28.46–29.6, *passim*. McCall, *Clan Fabius*, 143–6.
19. 'Unspeakable abuse': Liv. 29.8. (Yardley trans.).
20. Liv. 29.6–7; The account of Pleminius' governorship: Liv. 29.9.
21. Liv. 29.9.
22. Liv. 29.9.
23. Locrian embassy and debate in the senate: Liv. 29.16–20.
24. Ennius fragment book 12.360–2.
25. For Scipio's campaign in Africa: Hoyos, *Mastering the West*, (Oxford, 2015), 198–226.
26. Fabius' eulogy: Liv. 30.26.
27. Hoyos, *Mastering the West*, 200–212; R. Miles, *Carthage Must Be Destroyed* (Viking, 2010), 308–17.
28. Liv. 30.40–41.
29. Liv. 30.43.
30. Liv. 30.43.
31. Liv. 30.44.
32. App. *Pun.* 9.66. (White trans.)
33. Liv. 30.45.

Chapter 2

1. Cic. *Mor.* 59, *De or.* 1.227–8, *Brut.* 89–90; Liv. 39.40; Val. Max. 8.7.1, 9.6.2; Plut. *Cat Mai* 15.
2. Nep. *Cat.* 1; Plut. *Cat. Mai.*, passim; Plin. *NH Praef.* 30.
3. Liv. 38.5; Plut. *Cat. Mai.* 15; Gell. *N.A.* 4.18; Dio Cass. frag. 65. See A.E. Astin, *Cato the Censor*, (Oxford, 1978), 70–71 and note 64.
4. Not to be confused with (his son or grandson) Tiberius Gracchus, the subject of next chapter.
5. See the next few notes for sources on the trials of the Scipios.
6. Plut. *Cat. Mai.* 1.
7. Nepos. *Cat.* 1.
8. Plut, *Cat. Mai.* 3; Nepos *Cat.* 1; *De Vir. Ill.* 47.1.
9. Nepos *Cat.* 1.
10. Plut. *Cat. Mai.* 3. Nepos *Cat.* 1.
11. Plut. *Cat. Mai.* 3; Nepos *Cato* 1 is much more cursory: Cato was quaestor under Scipio in 205, had a falling out, and was opposed to him all his life.
12. Liv. 29.25.
13. Front. *Strat.* 4.7.12.
14. Plin *NH* Praef. 30.; See also *De Vir. Ill.* 47.1; See J.S. Ruebel, 'Cato and Scipio Africanus', *Classical World* 71 (1977), 163–164.
15. Ruebel, 'Cato and Scipio Africanus', 163.
16. Liv. 32.8, 27; Plut. *Cat. Mai.* 6.
17. Liv. 33.43.
18. Liv. 34.1; Val Max 1.1.3.
19. Zon. 9.17.

20. Cato's speech: Liv. 34.2–4. For the protest of the law, see Liv. 34.1–6; Zonar. 9.17. Val. Max. 9.1.3.
21. Liv. 34.13–21, 42.1.
22. Liv. 34.46–48. See Broughton, *MRR* 1.343 for sources.
23. Plut. *Cat. Mai.* 11
24. Liv. 35.1. This analysis is indebted to J.S. Ruebel, 'Cato and Scipio Africanus', *Classical World* 71 (1977), 166–169.
25. J.S. Ruebel, 'Cato and Scipio Africanus', *Classical World* 71 (1977), 165–168.
26. A point stressed by many and analyzed well by H. Mouritsen, *Politics in the Roman Republic* (Cambridge, 2017), 15–20, 24–30.
27. Liv. 31.1–8.
28. Liv. 36.2, 5–25.
29. See Astin, *Cato*, 57–9 for a succinct account of Antiochus and Glabrio in Greece, 189.
30. Liv. 37.58.
31. Astin, *Cato*, 70: Liv. 38, Plut. *Cat. Mai.* 15, Aul Gell., *N.A.* 4.18 and, seemingly, the vague Dio Cass. Fragment 65 (book 19).
32. Astin, *Cato*, 70, notes the sources and their lack of precision.
33. Liv. 38.50–56 is his main account. See also Plut. *Cat. Mai.* 15, Aul. Gell. *N.A.*, 4.18, Dio Cass. frag .65 (book 19).
34. For the chronology of the events and years between Cato's consulship and censorship, see Astin, *Cato*, 51–77, who offers this narrative in detail; also see Ruebel, 'Cato and Scipio Africanus', 161–73.
35. The battle of Magnesia: Polyb. 21.14–17; Liv. 37.37–44.
36. Astin, *Cato*, 61.
37. Liv. 38.50; Plut. *Cat. Mai.* 15, Aul. Gell. *N.A.* 4.18. Astin, *Cato*, 60–75; Broughton, *MRR* 1.367–70.
38. Liv. 38.56.
39. Polyb. 23.14 Liv. 38.55; Gell. *N.A.* 4.18; Broughton, *MRR* 1.369–70; Astin, *Cato*, 60–75.
40. Though Gell. 6.16.1–8 suggests Augurinus was a tribune in 184 and Broughton, *MRR* 1.376 follows him. See Astin, *Cato*, 61–63.
41. Gell. *N.A.* 4.18; Liv. 38.50–56; Ruebel, 'Cato and Scipio Africanus', 171; Astin, *Cato*, 61–62.
42. Broughton *MRR* 1.367; Aul. Gell. *N.A.* 4.18; Liv. 38.56.
43. Liv. 38.51.
44. Ibid.
45. Liv. 38.51 (Bettenson trans.).
46. The speech and the rounds to the Capitoline temples by Scipio and his well-wishers is also reported by Aul. Gell. *N.A.* 4.18.
47. Sen. *Ep.* 86.
48. Liv. 38.52. Astin, *Cato*, 70–73.
49. Liv. 38.53.
50. Liv. 38.55; 38.56.
51. Liv. 38.5; Plut. *Cat. Mai* 15; Gell. *N.A.* 4.18; Dio frag. 65. See Astin, *Cato*, 70–71 and note 64.

52. See Astin, *Cato*, 60–75 for discussion of motives.
53. Plut. *Cat. Mai.* 16; Liv. 39.41–2.
54. Liv. 39.42 says seven; Plut. *Cat. Mai.* 17 says 'a large number' (Waterfield trans).
55. Liv. 39.42.
56. Liv. 39.42; Val. Max 2.93 and Plut. *Cat. Mai.* 17 accounts seem to lean towards Antias.
57. J. Crook, '*Sponsione Provocare*: It's Place in Roman Litigation', *The Journal of Roman Studies*, 66(1976), 132–8; J.B. Churchill, '*Sponsio Quae in Verba Facta Est?* Two Lost Speeches and the Formula of the Roman Judicial Wager', *The Classical Quarterly*, 50(2000). 159–69.
58. Plut. 17.5; Liv. 39.43.
59. Plut. *Cat. Mai.* 18 (Waterfield trans.).
60. Plut. *Cat. Mai.* 18; Liv. 29; Astin, *Cato*, 81–2 suggests the forfeiture was not a disgrace but just the result of Cato instituting higher standards of physical fitness for the cavalry. It's hard to imagine Lucius accepted this with equanimity.
61. Liv. 39.44; Plut. *Cato* 18–19.
62. See J. Bartz, H. Engel, and S. Horacek, 'Basilica Porcia' in the *Digitales Forum Romanum* project for an overview of the building https://web.archive.org/web/20210428105154/http://www.digitales-forum-romanum.de/gebaeude/basilica-porcia/?lang=en
63. Plut. *Cat.Mai.*19 (Waterfield trans.).

Chapter 3

1. For a biography of Cornelia from the limited sources available, see S. Dixon, *Cornelia: Mother of the Gracchi* (Routledge, 2007).
2. Plut. *Ti. Gracch.* 1.
3. Plut. *Ti Gracch.* 1.
4. Plut. *C. Gracch.* 19 (Waterfield trans.).
5. Polyb. 6.19.
6. Plut, *Ti. Gracch.* 4. Diod. Sic. 29.26.
7. N. Rosenstein, '*Imperatores Victi*: The Case of C. Hostilius Mancinus', *Classical Antiquity* 5 (1986), 230–52.
8. Plut. *Ti. Gracch.* 7; Vell. Pat. 2.1; Dio 24.83; Liv. Per. 55; App *Hisp.* 13.83.
9. Vell. Pat. 2.1.
10. Dio Cass. 24.83.2.
11. Plut. *Ti. Gracch.* 8; App. *B Civ.* 1.7;
12. N. Rosenstein, *Romans at War: Farms, Families, and Death in the Middle Republic* (University of North Carolina, 2005), 107–69.
13. H.I. Flower, *Roman Republics*, (Princeton, 2010), 66–7.
14. For a recent discussion of the second century land problems, see Rosenstein, *Romans at War.*
15. Plut. *Ti. Gracch.* 9.
16. Plut. *Ti. Gracch.* 9.
17. App. *B Civ* 1.7–8, 11–12; Dio Cass. 24.83.7.
18. Again, see N. Rosenstein, *Romans at War.*
19. Vell. Pat. 2.2.3; Dio Cass. 24.83.7.

20. Plut. *Ti Gracch*. 9; Broughton, *MRR* 1.492–9 for their careers.
21. Plut. *Ti Gracch*. 9.
22. Plut. *Ti Gracch*. 9.
23. App. *B Civ*. 1.9.
24. See D. Stockton, *The Gracchi*, (Oxford, 1979), 41–60 for a discussion of Tiberius' agrarian law, and Rosenstein, *Romans at War*, 26–62 for a thorough critique of scholarly opinion.
25. On the interval between announcing a bill and the assembly vote, see A. Lintott, *The Constitution of the Roman Republic* (Oxford, 1999), 44, 62.
26. The Rostra: Liv. 8.14; Pliny *NH* 34.11.
27. Plut. *Ti. Gracch*. 9; App. *B Civ*. 1.9, 11.
28. Plut. *Ti. Gracch*. 10; Vell. Pat. 2.2.3; App. *B Civ* 1.12; Liv. *Per*. 58; Dio Cass. 24.4. For an overview of tribunes of the plebs, see Lintott, *The Constitution of the Roman Republic*, 121–8.
29. App. *B Civ*. 1.12; Dio Cass. 24.4–6; Plut. *Ti. Gracch*. 10.
30. Plut. *Ti. Gracch*. 10.
31. App. *B Civ*. 1.12; Plut. *Ti. Gracch*. 11.
32. Plut. *Ti. Gracch*. 12; App. *B Civ*. 1.12–13.
33. Flower, *Roman Republics*, 82–5 notes that the first violence was not the murder of Tiberius Gracchus but the laying of hands on the tribune Octavius. It's a fair point.
34. Plut. *Ti. Gracch*. 12; App. *B Civ*. 1.12.
35. Polyb. 6.11–18, especially 16–17. On the senate in the Republic and its relation to other political bodies: Lintott, *The Constitution of the Roman Republic*, 65–93 and Mouritsen, *Politics in the Roman Republic*, 7–53.
36. Plut. *Ti. Gracch*. 13
37. Plut. *Ti. Gracch*. 14; Liv. *Per*. 58.
38. J. Crook, '*Sponsione Provocare*: It's Place in Roman Litigation', *Journal of Roman Studies* – 66(1976), 132–8; J.B. Churchill, '*Sponsio Quae in Verba Facta Est?* Two Lost Speeches and the Formula of the Roman Judicial Wager', *The Classical Quarterly*, 50(2000). 159–69.
39. Plut. *Ti. Gracch*. 14 (Waterfield trans.).
40. Mouritsen, *Politics in the Roman Republic*, 165.
41. Plut. *Ti. Gracch*. 15.
42. Plut, *Ti. Gracch*. 16; App. *B. Civ*. 1.14.
43. Plut. *Ti. Gracch*. 16. One of these, putting a number of equestrians on the panel of eligible jurors equal to the existing senators, is a claim partially echoed by Dio Cass. 24.83.7, but Dio is quite late, quite condensed, and quite suspect in his account. Again, there is no compelling evidence that a law like this did pass, though later, under Gaius Gracchus, a law about the composition of juries would indeed be put into effect.
44. App *B Civ*. 1.14.
45. Plut. *Ti. Gracch*. 16; App. *B Civ*. 1.14.
46. Ibid.
47. Plut. *Ti. Gracch*. 17–19.
48. Plut. *Ti. Gracch*. 13.

49. Broughton *MRR* 1.499.
50. Vell. Pat 2.3.
51. P. Stadter, note to Waterfield, *Plutarch, Roman Lives* (Oxford, 1999), p. 449.
52. Plut. *Ti. Gracch.* 19.
53. App. *B Civ.* 1.15–16.
54. Vell. Pat. 2.3; Liv. *Per.* 58.
55. Vell. Pat 2.3; Plut. *Ti. Gracch.* 19; App. *B Civ.* 1.16.
56. App *B Civ.* 1.16.
57. Plut. *Ti. Gracch.* 20. App. *B Civ.* 1.16; Liv. *Per.* 58.
58. Sall. *Iug.* 31; Plut. *Ti. Gracch.* 20.
59. Plut. *Ti. Gracch.* 20–21; App. *B Civ.* 1.18.

Chapter 4

1. Stockton, *The Gracchi*, 88.
2. Plut. *C. Gracch.* 1.
3. Dio Cass. 25.85.1 (Cary trans.).
4. Cic. *De or.* 2.106, *Amic* 96; Liv. *Per.* 59.14; Vell. Pat. 2.4.
5. Stockton, *The Gracchi*, 97.
6. Stockton, *The Gracchi*, 98.
7. Liv. *Per.* 60.
8. Plut. *C. Gracch.* 1–2.
9. Cic. *Brut.* 109, *De Off.* 3.11; Stockton, *The Gracchi*, 94–5.
10. Stockton, *The Gracchi*, 95.
11. Liv. *Per.* 60.; Val. Max. 9.5.1.
12. G. Forsythe, *A Critical History of Rome: From Prehistory to the First Punic War* (University of California, 2005), 289–92; K. Lomas, 'Italy during the Roman Republic, 338–31 B.C.', *The Cambridge Companion to the Roman Republic* (Cambridge, 2004) 233–8.
13. Lomas, p. 238.
14. Stockton, *The Gracchi*, 106–13.
15. Stockton, 112–13; Lomas, 233–48.
16. Stockton, *The Gracchi*, 188–9.
17. Stockton, *The Gracchi*, 120–2; 186–7.
18. Stockton, 190–1.
19. App. *B. Civ.* 1.21.
20. Liv. *Per.* 60. Vell. Pat. 2.6.4; Plut. *C. Gracch.* 3.
21. Val. Max. 2.8.4.
22. Stockton, 97.
23. Plut. *C. Gracch.* 1 quotes Cicero.
24. Dio Cass. 25.1.
25. Plut. *C. Gracch.* 3.
26. Plut. *C. Gracch.* 3; App. *B Civ.* 1.21; Diod. Sic. 34.24.
27. Plut. *C. Gracch.* 3; Diod. Sic. 34.25.
28. Plut. *C. Gracch.* 4; Cic. *Rab. Post.* 12, *Cat.* 4.10, *Brut* 128; Vell. Pat. 2.7.4. Stockton, *The Gracchi*, 90, notes there may have been a special court set up for the investigations.

29. Dio Cass. 25.1.
30. Plut. *C. Gracch.* 5; Cic. *De Am.* 96.
31. Plut, *C. Gracch.* 1; *Ti. Gracch.* 1.
32. App. *B Civ.* 1.18. Stockton, *The Gracchi*, 166.
33. Plut. *C. Gracch.* 10.
34. Stockton, *The Gracchi*, 166.
35. Plut. *C. Gracch.* 5; Liv. *Per.* 60; Vell. Pat. 2.6; Flor 2.3. Stockton, 166.
36. Flower, *Roman Republics*, 66–7.
37. Stockton, *The Gracchi*, 98 (quoting Mommsen).
38. Cic. *Sest* 103, *Off.* 2.72; Liv. *Per.* 60; Vell. Pat. 2.6; Flor. 2.3; Plut. *C. Gracch.* 5.
39. Polyb. 6.21, 39.
40. Diod. Sic. 34.25.
41. Cic. *Brut.* 99; Plut. *C. Gracch.* 5; App. *B Civ.* 1.23, 34; Vell. Pat. 2.6; Stockton, *The Gracchi*, 156–8.
42. Stockton, *The Gracchi*, 138.
43. Plut. *C. Gracch.* 5.
44. App *B Civ.* 1.22. Also suggested by Diod. Sic. 34.25, 37.9; Vell. Pat. 2.6; Flor. 2.5.
45. Liv. *Per.* 60.
46. Stockton, *The Gracchi*, 136–42.
47. Plut. *C. Gracch.* 6–7.
48. Cic. *De or.* 2.106, *Amic.* 96; Liv. *Per.* 59; Vell. Pat. 2.4.
49. Sall. *Jug.* 37.
50. Stockton, *The Gracchi*, 169–71.
51. Ibid.
52. Plut. *C. Gracch.* 9.
53. Cic. *Brut.* 109; Plut. *C. Gracch.* 9 (Waterfield trans.); App. *B Civ.* 1.23; Stockton, *The Gracchi* 176.
54. Vell. Pat. 1.15, 2.7; Liv. *Per.* 60; App *B Civ.* 1.24; Plut. *C. Gracch.* 10; Stockton, 172.
55. Plut. *C. Gracch.* 10.
56. Plut. *C. Gracch.* 10.
57. Plut. *C. Gracch.* 11.
58. Plut. *C. Gracch.* 11.
59. App. *B Civ.* 1.24–25.
60. Plut. *C. Gracch.* 12; App. *B Civ.* 1.23.
61. Plut. *C. Gracch.* 12; App. *B Civ.* 1.23.
62. Plut. *C. Gracch.* 12.
63. Plut. *C. Gracch.* 12.
64. App. *B Civ.* 1.24. Plutarch *C. Gracch.* 13, asserts a number of Gaius' laws were on the table for repeal.
65. Stockton, *The Gracchi*, 195, Fragment quoted in 222–3; Plut. *C. Gracch.* 13.
66. Appian *B Civ* 1.24–25; Diod. Sic. 34.28 has Gracchus and his supporters coming to the assembly armed with swords. Oros 5.12 notes he went up with a crowd and that Gracchus' partisans killed Antullius.
67. Plut. *C. Gracch.* 13.

68. Plut. *C. Gracch.* 13–14.
69. Plut. *C. Gracch.* 13.
70. App. *B Civ.* 1.26; see also Orosius 5.12.
71. Plut. *C. Gracch.* 15.
72. Stockton, *The Gracchi*, 196.
73. Appian *B Civ.* 1.25 -26.
74. Plut. *C. Gracch.* 14.
75. Cic *Cat.* 1.4; Cic. *Phil* 8.14; Plut. *C. Gracch.* 14; Liv. *Per.* 61.
76. Plut. *C. Gracch.* 14–15.
77. Plut. *C. Gracch.* 15.
78. App. *B Civ.* 1.26; Plut. *C. Gracch.* 16.
79. Plut. *C. Gracch.* 16; Appian *B Civ.* 1.26.
80. Plut. *C. Gracch.* 16. Appian differs in suggesting that Flaccus was murdered in an associate's workshop. *B Civ.* 1.26.
81. Plut. *C. Gracch.* 17; App. *B Civ.* 1.26; Diod. Sic. 34.29; Cic. *Cat.* 1.4.
82. Plut. *C. Gracch.* 17; App. *B Civ.* 1.26; Diod. Sic. 34.29, Plin. *NH* 33.48.
83. App. *B Civ.* 1.26; Sall. *Jug.* 16, 31; Oros. 5.12.
84. Plut. *C. Gracch.* 17 (Waterfield trans.)
85. Plut. *C. Gracch.* 18.
86. Plut. *C. Gracch.* 19.

Chapter 5

1. See Polyb. 3.64.
2. Liv. 21.52–6, 22.44–9; Polyb. 3.68–74, 113–16.
3. Liv. 30.32–36 Polyb. 15.9–15
4. Some references to Numidian allied cavalry: Liv. 31.11; 35.11; 38.41; 42.35.
5. Sall. *Iug.* 8–11.
6. Sall. *Iug.* 16; Liv. *Per.* 62; Flor. 1.36.
7. Sall. *Iug.* 21–27.
8. Flor. 1.36, Liv. *Per.* 64.
9. Sall. *Iug.* 27–35.
10. Sall. *Iug.* 36–9.
11. Sall. *Iug.* 40.
12. Sall. *Iug.* 40–42; Flor. 1.36; Liv. *Per.* 64.
13. Sall. *Iug.* 43–47; Front. *Strat.* 4.1; Val. Max. 2.7.2; Eutr. 4.2.7.
14. Sall. *Iug.* 47–54.
15. Sall. *Iug.* 54–5; Liv. *Per.* 65 notes Metellus was successful in Numidia. Eutr. 4.27.
16. See also Plut. *Mar.* 7.
17. Sall. *Iug.* 46, 50.
18. Plut. *Mar.* 7; Diod. Sic. 34.38 agrees Marius earned a good reputation but implies he was under-appreciated by Metellus.
19. Plut. *Mar.* 1.
20. Diod. Sic. 34.38.
21. Plut. *Mar.* 3; Plut. *Ti. Gracch.* 13.
22. Plut. *Mar.* 3.

23. Plut. *Mar,* 4.
24. Plut. *Mar.* 5; Val. Max, 6.9.
25. Plut. *Mar.* 6.
26. Plut. *Mar.* 7.
27. Sall. *Iug.* 55–56.
28. Sall. *Iug.* 56–8; Flor. 1.36.
29. Sall. *Iug.* 60–61.
30. Plut. *Mar.* 4–6.
31. Sall. *Iug.* 63–4; Plut. *Mar.* 8.
32. Sall. *Iug.* 65.
33. Sall. *Iug.* 65–6.
34. Sall. *Iug.* 66–7.
35. Sall. *Iug.* 69.
36. Plut. *Mar.* 8.
37. Sall. *Iug.* 65–6; Plut. *Mar.* 8.
38. Plut. *Mar.* 8.
39. Sall. *Iug.* 73.
40. Sall. *Iug.* 73; Plut. *Mar.* 8; Vell. Pat. 2.11; Cic. *Off.* 3.79.
41. Sall. *Iug.* 73; Vell. Pat. 2.11.
42. Sall. *Iug.* 75; Flor. 1.36.
43. Sall. *Iug.* 75–6.
44. Sall. *Iug.* 80–82. Plut. *Mar.* 10.
45. Sall. *Iug.* 83.
46. Sall. *Iug.* 85.20–30 (Loeb Trans.).
47. Sall. *Iug.* 84–6. Plut. *Mar.* 9–10.
48. Sall. *Iug.* 88.
49. Vell. Pat. 2.12; *De Vir. Ill.* 62.
50. Sall. *Iug.* 87.
51. Sall. *Iug.* 89.
52. Sall. *Iug.* 89; Flor, 1.36; Oros. 5.15.
53. Sall. *Iug.* 92.
54. Sall. *Iug.* 92–4.
55. Sall. *Iug.* 95.
56. Plut. *Sull.* 1–2; Val. Max. 6.9 moralizes on Sulla's early lifestyle.
57. Sall. *Iug.* 96; Plut. *Sull.* 3; Val. Max. 6.9.6.
58. Sall. *Iug.* 98.
59. Sall. *Iug.* 97–100.
60. See also Front. *Strat.* 2.4.
61. Sall. *Iug.* 101.
62. Sall. *Iug.* 102–3.
63. Sall. *Iug.* 103–114; Plut. *Sull.* 3–4; Vell. Pat. 2.12; Val. Max. 6.9.6; Liv. *Per.* 66.
64. Plut. *Sull.* 3.
65. R. Evans, 'Rome's Cimbric Wars (114–101 BC) and their impact on the Iberian Peninsula', *Acta Classica* 48 (2005), 38–43. The most complete and detailed ancient account comes from Plut. *Mar.* 11–27 and Vell. Pat. 2.12.
66. Plut. *Mar.* 12.

272 Rivalries that Destroyed the Roman Republic

67. Plut. *Mar.* 14; Val. Max. 2.6.2 focuses on the training the consul Rutilius did.
68. Plut. *Mar.* 14.
69. Plut. *Mar.* 14.
70. Plut. *Sull.* 4.
71. Plut. *Mar.* 15.
72. Plut. *Mar.* 21 says over 100,000 were killed or captured at the subsequent battle of Aquae Sextiae.
73. Plut. *Mar.* 15–19.
74. Plut. *Mar.* 19–21.
75. Plut. *Mar.* 26–7.
76. Plut. *Mar.* 23–8.

Chapter 6

1. J.R. Patterson, 'Rome and Italy' in N. Rosenstein and R. Kallet-Marx (eds.), *A Companion to the Roman Republic* (Wiley-Blackwell, 2010) 606–24.
2. M.C. Alexander, 'Law in the Roman Republic', in N. Rosenstein and R. Kallet-Marx, eds., A *Companion to the Roman Republic*, (Wiley-Blackwell, 2010), 236–55.
3. Broughton, *MRR*, 1.567.
4. App. *B Civ.* 1.27; Broughton, *MRR* 1.563, 567, 571 on Saturninus' and Glaucia's tribunates and Metellus' censorship.
5. Plut. *Mar.* 28 has Marius seek Saturninus' and Glaucia's assistance for 100 and Liv. *Per.* 69 suggests Marius aided in the murder of Nonius. App. *B Civ.* 1.28 possibly suggests that the three joined forces only after the murder of Nonius and the election of Saturninus for 100.
6. Liv. *Per.* 69 asserts Marius' soldiers killed Nonius/Nunnius.
7. App. *B Civ.* 1.28.
8. Cic. *Brut.* 224.
9. App. *B Civ.* 1.29.
10. App. *B Civ.* 1.30.
11. Plut. *Mar.* 29; App. *B Civ.* 1.30 says Marius led the way by hypocritically saying he would swear the oath then changing his mind later.
12. Plut. *Mar.* 29.
13. Plut. *Mar.* 29; App *B Civ.* 1.31; Val Max 3.8.4; Liv. *Per.* 69.
14. See Broughton, *MRR* 1.575 for sources.
15. App. *B Civ.* 1.32. The critical analysis of these accounts came from Badian in his foundational 1984 article 'The Death of Saturninus', *Chiron* 14(1984) 101–147. Also see J.L. Benness and T.W. Hillard, 'The Death of Lucius Equitius on 1 December 100 BC', *Classical Quarterly*, 40 (1990), 269–72.
16. Senior magistrates were required to spend a year out of office between holding elected magistracies.
17. Badian, 'Death of Saturninus', esp 106–8.
18. E.D. Hunt, 'Orosius' in the *Oxford Classical Dictionary*.
19. Liv. *Per.* 69; Oros. 5.17. Badian, 'Death of Saturninus', 106–8.
20. App. *B Civ.* 1.32.
21. Oros. 5.17.

22. Cic. *Rab. Post.* 20 (Tyrrell trans.)
23. Cic *Rab Post.* 21 (Tyrrell trans.)
24. Val. Max. 3.2.18, Plut. *Mar.* 30, Liv. *Per.* 69. Again, Badian, 'Death of Saturninus', is the foundational scholarship for all these events.
25. Plut. *Mar.* 30.
26. Badian, 'Death of Saturninus', esp. 120–21.
27. Oros. 5.7–8.
28. Plut, *Mar.* 30.; Flor. 2.4.16 offers a similar version. App. *B Civ.* 1.32.
29. App *B Civ.* 1.36.
30. Vell. Pat. 2.14.
31. App. *B Civ.* 1.38–9.
32. F.C. Tweedie, '*Caenum aut caelum*: M. Livius Drusus and the Land', *Mnemosyne*, 64(2011), 573–90.
33. Vell. Pat. 2.14.3.
34. Liv. *Per.* 70; Flor. 2.4.16; Tweedie, 574–5.
35. Most of all Tweedie, 573–90.
36. App. *B Civ.* 1.35. Liv. *Per.* 71. See Tweedie, *passim*, for a relatively recent discussion.
37. App. *B Civ.* 1.35.
38. Tweedie, 579.
39. App *B Civ.* 1.35.
40. E.J. Weinrib, 'The Judiciary Law of M. Livius Drusus (tr. pl. 91 B.C.)', *Historia* 19 (1970), 415, makes this argument.
41. Vell Pat 2.13.2 (Shipley trans.).
42. Liv. *Per.* 71 (Chaplin trans.).
43. Cic. *Leg.* 2.14.31. Weinrib, 'The Judiciary Law of M. Livius Drusus', 415–17.
44. Tweedie, 'M. Livius Drusus and the Land', 581–2, points out Etruscan and Umbrian public lands were not touched by the Gracchan proposals so Drusus' proposals likely targeted their land in particular for reassignment.
45. App. *B Civ.* 1.35–7.
46. Vell Pat 2.13–14.
47. Suggested by Tweedie, 'M. Livius Drusus and the Land', 576–9.
48. Flor. 2.18.
49. App. *B Civ.* 1.39.
50. Ibid.
51. C.F. Konrad, 'From the Gracchi to the First Civil War', in N. Rosentstein and R. Kallet-Marx, eds., *A Companion to the Roman Republic*, (Wiley-Blackwell, 2010), 177–8.
52. Plut. *Sull.* 5; T.J. Luce, 'Marius and the Mithridatic Command', *Historia* 19 (1970), 165–9.
53. Luce, 'Marius and the Mithridatic Command', 186.
54. Luce, 186–7; Konrad, 'From the Gracchi to the First Civil War', p. 179. App. *Mith.* 3.21.
55. P.F. Cagniart, 'L. Cornelius Sulla in the Nineties: a Reassessment', *Latomus* 50 (1991), 285–303, especially 295–301. Konrad, 'From the Gracchi to the First Civil War', 179.

56. Luce, 'Marius and the Mithridatic Command', 161–94, especially 163–6.
57. Plut. *Mar.* 31–2.
58. Luce, 162–4.
59. Luce, 185.
60. Plut. *Sull.* 7.
61. T.N. Mitchell, 'The Volte-Face of P. Sulpicius Rufus in 88 BC', *Classical Philology* 70 (1975), 195–204; Powell, 'The Tribune Sulpicius', *Historia* 39 (1990), 447–9; Broughton, *MRR* 1.563–4. Cic. *Off.* 2.49; Cic *De or.* 2.88–9; 2.197–8, 2.202–203;
62. Vell. Pat. 2.18.
63. Plut. *Sull.* 8.
64. Plut. *Sull.* 8; App. *B Civ.* 1.55.
65. The *Lex Villia Annalis* of 180 BCE required that consular candidates previously had been praetors.
66. Cic. *Har. resp.* 43, Brut 226. Mitchell, 'The Volte-Face of P. Sulpicius Rufus', 197–204.
67. For sake of simplicity, I'm leaving out the *concilium plebis*.
68. Lintott, *The Constitution of the Roman Republic*, 50–61.
69. App. *B Civ.* 1.49; Vell. Pat. 2.20; Konrad, 'From the Gracchi to the First Civil War', 179.
70. Mitchell 'The Volte-Face of P. Sulpicius Rufus', 202 and n. 17. Mitchell counters A.W. Lintott, 'The Tribunate of P. Sulpicius Rufus', *Classical Quarterly* 21(1971), 450, who suggests the war against Mithridates was a consular province before the late 89 elections for the consuls of 88. See also P.F. Cagniart, 'L. Cornelius Sulla in the 90s: A Reassessment', *Latomus* 50(1991), 299–301.
71. Plut. *Mar.* 35, *Sull.* 8.
72. Plut. *Mar.* 35, *Sull.* 8. Powell, 'The Tribune Sulpicius', *Historia* 39 (1990), 450.
73. Powell, 451–3.
74. App. *B Civ.* 1.56.
75. App. *B Civ.* 1.57.
76. App. *B Civ.* 1.57; Powell, 450–1.
77. Lintott, 'The Tribunate of P. Sulpicius Rufus', 446.
78. Lintott, 446–53, though this has been challenged.
79. Plut. *Sull.* 9.
80. Plut. *Sull.* 8; App *B Civ.* 1.58.
81. Plut. *Sull.* 9.
82. Plut. *Sull.* 9.
83. Plut. *Sull.* 9–10; App. *B Civ.* 1.58; For the relevant geographical features of Rome, see L. Richardson, A *New Topographical Dictionary of Ancient Rome*, (Johns Hopkins, 1992), 263, 299, 416–17.
84. App. *B Civ.* 1.58.
85. Plut. *Sull.* 9.
86. App. *B Civ.* 1.58.
87. Plut. *Sull.* 10; App. *B Civ.* 1.59.
88. App. *B Civ.* 1.60.
89. Plut. *Sull.* 10.

Chapter 7
1. Plut. *Mar.* 36–9.
2. Plut. *Mar.* 40; App. *B Civ.* 1.62.
3. App. *B Civ.* 1.62.
4. A. Keaveney, *Sulla: The Last Republican 2d Ed.* (Routledge, 2005), 55–63; See Flower, *Roman Republics*, 118–134.
5. Keaveney, *Sulla*, 58–61.
6. Plut. *Sull.* 10.
7. App. *B. Civ* 1.62; P. Southern *Pompey the Great* (Tempus, 2002), 17–19 and n.17 lists the evidence and skepticism. Keaveney, *Sulla*, 55–63.
8. Plut. Sull. 10. Keaveney, *Sulla*, 59–63.
9. App *B Civ.* 1.64; Plut. Mar. 41; Vell Pat. 2.20.
10. App *B Civ.* 1.64; Plut. Mar. 41; Vell Pat. 2.20.
11. App. *B Civ.* 1.65.
12. App. *B Civ.* 1.65–6; Plut. Mar. 41.
13. Vell. Pat. 2.20.
14. App. *B Civ.* 1.66.
15. App. *B Civ.* 1. 66.
16. App. *B Civ.* 1.66–7.
17. App. *B Civ.* 1.67; Plut. Mar. 41.
18. Southern, *Pompey*, 18–19.
19. App. *B Civ.* 1.68.
20. App. *B Civ.* 1.68.
21. App. *B Civ.* 1.68; Vell. Pat. 2.21 Southern, *Pompey*, 19–20, on the plague comment.
22. App. *B Civ.* 1.69.
23. App. *B Civ.* 1.69.
24. App. *B Civ.* 1.70.
25. App. *B Civ.* 1.70; Plut. Mar. 43; Vell. Pat. 2.21.
26. App. *B Civ.* 1.71; Plut. Mar. 43; Vell. Pat 2.22.
27. App. *B Civ.* 1.71.
28. Plut. *Mar.* 42.
29. Vell. Pat. 2.22.
30. Vell. Pat. 2.22.
31. App. *B Civ.* 1.74.
32. App. *B Civ.* 1.74.
33. Plut. *Mar.* 44.
34. App. 1.72; Vell. Pat. 2.22.
35. Plut. *Mar.* 45; Vell. Pat. 2.23.
36. App. *Mith.* 51; Memnon 24; See G. Sampson, *The Collapse of Rome: Marius, Sulla and the First Civil War* (Pen & Sword, 2013), 109–10.
37. App. *Mith.* 38–50; Plut. Sull. 12–19; Samspon, *Collapse of Rome*, 109–12 for a brief narrative of Sulla's campaigns
38. App. *Mith.* 51; Sampson, *Collapse of Rome*, 109–10.
39. Memnon 24; Sampson, *Collapse of Rome*, 109–10.
40. App. *Mith.* 54–61. Plut. *Sull.* 19–26.

41. App. *Mith.* 59–60; Plut. *Sull.* 25.
42. Vell. Pat. 2.24.
43. App. *B Civ.* 1.77.
44. App. *B Civ.* 1.77; Liv. *Per.* 83.
45. App. *B Civ.* 1.78; Vell. Pat 2.24; Liv. *Per.* 83.
46. App. *B Civ.* 1.78.
47. App. *B. Civ.* 1.79.
48. App. *B Civ.* 1.79; Vell. Pat. 2.24.
49. Plut. *Sull.* 27.
50. G. Sampson, *The Collapse of Rome.* 116–17. Sampson marshals the poor evidence to provide a detailed narrative of this final phase of the Civil War, and I have followed him here.
51. Sampson, *The Collapse of Rome,* 117–24.
52. Sampson, *The Collapse of Rome,* 124–5.
53. Sampson, 125–8.
54. Sampson, 125–33.
55. Sampson, 134–45.
56. App *B Civ.* 1.95.; Plut. Sulla 31; Vell. Pat 2.28.
57. App. *B Civ.* 1.95.
58. App. *B Civ.* 1.96.
59. Plut. *Sull.* 33.
60. App. *B Civ.* 1.98.
61. App *B Civ.* 1.98–100.
62. H. Flower, *Roman Republics,* (Princeton 2010), 117–34.
63. H. Flower, *Roman Republics,* 117–34.
64. Flower, 117–34.
65. Ibid.
66. Flower, 129.
67. Flower, 117–34.
68. E. Gruen. *The Last Generation of the Roman Republic* (University of California, 1974).

Chapter 8

1. Plut. *Pomp.* 22.3 (Waterfield trans.).
2. Val. Max. 6.2.8.
3. Vell. Pat. 2.21; Plut. *Pomp.* 3. Southern, *Pompey,* 11–14.
4. Southern, *Pompey,* 14–18.
5. Plague: Vell. Pat. 2.21.4; Thunderbolt: Plut. *Pomp.* 1, App *B Civ.* 1.68.
6. Southern, 18–20; Plut. *Pomp.* 1.2 has no hook but the body is pulled off its bier.
7. Plut. *Pomp.* 4.
8. Southern, *Pompey,* 20–21. Plut. *Pomp.* 4.
9. Plut. *Pomp.* 6; App. *B Civ.* 1.80; Liv. *Per.* 85.; Cic. *Man.* 61.
10. Southern, *Pompey,* 21–3.
11. Plut. *Pomp.* 8.
12. Southern, *Pompey,* 21–3.
13. App *B Civ.* 1.90.

14. Plut. *Pomp.* 9; Southern, 27–8.
15. App. *B Civ.* 1.97.
16. Val. Max 5.3.5; Plut. *Pomp.* 10; App. *B Civ.* 1.95–96; Liv. *Per.* 89. Southern, *Pompey*, 32–3.
17. Plut. *Pomp.* 12–13; Liv. *Per.* 89; Southern, *Pompey* 33–36.
18. Plut. *Pomp.* 13; Southern, *Pompey*, 36–37.
19. App *B Civ.* 1.108.
20. Plut. *Pomp.* 17, 19.
21. Plut. *Pomp.* 17; App. *B Civ.* 1.108.
22. App. *B Civ.* 1.112.
23. App. *B Civ.* 1.113–114; Plut. *Pomp.* 20
24. App. *B Civ.* 1.115; Plut. *Pomp.* 20.
25. App. *B Civ.* 1.72.
26. Cic. *Sest.* 48; Cic. *De or.* 3–10.
27. Plut. *Crass.* 4.
28. App *B Civ.* 1.90.
29. Plut. *Crass.* 6; App *B Civ.* 1.93.
30. Sall. *Cat.* 37.6; Flor. 2.11.3.
31. Plut. *Crass.* 2.
32. Plin. *HN* 33.145 (Rackham trans.).
33. Plut. *Crass.* 3.
34. Plut. *Crass.* 3.
35. Plut. *Crass.* 7; Cic. *Brut.* 233 on Crassus as an effective orator.
36. Cic. *Brut.* 233 (Kaster trans.).
37. Plut. *Crass.* 3.
38. Front *Strat.* 1.5.21; Liv *Per.* 95; App *B Civ.* 1.116; Vell. Pat 2.30.
39. App. *B Civ.* 1.116; Plut. *Crass.* 9; Front *Strat.* 1.5.21.
40. Plut. *Crass.* 9; App. *B Civ.* 1.117.
41. Flor. 2.8.10; Liv. *Per.* 96; Plut. *Crass.* 9.
42. App *B Civ.* 1.118; Liv *Per.* 96 calls Crassus praetor.
43. Plut. *Crass.* 10; Oros. 5.24.5.
44. See Bruce Marshall, 'Crassus' Ovation in 71 BC', *Historia* 21 (1972), 669–73.
45. Marshall, 670, cleverly makes the case. Cicero *Para. Stoic* 45 seems to refer to Crassus' famous statement (reported in Plut. Crass 2) that one was only rich if they could support an army and specifically mentions six legions. Perhaps this is the episode Cicero had in mind.
46. App. *B Civ.* 1.118.
47. App. *B Civ.* 1.118; Plut. Crass 10.3–4.
48. Plut. *Crass.* 10.3–4.
49. Plut. *Crass.* 11.2.
50. Front *Strat.* 1.5.20 agrees on the breakout.
51. App. *B Civ.* 1.120; Plut. *Crass.* 11.4–7.
52. App. *B Civ.* 1.120
53. Ampelius *Liber Memorialis* 45.3.
54. Plut. *Crass.* 11.7–8; Plut. *Pomp.* 21.1–2, 31.6–7.
55. Much of this argument comes from Marshal, 'Crassus' Ovation'.

56. Marshal, 'Crassus' Ovation'.
57. App *B Civ.* 1.121.
58. Plut. *Pomp.* 21.3.
59. Vell. Pat. 2.30.
60. App. *B Civ.* 1.121.
61. Cic. *Man.* 62.
62. D. Stockton, 'The First Consulship of Pompey', *Historia* 22 (1973), 212. See also Seager, *Pompey*, 36–8.
63. App. *B Civ.* 1.121.
64. Plut. *Crass.* 12; Plut. *Pomp.* 22.
65. Plut. *Pomp.* 22.5
66. Cic. *Verr.* 1.1.45; Cic. *Leg.* 3.22; Sall. *Cat.* 38; Plut. *Pomp.* 22.
67. Stockton, 'The First Consulship of Pompey', 209; Asconius 66; C. Seager, *Pompey*, 32–34.
68. Stockton, 209; Cic. *Clu.* 110–12.
69. Stockton, 213.
70. Cic. *Ver.* 1.1.45, 2.3.223; Cic. *Phil* 1.20; Liv. *Per.* 97; Plut. *Pomp.* 22.4.
71. Plut. *Pomp.* 22 (Waterfield trans.).
72. E. Gruen, *The Last Generation of the Roman Republic* (University of California Press, 1974).
73.. Seager, *Pompey*, 44–7; R. Kallet-Marx, *Hegemony to Empire: The Development of the Roman Imperium in the East from 148 to 62 BC*, (University of California, 1996), 311–13; Cic. *Man.* 44, 52–4; Liv. *Per.* 99; Vell. Pat. 2.31; Plut. *Pomp.* 25–6.
74. Seager, *Pompey*, 45–9; Kallet-Marx, *Hegemony to Empire*, 317–18; Cic. *Man.* 33–35; Vell. Pat. 2.32; Liv. *Per.* 99; Plut. *Pomp.* 25–7; App. *Mith* 14.94–5; Dio Cass. 36.37.3–5.
75. Kallet-Marx, 299–322; Manilian law: Cic *Man.* 1–71; Liv. *Per.* 100; Plut. *Pomp.* 30, *Luc.* 35; App. *Mith.* 14.91.
76. Kallet-Marx, *Hegemony to Empire*, 323–4; Plut. *Pomp.* 30–43; App. *Syr.* 8.49–50; App. *Mith.* 14.91–17.121.

Chapter 9

1. Sall. *Cat.* 25 (Woodman trans.).
2. S. Pomeroy, *Goddesses, Whores, Wives, and Slaves: Women in Classical Antiquity* (Schocken Books, 1975, 1995) works this depiction of Sempronia on pages 171–2 into a larger investigation of the evidence for Roman matrons in Chapter 8, 'The Roman Matron of the Late Republic and Early Empire.'
3. Sall. *Cat.* 27–8.
4. Cic. *Cat.* 1.80–10, though he asserts two *equites* were sent to murder him. See also App. *B Civ.* 2.2–3; Plut. *Cic.* 16.
5. Sall. *Cat* 28; Plutarch *Cic.* 16; App *B Civ.* 2.3.
6. W. Batstone, 'Cicero's Construction of Consular Ethos in the First Catilinarian', *Transactions of the American Philological Association* 124 (1994), 211–13.
7. Sall. *Cat.* 31; Plut. *Cic.* 16.
8. Cic. *Cat.* 1.2, 5, 8–9.

9. Sall. *Cat.* 16–17; Plut. *Cic.* 10; E.G. Hardy, 'The Catilinarian Conspiracy in Its Context: A Re-Study of the Evidence', *Journal of Roman Studies* 7 (1917), 168.

10. K.H. Waters, 'Cicero, Sallust, and Catiline', *Historia* 19 (1970), esp. 198–204.

11. Sall. *Cat.* 56–61; Liv. *Per.* 102–103; Plut. *Cic.* 22; App. *B Civ.* 2.7; Dio Cass. 37.39.

12. A.J. Woodman, introduction, p. xviii in *Sallust: Catiline's War, The Jugurthine War, Histories* (Penguin, 2007).

13. Hardy, 'The Catilinarian Conspiracy in its Context: A Re-Study of the Evidence'. *Journal of Roman Studies* 7 (1917), 186, gives the example of the dating of the conspirators meeting at M Porcius Laeca's house, to which one could add Sallust's assertion that the senate issued the 'final decree (*senatus consultum ultimum*) after Catiline's meeting at Porcius' house (Sall. *Cat.* 29) when, according to Cicero, who is probably more reliable here, the *senatus consultum ultimum* came several weeks before (Cic. *Cat.* 1.7). See also Waters, 'Cicero, Sallust, and Catiline', 201 note 18.

14. Waters, 208–14.

15. Waters, 208; See also Seager, '*Iusta Catilinae*', *Historia* 22 (1973), 240–8 and E.J. Philips, 'Catiline's Conspiracy', *Historia* 25 (1976), 441–8 for rebuttals.

16. Sallust has Catiline continuously plotting as he ran for the elections of 64 and 63: *Cat.* 20–26, as does Plut. *Cic.* 11–17. App. *B Civ.* 2.2–3 only suggests Catiline ran for consul in 64, not again in 63.; Dio Cass. 37.29 places the whole plot after the elections of 63. See Hardy, 'The Catilinarian Conspiracy in its Context' for a good look at the evidence and an exceedingly helpful chronology.

17. Seager, '*Iusta Catilinae*', 240; Cic. *Mur.* 49; Plut. *Cic.* 14.

18. Sall. *Cat.* 26; Dio Cass. 37.30.

19. Sall. *Cat.* 32. Waters, 'Cicero, Sallust, and Catiline', 203–4.

20. Sall. *Cat.* 32; Plut. *Cic.* 16; Note that Appian *B Civ.* 2.3 has Catiline arrange the assassination during the night meeting and leave Rome before it is executed. Dio Cassius' version is too different to describe here, but his account gets Catiline leaving to the army in Etruria in 37.33.

21. Seager, '*Iusta Catilinae*', 240 asserts there is no proof, but if we are going to believe what can be corroborated in our sources, the Allobrogic envoys were given letters to deliver to Catiline.

22. Sall. *Cat.* 40–41.

23. Sall. *Cat.* 42–7; Plutarch *Cic.* 17–19; App. *B Civ.* 2.3–5; Dio Cass. 37.34.

24. Cic. *Cat.* 2.1–9.

25. Sall. *Cat* 48.

26. Sall. *Cat.* 48; compare Dio 37.35.

27. Sall. *Cat.* 49.

28. Sall. *Cat.* 50.

29. App *B Civ.* 2.5; Dio Cass. 37.36–7.

30. Sall. *Cat.* 50; App. *B Civ.* 2.5; Dio Cass. 37.5.

31. Sall. *Cat.* 51; App. *B Civ.* 2.6; Dio Cass. 37.6.

32. App *B Civ.* 2.6.

33. Woodman introduction p. xiv in *Sallust: Catiline's War, The Jugurthine War, Histories*.

34. Cic. *Cat.* 4.4 .

35. Cic. *Cat.* 4.

36. Plut. *Cat. Min.* 1–2.

37. Plut. *Cat. Min.* 7–9.

38. Plut. *Cat. Min.* 14.

39. Plut. *Cat. Min.* 16.

40. Sall. *Cat.* 52–3.

41. Sall. *Cat.* 53.

42. Sall. *Cat.* 55 (Woodman trans.). I replaced 'gaol' with 'jail' twice.

43. Sall. *Cat.* 56; App. *B Civ.* 2.7.

44. Sall. *Cat.* 58; App *B Civ.* 2.7.

45. Sall. *Cat.* 58.

46. Liv. *Per.* 103; App. *B Civ.* 2.7.

47. Sall. *Cat.* 61; App *B Civ.* 2.7 repeats the assertion.

48. Sall. *Cat.* 61.

49. Plut. *Cic.* 23; App. *B Civ.* 2.7.

50. Plut. *Cic.* 23; Dio Cass. 37.38; S.P. Haley, 'The Five Wives of Pompey the Great,' *Greece & Rome* 32 (1985), 49–54.

51. Plut. *Pomp.* 42.7; Cic. Att. 1.12; Dio Cass. 37.49.3.

52. Plut. *Pomp.* 43; Dio Cass. 37.20.

53. Plut. *Pomp.* 43.

54. Seager, *Pompey,* 74; Plut. *Pomp.* 44, *Cat. Min.* 30.1–2.

55. Plut. *Pomp.* 44.2–3; *Cat. Min.* 30.

56. Pliny *HN* 7.27 (Bostock trans.).

57. Seager, *Pompey,* 79–80.

58. Cic. *Off.* 1.78; Vell Pat. 2.40.3; Val. Max 8.15.8; Plut. *Pomp.* 45–6; App. *Mith.* 17.116–117; Dio Cass. 37.21.1–2.

59. Plin. *HN* 7.27.

60. Plut. *Pomp.* 45 (Waterfield trans.).

61. Seager, *Pompey,* 79–80.

62. T. Rising, 'Senatorial Opposition to Pompey's Eastern Settlement. A Storm in a Teacup?' *Historia* 62 (2014), esp. 203–11.

63. Seager, *Pompey,* 80–83; Plut. *Cat. Min.* 31.1–2, *Luc.* 42.5–6, *Pomp.* 46.3–5; *Flor.* 2.13.8–9; App. *B Civ.* 2.9; Dio Cass. 49–50

64. Plut. *Crass.* 13.

65. E.J. Parrish, 'Crassus' New Friends and Pompey's Return', *Phoenix* 27(1973), 357–80.

66. Plut. *Crass.* 7.

67. Plut. *Caes.* 7.

68. Plut. *Caes.* 11.

Chapter 10

1. A selective reading, in the hopes of illuminating Bibulus' perspective, of Suet *Iul.* 20; App. *B Civ.* 2.9–11. Plut. *Caes.* 14.; Dio Cass. 38.1–2; Dio Cass. 38.3 suggests Cato led the opposition to Caesar in the senate.

2. Suet *Iul.* 20; App. *B Civ.* 2.11.

3. App. *B Civ.* 2.11; Plut. *Caes.* 14 has a somewhat different version, that Caesar arrested Cato and had him hauled to prison initially, but relented when he saw how much the treatment of Cato offended those present. Dio Cass. 38.3 also mentions the arrest but suggests it took place in the initial senate meetings.
4. Suet *Iul.* 20; Plut. *Caes.* 14.; App *B Civ.* 12; Dio Cass. 38.6.
5. Suet *Iul.* 20.
6. Plut. *Caes.* 11–13; App. *B Civ.* 2.8 Dio Cass. 37.44, 52; Suet *Iul.* 18.
7. Plut. *Caes.* 12.
8. App. *B Civ.* 2.8
9. Suet *Iul.* 18; Dio Cass. 37.52.
10. Plut. *Cat. Min.* 31; *Caes.* 13; Suet *Jul.* 18. Appian *B Civ.* 2.8; Dio Cass. 37.54.
11. App *B Civ. 2.9* on Varro.
12. Dio Cass. 37.54; Suet *Iul.* 19; Plut. *Caes.* 13; App *B Civ.* 2.9.
13. Dio Cass. 37.54; App. *B Civ.* 2.9; Plut. *Caes.* 13.
14. Suet. *Iul.* 19
15. John Rich, 'Silvae Callesque', *Latomus*, 45 (1986), 510.
16. P. Freeman, *Julius Caesar*, (Simon & Schuster, 2008) 89–90; A. Goldsworthy, *Caesar: Life of a Colossus*, (Yale, 2006), 195.
17. Cic. *Att.* 2.3, written in December 60, shows that Cicero was aware of the pact between Caesar, Pompey, and Crassus by then at the latest. Most historians suspect, following the other ancient accounts, that Cicero simply was in the dark about the alliance until later.
18. K. Tempest, *Cicero: Politics and Persuasion in Ancient Rome*, (Bloomsbury, 2011). 116; Cic. Att. 2.3.
19. Cic. *Att.* 2.3; Tempest, *Cicero*, 114–17.
20. Tempest, 116, who notes Cicero's Jan 59 letter on the visit of Caesar's associate Balbus. Caesar suggested he would follow Cicero's guidance. Cic. *Att.* 2.3.
21. Goldsworthy, *Caesar*, 189.
22. One could probably do no better than the foundational chronological work of L.R. Taylor, 'The Dating of Major Legislation and Elections in Caesar's First Consulship', *Historia* 17 (1968), 173–93.
23. Cic. Att. 2.3.
24. Lintott, *Constitution of the Roman Republic*, 100; Goldsworthy, 202.
25. Goldsworthy, *Caesar*, 202; Lintott, *Constitution of the Roman Republic*, 44, says 17 days; Taylor, 'Major Legislation and Elections in Caesar's First Consulship', *passim.*
26. Plut. *Caes.* 14; App. B *Civ.* 2.10.
27. Dio Cass. 38.2.
28. Dio Cass. 38.3; See Taylor, 'Major Legislation and Elections in Caesar's First Consulship', 176.
29. Dio Cass. 38.4; Taylor, 'Major Legislation and Elections in Caesar's First Consulship', 176.
30. Plut, *Caes.* 14; App B *Civ.* 2.10; Dio Cass. 38.5–6.
31. Dio Cass. 38.6.
32. Dio Cass. 38; Taylor, 'Major Legislation and Elections in Caesar's First Consulship', 176–7.

33. Dio Cass. 38.6; Suet *Iul.* 20; App. *B Civ.* 2.11; Plut. *Cat. Min.* 42.

34. Suet. *Iul.* 20; Plut. *Caes.* 14; Dio Cass. 38.6. See Goldsworthy, *Caesar,* 208–210.

35. Cic. *Att.* 2.15, 16, 17, 18; Dio Cass. 38.7.3; Suet *Iul.* 2.3; See Goldsworthy, *Caesar,* 212–219 for Caesar's legislation and term as consul.

36. Goldsworthy, *Caesar,* 210.

37. Cic. *Plan.* 35; Suet. *Iul.* 20; App. *B Civ.* 2.13.

38. Cic. *Att.* 2.17; Plut. *Caes* 14; Plut. *Pomp.* 47; Goldsworthy, *Caesar,* 211.

39. Haley, 'The Five Wives of Pompey the Great', 49–54.

40. Cic. Att. 2.17, noted by Tempest, *Cicero,* 113.

41. Suet. *Iul.* 22.1; Dio Cass. 38.3–5; Plut. *Caes.* 14.10; App. *B Civ.* 2.13. Goldsworthy, *Caesar,* 212–15.

Chapter 11

1. Cicero *Att.* 1.12 (Shuckburgh trans).

2. The events and chronology surrounding Cicero and Clodius' rivalry is complex and based on critical readings of Cicero's letters and speeches, practically a complete field of study in its own right. W.J. Tatum, *The Patrician Tribune* (University of North Carolina, 1999) has been an invaluable guide to me, and those who want to do a deep dive on Clodius should look there as well as the ancient sources I have noted. K. Tempest, *Cicero: Politics and Persuasion in Ancient Rome* (Bloomsbury, 2011) is an excellent work to read in tandem for Cicero's perspective.

3. Suet *Iul.* 6.

4. HS Versnel, 'The Festival for Bona Dea and the Thesmophoria', *Greece & Rome* 39(1992), 32.

5. Cic. *Att.* 1.13; 1.16. Tatum, *Patrician Tribune* discusses the evidence on 67 and note 38.

6. Plut. *Caes.* 9; *Cic.* 28.

7. Plut. *Caes.* 10, Suet *Iul.* 6; App. *B Civ.* 2.145; Dio Cass. 37.45.

8. Cic. *Att.* 1.13; Liv. *Per.* 103 Plut. *Cic.* 28–29; Plut. *Caes.* 9–10; Dio Cass. 37.45, though Dio asserts the two lovers actually united that evening Suet *Iul.* 6; Cic. *Har.* 44. Epstein makes helpful sense of all the evidence, 'Cicero's Testimony at the Bona Dea Trial', *Classical Philology* 81(1986), 229–35; Tatum, *Patrician Tribune,* 62–68.

9. Some of Clodius' family and friends at the time of the Bona Dea scandal: Tatum, *Patrician Tribune,* 33, 62–69; Caesar's Testimony: Plut. *Caes.* 10; Plut, *Cic.* 29; Suet. *Iul.* 74. Tatum, *Patrician Tribune,* 62–8.

10. Dio Cass. 37.46.

11. Cic. *Att.* 1.13; Suet. *Iul.* 6; Dio Cass. 37.46; Epstein, 'Cicero's Testimony at the Bona Dea Trial', 231. Tatum, *Patrician Tribune,* 72–5.

12. Plut. *Cic.* 28–29; Plut. *Caes.* 10. Caesar did not charge Clodius, App. *B Civ.* 2.14; Dio Cass. 37.45, and though it is an argument from silence, it's worth noting Cicero does not say that Caesar brought the charge in his letter to Atticus detailing the trial (*Att.* 1.16.) but names the Tribune Fufius; Epstein, 'Cicero's Testimony at the Bona Dea Trial', 231–2.

13. Cic. *Att* 1.13, Epstein, 231–2.
14. Cic. *Att.* 1.16; Dio Cass. 37.46.
15. Plut, *Caes.* 10; Dio Cass. 37.45.
16. Plut. *Caes.* 10.
17. Cic *Att* 1.16 (Shuckburgh trans.) Val. Max. 8.5.5.
18. Cic *Att* 1.16 (Shuckburgh trans.) Val. Max 8.5.5; Plut. Cic. 29; Epstein, 'Cicero's Testimony at the Bona Dea Trial', 229–35.
19. Plut. *Cic.* 29; Terentia's role as Cicero's partner and advisor: Plut. Cic. 20; Epstein, 232–4.
20. Plut. *Cic.* 29; Epstein, 232–4.
21. Val. Max. 9.1.7.
22. Cic *Att* 1.16 (Shuckburgh trans.).
23. Cic. *Att.* 1.16 (Shuckburgh trams.); Repeated by Plutarch *Cic.* 29.
24. Tatum, *Patrician Tribune*, 87–9; Cic. *Att.* 1.16, 1.17.
25. Cicero enjoyed the clientage of Sicily for his service prosecuting one of its more corrupt governors, Verres.
26. Cic. *Att.* 2.1.5; Tatum, *Patrician Tribune*, 89–90.
27. Cic *Att.* 1.19, 2.1; For a detailed analysis of the legal and technical parts of a *transitio ad plebem*, and Clodius' efforts in 60 to achieve this, see Tatum, *Patrician Tribune*, 90–103.
28. Plut. *Pomp.* 46–7, *Cat. Min.* 31; Tatum, 102.
29. Cic. *Att.* 8.3, *Dom.* 35; Liv. *Per.* 103; Plut. *Caes.* 14, Suet. *Iul.* 20.
30. Tatum, 101–3; Tempest, *Cicero*, 117–18. Cicero annoying Caesar with his speeches in 59: Cic. *Prov. Cons.* 42; Suet. *Iul.* 20.4, Dio Cass. 38.10.
31. Cic. *Att.* 2.12 (Shuckburgh trans.).
32. Cic. *Dom.* 36–42; Dio Cass. 39.11; Plut. *Cat. Min.* 33; App. *B Civ.* 2.14; Dio Cass. 38.12; Tatum, *Patrician Tribune*, 104–7 investigates the technicalities and legalities of brought up by Cicero's 57 analysis in *De Domo Sua*.
33. On Vatinius' role see Cic. *Vat.* 24.
34. Cic. *Att.* 2.24; *Vat.* 24; Plut. *Luc.* 42; Dio Cass. 38.10. Tempest, *Cicero*, 119–21. Tatum, *Patrician Tribune*, 111–12.
35. Cic. *Att.* 2.12, 2.21.
36. Cic. *Att.* 2.12, 2.22.
37. Cic. *QFr.* 1.2 (Shuckburgh Trans.).
38. Tatum, *Patrician Tribune*, 110–113.
39. Tatum, 114–49 carefully investigates Clodius' initial legislative package for 58.
40. Cic. *Att.* 3.15, *Pis.* 9, *Sest.* 34,55; Dio Cass. 38.13.
41. Tatum, *Patrician Tribune*, 24–6. See note 126 for a bibliography on *collegia*.
42. Cic. *Pis.* 8.
43. Tatum, 116–18.
44. Cic. *Dom.* 25; Dio Cass. 38.13.
45. Stockton, *Gracchi*, 126–29.
46. Plut. *Cat. Min.* 26, *Caes.* 8.
47. Tatum, *Patrician Tribune*, 118–24.
48. Tatum, *Patrician Tribune*, investigates this law in detail, p. 125–32.
49. Dio Cass. 38.13, 42.57; Cic. *Har.* 58. Tatum, 132–5.

50. Tatum, 134–5.
51. Tatum, *Patrician Tribune*, 150–2.
52. Cic. *Dom.* 23–25, *Sest.* 55, *Red. sen.* 18; Plut. *Cic.* 30; Tatum, 150–1; note that the provinces were amended and Gabinius was assigned to Syria, before the year ended.
53. Vell. Pat. 2.45, App. *B Civ.* 2.15; Dio Cass. 38.14.
54. Tatum, *Patrician Tribune*, 153–4; Tempest, *Cicero*, 119.
55. Plut. *Cic.* 30; App. *B Civ.* 2.15.
56. On Cicero's support: Cic. *Red. sen.* 12, *Dom.* 55–6; Plut. *Cic.* 31, *Crass.* 13; Dio Cass. 38.16.
57. Cic. *Dom.* 20–23; Tatum, 154–5; Tempest, 121.
58. Cic. *Red. sen.* 33–34, *Dom.* 63–64; Plut. *Cic.* 31–32; Dio Cass. 38.17.
59. Cic. *Dom.* 43–53, *Sest.* 53–55; Plut. *Cic* 32; Dio Cass. 38.17.
60. Cic. *Sest.* 54 (Yonge trans.).
61. Cicero's *De Domo Sua* throughout deals with his loss of his property. See also Cic. *Pis.* 22–26; Vell. Pat. 2.45; App. *B Civ.* 2.15. On the Temple, see Cic. *Dom.* 131–4 and Plut. *Cic.* 33. Tatum, *Patrician Tribune*, 155–62.
62. Plut. *Cic.* 32. Tempest, *Cicero*, 122.
63. Plut. *Cic.* 33, *Pomp.* 48.
64. Asc. 47(C) Cic. *Har.* 58; *Dom.* 66; Plut. *Pomp.* 48; Dio Cass. 38.30; Tatum, 170.
65. Cic. *Pis.* 27–29; Dio Cass. 38.30; Tatum, *Patrician Tribune*, 162–70
66. Cic. *Red. sen.* 3–4,8, *Dom.* 68. Dio Cass. 38.30.
67. Cic. *Att.* 3.15, 3.18.
68. Cic. *Att.* 3.15, 3.18. *Pis.* 76–77; Plut. *Cic.* 31.
69. Tatum, *Patrician Tribune*, 170–3.
70. Cic. *Pis.* 28–29, *Mil.* 18, *Dom.* 66–67; Plut. *Pomp.* 48–9.
71. Cic. *Att.* 3.23, *Sest.* 69–70; Tatum, *Patrician Tribune*, 173–4.
72. Quotation Cic. *Sest.* 77 (Yonge trans.). Cic *Sest.* 71–89; Dio Cass 39.6–8. Tatum, *Patrician Tribune*, 177–8.
73. Milo: Cic. *Mil.* 35; Cic. *Sest.* 88–90; Dio Cass. 39.7–8; Sestius: Cic. *Sest*: 80, 84; Pompey: Plut. *Cic.* 33; Tatum, 178–80; Tempest, 123.
74. Cic. *Sest.* 116–123.
75. Cic. *Dom.* 74, *Pis.* 41.
76. Cic. *Red. sen.* 25–6; *Sest.* 129.
77. Tempest, *Cicero*, 122–23. Tatum, *Patrician Tribune*, 180–84.
78. Tatum, 180–84.
79. Cic. *Att.* 4.1, translated by Tempest, *Cicero*, 125.
80. Plut. *Cic.* 33; See also Cic. *Att.* 4.1, *Dom.* 75–6.
81. Cicero mentions some of the challenges to getting his property back in a letter to Atticus 4.1. Getting his religiously-devoted property back and cleared for secular construction is the subject of Cicero's extant speech, *De Domo Sua*.

Chapter 12
1. Plut. *Caes.* 32.5–8 (Waterfield trans.)
2. Tatum, 150–1 notes that, as with the last two chapters, the historical challenges the evidence for the end of the Republic presents is of a different kind for

those accustomed to studying earlier periods. Simply put, there are orders of magnitude more evidence available for this decade 59–49 than there were for earlier periods. The secondary sources – Plutarch, Appian Dio Cassius – that refer to the period increase in the detail and volume of their accounts. Many other secondary historians have left still-surviving scraps. In addition there are the primary sources of the like that we simply do not have for third and second century BCE Rome. Most of all, Cicero wrote hundreds of letters that still survive for the period 59–49 in addition to dozens of surviving speeches. Caesar also left two commentaries of the period, additional primary sources, in his *Gallic Wars* and *Civil Wars*. Even the chronology gets more complex. The volume of evidence, and Cicero's helpful habit of dating his letters (using a Roman system, of course) means that, in many cases, historians of this period can talk about the days in the months various events occurred. So I have again looked to the work of several modern historians to help navigate through the complex and voluminous evidence for this period, especially R. Seager, *Pompey the Great: A Political Biography* (Wiley-Blackwell, 2002); A. Goldsworthy, *Caesar: The Life of a Colossus* (Yale, 2006); K. Tempest, *Cicero: Politics and Persuasion in Ancient Rome* (Bloomsbury, 2011). Special mention must also be made of the fantastic web resource that is Andrew Smith's attalus.org. Smith has collected a truly vast number of ancient source references to all manners of topics in Roman history, with links to credible online texts of those sources. It is an invaluable aid for anyone studying the period.

3. 'All Gaul is divided into three parts' Caes. *BGall.* 1.1.
4. Goldsworthy, *Caesar*, 237–40.
5. Liv. 5.38–49.
6. Goldsworthy, 237–40.
7. Map, Goldsworthy, 239.
8. Goldsworthy, 237–40.
9. Goldsworthy, *Caesar*, 248–58.
10. Goldsworthy, *Caesar*, 263–9, 272. 282–3. Caes. *BGall.* 1.1–40 describes the campaign against the Helvetii. See also Plut. *Caes.* 18.
11. Caes. *BGall.* 1.31–52 for Ariovistus and Caesar's campaign against him. See also Plut. *Caes.* 19.
12. Goldsworthy, *Caesar*, 257.
13. Caes. *BGall.* 2.35; Plut. *Caes.* 21; Dio Cass. 39.5. Goldsworthy, *Caesar*, 286–304. Campaign against Belgae.
14. Cic. *Att.* 4.1.
15. Cic. Red. sen. 31. See Tempest, *Cicero*, 125.
16. The most obvious example of this is the command over the grain supply Cicero proposed for Pompey almost immediately upon his return to Rome. Cic. *Att.* 4.1; Tempest, 125–8.
17. K. Tempest, *Cicero*, 128–30.
18. Cic. *Att.* 4.1; Liv. *Per.* 104; Dio Cass. 39.9; Plut. *Pomp.* 49.
19. Cic. *Att.* 4.1.
20. See Seager, *Pompey*, 107–09.

21. Cicero's *De Domo Sua* speech is devoted to this issue; see also Cic. *Att.* 4.2; App. *B Civ.* 2.16. Dio Cass. 39.11. K. Tempest, *Cicero*, 125–8.
22. Tempest, 128–9.
23. Cic. *QFr.* 2.3.
24. Seager, Pompey, 114–15.
25. Tempest, *Cicero*, 128–30. For Pompey's position on the Campanian Law, see Seager, 111–14.
26. Suet. *Iul.* 24; Cic. *Att.* 4.8 corroborates that Domitius was a candidate.
27. Cic. *Att.* 4.8; Suet *Iul.* 24; Plut. *Caes.* 21; App. *B Civ.* 2.17; Dio Cass. 39.5.
28. Plut. Caes. 21; App. *B Civ.* 2.17; Dio Cass. 39.5.
29. Plut. *Cat. Min.* 41, *Crass.* 15, *Pomp.* 52.
30. Plut. *Crass* 15.
31. Seager, *Pompey*, 120–22 works through this. The sources that touch on the consular elections for 55. App. *B Civ.* 2.17; Plut. *Pomp.* 52, Crass. 15, *Cat. Min.* 41; Suet. *Iul.* 24. Dio Cass. 39.27–31.
32. Plut. *Pomp.* 52; App. *B Civ.* 2.17; Dio Cass. 39.31
33. Seager, 120–22.
34. Cato's efforts to win a praetorship of 55: Plut. *Cat. Min.* 42, *Pomp.* 52; Liv. *Per.* 105; Dio Cass. 39.32.
35. Trebonian Law on provinces: Plut. *Pomp.* 52, Liv. *Per.* 105; Vell. Pat. 2.46; App. *B Civ.* 2.18; Dio Cass. 39.33
36. Plut. Pomp. App. B Civ. 2.18.
37. Dio Cass. 39.34; Plut. *Cat. Min.* 43.
38. Cato hauled to prison for his rhetorical tactic delaying Trebonius' law: Plut. *Cat. Min. 43*; Dio Cass. 39.34.
39. Plut. *Caes.* 21, *Pomp.* 52, *Crass.* 15; Suet. *Iul.* 24; App. *B Civ.* 2.18; Dio Cass. 39.33. Dio 44.43 seems to double down on the figure of an eight-year command (the original 5 plus a 3-year extension) in the speech he gives to Caesar.
40. Cic. *Cos. Prov.* 38.
41. Cic. *Att.* 4.15.
42. Cic. *Fam.* 7.1.
43. Tempest, *Cicero*, 134–7.
44. Tatum, *Patrician Tribune*, 214–36
45. Crassus leaves for Syria: Plut. *Crass.* 16.
46. Pompey's theatre: Plut. *Pomp.* 52; Dio Cass. 39.38. See Goldsworthy, *Caesar*, 416–17.
47. Dio Cass. 39.38.
48. Plut. *Pomp.* 52–3.
49. Julia's death Plut. *Pomp.* 53; Liv. *Per.* 106; Dio Cass. 39.64; App. *B Civ.* 2.19; Suet. *Iul.* 84.
50. Dio Cass. 40.45–6; Plut. *Pomp.* 54; App. *B Civ.* 2.19.
51. App. *B Civ.* 2.19.
52. Plut. *Pomp.* 54. (Waterfield trans.).
53. Dio Cass. 40.45–6; Plut. *Pomp.* 54; App. *B Civ.* 2.19. Plutarch names the tribune Lucilius as the first to publicly propose the dictatorship and notes Cato's objection.

54. Plut. *Pomp.* 54.
55. Dio Cass. 40.45; Plut. *Pomp.* 54.
56. Carrhae is modern day Harran, Turkey.
57. Plut. Crass. 16–33; Dio 40.12–30; Liv. Per. 106. See also Mattern-Parkes, 'The Defeat of Crassus and the Just War', *The Classical World*, 96 (2003), 387–96. Goldsworthy, *Caesar*, 378–9.

Chapter 13
1. Plut. *Cat. Min.* 47; Dio Cass. 40.46–7. Tatum, *Patrician Tribune*, 231–8 goes into incredible detail about the elections, the candidates, and Clodius' goals.
2. Plut. *Sull.* 34. Notes her mother's birth, Sulla's daughter, alongside a twin brother, Faustus.
3. Asc. *Mil.* 31–32C. J.P. Adam's unpublished translation (https://web.archive.org/web/20210410174745/http://www.csun.edu/~hcfll004/asconius.htm) was very helpful for working through the Latin text and can offer readers access to Asconius in English.
4. Asc. *Mil.* 32. J.P. Adam.
5. Asc. *Mil.* 32. J.P. Adam.
6. Asc. *Mil.* 33–4. J.P. Adam. See Cic. *Mil.* 33, 61; Liv. *Per.* 107; App. *B Civ.* 2.21; Dio Cass. 40.49.
7. Asc. *Mil.* 33; App. *B Civ.* 2.22; Liv. *Per.* 107.
8. Cic. *Mil.* 70; Caes. *BGall.* 7.1; Asc. *Mil.* 33–36; Dio Cass. 40.49–50.
9. Asc. *Mil.* 36.
10. Cato supports Pompey's sole consulship: Plut. *Cat. Min.* 47; App. B Civ. 2.23 mistakenly says Cato was sent to Cyprus to get him out of the way (which happened in 58).
11. Pompey named sole consul: Plut. *Pomp.* 54, *Caes.* 28, *Cat. Min* 47; App. *B Civ.* 2.23; Liv. *Per.* 107; Asc *Mil.* 35–36; Seager, *Pompey*, 134–5.
12. Seager, *Pompey*, 135–6.
13. Tatum, Patrician Tribune, 241.
14. Trial: All of Cicero's *Pro Milo* and Asconius' commentary on the *Pro Milo*, Plut. *Cic.* 35; App. *B Civ* 2.24; Dio Cass. 40.54; Seager 136–7.
15. Suet. *Iul.* 27.
16. Vell. Pat 2.54; Plut. *Pomp.* 55.
17. Plut. *Pomp.* 55 (Waterfield trans.).
18. Seager, *Pompey*, 131.
19. Seager, 131–2.
20. Val. Max. 9.5; Plut. *Pomp.* 55; App. *B Civ.* 2.24.
21. Plut. *Pomp.* 55; App. *B Civ.* 2.25; Dio Cass. 40.51.
22. Seager, *Pompey*, 137–8.
23. Cic. *Att.* 8.3.
24. Plut. *Caes.* 28.8; Dio Cass. 40.56.
25. See Seager's explanation, *Pompey*, 138.
26. Cic *Att.* 8.3; Suet. *Iul.* 28; Dio Cass. 40.56; Seager, *Pompey*, 137–39.
27. Goldsworthy, *Caesar*, 325–46.
28. Goldsworthy, *Caesar*, 338–54.

29. Goldsworthy, *Caesar*, 359–69.
30. Caes. *BGall.* 7.90; Dio Cass. 40.50.
31. Goldsworthy, 381–427.
32. D. Epstein, *Personal Enmity in Roman Politics 218–43 BC* (Croom Helm, 1987), 85; Goldsworthy, *Caesar*, 488.
33. Cic. *Fam.* 8.1; Liv. *Per.* 108; Plut. *Caes.* 29; Dio Cass. 40.59.
34. Suet. *Iul.* 28.
35. Caesar's loyal agent, Hirtius, derides Marcellus for his illegal proposal, noting the law of 55. Hirt. *BGall.* 8.83. Note too that Hirtius seems to take for granted that Marcellus was simply an enemy.
36. Cic. *Att* 8.3; Dio Cass. 40.59; Suet *Iul.* 29. It is daunting for anyone to wade into the mass of extant letters with uncertain dates from Cicero and his friends and colleagues in addition to accounts of Plutarch, Appian, and Dio without a guide to the chronology. And so I have relied considerably on Robin Seager, *Pompey*, 140–52, for a chronology of major events in the growing standoff between Caesar and Pompey in the years 50–49 BCE and for insight into Pompey's position.
37. Cic. *Att.* 8.3 App. *B Civ.* 2.26; Dio Cass. 40.59.
38. Hirt. *B.Gall* 8.53. Seager, *Pompey*, 140.
39. Suet *Iul.* 28.
40. App. *B Civ.* 2.26.
41. Suet. *Iul.* 28; Plut. *Caes* 20; App. *B Civ.* 2.28.
42. Cic. *Att.* 5.11 (Shuckburgh Trans); Seager, *Pompey*, 140.
43. Epstein, *Personal Enmity in Roman Politics*, 85.
44. So Caelius reports to Cicero Cic. *Fam.* 8.9. Seager, *Pompey*, 141.
45. Caelius Cic. *Fam.* 8.8; Dio Cass. 40.59; App. Bciv 2.26. Seager, 140–42.
46. Caelius Cic. *Fam.* 8.8.
47. Goldsworthy, *Caesar*, 441–2.
48. Cael. *Fam.* 8.8, *Att.* 6.1. (Shuckburgh trans.) Seager, *Pompey*, 143.
49. So suggests Seager, *Pompey*, 142–3.
50. Here, I am following C.T.H.R. Ehrhardt, 'Crossing the Rubicon', *Antichthon* 29 (1995), 30–41, and R. Morstein-Marx, 'Caesar's Alleged Fear of Prosecution and His 'Ratio Absentis' in the Approach to the Civil War'. *Historia* 56 (2007), 159–78.
51. Suet. *Iul.* 30.
52. Suet. *Iul* .30. (Rolfe trans.).
53. Cic. *Att.* 7.9. Cic. *Fam.* 16.1
54. Again, see Morstein-Marx, 159–78.
55. Ibid.
56. Caelius Cic. *Fam.* 8.4. Seager, *Pompey*, 140–41.
57. App. *B Civ.* 2.26.
58. Cic: *Att.* 6.3; Vell. Pat. 2.48; Plut. *Caes.* 29, *Pomp.* 58; Dio Cass. 40.60.
59. Suet *Iul* 29; App *B Civ.* 2.26; Plut. *Pomp.* 58, *Caes.* 29.
60. Vell. Pat. 2.48; Liv. *Per.* 109; Plut. *Pomp.* 58; App. *B Civ.* 2.27. Vell. Pat. 2.48; Hirt. *BGall* 8.52. Seager, *Pompey*, 144.
61. App. *B Civ.* 2.28. Seager, *Pompey*, 144–5.

62. Vell Pat. 2.48; Seager, *Pompey*, 145–6.
63. App. *B Civ.* 2.30. Plut. *Pomp.* 58 is somewhat different in the proposal. Seager, 147, prefers Appian. The operative point is that in the end Curio was able to take the temperature of the senate, and the senate, overwhelmingly, supported the proposal that Caesar and Pompey both resign.
64. App. *B Civ.* 2.31; Plut. *Pomp.* 59; Dio Cass. 40.64. Seager, *Pompey*, 147.
65. See Seager, 146–7.
66. Seager, 147.
67. Both because it is traditional, and because there is little to be gained from attempting a revision even if one possessed the necessary calendrical skills (which I do not), I have followed the dates that modern historians use, which are based on the Roman calendar at the time. The Roman calendar, however, was out of synch with the solar calendar at this point. So according to our reckoning, January 49 for the Romans, the month in which the Civil War started, was several months earlier on the solar calendar, sometime in late 50.
68. Cic. Fam. 16.11.
69. Plut. Pomp. 59, *Caes.* 30 Dio Cass. 41.1 App 2.32. Seager, *Pompey*, 148.
70. Caes. *B Civ.* 1.1.
71. Caes. *B Civ.* 1.1.
72. Caes. *B Civ.* 1.5; Cic. *Fam.* 16.11; Plut. *Caes.* 31; App *B Civ.* 2.33. Liv. *Per.* 109; Seager, *Pompey*, 150.
73. Cic. Fam 16.11 (Shuckburgh trans.).

Conclusion
1. C.T.H.R. Ehrhardt, 'Crossing the Rubicon', *Antichthon* 29 (1995), 37. The article is a must-read for looking at Caesar's preparations up to and after he crossed the Rubicon; Goldsworthy, *Caesar*, 468.
2. Ehrhardt, 'Crossing the Rubicon', 37–9.
3. Seager, *Pompey*, 153.
4. Cic. Att. 7.11.
5. For the core narrative of 49–44, I've followed Goldsworthy, *Caesar*, 461–70.
6. F.A. Sirianni, 'Caesar's Peace Overtures to Pompey', *L'Antiquité Classique* 62 (1993), 219–24.
7. Seager, *Pompey*, 157–8
8. Goldsworthy, *Caesar*, 472
9. D. Konstan, 'Clemency as a Virtue', *Classical Philology*, 100(2005), 337–46. Konstan also suggests that Cato's famous choice to commit suicide rather than being forgiven by Caesar can be understood as a refusal to be in Caesar's debt, not a philosophical problem with clemency as a policy.
10. Seager, *Pompey*, 161–62.
11. Goldsworthy, *Caesar*, 475–79; Sirianni, 'Caesar's Peace Overtures to Pompey', *L'Antiquité Classique* 62(1993), 224.
12. Goldsworthy, *Caesar*, 461–93.
13. Goldsworthy, 494–522. Seager, *Pompey*, 166–7.
14. Seager Ch 13 *Pompey*; Goldsworthy, Caesar, 522–3.
15. Goldsworthy, 535–9.

16. Goldsworthy, 553.
17. Battle of Thapsus: Goldsworthy, 560–67.
18. Goldsworthy, *Caesar*, 522–570.
19. Plut. *Cat. Min.* 64–73 retells the epic tradition about Cato's suicide. African Campaign: Goldsworthy, *Caesar*, 553–68.
20. Goldsworthy, 586–91.
21. Goldsworthy, *Caesar*, 582–86. Goldsworthy discusses possible interpretations 574–79.
22. Goldsworthy, *Caesar*, 600–622.
23. He never went by the name Octavian, choosing purposely to take his adoptive father's name and call himself Gaius Julius Caesar. We call him Octavian so as not to confuse them.
24. Though written quite some time ago, on the eve of the Second World War, R. Syme, *Roman Revolution*, is still the best narrative of the political and military events from the death of Caesar in 44 to the monarchy of Augustus in 27 and beyond.
25. Suggested by A. Lintott, *Violence in Republican Rome* (Clarendon, 1968).
26. This is essentially P.A. Brunt's classic argument in his introductory essay (pages 1–92) for: *The Fall of the Roman Republic* (Clarendon, 1988).
27. So E. Gruen, *The Last Generation of the Roman Republic* (University of California, 1974). This book was received with a range of criticism and respect. See D. Stockton's review in *Gnomon* and A.W. Lintott's review in *Classical Review* 26(1976), 241–43 and S. Treggiari in *Phoenix* 30(1976) 91–94.
28. H. Flower, *Roman Republics* (Princeton, 2010).
29. See the excellent work of H. Mouritsen, *Politics in the Roman Republic* (Cambridge, 2017).
30. See Mouritsen, quotation from page 165.

Bibliography

Adam J.P. Unpublished translation of Asconius, *Pro Milo*. Accessed online https://web.archive.org/web/20210410174745/http://www.csun.edu/~hcfll004/asconius.htm

Alexander, Michael C. 'Law in the Roman Republic,' in N. Rosenstein and R. Kallet-Marx, eds., A *Companion to the Roman Republic*, (Wiley-Blackwell, 2010), 236–55.

Astin, Alan E. *Cato the Censor* (Oxford, 1978).

Badian, Ernst. 'The Death of Saturninus', *Chiron* 14 (1984) 101–47.

Bartz, Jessica, Engel, Henriette, and Sophie Horacek, 'Basilica Porcia' in *Digitales Forum Romanum* http://www.digitales-forum-romanum.de/gebaeude/basilica-porcia/?lang=en

Batstone, William W. 'Cicero's Construction of Consular Ethos in the First Catilinarian', *Transactions of the American Philological Association* 124 (1994), 211–66.

Benness, J. Lea, and T.W. Hillard, 'The Death of Lucius Equitius on 1 December 100 BC', *The Classical Quarterly*, 40 (1990), 269–72.

Broughton, Thomas Robert. S. *Magistrates of the Roman Republic*. 3 vols. (American Philological Association, 1951–60).

Brunt, Philip A. *The Fall of the Roman Republic and Related Essays* (Clarendon, 1988).

Cagniart, Pierre F., 'L. Cornelius Sulla in the Nineties: a Reassessment', *Latomus* 50 (1991), 285–303.

Churchill, J. Bradford. "*Sponsio Quae in Verba Facta Est?*' Two Lost Speeches and the Formula of the Roman Judicial Wager', *The Classical Quarterly*, 50 (2000). 159–69.

Crook, John. '*Sponsione Provocare*: It's Place in Roman Litigation', *The Journal of Roman Studies*', 66 (1976), 132–8.

Dixon, Suzanne *Cornelia: Mother of the Gracchi* (Routledge, 2007).

Ehrhardt, C.T.H.R. 'Crossing the Rubicon', *Antichthon* 29 (1995), 30–41.

Epstein, David F. 'Cicero's Testimony at the Bona Dea Trial', *Classical Philology* 81 (1986), 229–35;

Evans, Richard 'Rome's Cimbric Wars (114–101 BC) and Their Impact on the Iberian Peninsula', *Acta Classica* 48 (2005), 37–56.

Flower, Harriet I. *Roman Republics* (Princeton, 2010).

Forsythe, Gary, *A Critical History of Rome: From Prehistory to the First Punic War* (University of California, 2005), 289–92.

Freeman, Philip. *Julius Caesar*, (Simon & Schuster, 2008).

Goldsworthy, Adrian, *Caesar: Life of a Colossus* (Yale, 2006).

Gruen, Erich, *The Last Generation of the Roman Republic* (University of California, 1974).

Haley, Shelley P. 'The Five Wives of Pompey the Great', *Greece & Rome* 32 (1985), 49–59.

Hardy, E.G. 'The Catilinarian Conspiracy in Its Context: A Re-Study of the Evidence', *Journal of Roman Studies* 7 (1917), 153–228.

Hoyos, Dexter *Mastering the West: Rome and Carthage at War* (Oxford, 2015).

Hunt, E.D. 'Orosius', *Oxford Classical Dictionary*, accessed online

Kallet-Marx, Robert, *Hegemony to Empire: The Development of the Roman Imperium in the East from 148 to 62 B.C.*, (University of California, 1996).

Keaveney, Arthur, *Sulla: The Last Republican 2d Ed.* (Routledge, 2005).

Konrad, C.F. 'From the Gracchi to the First Civil War', in N. Rosenstein and R. Kallet-Marx (eds.), *A Companion to the Roman Republic*, (Wiley-Blackwell, 2010), 167–89.

Konstan, David. 'Clemency as a Virtue', *Classical Philology*, 100 (2005), 337–46.

Lintott, Andrew, *Violence in Republican Rome* (Clarendon, 1968).

Lintott, Andrew, 'The Tribunate of P. Sulpicius Rufus', *Classical Quarterly* 21 (1971), 442–53.

Lintott, Andrew, *The Constitution of the Roman Republic* (Oxford, 1999).

Lomas, Kathryn. 'Italy during the Roman Republic, 338–31 B.C.' in H.I. Flower (ed.) *The Cambridge Companion to the Roman Republic* (Cambridge, 2004) 233–59.

Luce, T.J. 'Marius and the Mithridatic Command', *Historia* 19 (1970), 161–94.

Marshall, Bruce. 'Crassus' Ovation in 71 BC', *Historia* 21 (1972), 669–73.

Mattern-Parkes, Susan P. 'The Defeat of Crassus and the Just War', *The Classical World*, 96 (2003), 387–96.

McCall, Jeremiah. *Clan Fabius, Defenders of Rome: A History of the Republic's Most Illustrious Family* (Pen & Sword, 2018).

Miles, Richard, *Carthage Must Be Destroyed: The Rise and Fall of an Ancient Civilization* (Viking, 2010).

Mitchell, Thomas N. 'The Volte-Face of P. Sulpicius Rufus in 88 B.C.', *Classical Philology* 70 (1975), 197–204

Morstein-Marx, Robert. 'Caesar's Alleged Fear of Prosecution and His 'Ratio Absentis' in the Approach to the Civil War', *Historia* 56 (2007), 159–178

Mouritsen, Henrik. *Politics in the Roman Republic* (Cambridge, 2017).

Parrish, Eve J. 'Crassus' New Friends and Pompey's Return', *Phoenix* 27 (1973), 357–80.

Patterson, John R. 'Rome and Italy' in N. Rosenstein and R. Kallet-Marx (eds.), *A Companion to the Roman Republic*, (Wiley-Blackwell, 2010), 606–24.

Philips, E.J. 'Catiline's Conspiracy', *Historia* 25 (1976), 441–48.

Pomeroy, Sarah. *Goddesses, Whores, Wives, and Slaves: Women in Classical Antiquity* (Schocken Books, 1975, 1995).

Powell, Jonathan G.F. 'The Tribune Sulpicius', *Historia* 39 (1990), 446–60.

Rich, John W. 'Silvae Callesque', *Latomus*, 45 (1986), 505–21.

Richardson, Lawrence. A *New Topographical Dictionary of Ancient Rome*, (Johns Hopkins, 1992).

Rising, Thilo 'Senatorial Opposition to Pompey's Eastern Settlement. A Storm in a Teacup?' *Historia* 62 (2014), 196–221.

Rosenstein, Nathan S. "Imperatores Victi': The Case of C. Hostilius Mancinus', *Classical Antiquity* 5 (1986), 230–52.

Rosenstein, Nathan S. *Romans at War: Farms, Families, and Death in the Middle Republic* (University of North Carolina, 2005).

Ruebel, James S. 'Cato and Scipio Africanus', *Classical World* 71 (1977).

Sampson, Gareth C. *The Jugurthine and Northern Wars and the Rise of Marius* (Pen & Sword, 2010).

Sampson, Gareth C. *The Collapse of Rome: Marius, Sulla and the First Civil War* (Pen & Sword, 2013)

Seager, Robin, *Pompey the Great: A Political Biography, 2nd Edition* (Wiley-Blackwell, 2002).

Seager, Robin, 'Iusta Catilinae', *Historia* 22 (1973), 240–48.

Sirianni, Frank A. 'Caesar's Peace Overtures to Pompey', *L'Antiquité Classique* 62 (1993), 219–37.

Smith, Andrew. *Attalus.org: Sources for Greek and Roman History.* Accessed Online http://attalus.org/.

Southern, Patricia, *Pompey the Great* (Tempus, 2002).

Stadter, Philip A. Introduction and notes to Robin Waterfield (trans.) Plutarch: *Roman Lives: A Collection of Eight Roman Lives* (Oxford, 1999).

Stockton, David, 'The First Consulship of Pompey', *Historia* 22 (1973), 205–18.

Stockton, David, *The Gracchi*, (Oxford, 1979).

Syme, Ronald, *Roman Revolution*, (Oxford, 2002).

Tatum, W. Jeffrey, *The Patrician Tribune* (University of North Carolina, 1999).

Taylor, Lily Ross, 'The Dating of Major Legislation and Elections in Caesar's First Consulship', *Historia* 17 (1968), 173–93.

Tempest, Kathryn, *Cicero: Politics and Persuasion in Ancient Rome* (Bloomsbury, 2011).

Tweedie, Fiona C. '*Caenum aut caelum*: M. Livius Drusus and the Land', *Mnemosyne*, 64 (2011), 573–90.

Versnel, H.S. 'The Festival for Bona Dea and the Thesmophoria', *Greece & Rome* 39 (1992), 31–55.

Waters, K.H. 'Cicero, Sallust, and Catiline', *Historia* 19 (1970), 195–215.

Weinrib, E.J 'The Judiciary Law of M. Livius Drusus (tr. pl. 91 B.C.)', *Historia* 19 (1970), 414–43.

Woodman, A.J. *Sallust: Catiline's War, The Jugurthine War, Histories* (Penguin, 2007).

Index